LUSITANIA

LUSITANIA
Saga and Myth

DAVID RAMSAY

W · W · NORTON & COMPANY
NEW YORK · LONDON

Copyright © 2001 by David Ramsay
First American edition 2002

First published in Great Britain in 2001
by Chatham Publishing, 99 High Street,
Rochester, Kent ME1 1LX

Published in the United States of America and Canada
by W. W. Norton & Company

Printed in Great Britain

The text of this book is composed in 11 point Baskerville
with the display set in Baskerville
Composition by Dorwyn Limited
Map by Venture Graphics
Manufacturing by The Cromwell Press

Library of Congress Cataloging-in-Publication Data
is available on request

ISBN 0-393-05099-8

W. W. Norton & Company, Inc., 500 Fifth Avenue, New York, N.Y. 10110
www.wwnorton.com

2 3 4 5 6 7 8 9 0

Contents

This book is dedicated to the memory
of all those who sailed from New York
on the 101st Eastbound Voyage
of RMS *Lusitania*
on May The First 1915
and especially to Alice Lines Drury
December 1896–November 1997
Centenarian and *Lusitania* Survivor
who in those terrible minutes of adversity
on the afternoon of May The Seventh
by virtue of her courage and tenacity
brought to safety the two young children
who had been entrusted to her care
one of them a baby of only three months.

Semper fidelis

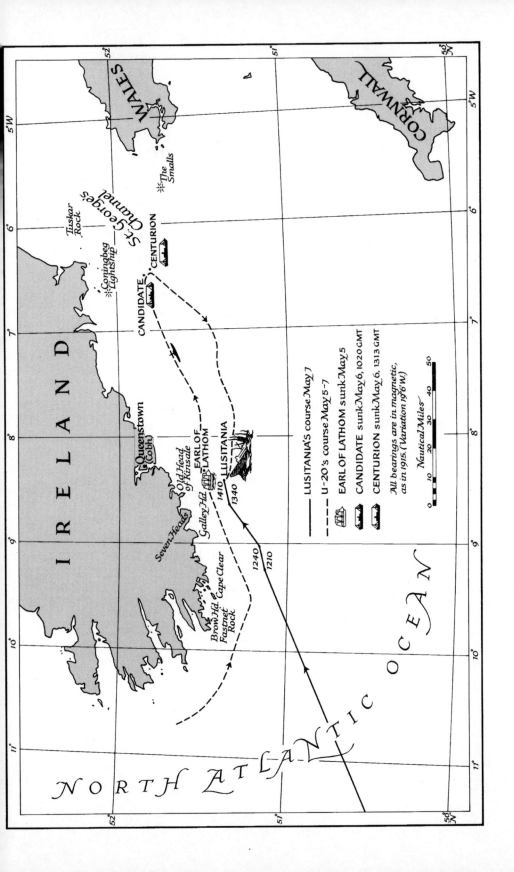

WALES

CORNWALL

5°W

5°W

5°

6°

The Smalls

St. George's Channel

Tuskar Rock

Coningbeg Lightship

CENTURION

CANDIDATE

6°

7°

IRELAND

Queenstown (Cobh)

Old Head of Kinsale

EARL OF LATHOM

Galley Hd.

LUSITANIA

1410

1340

Seven Heads

Brow Hd.

Fastnet Rock

Cape Clear

1240

1210

8°

9°

10°

11°

LUSITANIA'S course May 7

U-20's course May 5-7

EARL OF LATHOM sunk May 5

CANDIDATE sunk May 6, 1020 GMT

CENTURION sunk May 6, 1313 GMT

All bearings are in magnetic, as in 1915. (Variation 19°6'W.)

Nautical Miles

0   10   20   30   40   50

NORTH ATLANTIC OCEAN

52°

51°

50° N

7°

8°

9°

10°

11°

52°

51°

50° N

List of Illustrations

Between pages 148 and 149

Lusitania on the slipway. (Glasgow University Archives)
Lusitania fitting out. (Glasgow University Archives)
Lusitania steaming at speed. (Imperial War Museum)
Lusitania in New York. (Arnold Kludas Collection)
Captain William Thomas Turner. (Cunard Archives, University of Liverpool)
Series of drawings by Oliver Bernard. (The *London Illustrated News*)
'Track of the Lusitania'. (Chatham Publishing)
Headstone in Cobh cemetery. (Author's Collection)
Captain Turner, the day after the sinking. (Alister Satchell Collection)
Henry Oliver. (By kind permission of Commodore J F Rodley RN, School of Maritime Operations, HMS *Dryad*)
Winston Churchill. (Hulton Getty Collection)
Admiral of the Fleet Lord Fisher. (The Royal Collection Copyright 2001. Her Majesty Queen Elizabeth II)
Woodrow Wilson. (Imperial War Museum)
Kaiser Wilhelm II. (Imperial War Museum)
'Take up the Sword of Justice'. (Imperial War Museum)

Acknowledgements

The saga of the liner *Lusitania* has intrigued me for many
years in the same way that others have been fascinated by
the drama of the maiden voyage of *Titanic*. In the early
1970s a former Director of Cunard told me that the liner's history
and the reasons behind her sinking had never been adequately
told and that it was a far bigger and much more important story
than that of her contemporary. My interest in the liner was rekindled by Dr Robert Ballard's exploration of her wreck with submarines and by a conversation my wife Pamela and I had when we
were travelling on *QE2* with a well-known maritime historian who
was lecturing on *Titanic*. He remarked on the number of books
which had recently been published on that ill-fated liner, which
had found a ready sale although some of them were frankly
mediocre. His conversation spurred me to write this book which I
have based on detailed research on both sides of the Atlantic. The
saga which unfolded in front of me was even more intriguing than
I had assumed. Over the years it has become encrusted with
myths, some of which can be traced back to German propaganda
in the aftermath of the sinking, and others which have their orgin
in the understandable desire of the British Admiralty to 'let sleeping dogs lie'. My intention has been to examine and rebut the
many myths of *Lusitania*.

The passing of the years has carried away not only almost all the
survivors but sadly some valuable source material. In the 1960s the
late John Light carried out some forty dives on *Lusitania*'s hull,
which at one time he owned. He also built up an archive on the
liner which reputedly contained about 15,000 items. Following
the death of his widow a few years ago, the present location of
these documents is unknown. Although Light's conclusions were
often debatable, the apparent disappearance of his archive is a
serious loss to anyone writing on the liner. The correspondence
between Alfred Booth, the then Chairman of Cunard, and his
cousin George, the Managing Director of the family firm of Booth
& Co and a major figure in the City of London, together with
George Booth's papers and his unfinished autobiography, which

was made available to at least one earlier writer, also seem to have disappeared. The admirable Cunard Archives at Liverpool University include remarkably few papers on the line in the First World War. A file marked Chairman's Correspondence with the Admiralty 1914–19 contains a mere handful of papers, none of them relevant to *Lusitania.*

I owe a very considerable debt to Captain David Garstin RN, naval engineer by profession and enthusiastic naval historian, for the quite invaluable help he has given me particularly in the technical aspects of the liner's design and in establishing the reasons why she sank in only eighteen minutes. He has corrected many of my errors and I have incorporated almost all of the suggestions he made to me after he read my various drafts. Last but not least, he warned me of the dangers of hindsight in making judgments about those who were involved in the events which preceded and followed the sinking of *Lusitania*, both aboard the liner and ashore. I would also thank Lieutenant-Commander Paul Satow RN for his advice about navigation and Rear-Admiral Geoffrey Mitchell RN, a former Director of Naval Operations and Trade, for reading the chapters that discuss what degree of responsibility the Admiralty bore for the tragedy.

Lord Bridgeman, the grandson of a distinguished First Lord of the Admiralty, kindly delved into the House of Lords Library and provided me with copies of contemporary issues of *The Times* and *The Morning Post*, which I have found to be high quality source material as are the books written by the *Lusitania* survivors, Oliver Bernard and Charles Lauriat. The late Philip Bates, a former Managing Director of Cunard, gave me the benefit of his considerable knowledge of the line and of the Liverpool shipping world in general. David Inglefield and Imelda Lutyens kindly gave me access to the papers of their grandfather, Admiral Sir Frederick Inglefield, Senior Naval Assessor at the Mersey Inquiry into the loss of *Lusitania*. Audrey Lawson Johnson, who was rescued from the disaster when she was only three months old, lent me a most useful collection of newspaper cuttings and documents and told me of her memories of her parents, Warren and Amy Pearl, who also survived the sinking. Sadly, I was unable to meet the intrepid Alice Lines Drury, the nanny who had saved her, who died, aged 100, a few months after my meeting with Mrs Lawson Johnston. Tom Johnson and his staff at the Rancho Mirage Public Library went out of their way to obtain books as source material from the admirable Interlibrary Loan System. The distinguished marine artist, Harley Crossley, painted the picture for the dust jacket. Alec Herzer (Venture Graphics) compiled the chart of the the waters off the South Coast of Ireland, which uses the latest data.

I express my gratitude to the staff of the Public Record Office, Kew, the National Maritime Museum, Greenwich and the Cunard Archives and also to Carole Leadenham, Assistant Archivist at the Hoover Institution, Stanford University, Piers Brendon, Keeper of the Churchill Archives Centre, Churchill College, Cambridge and his archivist, Alan Kucia, Peter Simpkins and his colleagues at the Imperial War Museum, Professor Michael Moss and Moira Rankin, University of Glasgow, and Rachel Mulhearn, Merseyside Maritime Museum, all of whom gave me full measure of assistance. My son James, in the interval between receiving his MBA and his appointment to run an executive relocation company, undertook some research for me at the Imperial War Museum and in the Booth family papers at London University. Judy Collingwood carried out additional research for me into the Admiralty files at the PRO.

My thanks are also due to all those in Great Britain, the United States, Belgium, Canada, Germany and Ireland who helped me in my research, particularly Paul Banfield (Queen's University, Kingston, Ontario), Captain Edward Beach USN, Count Bertil Bernadotte, Tobias Graf Von Bernstorff, Lady Bridgeman and her staff at the Bridgeman Art Gallery, David K Brown, Wim Coumans and Luc De Munck (Belgian Red Cross), Richard Crissman, Chris Doncaster, who alerted me to the heroic efforts of the Manx fishing boat *Wanderer* in saving lives after *Lusitania* was sunk, William H Garzke, Graham C Greene, Oliver Greene, Dr Alan Jamieson, Sir Ludovic Kennedy, Arnold Kludas, David Mackay, Professor Walter McDougall (University of Pennsylvania), Dr Joe A Martin, Roy Martin, John Maxwell (Hill Dickinson), Ranald and Patricia Noel-Paton, Belinda Norman-Butler, Sir Thomas Pilkington and Captain Graeme Cubbin (Harrison Line), Maighread Rutledge (Cobh Heritage Centre), Lord Rees-Mogg, Max Roberts, who gave me details about the life of Captain Turner, General Michael Rogers USAF, Arthur Sandiford, Rupert Graf Strachwitz, Major-General Julian Thompson, Steve Torrington (Library Editor, Associated Newspapers) and Captain Ronald Warwick.

I acknowledge the authors and publishers of the following works from which I have quoted:

Thomas Bailey & Paul Ryan, *The Lusitania Disaster* (Free Press); Correlli Barnett, *Engage The Enemy More Closely* (W W Norton); Oliver Bernard, *Cock Sparrow* (Jonathan Cape); W S Chalmers, *Full Cycle* (Hodder & Stoughton); Kendrick Clements, *Woodrow Wilson – World Statesman* (Twayne); Allan Crothall, *Wealth From The Sea* (Starr Line); Reinhard Dorries, *Imperial Challenge: Ambassador Count Bernstorff and German-American Relations 1908–1917* (University of North Carolina); Niall Ferguson, *The Pity Of War* (Allen Lane); James Gerard, *My Four Years in Germany* (Hodder & Stoughton); Martin Gilbert, *Winston S. Churchill,* Vol 3 and Companion Vol III, Part 1 (Heinemann); Peter Gretton, *Former Naval Person: Winston Churchill and The Royal Navy* (Oxford); J J Horgan, *From Parnell To Pearse* (Browne & Nolan); Micheal Hurley, *Home From The Sea: The Story Of The Courtmacsherry Lifeboat 1825–1995* (Privately Published); Francis Hyde, *Cunard and the North Atlantic* (Macmillan); J H Isherwood, *Steamers of the Past* (The Journal of Commerce and the Shipping Telegraph); Charles Lauriat, *The Lusitania's Last Voyage* (Houghton Mifflin); Walter McDougall, *Promised Land: Crusader State* (Houghton Mifflin); Arthur Marder, *From Dreadnought to Scapa Flow* (Oxford); Avner Offer, *The First World War: An Agrarian Assessment* (Oxford); Norman Rose, *Churchill The Unruly Giant* (Free Press); Charles Seymour, *The Private Papers of Colonel House* (Houghton Mifflin); David Stafford, *Churchill And Secret Service* (John Murray); Barbara Tuchman, *The Zimmermann Telegram* (Macmillan); Evelyn Waugh, *Scoop* (Chapman & Hall)

Finally, my undying debt to Pamela who bought me a second-hand computer one Christmas. Without her gift and her tolerance of the hours I have spent on research and writing, this book would not have been possible. Pamela Collaro kindly gave me some basic lessons in the art of computers and word processing. I am sad that my former computer consultant, the late Duke Janus, who took a great interest in this book, did not live to see it published.

DAVID RAMSAY
Indian Wells, California
February 2001

Prologue

The Old Head of Kinsale and its sentinel lighthouse stands on the tip of a promontory jutting into the Irish Sea some six miles south of the town of the same name. In the days of the great transatlantic liners which plied to and from the port of Liverpool, their regular route passed within a couple of miles of the Old Head. Generations of sea captains have taken their bearings from the famous point. Even on a dark day with scudding low cloud driven by a westerly wind, it is a place of sombre beauty. Gulls soar and kestrels hover above a background of rolling green fields and grey and black cliffs which sweep steeply down to the sea. From a vantage point below the lighthouse spectacular views delight the eye. To the east are the entrances to the harbours of Kinsale, Oysterhaven and Cork and beyond them lie Knockadoon and Ram Head. Westward the great half-moon sweep of Courtmacsherry Bay leads towards the cape known as the Seven Heads. On a warm spring day when the sun is shining and there is not a hint of wind, there can be few places as serene or as near to heaven on earth as the Old Head of Kinsale.

On one such day in the spring of 1915, a family named Henderson drove from their home in the nearby town of Bandon to have a picnic on one of the cliffs close to the Old Head. As they enjoyed their meal amid the magnificent views a large four-funnelled liner rounded the Seven Heads steaming east and parallel to the coast. The Henderson children, who had never seen a ship of such size before, were fascinated by the sight. As they watched the liner's progress they noticed a column of water and smoke suddenly rise above her decks and the great ship list to starboard. Before their horrified gaze the liner's bows started to sink and her stern, with her four great propellers clearly visible, rose into the air. For a second it seemed to them that she hung there motionless and then she plunged into the sea. She had gone in less than twenty minutes. More than seventy years later, George Henderson recalled the event. 'As a six year old boy it is something which has stuck in my mind for the rest of my life. Although time fades and grey cells wear out, I can still sit here now and see that great liner just sliding below the waves.'[1]

The Henderson family were not alone in watching the disaster unfold. The lighthouse keepers on the Old Head and Galley Head instantly sent out a warning message, alerting the naval and civil authorities. Several miles away from the Hendersons, Tim Keohane, coxswain of the Courtmacsherry lifeboat, was on coast-guard duty. Aghast at the sight of the stricken liner, he instinctively started to run back to the little town to summon his lifeboat crew for what was obviously going to be an urgent mission. Alerted by his lookout, Thomas Woods, William Ball, the skipper of *Wanderer*, a small fishing boat from the Isle of Man, and his crew, searching for mackerel in the rich grounds off the Old Head, watched the liner start to sink by the bows approximately three miles SSW from their position. Without any hesitation, they set course for the sinking ship. The schoolchildren of Butlers-town, a village two miles from the Seven Heads, were in the school yard enjoying a break in the afternoon sunshine when they heard the sudden crack of an explosion. Looking out to sea, they watched in horror as the liner listed, her bows went under and finally she disappeared. Once the schoolmistress had summoned the children back to the classroom, she told them to write an essay describing what they had seen. These spectators, afloat and ashore, had witnessed one of the greatest and, in retrospect, one of the most avoidable sea disasters of the twentieth century, the sinking of the Cunard liner *Lusitania*.

The tragedy which overtook her has always been overshadowed by the sinking of *Titanic* three years earlier. One *Lusitania* survivor used to complain that she had been rescued from the wrong shipwreck! There is more than an overtone of Hollywood drama in the saga of *Titanic* and, indeed, Hollywood has returned to the sinking time after time, most memorably in the 1958 film *A Night to Remember* based on Walter Lord's bestselling book. The latest of these films, simply named *Titanic*, whose production cost more than $200m, was released for Christmas 1997 and became a huge commercial success, the highest-grossing film in cinema history. The real-life drama was played out on the deck of the doomed liner and such scenes as the indomitable Ida Straus declining a place in the lifeboat, declaring that as she and her husband Isador had lived together, they would die together, linger in the memory. Meanwhile, the hero of the hour, Arthur Rostron, the Captain of *Carpathia*, who had once been Chief Officer on

Lusitania, known in Cunard as the Electric Spark, was steaming north at full speed through the night and the ice floes on his rescue mission, as in countless Westerns the cavalry have galloped to the rescue of the embattled settlers. Sadly, the recent film almost totally ignored his contribution to saving the survivors.

In contrast, the more complex saga of *Lusitania*, much of which took place away from the ship, bears a remarkable resemblance to the plot of a Tom Clancy novel, shorn of its high technology. It is a saga of a mighty liner, which in her time had herself been state-of-the-art. *Titanic* was lost on her maiden westbound voyage, before she could establish herself. *Lusitania* was torpedoed on her eastbound hundred-and-first voyage; she was a proven commercial success and had a considerable following among regular travellers on the North Atlantic. It is a saga of an almighty clash among three powerful nations, a story of potentates and presidents, ambassadors and ministers of state, admirals and generals, bankers and shipping magnates and lawyers, newspapermen and spies, sea captains and submariners and not a few of the most towering egos of the first part of the twentieth century. It is also a story of ordinary people, who found themselves in peril on the sea. In their hour of adversity they were to do the most extraordinary things to help their fellow human beings.

CHAPTER 1

Challenge and Response

In 1840, seventy-five years before *Lusitania*'s sinking, Samuel Cunard had introduced the first transatlantic steamship service and the company which he had founded had become a major force in travel between Europe and the United States. Wooden hulls gave way first to iron and then to steel and the paddle wheel was replaced by the propeller powered by the reciprocating or compound engine. Others had followed Cunard on the North Atlantic, some of them British like Guion and Inman and White Star, controlled by the astute Thomas Ismay from 1869, and shipping lines from those European nations with long maritime traditions, the Dutch and the Norwegians and the city states of the old Hanseatic League, Bremen and Hamburg, now united into Imperial Germany. By the turn of the century Germany had become the most populous and economically the most powerful state in Europe. Its merchant marine was second in size only to Britain's.[1] In the seaports of every continent, liners flying the Red, Gold and Black of Imperial Germany lay alongside those displaying the British Red Ensign. The Red Duster had for decades dominated the sea lanes of the world just as the Royal Navy had, since Trafalgar, kept the peace and protected the freedom of the seas on which every trading nation had come to rely. A formidable new power had now arrived to challenge the long-lasting British supremacy.

The rapid growth of the German merchant marine reflected the country's impressive industrial and commercial strength, the rise in exports and its predominant position in the all-important emigrant traffic. James Gerard, the American ambassador in Berlin from 1913 to 1917, and a perceptive observer of Imperial Germany, noted that 'much of the commercial success of the Germans during the past forty years is due to the fact that each manufacturer, each discoverer, each exporter knew that the whole weight and power of the Government was behind him in his efforts to increase his business'.[2] Ocean liners flying the German flag and carrying German products to markets around the world were a tangible symbol of the country's new-found

4

economic strength and influence. The two main shipping lines, the Bremen-based Nord Deutscher Lloyd (NDL) and its great rival Hamburg-Amerika (HAPAG) were extremely well-managed and highly innovative.

In 1888, Wilhelm II, then only twenty-nine, succeeded as Kaiser. He had an acute understanding of the importance of sea power and indulged himself by designing and building the magnificent *Hohenzollern*, a steam yacht to rival any in the world, which he relished as she eclipsed all the British royal yachts. Wilhelm was also an unstable, arrogant and impulsive man with an inflated belief in his own ability and an ingrained love-hate relationship with the British.

In 1878, when Britain came close to going to war with Russia, Thomas Ismay had suggested to the then First Lord of the Admiralty, W H Smith, that he would make some of his fast White Star liners available to the Admiralty as auxiliary cruisers in time of war, with a crew of whom half would be naval reservists, providing he received a suitable subsidy. He met with no immediate response. In 1885, when relations with Russia again deteriorated, the Admiralty commandeered and converted sixteen liners including the Cunarder *Oregon*. Two years later Ismay's scheme was revived and it was agreed that the Admiralty would finance the installation of gun fittings and platforms on three Cunarders and two White Star liners.[3] When, in 1889, Victoria invited the new Kaiser to attend the Naval Review at Spithead, Thomas Ismay welcomed him aboard the new White Star liner *Teutonic*, which was one of the ships representing the Merchant Navy at the review. *Teutonic* was the first liner which had been specifically designed for conversion into an armed merchant cruiser in time of war under the scheme which Ismay had originally suggested and which had been introduced two years before. Wilhelm was highly impressed and told his aides that Germany must build ships like her.[4]

The two chief German lines had inherited, and enthusiastically continued, the deep-seated rivalry which had long existed between the old Hanseatic ports of Bremen and Hamburg. The Managing Director of NDL, Heinrich Wiegand, was a manager of considerable ability and Albert Ballin, who by the 1890s had become the driving force in HAPAG, was to become a major figure in the shipping world. HAPAG had been founded by a number of Hamburg shipowners and merchants in 1847, seven years after Cunard, with the express objective of operating 'a regular connection between Hamburg and North America by means of sailing ships under the Hamburg flag'. Forty years later HAPAG was the dominant shipowner in Hamburg. Its Bremen-based rival, NDL was, however, twice its size. HAPAG had only twenty-four ships on the North Atlantic against NDL's forty-seven. In terms of tonnage operated, HAPAG was only the world's twenty-second largest shipping line.

In 1886, Carl Laeisz, a director of HAPAG and an influential figure in Hamburg shipping circles, engineered a takeover bid for the much smaller Union Line. The astute Laeisz had two objectives: first, he intended curtailing an interloper whose rate-wars were eroding the lucrative profits HAPAG had been making in the emigrant trade; secondly, and more significantly, he wanted to secure for HAPAG the services of Albert Ballin, a native Hamburger in his late twenties, who had been the driving force behind the growth of Union Line. Under the terms of the con-tract, Ballin became the head of HAPAG's passenger division. He was a man of considerable personality, an innovative entrepre-neur and a perfectionist with an eagle eye for the smallest detail. He had an iron determination to make HAPAG a leader in world shipping worthy of the traditional Hanseatic motto, which the line had adopted: *Mein Feld ist die Welt* – My Field is the World. Two years later Ballin joined the HAPAG board and from then on he became the dominant influence in its development. Over the following ten years the line added eleven new routes and had sur-passed NDL to become Cunard's chief rival on the North Atlantic. By the time Ballin became its managing director in 1899, his dynamic management talents had built HAPAG into the largest shipping line in the world.[5] In 1914, when HAPAG was operating almost worldwide, its fleet numbered 175 ships compared with Cunard's 28.

The years between 1870 and 1914 witnessed the zenith of mass European emigration to the United States. Although the glamour and refinements of first-class sea travel held the public imagin-ation, the bread-and-butter of the North Atlantic passenger ship-ping trade literally lay several decks below in steerage. Cunard and its British competitors had originally pioneered this segment of the trade in the 1850s to meet the surge in Irish emigration after the potato famine, instituting a port of call at Queenstown (now Cobh) in County Cork to cater for this traffic. After 1870, the majority of emigrants came from central and eastern Europe and by virtue of geography the two German lines came to dominate the emigrant traffic. The extent of their influence can be illustrated by the figures for 1891 for westbound steerage passengers, embarking from Northern European ports. HAPAG carried nearly 76,000 and NDL a further 68,000 while White Star and Cunard carried only 35,500 and 27,300 respectively.[6] By 1900 steerage provided more than half of HAPAG's profits.

Hamburg, in particular, had for centuries been the gateway to central Europe. The development of a comprehensive European railway system serving Germany and its neighbours from 1850 onwards enabled would-be emigrants for the first time to reach the North Sea ports quickly and cheaply. The railways brought Germans and Austrians, Poles and Russians, Hungarians and Czechs and others by the thousand to Hamburg and Bremen. The methodical Ballin had built a hostel complex to house them until the next HAPAG liner could carry them across the Atlantic to the line's American terminal at Hoboken, New Jersey, opposite New York and thence to Ellis Island, that forbidding portal to the land of opportunity. (There was an element of enlightened self-interest in the provision of this facility. All immigrants were subjected to a stringent medical examination at Ellis Island and those who failed were sent back at the expense of the shipping lines. Ballin instituted a similar examination in his Hamburg hostel thus eliminating the liability to this tiresome overhead.)

When Ballin joined HAPAG in 1886, passenger liners were powered by a single screw and the not infrequent breakdowns wreaked havoc with timetables. The first liner fitted with twin screws, *City of New York*, flagship of the Inman Line, by then American controlled, had entered service in 1888. Twin screw liners had an obvious advantage. As their liability to breakdowns was greatly reduced they could offer a much more reliable service. Soon after his appointment, Ballin commissioned a new generation of fast twin-screw passenger liners designed to provide superior standards of comfort and service. In essence, he had introduced the concept of the liner as a floating hotel, offering similar amenities to their counterparts ashore. The first of these vessels, *Augusta Viktoria* (7,661 tons), named for the Kaiser's wife, was launched in 1890, and was the first European liner to be equipped with twin propeller shafts. She had been under construction when, after he inspected *Teutonic*, the Kaiser induced HAPAG and NDL to design liners which could be converted to serve as auxiliary cruisers. Like every subsequent German express liner built before 1914, she had been fitted with specially strengthened decks to support gun platforms.[7] In the following year the Kaiser came to Hamburg with the Kaiserin and met Ballin for the first time, when he showed them round the new liner before she sailed on her maiden voyage. A lasting friendship developed between these two very different men, who shared a fascination with the sea and a love of travel. From the time they first met, the Kaiser took a deep personal interest in HAPAG, often sending Ballin his detailed ideas for the line's future and sketches of designs for new ships.

Ballin was an astute student of human nature and well understood the Kaiser's susceptibility to flattery and love of pomp and circumstance. He boosted HAPAG's prestige by providing liners for the Kaiser's use during his overseas journeys. During Kiel Week, which the Kaiser had founded in imitation of Cowes, one of his newest liners, immaculate in its house colours, black hull, white superstructure and blue trim, was always prominently moored to house royal or government guests. Ballin's assiduous cultivation of the Kaiser won him an influence which no British or American industrialist could rival and the Kaiser came to regard him as a valued adviser on economic and naval policy. His feat was all the more remarkable as he was Jewish and Imperial Germany had an unmistakable culture of anti-Semitism with many doors firmly closed to Jews. The Kaiserin, notoriously both anti-British and anti-Semitic, strongly disapproved of her husband's friendship with Ballin. Maximilian Harden, editor of the outspoken *Zukunft*, the *Private Eye* of Imperial Germany, loved to chide his friend Ballin as Der Hof-Ozean-Jude, which roughly translates as the Oceanic-Jewish-Courtier.[8]

In pursuit of excellence Ballin hired the best talent he could find. The hotelier Cesar Ritz was retained as head of catering and customer services. He engaged the British firm of Mewes and Davies, architects of the magnificent *fin-de-siècle* London Ritz, to design the interiors of new HAPAG liners. As a result of Ballin's innovations, a voyage on the North Atlantic, which in the past had too often been disagreeable, was to become a much more pleasant experience, at least for HAPAG's first-class passengers. Ballin also introduced cruising into HAPAG in the winter of 1891, with the objective of increasing off-season earnings.[9] Within a few years, Ballin had revolutionised the management of passenger shipping lines, setting new and much higher standards of amenity and service, standards which his competitors would inevitably be forced to emulate.

Unlike its German contemporaries, Cunard had not been noted for innovation and was vulnerable to the full vigour of German competition. Samuel Cunard, in particular, had reservations about propeller-driven ships and preferred to stick to the tried and tested paddle steamers, long after other shipping lines had abandoned them. His lodestar was reliability and he was determined to see that his line achieved a reputation for operating a dependable service. His American competitor, Edward Collins, built faster ships and drove them hard. As a result breakdowns were frequent. The loss of two Collins liners – *Arctic*, sunk in a collision in fog in September 1854, with heavy loss of life, including Collins's wife, son and daughter, and *Pacific*, which disappeared without trace outward bound from Liverpool in January 1856 – led to the line's demise in 1858. Samuel Cunard's insistence on reliability had served his line well for many years.

Although in 1881 Cunard had commissioned its first steel-hulled liner *Servia* (7,392 tons), the first ship in the world to be fitted with electric power, the line's management had, by the end of the decade, become complacent and slow to accept technical innovation. The first twin-screw Cunarder, *Campania* (12,950 tons), did not enter service until 1893, five years after Inman had commissioned *City of New York* and two years later than *Augusta Viktoria*. Their ships had always enjoyed a somewhat spartan reputation and Samuel Cunard's partner, Charles MacIver, had once famously rebuked a passenger who had complained about poor service by telling him that 'going to sea was a hardship; the company did not seek to make anything else out of it'.[10] The banker, Pierpont Morgan, a discerning as well as a regular traveller, crossed eastbound on the newly commissioned *Servia* in December 1881. Despite the electric light, he found her inferior to her White Star contemporaries and thereafter he always travelled by White Star in preference to Cunard.[11]

At a board meeting in November 1897, a Cunard director, Sir William Forwood, found it necessary to advise his colleagues that they should see more of their ships both in port and at sea and complained about their cleanliness. As a result of Forwood's prodding, Leonard Peskett, the line's naval architect, was dispatched to New York to have a good look at the German competition and in particular at their passenger accommodation.[12] Earlier that year and much to Cunard's chagrin, the prestigious Blue Riband for the fastest Atlantic crossing, previously held by *Campania*, was captured by an NDL liner, *Kaiser Wilhelm Der Grosse*

(14,349 tons) with a speed of 21.3 knots. Customary and fierce rivalry between the two German lines ensued. In 1900 a new HAPAG liner, *Deutschland* (23,620 tons), wrested the trophy from NDL, and three years later, another NDL liner, *Kaiser Wilhelm II* (20,000 tons), won the award back, raising the record to 22.6 knots.

The growth of the German merchant marine ran parallel to the vast expansion of the Imperial German navy, the Kriegsmarine, under the leadership of Admiral Alfred Tirpitz, whom the Kaiser had appointed State Secretary for the Navy in 1897. When Tirpitz took office the Kriegsmarine was only the world's sixth largest navy. The Kaiser had given him the mission of making the largely landlocked Germany second only to Britain as a naval power. Albert Ballin became one of the most vocal advocates of the larger German navy, and like other leading industrialists, he was closely involved in the influential Flotten-verein or Navy League, which Tirpitz, a master of public relations, set up to promote public support for German sea power. Following the example of Cunard and White Star, HAPAG and NDL agreed that their ships could be requisitioned for service as armed merchant cruisers in time of war and encouraged their officers and crews to join the naval reserve, and in 1900 Tirpitz introduced the Second Navy Law which effectively doubled the size of the battlefleet. The Admiralty quickly perceived that the expansion of the German navy was aimed at Britain's maritime superiority and threatened the freedom of the sea lanes on which the country's survival so crucially depended.

By the turn of the century, the North Atlantic passenger trade had become an intensely competitive high-volume and low-margin business increasingly dominated by the two German lines. Commentators have concluded that their rapid growth – especially that of HAPAG – was due at least in part to government subsidies but German maritime historians maintain that the North Atlantic routes were not subsidised and ascribe the success of the lines to Imperial Germany's rapid economic growth, their pre-eminent position in the emigrant traffic and their strong management.

The evidence for subsidisation is mixed. The shipping lines do not seem to have resorted to government construction loans and the historians insist that the gun platforms installed to permit the conversion of the new liners into merchant cruisers were funded by the lines as a patriotic gesture. On one occasion, in 1900,

Ballin negotiated a subsidy for HAPAG's new routes in the Far East, but with his entrepreneurial background, he was wary of its implications and three years later he cancelled the arrangement to preserve his freedom to manage the line without government interference. (Only when it was too late did the Cunard board realise the Faustian implications of accepting a government subsidy.) NDL took a different view to its main competitor. From 1886 until 1914 it accepted subventions for operating its routes to the Far East and Australia. In Britain, with its long parliamentary tradition, naval estimates were thoroughly scrutinised by and debated in the House of Commons, with major items of expenditure disclosed to the public. In Imperial Germany the Reichstag had much less influence over government expenditure and hidden agreements were by no means unknown. In any case, subsidies emerge in many shapes and sizes, sometimes including inflated mail contracts. In 1902, Lord Inverclyde, the recently appointed Chairman of Cunard, testifying before the House of Lords Committee on Merchant Cruisers, was asked how the Germans could run four vessels on the North Atlantic at speeds of between 22 and 23 knots. His reply was explicit: NDL was receiving an operating subsidy of £280,000 per annum and a further £9,000 in respect of each of their new ships for fitting gun platforms. Inverclyde was a man of considerable integrity who could have had little reason for misleading the Committee.[13]

HAPAG and NDL had successfully driven rates down to the extent that their European and American rivals were finding it difficult, if not impossible, to finance the construction of newer, larger and faster liners which would allow them to provide effective competition. The German lines had another inbuilt advantage. While Cunard's fleet was made up almost entirely of fast passenger and mail liners, NDL and HAPAG operated fast and intermediate liners and cargo vessels. Intermediate liners had a top speed of 18 knots, some passengers preferring a longer voyage, and had a much larger cargo capacity. They were consistently profitable, and the largest German shipping lines, including HAPAG and NDL, enjoyed a virtual and lucrative monopoly of the country's import and export trade. Unlike the passenger trade, cargo was not seasonal and the revenue from the intermediate and cargo operations could be used to cross-subsidise their fast liners.

A downturn in freight traffic from British ports further weakened Cunard's position and in March 1902 it was forced to cut its

dividend by 20 per cent. Two years later it was eliminated alto-
gether and by the summer of 1902 Cunard was facing financial
disaster; its fleet was inferior to its German competitors and the
line's future as an independent entity was in doubt. Its Board,
with its responsibility to its shareholders in mind, might well have
been forced into accepting an offer for the line.

Although the combination of Ballin's entrepreneurial abilities
and his influence in the halls of power in Berlin made him a most
formidable rival, the German lines did not pose the only threat
to the future of the British merchant marine and particularly that
of Cunard. The American banker, Pierpont Morgan, a man so
powerful that, in 1907, he almost single-handedly saved his
country from a catastrophic financial meltdown, had recognised
the opportunity to rationalise the North Atlantic shipping lines.
He habitually worked on a colossal scale, creating such industrial
giants as General Electric, American Telephone and Telegraph
and United States Steel. Morgan and his allies virtually controlled
the American railroad system through a number of strategic
holdings. The project was allegedly suggested to Morgan when
he was on a transatlantic liner returning from a business trip to
Europe. A later Chairman of Cunard, Sir Percy Bates, once noted
that the American mercantile marine of that day had been killed
off by the American railroads after the completion of the first
trans-continental line in 1869.[14] In his vivid phrase: 'They were
opening up the continent and they naturally went inland instead
of round the Horn'. Morgan intended to re-establish a significant
American presence on the North Atlantic, currently dominated
by British and other European lines.

In 1900 he created a shipping operation, International
Merchant Marine (IMM), which was controlled and funded by
the Morgan Bank, and he set about buying control of American
and European lines. He was fully prepared to pay over the top for
his acquisitions and early in 1901 he made an offer of $11 million
cash for the British-owned Frederick Leyland & Co, the largest
freight carrier on the North Atlantic, which was so clearly over-
pricing the company that its Chairman, John Ellerman, could not
afford to refuse it. The Annual Shipping Review of 1901 accurately forecast that 'The vendors have made an exceptionally
good bargain, which it is probable that the purchasers will shortly
find out.'[15] In July of the same year Morgan bought Cunard's
principal British rival White Star Line for $32 million.
Strategically, this was an important acquisition. White Star had

been effectively controlled by two major shareholders, J Bruce Ismay, its managing director and son of Thomas Ismay, who had died in 1899, and William (later Lord) Pirrie, the chairman of the Belfast shipbuilders, Harland & Wolff. Pirrie, whom Morgan made a Director of IMM, was an influential figure in the world of European passenger shipping and a major investor in the leading Dutch line, Holland Amerika. Harland & Wolff was the builder of choice for White Star and Holland Amerika and also built liners for HAPAG.

Morgan moved with circumspection in his relations with governments. At the time he acquired White Star, he sought the views of two of the most powerful men in the British Cabinet, Arthur Balfour, the nephew and acknowledged political heir of the great Lord Salisbury, then approaching the end of his distinguished career, and the Colonial Secretary, Joseph Chamberlain. The latter had been a successful businessman before entering politics and was more sympathetic to the concept of official intervention in industry than most of his contemporaries. Although the two ministers expressed no opposition to Morgan's purchase of White Star and Leyland, they insisted that their ships remain under British registry and told the banker that their colleagues at the Admiralty and the Board of Trade would require IMM to meet further conditions. As Morgan did not wish to jeopardise the standing of his bank's profitable London branch, he readily agreed to the Government's stipulations.

Berlin quickly saw the danger that IMM would offer preferential rates for traffic offered by Morgan's railroads, cutting into business currently being carried by the German lines. At the Kaiser's instigation, Wiegand and Ballin met Morgan in New York in February 1902 to negotiate what was euphemistically called a Community of Interest between IMM, HAPAG and NDL. Morgan, who had created so many cartels, well understood such a concept. On 20 February they reached an agreement, ambitious in its scope, to fix rates, allocate routes, share profits and co-operate on ventures of mutual interest including the acquisition of both Cunard and Holland-Amerika. With Pirrie's assistance, the cartel was able to buy a 51 per cent stake in the Dutch line, completed in April 1902. In less than two years, Morgan had achieved control of, or an operating alliance with, every important North Atlantic shipping line other than Cunard and the French CGT. On 2 April, he set off once again for Europe. On his arrival in Britain, he made a takeover bid for Cunard, but the staunchly independent Liverpool and Glasgow shipowners, who controlled the line, politely showed him to the door. He brushed off this setback and boarded his magnificent yacht, *Corsair III*, and sailed for Kiel where he had been invited to be guest of honour at Kiel Week.

The Kaiser delighted in welcoming rich and successful entrepreneurs like Morgan, thus showing the world that Germany was realistic and forward looking. To secure the presence of the great banker, arguably one of the most powerful men in the world, was a considerable coup. He loved to point out that the aristocrats of the Royal Yacht Squadron, who ran Cowes, had once again black-balled Thomas Lipton, despite his valiant efforts to recapture the America's Cup, for no better reason than he was 'in trade'.

Corsair III had hardly dropped anchor at Kiel when Morgan was summoned to lunch with the Kaiser on board *Hohenzollern*. After the meal, Kaiser and banker repaired to deck chairs for a talk about business in general and shipping in particular. Both men were in good form and expressed the hope that the alliance between IMM and the German lines would help to foster a close and profitable commercial connection between their two countries. The Kaiser could not resist adding that he did not think it unfair to make a little trouble over ships with the British. On the following day Wilhelm, accompanied by the Imperial Chancellor, Von Bulow, returned the compliment, spending an hour and a half on board *Corsair III*, dressed overall to mark the occasion. Morgan and his party were regally fêted throughout their visit, which concluded with a dinner Wilhelm gave for them at his palace at Potsdam. The two men parted on the most amicable terms.

In the event, IMM was to prove a paper tiger, Morgan's only unsuccessful major venture. As a result of the Balfour government's insistence that its British subsidiaries remained under British management and its ships in British registry, the company never achieved the synergy or the economies of scale in construction costs which Morgan had foreseen. It was initially plagued by management problems and in 1904 Morgan even sought, unsuccessfully, to lure Ballin away from HAPAG to become IMM's President. The loss of *Titanic* in 1912 dealt it a near fatal blow, and after the First World War, IMM's British cargo liner subsidiaries were sold to a City of London syndicate for less than a third of what they had cost twenty years before.[16]

The implications of Morgan's alliance with HAPAG and NDL and his visit to Germany had not gone unnoticed in Britain either in Whitehall or in Cunard's boardroom in Liverpool. An unwelcome result of the agreement had been an intensified commercial war against Cunard and other British companies. At the Cunard Annual General Meeting in 1905, their Chairman, Lord Inverclyde, quoted from a German shipping publication which had boasted that the agreement between IMM and the two German lines had established an alliance, offensive and defensive, which was splendidly proved during the war against Cunard. As an instance of this hostility, he mentioned that travel agents in the US, who had booked passengers on Cunard, had subsequently been boycotted by the cartel. He bluntly told his shareholders that the Board could not ignore such a state of affairs.[17]

Fortunately for Cunard, their newly-appointed chairman was a resourceful and determined man. George Arbuthnot Burns, second Lord Inverclyde, was a member of a successful Glasgow shipping family and his grandfather had been one of Samuel Cunard's original partners. He firmly believed that, despite its current financial problems, Cunard could escape from Morgan's blandishments and remain independent. He did not hesitate in seizing his opportunity. From the time that Samuel Cunard had signed the first mail contract, the line had enjoyed a close relationship with Whitehall and had played a conspicuous role in wartime. The 1840 contract had required that his ships be designed to carry guns. During the Crimean War eleven Cunarders had been requisitioned by the Admiralty. Most of them were employed as troop transports but one steamer, *Arabia*, was converted to carry the Light Brigade's horses to the war zone. Only one Cunard route, to Boston, remained operational until the Admiralty returned the requisitioned ships. More recently, during the Boer War, a number of Cunard liners and freighters had been chartered by the Admiralty, resulting in a welcome if short-lived boost to the line's profits.

Inverclyde reasoned that the Admiralty, with its experience in the recent war vividly in its mind and a far-flung Empire to defend, would understand the strategic importance of maintaining a strong merchant navy. Taking his argument a stage further, he concluded that, faced with the combined menace of the expansion of the Kriegsmarine, the increasing power of HAPAG and NDL and the Morgan Bank's vast financial resources, the traditionally laissez-faire British Government could be persuaded to take the unprecedented step of subsidising Cunard as the remaining British-owned flag carrier on the North Atlantic. In their book *The Lusitania Disaster*, Thomas Bailey and Paul Ryan, described the situation concisely:

> Morgan's manoeuvres threatened Britain's prestige as well as her profitable shipping business. Wealthy passengers have a passion for the fastest and most luxurious forms of transportation as manufacturers of motor cars have discovered. For a nation that lived by the sea, the impulse was strong to do something spectacular that would recapture Britain's fading glory, while simultaneously countering Germany's potential armed merchant cruisers. These were the motives behind the building of two palatial Cunarders . . .[18]

The IMM takeovers had not been well received in Britain and Inverclyde could safely count on the support of public opinion. By the summer of 1902 the British Government was ready to take a harder line against Morgan and the First Lord of the Admiralty, Lord Selborne, told Inverclyde that he strongly objected to Cunard joining the combine. He wrote: 'we will do whatever we can to assist you to justify yourself to your shareholders'.[19] In essence, Selborne had assured Inverclyde that the Government would take the necessary action to facilitate Cunard's continued independence. Three senior cabinet ministers, Selborne, Gerald Balfour, President of the Board of Trade and brother of Arthur Balfour, who had by now succeeded Salisbury as Prime Minister, and the formidable Colonial Secretary, Joseph Chamberlain, were entrusted with the twin tasks of securing Cunard's future as an independent and viable presence on the North Atlantic and of negotiating the terms under which IMM's British-registered liners could operate. Knowing that Whitehall would have to deliver on the assurances that they had given to his shareholders, Inverclyde then opened detailed negotiations with the three ministers for government assistance in the construction of two new fast liners. A table, which was prepared for these negotiations, indicated that the higher the maximum speed of the proposed liners, the greater would be their construction costs and the amount of the required annual operating subsidy.[20]

Under the final terms of the agreement, the Government provided a construction loan of £2.6 million for the two proposed Cunarders, repayable in annual instalments over twenty years from the date each liner went into service, together with an annual operating subsidy of £75,000 for each ship and a further annual mail subsidy of £68,000. The loan carried interest of 2¾ per cent as against the going commercial rate of 5 per cent.

The financial terms were clearly attractive to Cunard but in certain respects the Government had in return struck a hard bargain. The Admiralty had the power to take over the liners in wartime and insisted on a right of veto over their proposed specification. This was exacting, stating that special attention be paid to stability. In the wording of the contract:

> The ship must be as steady as possible under the varying conditions to which a ship of the high speed defined in the contract would be subjected in the North Atlantic Trade and the stability should be so arranged that, by the use of water ballast, the ship may have a positive metacentic height in the worst condition when fitted as an armed cruiser.[21]

The agreement stipulated that the new liners achieve a maximum speed of 25 knots and could be speedily converted into merchant cruisers, carrying an armament of twelve 6in guns. Four of these were to be installed on the forecastle, six on the shelter deck amidships and two more on the shelter deck aft. In line with current Admiralty practice, the ships were to be equipped with longitudinal bunkers and their engine and boiler rooms were to be located below the water line, as were the magazines.

The Admiralty insisted on these design features as a protection against gunfire and it should be remembered that in 1903 the submarine was not a significant factor in naval warfare. As gunfire, rather than the torpedo, represented the principal threat to warships, protection was required above and not below the waterline. The presence of coal in longitudinal bunkers was thought to provide additional defence against gunfire and the Royal Corps of Naval Constructors had a maxim that one foot of coal equalled one inch of armour.[22] The agreement effectively reflected nineteenth-century naval strategy in which merchant raiders, such as CSS *Alabama* in the American Civil War, had played a significant role. The deck officers and half the crew of the two new ships were required to enlist in the Royal Naval Reserves. Cunard was to remain in British ownership and its fleet in British registry. The company's entire fleet was to be placed at the disposal of the Government in time of war and the Admiralty's interest was further protected by a floating charge over all Cunard's assets and by what would now be called a golden share which effectively gave it a veto over its operations.

Inverclyde's shrewd negotiating tactics had achieved his objective and the agreement was signed on 30 June 1903. It was then published and debated in, and duly approved by, Parliament. It was not well received in Berlin when the German establishment regarded the Inverclyde/Selborne agreement as an unnecessary provocation, overlooking the fact that its own agreements with HAPAG and NDL provided that their liners could be converted into auxiliary cruisers in wartime.

CHAPTER 2

The Birth of a Star

Inverclyde realised that the new Cunarders, now codenamed Nos 367 and 735, would have to constitute as significant an advance over the competition both technically and in terms of customer service as Ballin's twin-screw liners had a decade earlier. On the technical side he set up a committee to decide the motive power to be installed on the new liners. It was headed by Cunard's Marine Superintendent, James Bain, and included Rear-Admiral H J Oram, Deputy Engineer-in-Chief of the Royal Navy, who had played a major part in the Navy's decision to adopt turbines, and senior managers of the major shipbuilders who would bid for the contracts to construct the new Cunarders or had experience of designing and building turbine-driven merchant ships, chiefly cross-channel ferries.

The most significant member of the committee was Charles Parsons, an Anglo-Irish aristocrat with a penchant for innovative engineering, who during a long and distinguished career, took out over 800 patents. In 1893 Parsons, now running his own engineering business in Newcastle-upon-Tyne, began to devote much of his considerable energy to marine propulsion, focussing on the development of the steam turbine – this at a time when steamships were powered by the ubiquitous reciprocating engine. He launched his demonstration ship *Turbinia* in December 1894. Her initial trials proved to be disappointing when she achieved a maximum speed of only 19.75 knots, little higher than that of contemporary battleships and less than that of torpedo-boats. With dogged tenacity, Parsons persevered and, by the end of 1895, he had perfected the design of an effective marine turbine. *Turbinia* was only 100 feet long, with a beam of 9 feet. Her displacement was less than 45 tons and her remarkable power-weight ratio gave her a hitherto unmatched top speed of 34 knots enabling her to outrun any contemporary warship.[1]

Parsons had ensured that the Royal Navy was well aware of the potential of his steam turbine. He had been encouraged by the positive reaction which he had received from senior figures within the Admiralty, thus belying its reputation for opposition to

19

technological change. Foremost among his supporters was the formidable and ever forward looking Jacky Fisher, who was then Third Sea Lord responsible for warship design and construction. Parsons had a flair for public relations and *Turbinia* had caused a stir at the Naval Review at Spithead at the time of Queen Victoria's Diamond Jubilee in 1897. The legend, carefully fostered by Parsons, that *Turbinia*'s appearance at Spithead was entirely unauthorised and that her agility enabled her to evade the Navy's patrol boats should be taken with a pinch of salt. She did manage to clip a picket-boat's stern. Parsons had invited a number of distinguished guests to join him aboard the vessel, one of whom later insisted that the spectacular high-speed run she made between the two main lines of British battleships had been expressly authorised by the Admiral commanding the Review.

In the event, Parsons' publicity coup at Spithead did not endanger his relations with the Sea Lords. Within a year the Admiralty had ordered HMS *Viper*, the Navy's first destroyer powered by Parsons marine turbines. *Viper* could achieve a speed of 37 knots and the superior performance of HMS *Amethyst*, the first turbine-driven cruiser, effectively confirmed the Admiralty's favourable view of Parsons and his invention. Shipping lines were equally quick to appreciate the advantages offered by the turbine, relative lightness and economy at speed. Turbines had another virtue in that their reduced vibration increased passenger comfort. In addition, engine rooms in ships fitted with turbines required less space than in comparable vessels with reciprocating engines, releasing more room for passenger accommodation. The first turbine-powered merchant ship, the Firth of Clyde ferry *King Edward*, went into service in 1901.[2]

Parsons maintained that, fitted with turbines, the new Cunarders could achieve a maximum speed of over 25 knots and maintain a cruising speed of 24 knots. The turbine represented a considerable quantum leap over the conventional reciprocating engine, not least because at high speed it was noticeably more economic. At Inverclyde's request, tests carried out on cross-Channel ferries indicated that turbine-equipped vessels achieved savings over comparable ships fitted with reciprocating engines of 23 per cent at full speed and 16 per cent at cruising speed.

By March 1904 the committee had decided that if the new Cunarders were to outclass their German rivals, there was no alternative to installing turbines. The Cunard Board, originally opposed to turbines as a power source, accepted their conclusion that the two new liners should be powered by four turbines driving quadruple screws.[3] Cunard had taken a high risk in opting for this technology as the power source for their two large new liners, the more so since, once taken, the decision was irrevocable. In 1904 those turbine-powered merchant ships which were already at sea were relatively small and the design of the much larger turbines to be installed in the new Cunarders caused considerable problems for the engine builders and their suppliers.

To illustrate the difficulty, the turbines for Nos 367 and 735 were designed to develop 68,000 brake horsepower, whilst those installed in contemporary warships such as HMS *Dreadnought* and the Royal Navy's first battlecruisers, the *Invincible* class, could generate 23,000 and 41,000bhp respectively. Although the engines performed well from the time of the two vessels' acceptance trials, Cunard and Parsons had taken an extremely courageous decision in committing to such an innovative design at a time when its application to large vessels was utterly unproved. It was the British, allegedly reluctant to adopt new technological advances, who had committed such important vessels to a new and untried propulsion system, while the Germans were far more cautious. The German navy's first eight dreadnoughts were powered by reciprocating engines and it was not until 1911 that the first turbine-powered German capital ship, the battlecruiser *Von Der Tann,* was commissioned. *Imperator,* the first German express liner fitted with turbines, did not enter service until 1913.

The specification of *Carmania* (19,524 tons), one of two liners who became known in Cunard as the Pretty Sisters, then under construction at Clydebank, was altered to serve as a test bed for the new technology. She was now to be powered by three direct-acting Parsons steam turbines. On her trials she smartly outperformed her sister *Caronia,* proving to be 1½ knots faster, and she ran more smoothly with a noticeable reduction in engine noise and vibration and improved fuel consumption. A number of marine engineers sailed on *Carmania*'s maiden voyage to New York in December 1905 and were impressed by the efficiency of her turbines in operation. Parsons' turbines had been proven beyond doubt as an effective and viable power source for North Atlantic liners, representing a huge advance over the noisy reciprocating engines used on all earlier liners including the HAPAG and NDL fleets.

The hull design for Nos 367 and 735 incorporated the results of detailed tests carried out in the Admiralty tank at Haslar, near

Portsmouth. The specification called for 'five of Lord Kelvin's most recent patent (magnetic) compasses'. On the marketing side, Cunard's catering and customer service departments were extensively reorganised to provide the exacting standards which would be required to assure a high degree of passenger satisfaction aboard the new liners.

In May 1904, the construction contracts for Nos 367 and 735 were awarded respectively to John Brown on Clydebank and Swan Hunter on Tyneside. In Cunard they were respectively nicknamed the Scottish and the English ship. No 367's keel was laid on 16 June 1904, about three months earlier than that of her sister. John Brown had to reorganise its shipyard to accommodate such a large project. A new berth was installed taking up the area previously occupied by two slips. As the Clyde was only 610 feet wide opposite Clydebank and No 367 was 786 feet long the new slip was constructed at an angle of 40 degrees to the river's banks to take advantage of the junction between the Clyde and its tributary, the Cart. This junction was widened so as to permit the newly-launched giant a run from the slips of up to 1,200 feet.

In February 1906 the Cunard Board named No 367 *Lusitania* and No 735 *Mauretania*. Cunarders had traditionally been given names ending in 'ia', and the two new giants were called after the Roman names for Portugal and Morocco. Sadly, Inverclyde, who died in October 1905, never lived to see the launch of the two mighty ships which he had conceived and championed. At 12.30pm on 7 June 1906, watched by 600 invited guests and with thousands of spectators occupying every conceivable vantage point and the town of Clydebank *en fête*, his widow Mary broke the traditional bottle of champagne over *Lusitania*'s bows and, to thunderous applause, her 20,000-ton hull slid smoothly down the slipway into the Clyde. The launch had gone like clockwork, taking only 86 seconds from the time she started to move until 1,600 tons of dragging chains brought her to rest with her bows only 110 feet from the end of the slipway – a very satisfactory result as a contemporary account declared.

The trade journal *The Shipbuilder* marked the occasion in a thoughtful editorial:

> Transcending in interest every event of the kind for many years, if not in the entire annals of shipbuilding on the Clyde, the launch of the Cunard liner, the *Lusitania*, from the stocks of the Clydebank ship-

building establishment of John Brown and Co. Ltd., attracted almost universal attention, and was observed by a vast concourse of spectators, drawn not only from local shipping circles, but from associated sources throughout the kingdom and abroad.

The launch and the coming advent of this triumph in marine architecture must undoubtedly mark an epoch in the development of the steamship, and it is peculiarly appropriate that they should signalise the centenary of practical steam navigation. The *Lusitania* and her sister ship, *Mauretania* which will follow her from the stocks of Swan Hunter and Whigham Richardson on the Tyne in September, are expected to sail two miles per hour faster than any of their predecessors on the Atlantic – an increase at one step which involves an addition of about 70 per cent to the 40,000 indicated horse-power developed by the fastest of merchant steamers now afloat.

Not only are they the largest, most powerful and, by intention, the fastest ocean liners ever constructed, but they are specially interesting and significant as factors in technical development because of the adoption of quadruple screws, and of the turbine system of propulsion in a much more comprehensive form than in any preceding steamships.[4]

A year later *Lusitania* was fitted out and ready for her sea trials, which were conducted under the eagle eye of that extremely interested party, the Admiralty, and were far more extensive than those of *Titanic* five years later. James B Watt, Cunard's highly respected senior captain, who had first gone to sea on clipper ships, was appointed as her first Master, and one of the line's most remarkable personalities, Arthur Rostron, as Chief Officer. Rostron became famous for his inspired rescue of the *Titanic* survivors when he was captain of *Carpathia* and was later to command *Mauretania* and become Commodore of the line. Her Chief Engineer, Alexander Duncan, like his colleagues, transferred from *Campania*. Like so many of Cunard's senior officers, all three were Scotsmen.

On 27 June 1907, escorted by six tugs, *Lusitania* left Clydebank and sailed proudly down the Clyde to the Tail of the Bank off Gourock to begin her trials, safely negotiating the sharp, 90-degree bend in the river on which *Queen Mary* grounded on her voyage 'doon the watter' nearly thirty years later. Early in her trials her designers discovered to their chagrin that *Lusitania* was not entirely flawless. Her stern vibrated severely at speed and she was returned to John Brown for alterations to the cabin-class public rooms, which substantially reduced the fault although it was never entirely eliminated. Her English sister *Mauretania* also suffered from vibration. During her high speed trials, her Captain, Pritchard, ordered the engine room to slow down, explaining that 'he was being shaken off his bridge'.[5] Excess vibration in large ocean liners repeatedly plagued naval architects and *Queen Mary* and *Normandie* both suffered badly from this defect when they first went into service. The British Second World War battleships of the *King George V* class, fitted with four screws, vibrated severely above 25 knots.[6] All ships vibrate to some degree, particularly those which have high power and can steam at high speed. This problem was not to be resolved until well after the Second World War when detailed research and computer-aided design resulted in a dramatic improvement in the incidence of vibration, especially in fast ships.

By the end of July these alterations were complete and *Lusitania* was ready for her speed trials. On 27 July, 600 guests of Cunard and John Brown went aboard for a 48-hour shakedown cruise round Ireland. After they had transferred to tenders at the Mersey Bar, the liner then sailed for the Firth of Clyde to undergo the most exacting tests. On the measured mile in the Firth, and drawing 33 feet she achieved a speed of 26 knots and on two 60-mile runs with a draft of 31 feet 7 inches she recorded 26.45 knots. On four successive 300-mile runs between Corsewall Point on the Wigtonshire coast and the Longship light at Land's End she averaged 25.4 knots. The mighty ship had triumphantly surpassed the Admiralty's specifications. Despite her size, *Lusitania* was remarkably agile and manoeuvreable. During her sea trials, the order to go to full speed astern was telegraphed to the engine room when she was travelling at 22.8 knots, bringing her to a full stop in 3 minutes and 55 seconds during which time she had covered ¾ mile. Tests showed that her rudder could be put from amidships to hard over to port or starboard in 15 seconds. Sailing at 22 knots she steered a complete circle in 7 minutes and 50 seconds.[7]

In August 1907, *Lusitania*, her trials successfully completed, was accepted into Cunard's service and she sailed for Liverpool to go into drydock before her miden voyage. In every aspect – size, technology, comfort and speed – she was state-of-the-art, outclassing her German rivals. At 30,396 tons she was the largest ship afloat, half as large again as the revolutionary all-big-gun turbine-powered battleship HMS *Dreadnought* which had been commissioned into the Royal Navy less than a year before.

Dreadnought had made all existing battleships obsolete and *Lusitania* was similarly to render every liner on the North Atlantic out of date. For the first time since Samuel Cunard had introduced his four pioneering paddle ships, his line was at the cutting edge of change and their new liner was hailed as a star. At 786 feet *Lusitania* was nearly 80 feet longer than the current Blue Riband holder, *Kaiser Wilhelm II.* She was 10,000 tons larger, 70 feet longer and at least 2 knots faster than the most recently completed German liner *Kronprinzessen Cecilie,* in her own right a fine ship. Her turbines could develop 68,000 brake horse-power whilst her German rival, fitted with the latest model quadruple expansion reciprocating engines, could only provide 45,000bhp. She was equipped with Marconi's wireless telegraph system, invented less than ten years before and among other innovations were electrically-powered lifts and the Thermo-Vent forced air heating and cooling system, a forebear of today's air-conditioning. As a safety feature she had an extensive system of hydraulically powered watertight bulkhead doors, controlled from the bridge.

The space allotted to passenger accommodation was half as large again than on any liner then in service. She could carry 552 passengers in first class, or saloon in Cunard terminology, 460 in cabin or second class and 1,186 in third class, as steerage had politely been renamed. She would have a crew of 827, 69 in the deck departments, 369 in the engine and boiler rooms and 389, including cooks and stewards, in passenger service.

Cunard had built not only a mighty ship but a beautiful one. Sixty years later the maritime historian, J H Isherwood, remembered her:

> *Lusitania* was the world's most magnificent ship. The fine bow, long forecastle carried well back into the superstructure, graceful stern and four huge heavily raked funnels gave an impression of power, speed and seaworthiness never since equalled. No ships before or since have had such a dominating, purposeful personality. She, and her sister, looked superb from any angle and they became from the first national symbols of the country's prestige and prowess at sea. I remember being overtaken in mid-Atlantic by *Mauretania* just after sunset. She passed close just as all her lights were coming on, dipping gently to the same sea that we were throwing over the forecastle head, smoke trailing astern from her four funnels. It was a memorable, even awe-inspiring sight.[8]

Lusitania was also highly resilient – in January 1910 she ran into an exceptionally severe storm en route for New York and she was hit head on by an 80-foot wave which crashed over her forecastle with colossal force. The most serious damage was to the front of her bridge which was pushed back several inches.

In comparison to their ornate German contemporaries, the standard of decor and comfort of British liners had been mediocre. Inverclyde, determined that his new Cunarders would provide the highest standards of decoration and passenger appeal, emulated Ballin by appointing distinguished architects to design their interiors. Almost his last decision as Chairman was to select the Scottish architect, James Millar, as *Lusitania*'s interior designer.[9] Millar was an inspired choice. He had started his professional life in the civil engineering department of the Caledonian Railway, well known for the importance it placed on design, and his layout of the 1901 Glasgow Exhibition had earned him considerable recognition. During a long and successful career, which stretched well into the 1930s, he designed many highly-admired commercial buildings and banks, mostly in and around Glasgow.

Millar worked in an eclectic period style, then much admired. His treatment was lavish, most notably the magnificent domed two-deck, white-panelled Louis Seize saloon-class dining saloon. The saloon-class lounge was Georgian with inlaid mahogany panels and massive marble fireplaces surmounted by a spectacular skylight with twelve stained glass panels, one representing each month of the year. The smoking room was Queen Anne, panelled in Italian walnut complemented by furnishings in Italian red, which acted as a contrast to the prevailing white and gold decor of the other public rooms. The saloon-class writing-room, with its mahogany furniture and silk curtains, looked if it had been moved from an Adam house. In designing *Lusitania*'s eighty-seven two-room suites, Millar gave his eclecticism full rein and passengers could choose between suites decorated in a range of styles from William and Mary to Adam, from Sheraton to eighteenth-century Colonial and from Louis Quinze and Louis Seize to Empire. His pièce de résistance was the portside six-room Regal suite on the promenade deck modelled on the Petit Trianon at Versailles with a walnut dining-room and gold mouldings and a white drawing-room with gilt mouldings and panels with floral paintings. The striking grand stairway connecting her six main decks was much admired. At each deck a spacious hall ran the breadth of the liner and in its centre were the two lifts.

Lusitania's second- or cabin-class public rooms, a Georgian dining-room with an ornate mahogany sideboard and a drawing-room with satinwood furniture in a grey Louis Seize style, were almost as comfortable as first class had been in earlier Cunarders and her third-class accommodation, although spartan, almost certainly offered better amenities than the homes which most immigrants had left behind. In contrast to the open dormitories provided in earlier liners, *Lusitania*'s third-class passengers were accommodated in 302 cabins, most of them with four or six beds. Millar had succeeded in creating a magnificent interior which won him many eloquent tributes from passengers and critics alike and a letter of appreciation from the Cunard Board.

Particular care had been devoted to planning the state-of-the-art galleys, the twenty pantries and still rooms and 13,000 cubic feet of refrigerators. The main galley served both the saloon and cabin class dining rooms and boasted a 250 square foot hot-plate and the third-class galley had the capacity to serve 3,000 meals if the liner was ever to be converted into a troopship. The first-class menus rivalled those of the best restaurants ashore and the food in third class was remarkably wholesome, with steak and onions for breakfast twice a week and roast beef and plum pudding for Sunday dinner.

On 3 September Cunard opened *Lusitania* to the public and 20,000 people seized the chance of visiting her, and the mighty ship ever after held a particular place in the hearts of the people of Liverpool, who affectionately called her Lucy. The weekly periodical, *The Sphere*, estimated that almost ten times that number came to see her off when she sailed on her maiden voyage to New York on the evening of 7 September, calling at Queenstown on the following day. On 13 September she reached New York, sailing in triumph up the Hudson to receive the tumultuous welcome traditionally given to ocean liners on their first arrival in the city. Thousands of spectators, primed by extensive Cunard publicity, lined both banks of the Hudson to catch a sight of the splendid new ocean giant, the sirens of every boat on the river sounded their greetings, and the city's firefloats saluted her with spectacular fountains of water. *Lusitania* had crossed the Atlantic in 5 days and 54 minutes and on one day she had run 593 miles. Slowed by fog on the last day of the voyage, she had failed to break the record for the crossing by only 30 minutes.

On her second westbound voyage *Lusitania* triumphantly won back the Blue Riband, steaming the 2,780 miles from

Queenstown to the Ambrose Lightship in 4 days, 19 hours and 52 minutes. Her average speed on this record-breaking voyage was almost 24 knots and for the first time the Atlantic had been crossed in less than five days. At a stroke, Britain had regained her previous supremacy on the North Atlantic.[10] The news that Germany had lost the Riband caused considerable irritation in Berlin, Bremen and Hamburg, with Ballin publicly denouncing the provision of a subsidy for *Lusitania* to secure a slight advantage over German shipping.

That November *Lusitania* carried 10 million dollars in gold bullion dispatched by the Bank of England to the Morgan Bank as much needed collateral for Pierpont Morgan's audacious and successful rescue effort after the October financial panic.[11] None of Morgan's liners were fast enough for the task. In the same month she was joined on the route by her sister *Mauretania* and between them the two great Cunarders were to hold the Blue Riband for the remarkable span of twenty-two years. There was a great rivalry between the two new liners and the English ship *Mauretania* was always marginally the faster. From the time she went into service, and despite the intense competition provided by the arrival of larger and even more luxurious liners, White Star's *Olympic*, sistership of the doomed *Titanic* and more than half her size again, and HAPAG's *Vaterland* and *Imperator*, of over 50,000 tons, *Lusitania* remained highly popular with travellers on the North Atlantic due to her speed, her record for punctuality and reliability, the splendour of her decor and Cunard's newly-acquired reputation for service. She proved to be the more popular of the two sisters, largely because regular passengers preferred Millar's spectacular interior decorations to those designed for *Mauretania* by the English architect Harold Peto. The two sisters were able to operate a consistent 16-day Liverpool/New York/Liverpool round voyage. In 1911 *Lusitania* completed sixteen round voyages. In marketing terms, Cunard had a particular niche. White Star never even attempted to emulate the five-day Transatlantic crossing offered by their two popular express liners.

Six months after *Lusitania* went into service, Albert Ballin sued for peace and called off the rate war. Berlin had become increasingly concerned that the combine was engaged in a destructive commercial battle with Cunard which neither side could win. William Watson, Inverclyde's successor as chairman, noted that the Kaiser himself intervened saying that ' he was going to tell Mr Ballin that he must settle things with Cunard . . . it was absurd this fighting and cutting of rates and throwing away money.'[12] The timing was advantageous as traffic had fallen sharply following the American financial crisis and Ballin rightly feared that the introduction of *Lusitania* and *Mauretania* had enabled Cunard to operate a premium service which could cream off what trade was available. The effect of introducing new ships, which can offer superior service and amenities to those of existing vessels, was highlighted when the new NDL liners *Bremen* and *Europa* went into service in July 1929 and March 1930 respectively. At that time Cunard was operating a weekly service with three liners, all of which had been commissioned before the First World War. Between 1928 and 1931 passenger traffic and revenue on the North Atlantic dropped rapidly due to the Depression but the new German liners proved so attractive that in 1931 the two German lines carried more than twice the number of first-class passengers they had in 1926. During the same period Cunard's first class bookings fell by nearly 60 per cent.[13] Ballin had another reason for ending the war. He did not wish to prejudice funding for the 50,000-ton giants now on the HAPAG drawing boards which would constitute his line's response to the new Cunarders.

The two new ships were now operating a weekly Liverpool–New York service on a three ship basis together with the older *Campania*, a voyage pattern which had previously required using four ships. The resultant operating economies had permitted Cunard to introduce a second weekly crossing with four more ships. For the first time in more than a decade the imperative on the North Atlantic had moved away from the German lines. In 1909, both sisters were equipped with four-bladed propellers of an improved design which effectively increased their speed by a knot and later that year *Lusitania* steamed from Queenstown to Sandy Hook on Long Island in 4 days, 11 hours and 42 minutes averaging 25.85 knots.[14] In October, Alfred Booth, then only thirty-seven, became Chairman of Cunard. He came from a strongly entrepreneurial background and was a member of one of Liverpool's most successful and well-connected merchant families, who had extensive interests in construction, manufacturing and service industry, including their own shipping line, the Booth Steamship Co, and who owned a stake in Cunard. In 1912 he was also appointed managing director. Like Albert Ballin, whom in some ways he resembled, he was an energetic hands-on manager, who habitually worked long hours. He could be autocratic and he was not a great delegator but during his reign Cunard ran like clockwork. His personal life, on the other hand, was not so, as he was burdened with a wife who was mentally distressed.[15]

*   *   *

The inquiry into the loss of *Titanic* in April 1912 generated a controversy over the location of bunkers in passenger liners. *Titanic* was equipped with transverse bunkers and had remained on an even keel for two hours and forty minutes before she sank. All her lifeboats were successfully launched. Some authorities suggested that *Lusitania* was a safer ship than *Titanic* and that if the latter had been equipped with longitudinal bunkers, the coal might have restricted the amount of water which flooded into the ship, thus allowing her to stay afloat for longer. However, coal absorbs water and its weight increases and with it the tendency of the damaged ship to list. Counsel for the White Star Line argued persuasively before the inquiry that if *Titanic* had been equipped with longitudinal bulkheads, she would have developed such a serious list that it would have been difficult if not impossible to have launched the lifeboats. *Lusitania*'s subsequent fate confirms this contention. The *Titanic* inquiry is chiefly remembered for its recommendation that liners must carry sufficient lifeboats for every passenger and every member of the crew. The number of lifeboats carried on *Lusitania* was accordingly increased from sixteen to twenty-two and a further twenty-four collapsible lifeboats were installed.

One writer has suggested that *Lusitania*'s longitudinal bunkers constituted a major design fault and alleged that she should have been equipped with transverse or cross-ship bunkers. The latter assertion is pure hindsight. Early steam-powered warships and merchant vessels had engines of relatively small power and thus did not carry a great quantity of coal. As their size and speed increased, so did the requirement for larger coal bunkers. In particular, fast warships and express liners, such as *Lusitania* and the *Olympic* class, burned large amounts of coal. The most practical location for bunkers in such vessels was outboard of the boiler rooms thus enabling fuel to be readily transferred from the bunkers to the firing floors. This necessitated the provision of longitudinal bulkheads between boiler rooms and bunkers, permitting large stocks of coal to be carried adjacent to the point of use.

At the time *Lusitania* was designed, shipbuilders and naval architects believed that longitudinal bunkers were a desirable safety feature, protecting vessels in case of collision. The Admiralty required that the new Cunarders should be equipped with longitudinal bunkers in line with normal warship design. Many shipping lines, including HAPAG and NDL, following the accepted conventional practice, specified these bunkers for their passenger liners, including *Lusitania*'s contemporary, the elegant *Kronprinzessen Cecilie* and the later *Imperator* class, which were under construction when *Titanic* was lost. Both German lines were noted for the attention they paid to safety. It is not clear why the naval architects department of the shipbuilders Harland & Wolff, which was responsible for designing the *Olympic* class, departed from the conventional practice and specified transverse bulkheads but in retrospect their decision was correct.

In the aftermath of the inquiry a committee was set up, headed by the Scottish shipbuilder Archibald Denny, to advise on the internal division of merchant ships. The committee, like its successors, concluded that that longitudinal wing bunkers, with which *Lusitania* (and her German contemporaries) were equipped, were dangerous features, which could hazard a ship's stability. Centreline longitudinal bulkheads, which were usually installed in the cavernous engine rooms of liners with reciprocating engines, were considered to be even more dangerous. The loss of so many ships with longitudinal bunkers to torpedo attack or to mines during the First World War confirmed the validity of the Denny committee's recommendation and led to a general rearrangement of the positioning of bulkheads. The replacement of coal by oil made bunkers redundant. Oil tanks do not have to be located close to boiler rooms and can, for instance, be placed in double bottoms.

Cunard's financial statements clearly reveal the improvement in the company's position from the time *Lusitania* and *Mauretania* went into service. From a low point in 1908, when traffic had been adversely affected by the American Depression of the previous year, profits and return on capital rose steadily. The annual dividend which had been passed in 1904 and again in 1908 and 1909 more than doubled between 1910 and 1914. By that year almost £800,000 of the Government's construction loan had been repaid on schedule.[16] This strong performance reflects the benefit from the ending of the rate war as well as the significant operating efficiencies built into the two new Cunarders, their considerable popularity with the travelling public and the resultant increase in market share.

By 1910 Cunard was able to order another large express liner, *Aquitania* (45,646 tons), whose construction was entirely funded from the line's own resources.[17] The new ship, effectively an improved *Lusitania* with an additional deck and 80 feet longer, was approximately the same size as the *Olympic* class. She was delivered to Cunard less than three months before the outbreak of war. The line could now operate a weekly transatlantic service with three modern liners of similar speed with a combined passenger capacity of almost 8,000. Inverclyde's initiative in negotiating the 1903 agreement had been fully justified. Britain's predominance on the North Atlantic had been triumphantly restored and in time of peace the deal had proved to be extremely fruitful for Cunard and its shareholders. With the advent of war in August 1914, the advantage was to alter sharply in favour of the Admiralty.

CHAPTER 3

The Brief Life of the Armed Merchant Cruiser

At 2.30pm 1430 GMT on 25 July 1914, *Lusitania*, Captain Daniel Dow in command, sailed from Liverpool on her ninety-second westward voyage, the last she was to make in time of peace. It was the height of the travelling season, all three classes were well-booked and the usual large crowd had gathered at the waterfront to see her off. As the mighty ship cleared Fastnet, leaving Ireland behind her, and headed out into the Atlantic, few aboard would have realised that the long European peace, the *Pax Britannica*, which had brought such unprecedented progress, was crumbling by the day. Her third-class passengers, looking forward to the challenge of a new life in the New World, little knew that they were almost the last of the millions who had crossed the Atlantic in response to the lines of the poet Emma Lazarus:

> 'Keep, ancient lands, your storied pomp!' cries she
> With silent lips. 'Give me your tired, your poor,
> Your huddled masses yearning to breathe free,
> The wretched refuse of your teeming shore.
> Send these, the homeless, tempest-tossed to me.
> I lift my lamp beside the golden door.'

While *Lusitania* steamed serenely westward under the blue skies and through the calm seas of high summer the lamp beside that golden door was soon to go out, never to be rekindled.

If her British saloon-class passengers on this voyage ever discussed politics, they would probably have talked about the latest in an apparently perennial succession of Irish political crises and not about the implications of the murder of the heir to the Austrian throne and his wife, nearly a month before. On 5 July, the Kaiser had assured the Austrian ambassador in Berlin that Austria could depend on Germany's full support in any action it might take to punish Serbia for its involvement in the murders.

In giving Vienna what historians have called the blank cheque, Wilhelm, ignoring Bismarck's precept that Balkan adventures were not worth the bones of a single Pomeranian Grenadier, had taken the fateful act which was to precipitate the First World War.

By the time *Lusitania* reached New York on the evening of 30 July, the European crisis had become front-page news. Austria and Serbia were already at war and Austria-Hungary and Russia had both mobilised, although the British Government still believed that the conflict would be confined to the east. Two days later Imperial Germany declared war on Russia and then prepared to invade France. The Schlieffen plan, involving the breach of Belgian neutrality, brought Britain into the conflict.

On 3 August, the day before Britain declared war on Imperial Germany, the Admiralty requisitioned both *Lusitania* and the westbound *Mauretania,* two days out of Liverpool and hastily diverted into Halifax, Nova Scotia, for war service under the terms of the 1903 agreement. Captain Vivian Bernard RN was appointed to command *Lusitania.* Captain Cole Fowler RN was dispatched post-haste to Halifax to take over command of *Mauretania* for her eastbound voyage. The General Manager of Cunard, A D Mearns, successfully insisted that neither vessel would sail for Liverpool until the Admiralty had agreed to indemnify the line against war risks on their eastbound voyage. *Lusitania* slipped out of New York at 1.00am on 5 August, arriving safely in Liverpool on August 11. A third captain RN was sent to Liverpool to supervise the conversion of the two liners into auxiliary cruiser role. He took with him a comprehensive list of instructions. Gun platforms had already been installed on their open decks and the Admiralty now required the clearing of space on the open deck around the gun foundations, prior to fitting the guns, thus creating an arc of fire. More space was to be cleared for the installation of magazines.[1]

The War Staff soon reassessed the desirability of using liners as auxiliary cruisers. Their limitations were sharply illustrated in the only encounter of the war between two armed merchant cruisers, which took place on 14 September 1914 off the Brazilian coast between the requisitioned Cunarder *Carmania,* equipped with eight 4.7in guns, and *Cap Trafalgar* of HAPAG's subsidiary, the Hamburg Sud-Amerika Line. The liner had been commandeered by the German Naval Attaché in Buenos Aires and repainted in Cunard colours. On 1 September she met the gunboat SMS *Eber* off the Brazilian port of Bahia and was fitted with two 4.1in guns.

Although she was outgunned, *Cap Trafalgar* put up a doughty fight before she went down. In the process *Carmania* suffered such heavy damage that she barely made port.

At the outset of the war the British blockade had effectively bottled up almost all the German liners which were in their home ports. No fewer than eighteen liners, including Ballin's huge *Vaterland* were laid up in New York and other American ports to keep them from falling into British hands.

The 1897 Blue Riband winner *Kaiser Wilhelm Der Grosse* sailed from Bremen on the morning of 4 August before Britain had declared war and took a circuitous route between Iceland and Greenland to reach her patrol area off the Canary Islands. She had only sunk two small ships and a trawler totalling 10,000 tons when the cruiser HMS *Highflyer* found her coaling off West Africa on 26 August and opened fire even though she was in the territorial waters of a Spanish colony. The liner was so heavily damaged that her crew scuttled her.

Only two German auxiliary cruisers were to survive for long. *Kronprinz Wilhelm* left Hoboken on 3 August and rendezvoused two days later off the Bahamas with the cruiser SMS *Karlsruhe* who transferred two 3.4in guns and her navigating officer, KapitanLeutnant Paul Thierfelder, who took over as captain. The process was interrupted by the arrival of the cruiser HMS *Suffolk*. *Karlsruhe* broke off and succeeded in outrunning her British pursuer and *Kronprinz Wilhelm* also managed to escape, sailing for the Azores where she was refueled from a German collier. By consummate seamanship, Thierfelder kept the liner, designed for an Atlantic crossing lasting a week, at sea for eight months in which time she sank fifteen ships totalling 60,000 tons. Whilst she was able to secure coal supplies from the prize ships which she captured, the process of coaling at sea caused considerable damage to her sides as the ships inevitably bumped each other in the swell. The once proud liner was in poor condition, leaking heavily, her engines and boilers failing and her crew suffering from a lack of fresh food, when Thierfelder eventually surrendered her to the US Coast Guard at Hampton Roads, Virginia, on 11 April 1915. A month earlier and for similar reasons, the other surviving merchant cruiser, *Prinz Eitel Friedrich*, which had sailed from the Chinese port of Tsingtao at the start of the war and which had accounted for over 30,000 tons of Allied shipping, had also surrendered to the American authorities. Their considerable appetite for coal, the increasing difficulty in supplying them in face of British control of the seas and their lack of armour and resultant vulnerability to gunfire, had rendered the German passenger liners completely unsuitable for use in the merchant cruiser role.[2]

Within a week of the outbreak of war, the Admiralty reconsidered their order requisitioning *Lusitania* and *Mauretania*. With the majority of the German liners now bottled up in port, they had less need for auxiliary cruisers than they had anticipated. They decided, correctly, if rather belatedly, that the two great Cunarders were too large and vulnerable and their fuel consumption too great for their effective deployment as merchant cruisers.[3] Although early steam turbines were markedly more economical than reciprocating engines at high speed, the reverse was true if they were cruising at slow speed. On 11 August, the day *Lusitania* returned to Liverpool, the Admiralty instructed Cunard that the two express liners would no longer be required in auxiliary cruiser role and that they would be held in Liverpool to Admiralty requirements. Pending further instructions, the third-class passenger accommodation on *Lusitania*'s D, E and F decks would be cleared and a number of bulkheads taken down to provide additional cargo space.[4] Cunard strongly protested against this decision on the grounds of resultant expenses and losses incurred. The executive committee of the line, meeting on August 19, noted that the Admiralty had agreed to pay one month's rent for *Lusitania* commencing from 12 August, as compensation for her enforced inactivity. Meanwhile, *Mauretania* made a rapid five-day crossing from Halifax, arriving in Liverpool on 19 August. After making one further round trip voyage to New York leaving on 29 August, she was laid up in the Mersey. On 12 September, with her month's rent concluded, *Lusitania*, her Cunard Red funnels and her brass nameplates painted black, sailed for New York on her ninety-third voyage, carrying a large number of American passengers who had been marooned in Europe by the outbreak of hostilities. She was to make nine wartime voyages. *Aquitania*, which had only completed three round voyages before the declaration of war, briefly served as an auxiliary cruiser, but after colliding with the Leyland liner *Canadian* in thick fog on 22 August she was forced to return to Liverpool for repairs. The Admiralty concluded that, like her sister Cunarders, she was too large for use as an auxiliary cruiser and she was handed back to the line and laid up.

*   *   *

At the onset of the war, the conventional wisdom decreed that it would be over by Christmas. Lord Kitchener, appointed as Secretary of State for War on 4 August, had disagreed with this thesis and had persuasively argued that the British Government should plan for a war which would last at least three years. This would entail a concerted programme to purchase munitions, metals, textiles and other military supplies for a greatly enlarged army on a huge and hitherto unprecedented scale. Imperial Germany, who had long been actively preparing for war, had built up a large store of war supplies. Britain had been less provident and the country was almost totally unprepared to fight a large-scale war. In peacetime it had come to depend on importing much of the manufactured products and raw materials, which would prove essential for maintaining the war effort.[5] Germany had supplied many of these goods and the resultant shortfall could only be overcome by placing large orders with American industry. Alfred Booth's cousin, George, ran Booth & Co in London and his ability was recognised by his appointment as a director of the Bank of England in 1915, when he was only thirty-eight. The Booth family had powerful connections in the business establishment. From the outset of the war, George Booth had worked with the War Office in developing their contacts with leading industrialists who could provide some of their urgently needed requirements. This involvement led to his appointment in April 1915 as head of the Armaments Output Committee, a group of businessmen, whom Lloyd George nicknamed the Men of Push and Go, whose function was to plan and implement this considerable enterprise, including controlling the purchases to be effected in America. Time being of the essence, *Lusitania* and the other Cunard liners on the North Atlantic run, far faster than freighters, would be useful in transporting these much-needed supplies as rapidly as possible across the North Atlantic.

The Admiralty's relations with Cunard and the other major shipping lines were handled by the Secretary to the Admiralty, Sir William Graham Greene, uncle of the novelist. Greene had served in the Admiralty for over thirty years and had been Private Secretary to four successive first lords. He was a man who welded considerable influence and was widely regarded as one of the most able civil servants of his time. Towards the end of September he told Alfred Booth that the cargo space of the Cunarders on the North Atlantic run, including *Lusitania*, was to be placed at the Admiralty's disposal to facilitate the rapid transport of vital military supplies, which would take priority over all other cargo. *Lusitania*'s cargo space had already been increased at the Admiralty's instruction so that with her speed and size she would play a valuable part in the war effort. The masters of these liners would be subject to Admiralty instructions and Cunard would only be permitted to contact their ships at sea through naval channels. The line would continue to be responsible for the provision of ships, crews and fuel.

Booth objected to the Admiralty's decision, particularly the proposal to use the liner to run military supplies. He could see no economic justification for keeping *Lusitania* on the North Atlantic run over the winter. Passenger traffic was falling dramatically after the marooned Americans had secured passage home and could be accommodated on the other smaller Cunarders. He told Greene that he would have preferred to lay her up for the duration like her sisters, no doubt pointing out that the White Star Line had already decided to withdraw their sole express liner, *Olympic*, from service at the end of October as their smaller intermediate liners had sufficient capacity to carry the reduced traffic. The *Olympic* class had been funded by White Star's ultimate parent, the Morgan Bank, and the line was not fettered by any agreement with the Government regarding their use in wartime. Greene overruled him and under the terms of what now looked suspiciously like a Faustian deal struck by his predecessor, Alfred Booth had little option but to agree to the Admiralty's demands. He had every reason to be annoyed as, by virtue of this order, the Admiralty had effectively reduced Cunard to the level of a sub-contractor with responsibility only for crewing, fuelling and provisioning their own flagship. This enforced degree of dual control was hardly ideal, especially in time of war, and sowed some of the seeds of the ensuing disaster.

Lusitania's Captain, Daniel Dow, was known in Cunard as Fairweather for his reputation both as a cautious and canny Scot and for being notoriously prone to seasickness. In October Alfred Booth appointed one of Cunard's rising stars, the burly and affable John C Anderson, as *Lusitania*'s Staff Captain or second-in-command. Jock Anderson was then forty-nine and had commanded three Cunarders, most recently the former Blue Riband holder, *Campania*. After the loss of *Titanic*, Booth had instituted the position of Staff Captain on *Lusitania* and *Mauretania*, with the objective of easing the multitude of responsibilities borne by their captains thus allowing them to concentrate on navigation and chief officers on watch-keeping. The terms of reference for staff captains required that they take responsibility for all aspects of discipline on board the liners including all drills and the stowage of cargo. They were to dine in the saloon dining-room at a table other than the captain's and in a picturesque phrase they were required to be on duty from 7am to 9pm, or after the third-class women had been ordered below![6]

George Booth, who had crossed the Atlantic regularly on *Lusitania* in peacetime, was among her first-class passengers when she sailed from Liverpool on 24 October, her third wartime crossing. He prided himself on having good sea legs and he was somewhat disconcerted to find himself prostrated by seasickness when the mighty ship ran into heavy weather. A relatively minor sea could make a voyage unpleasant for passengers and even large ships were thrown around by North Atlantic gales, which were all too frequent in winter. When Booth recovered, he went to see Captain Dow and the two men doubtless consoled each other on their recent bout of seasickness. As a senior Cunard captain, accustomed to wielding untrammelled authority aboard his ship, Dow was understandably concerned that he was now subject to Admiralty instructions when he went to sea. He was thus only too ready to confide in his chairman's cousin and confidant. He went as far as to show Booth the gun mountings concealed under coiled ropes on the shelter deck.

Booth asked the Captain why he should have suffered so badly from sickness on this particular voyage when he had suffered no ill-effects during bad weather on earlier voyages aboard the mighty ship. An apologetic Dow ascribed the liner's uncomfortable performance in the gale to the Admiralty's decision to remove the forward passenger accommodation on the three lower decks, which made her light in the bow and prone to ride higher in the water. To make matters worse, she was carrying little or no cargo on her wartime westbound voyages. Dow explained that as a result the vessel was both rolling and pitching in heavy seas, which in seaman's parlance he described as 'corkscrewing'. This is a particularly uncomfortable motion, caused by a quartering sea from aft. As it is only necessary to remove a relatively small amount of passenger accommodation to affect the stability of even a large ship, Dow's explanation seems reasonably well-founded. He added that he thought the liner would handle better when she would be carrying a full cargo on her eastbound voyages. Booth was able to reassure Dow on this point as he had some large orders to place for leather goods and other war supplies on a war office contract with Booth & Co. He was as good as his word, writing to Alfred from New York: 'The accoutrement business goes well, which should please the War Office and settle poor Fairweather's stomach'.[7]

George Booth had gone to America on his company's business but he had no sooner arrived in New York than the War Office asked him as a matter of urgency to develop the contacts with American industry and arrange the financial credits which would be necessary for an extended purchasing programme. To this end, Booth approached the Morgan Bank. The great Pierpont Morgan had died in 1913 and his bank was now run by his son Jack, a committed anglophile, who had managed its London operations for eight years, supported by an array of able partners. Prominent among them were Thomas Lamont, reckoned by many to be the most powerful man on Wall Street, and Dwight Morrow, later to become Charles Lindbergh's father-in-law. Booth was also able to enlist the invaluable support of Captain Guy Gaunt, the energetic and resourceful British naval attaché in Washington. Gaunt would oversee the arrangements for assembling the cargo and allocating it to the Cunarders and other British-flagged ships on the Atlantic run.

Mainstream American public opinion was strongly pro-Allies and was a factor in the success of George Booth's mission. This sentiment had been generated by Germany's breach of Belgian neutrality despite their guarantee of that country's integrity, the random brutality, including executions, handed out by the army to the civilian population and the wanton torching of the irreplaceable mediaeval library at Louvain. It was fully shared by the business community, who had quickly spotted the opportunity for profiting from the British and French need for munitions and war supplies on a colossal scale. In 1916 alone, American industry provided Britain and France with goods totalling $2.3 billion. The credit for these supplies was largely funded by the Morgan Bank.

On 30 October, the day *Lusitania* reached New York, an important change took place at the Admiralty. The First Sea Lord, Prince Louis of Battenberg, born in Germany and who had come to England to enter the Navy as a boy of thirteen almost fifty years before, was forced to retire, although his integrity and loyalty to his adopted country were unquestionable. An outbreak of xenophobia directed at anyone of German origin was largely to blame but the First Lord of the Admiralty, Winston Churchill, and the Prime Minister, H H Asquith, had both lost confidence in him. To succeed Prince Louis, Churchill brought back from retirement the veteran Lord Fisher, who had driven through so many far-reaching naval reforms during his previous tenure as First Sea Lord from 1904 to 1910. As the creator of HMS *Dreadnought*, which at a stroke had made every battleship in the world obsolete, the flamboyant Jacky Fisher was a true national hero. He was a volcano of a man, with boundless energy and a single-minded determination to achieve his objectives. Like Ballin he had a motto: Fear God and Dread Nought, and he liked to sign his letters to his close allies: 'Yours until Hell Freezes Over.'

The Navy's achievements at the outset of war had been considerable. Exploiting Britain's strategic position abreast of the sea routes connecting Germany with the rest of the world, the German merchant marine had been swept from the seas, an effective blockade had been enforced and the British Expeditionary Force had been escorted to France without any loss of life. Despite these successes, the Navy had experienced several setbacks. In the Mediterranean, during the first week of the war, the German battlecruiser *Goeben* and the light cruiser *Breslau* had successfully evaded a much larger British force including three battlecruisers and had sought refuge in Turkish waters. The resultant loss of British prestige was a considerable factor in Turkey's decision to join the war on the German side. On 22 September, the three old cruisers *Aboukir*, *Cressy* and *Hogue*, on blockade patrol off the Dutch coast, were attacked by a U-boat. *Aboukir* was torpedoed first and quickly developed a heavy list, caused by asymmetrical flooding, and then capsized. Her sisters came to her aid and were themselves torpedoed. 1,459 officers and men, including a number of naval cadets, were lost. Churchill, who had just made an ill-timed speech threatening that 'if the German fleet did not come out and fight they would be dug out like rats in a hole' was strongly criticised for this disaster. In reality, he had been alerted to the risks involved in keeping the cruisers in such an exposed position but, against his better judgement, Prince Louis had been persuaded by the Naval War Staff not to implement Churchill's order for their withdrawal, made four days before their sinking. Only a day before Fisher's return the new battleship *Audacious* had struck a mine and her crew were taken off. Three hours later, when in tow and without any warning, she blew up.

Churchill reasoned that Fisher would serve to restore public confidence in the Admiralty which had inevitably been undermined by this series of disasters. Fisher was, however, seventy-three and past his best. King George V, amongst others, had serious misgivings about the appointment, doubting that Churchill, who was notorious for interfering in operational matters to a far greater extent than any of his predecessors, could work successfully with the formidable old Admiral, who had always insisted that operations were the sole prerogative of the First Sea Lord. They feared that the Admiralty was not large enough to house these two men and their huge egos. Before six months had passed, their forebodings were to be realised.

CHAPTER 4

A Winter of Discontent

During the winter of 1914, the German navy sought to counter the increasingly effective British blockade by directing its best weapon, its U-boats, against merchant shipping. In the early months of the war, they had adhered to the internationally accepted rules of cruiser warfare, which stipulated that a warship could enforce a stop-and-search order against a merchant ship. If a vessel attempted to escape or resist, or if it was escorted by a warship, it lost its immunity to attack and could be sunk by gunfire or torpedo. If it was found to be an enemy vessel or if it was carrying contraband it could only be sunk after all passengers and crew had been allowed to take to the boats. Mere suspicion of contraband did not constitute grounds for attacking a vessel without warning. Throughout his career, Churchill believed that attack was the best method of defence and from October 1914, he issued a series of aggressive instructions to British shipping companies requiring masters to disregard any instruction to heave to and authorising them to attack or ram U-boats. They were also told to paint out their names and were permitted to fly a neutral flag. These orders were a clear breach, at least in spirit, of cruiser rules. In the following month, the Admiralty tightened the blockade by designating the North Sea as a military zone which neutral shipping entered at their peril.

On 4 February 1915, Germany retaliated. Addressing his submarine commanders at Wilhelmshaven, the Kaiser announced that from 18 February, the waters surrounding the British Isles, including Ireland, would become a war zone in which any enemy vessels could be sunk. In a clear attempt to deter neutral shipping from sailing into the new zone, neutral citizens were strongly warned against either travelling or shipping goods on Allied ships. The Kaiser told his U-boat captains that: 'if it is possible . . . to save the crews . . . do it . . . if you cannot save them, then it cannot be helped'. Both sides were thus shifting away from the concept of cruiser rules and, in essence, Germany was adopting a policy of unrestricted submarine warfare, which had been strongly advocated by Tirpitz and other admirals and supported, amongst others, by Ballin. In Washington, President Wilson and his administration reacted forcefully to the Kaiser's announcement.

Thomas Woodrow Wilson, twenty-eighth President of the United States, descended on both sides of his family from Presbyterian ministers, was the first southerner to occupy the White House since the Civil War. During that conflict, his father, Joseph, had been the minister in Augusta, Georgia. The town had been an important military centre and Confederate wounded had often been billeted in his father's church. Unlike so many of his contemporaries, the young Woodrow had seen the reality of war at first hand and it had left an indelible impression on him. At an early age Joseph had instilled into his son, on whom he doted, the Calvinist concept that he was destined for great achievements and that he should do good on this earth.[1] Although Wilson was in many ways a Gladstonian liberal, he also admired the conservative philosopher, Edmund Burke, and the Prussian autocrat, Otto von Bismarck. His idealism was tempered with a strong authoritarian streak and a mighty zest for power.

The late Dr Edwin Weinstein, a leading neurologist, who made a study of the medical histories of prominent political figures, wrote a detailed medical and psychological biography of Wilson. He discovered that he had suffered a series of strokes, one as early as 1896 when he was forty, in which he lost the use of his right hand for almost a year. Ten years later another stroke resulted in Wilson temporarily losing sight in his left eye. A third rather minor stoke occurred shortly after he became President. Weinstein concluded that the authoritarian bent in Wilson's character and his tendency to pay scant attention to other people's opinions had increased after these strokes.[2]

King George V, a shrewd judge of character, summed Wilson up as an arrogant professor. Indeed, for most of his life, Wilson had been an academic and in 1902 he had become President of Princeton. Although he achieved much for the university, his inability to reach a compromise over the status of the fraternity houses, known as eating clubs, on the campus, had united faculty, students and alumni against him. He took the rather extravagant stance that the clubs stood for the agents of evil and disease to whom he would make no concessions.[3] He suffered a serious defeat on this issue and lost another battle over a proposed new graduate college. His position as President became impossible and he was rescued by the local Democratic party bosses who secured for him the nomination for Governor of New Jersey. Once elected in November 1910, he soon announced his candidacy for President. On the forty-sixth ballot of the 1912 party convention he was finally nominated. Theodore Roosevelt and his Bull Moose party split the Republican vote and Wilson won the presidency with only 41 per cent of the electoral vote. He had become President only three years after entering the political arena – by any standard a formidable achievement.

In August 1914 Wilson's wife, Ellen, had died from nephritis and for several months afterwards he had suffered from depression, which was to some extent influenced by a severe guilty conscience. In the last few years of her life, Wilson had conducted a romantic friendship with one Mary Allen Peck, a divorcee, whom he often met in New York and when he went on holiday to Bermuda. Although the relationship may well have been platonic, as Mary Peck had the reputation of being a flirt, shortly before she died, Ellen Wilson had told the White House physician, Cary Grayson, that it had caused her the only grief of her married life.

Although the President had officially declared American neutrality in August 1914, most of his Cabinet and senior advisers, notably his political secretary, Joseph Tumulty, were sympathetic to the Allies. He himself had no objection to American industry profiting from supplying goods of war to the Allies. The German edict, delivered to the State Department on 6 February by their ambassador in Washington, Johann-Heinrich Count von Bernstorff, was not well received. Bernstorff was a member of a distinguished German family, his father Albrecht having served for nearly twenty years as ambassador in London and briefly as Prussian foreign minister. He had been born in England and had himself served as minister in the London embassy before his appointment to Washington in 1908. By German standards he was a liberal with little sympathy for the bellicose ultra-nationalists who surrounded the Kaiser, and whose contempt for America was only matched by their ignorance of its potential. The genial Bernstorff was well-liked in America.[4]

The German declaration conflicted with the President's rigid insistence that the freedom of the seas included the untrammelled right of American citizens to travel on Allied ships. The strongly-worded American reply, drafted in the absence of the Secretary of State, William Jennings Bryan, by Robert Lansing, Counsellor to the State Department and a committed Allied

supporter, threatened: 'that in the event that German submarines should destroy an American vessel or the lives of
American citizens, it would be difficult for the Government of the
United States to view the action . . . other . . . than as an indefensible violation of neutral rights.'[5] If such a situation should arise
Berlin would be held strictly accountable. This decisive reaction
caused the Kaiser to backtrack. On 15 February he ordered his
submarine commanders that on no account were they to attack
ships flying neutral flags unless they were positively recognised as
being enemy ships in disguise. In fact, the American position disregarded precedents in international law dating back as far as the
War of 1812. During the Civil War a Federal warship had actually
stopped a British merchant ship at sea and forcibly removed two
Confederate agents. Lincoln had ignored the vigorous but
unavailing protests of the British Government. The American
response was the first of an increasingly acrimonious exchange of
notes between Berlin and Washington over the ensuing year.

In a rather facile attempt at even-handedness, the State
Department protested strongly to London about British ships
who had been flying the Stars and Stripes, aimed amongst others
at *Lusitania*. The background to this contretemps is worthy of
examination. On 30 January *U-21* had sunk three unarmed merchant ships in the Irish Sea, close to the entry to the port of
Liverpool. Although the U-boat had obeyed cruiser rules, the
Admiralty was sufficiently concerned to divert two eastbound
Cunarders, *Transylvania* and *Ausonia,* into the Irish port of
Queenstown where they arrived on 31 January and 3 February.
Both liners were carrying war cargo including two pairs of 14in
guns, complete with turrets, which the Admiralty had purchased
from Bethlehem Steel, one of the principal American suppliers
to the British war effort. The turrets were clearly visible lashed to
the Cunarders' foredecks. The two liners were detained in
Queenstown incommunicado for several days, to the annoyance
of American passengers, some of whom protested vehemently to
the embassy in London. The two diverted Cunarders were followed on the busy shipping lanes off the south coast of Ireland by
a stream of merchant shipping including *Lusitania* who cleared
Fastnet Rock on the southwestern approach to the island, eastbound for Liverpool, early on the morning of 5 February.
Fortunately, *U-21* had only one torpedo left and her commander
decided to save it for his homeward voyage, although he had
identified a number of potential targets whom the copies of

Brassey's Naval Annual, which all German submarines carried, listed as being armed.

Lusitania arrived in Liverpool on 6 February with the President's emissary to Europe, Colonel Edward House, among her passengers. House had had a rough passage, and wrote in his diary on 5 February:

> Our voyage is about to come to an end. The first two days we had summer seas but just after passing the Banks a gale came shrieking down from Labrador and it looked if we might perish. I have never witnessed so great a storm at sea. It lasted for 24 hours and *Lusitania,* big as she is, tossed about like a cork. This afternoon, as we approached the Irish coast, the American flag was raised. It created much excitement and comment and speculation ranged in every direction.

On the following day, House noted Dow's reservations about his ship's vulnerability to torpedo attack:

> I found from Mr. Beresford, Lord Decies' brother, who had crossed with us, that Captain Dow had been greatly alarmed the night before and had asked him [Beresford] to remain on the bridge all night. He expected to be torpedoed and that was the reason for raising the American flag. I can see many possible complications arising from this incident. Every newspaper in London has asked me about it but, fortunately, I was not an eye-witness to it and have been able to say that I only knew about it from hearsay. The alarm of the captain for the safety of his boat [*sic*] caused him to map out a complete pro-gramme for the saving of passengers, the launching of lifeboats etc. etc. Dow told Beresford that if the boilers were not struck the boat could remain afloat for at least an hour and in that time he would endeavour to save the passengers.[6]

Dow's innate caution and attention to detail might have helped to save more lives had he still been in command of *Lusitania* three months later. Events were to dictate otherwise. Throughout the winter the British purchasing programme had been brought to a high degree of efficiency. Whilst some war supplies could legally be carried on passenger ships, notably rifle ammunition by virtue of a Commerce Department decree enacted in 1911, others had to be concealed in the manifests under such designa-tions as foodstuffs, furs and textiles. In the early months of 1915 Dudley Field Malone, Collector of the Port of New York, was hav-ing to cope with the problems caused by the vast increase in cargo being shipped through the port for the Allied purchasing programmes. Malone was a lawyer and a political appointee of the Federal Government. Wilson had nominated him as a favour to his father-in-law, Senator James O'Gorman of New York, an influential figure in Democratic politics, with whom he was not on good terms.

In his report to the Treasury Department compiled after the sinking, which he published in the magazine *The Nation* in January 1923, Malone outlined the system which he operated. He wrote that:

> it would have been impossible to discover . . . whether there were explosives on the *Lusitania* or on other ships unless [they] were enumerated in the manifests . . . or unless suspicious circumstances attracted the attention . . . of the Neutrality Squad . . . It is practically a physical impossibility to examine the contents of each case and package that is put on each outgoing ship . . . During the early stages of the European War, . . . I gave great thought to the question of verifying the contents of cases and packages to be shipped on outgoing steamers. The . . . purpose of such examination would be to ascertain if the contents . . . corresponded with [its] description in the sworn manifest. I called a conference . . . of the larger shippers . . . and the more experienced men of the customs service . . . after a long discussion, it was decided that . . . it would be . . . impracticable to make a physical examination of each package or case going into the cargo of an outgoing ship . . . it would take an army . . . to open and verify the contents of closed cases, replace the goods, and reseal the cases. The expense to the Government would make it . . . prohibitive. The delay to shippers and steamship companies would make it an untold . . . inconvenience. The damage to goods would be immeasurable. . . . these reasons, in the judgment of the conference . . . would be sufficient to make . . . impracticable . . . the physical examination of all closed cases in outgoing cargoes. . . . orders were issued to the customs and particularly to the Neutrality Squad to report at once any circumstance of a suspicious nature with respect to any cargo . . . in which case a complete examination and verification of the contents . . . would immediately be made by the customs.

Malone concluded this convincing analysis by telling his superiors that this random degree of surveillance was the utmost that could be done with the resources he controlled.[7]

The winter of 1914 had indeed proved difficult for Cunard. *Lusitania* consumed nearly 1,000 tons of coal per day at full speed. The combination of falling passenger traffic and a rising coal price resulted in her losing money at a rate well in excess of the subsidy, the very situation which Booth had feared. As competent managers, Cunard cut operating expenses. With effect from Voyage 96, sailing on 21 November, *Lusitania*'s No 4 boiler room was taken out of service, saving 1,600 tons of coal per voyage, reducing crew numbers and enabling the ship to break even. After she was sunk, Booth told Charles Sumner, the Cunard manager in New York, that even with these economies, the liner could hardly be expected to earn more than depreciation and interest on the construction loan. With only three boiler rooms in operation, *Lusitania*'s top speed was cut to 21 knots and her regular cruising speed to 18 knots, entailing a six-and-a-half day crossing. Many of the reservists in the liner's elite crew had joined the Navy and it was becoming increasingly difficult for Cunard to maintain peacetime standards in wartime conditions. The replacements which were found were seldom up to scratch and these staffing difficulties added considerably to the stress on the liner's officers.

Alfred Booth's reservations about carrying contraband on his liners were forcibly shared by both Sumner and Dow. Booth persuaded Sumner to accept the necessity of the situation and in January 1915 increased his annual salary from $20,000 to $25,000.[8] When Dow brought *Lusitania* into Liverpool on 8 March at the end of her seventh wartime voyage, during which a U-boat had sunk two merchant ships uncomfortably close to the liner's course, he asked to be relieved of his command. He bluntly told his Chairman that although he did not object to commanding his ship in a war zone, he could no longer accept the responsibility of carrying munitions or contraband on a passenger liner. Booth decided that Dow was suffering from nervous strain and sent him on leave.

His replacement was one of Cunard's most senior captains. William Thomas Turner, a native of Liverpool, was fifty-eight. He was a stocky man of great physical strength with piercing blue eyes, whose seagoing career stretched back nearly fifty years. The son of a sea captain, he had run away to sea as a cabin boy on the barque *Grasmere* and had survived when she ran onto a reef off the Northern Ireland coast in a gale and foundered. At the age of thirteen, he had signed on the clipper *White Star* as a deck hand, sailing round the Cape of Good Hope. During the voyage, he had a chance meeting with his father, who was then master of a sailing ship *Queen Of The Nations* and transferred to serve under him. When he was second mate of the clipper *Thunderbolt* in the

Indian Ocean outward bound for Calcutta, he had been swept overboard by a wave. The first mate had thrown him a lifebuoy to which he clung for over an hour, fighting off sharks while the clipper's crew hove to so that they could lower a boat to rescue him. In 1883 he was awarded the Liverpool Humane Society's Silver Medal for rescuing a fourteen-year-old boy who had fallen into the Alexandra Dock on the city's waterfront. That same year he rejoined Cunard, with whom he had served briefly as a third officer in 1877, and had since remained in the line's service with only one year's gap. He had been given his first command in 1903 and had since been master of nine Cunarders. When her first captain, James Watt, retired in 1908 he had succeeded to the command of *Lusitania*. Between 1910 and 1914, he had been master of Cunard's other express liners, *Mauretania* and *Aquitania*. He was currently captain of the intermediate liner *Transylvania*, one of the Cunarders which had been diverted into Queenstown at the end of January 1915.

Like many of his kind, Turner was a practical man without much formal education, who had risen to the top on ability. He had earned a reputation as a strict disciplinarian, who ran a tight ship and went by the book. Nonetheless, he enjoyed the respect, almost amounting to affection, of the officers and crews who had served under him. Unlike Dow or E J Smith of *Titanic*, Turner was one of those captains who disliked the social part of his duties. He did not enjoy dining at the Captain's table and succeeded in taking most of his meals in his day cabin below the bridge. Anderson, who had served as Turner's chief officer on the liner *Umbria* several years earlier, remained as *Lusitania*'s staff captain.

Like Alfred Booth, Turner had a troubled personal life; his wife had left him and his sisters had found him a housekeeper, one Mabel Every. She was still alive in January 1972, past ninety but mentally alert, when she was interviewed by a researcher for the author Colin Simpson, whose book *Lusitania* was published later that year. According to Simpson, she referred to Turner as Tom and disclosed that, despite a reputation for being uncommunicative, he had occasionally discussed Cunard affairs and the state of his ship with her.

CHAPTER 5

The Last Voyage

When he took command of *Lusitania*, Turner soon discovered that she was not the smoothly-running ship he remembered. Whilst her officers were experienced and capable, he was far from satisfied with the crew. He also found that maintenance of the lifeboats had been neglected. When Turner berthed *Lusitania* in Liverpool on the completion of his first voyage as her captain on 11 April he was not in a good mood. According to Miss Every he complained bitterly to Alfred Booth about these deficiencies and demanded and secured a Board of Trade inspection. The lifesaving equipment was examined by Mr Alfred Laslett, the Board of Trade surveyor in Liverpool and Captain Barrand, responsible for inspecting all liners which, like *Lusitania*, were certified to carry emigrants. They ordered four lifeboats and two hundred lifebelts, together with a number of other items which Turner and Anderson had identified as being defective, to be replaced immediately. As far as the Board of Trade was concerned, the liner was in good shipshape condition when she sailed from Liverpool on her 101st voyage on 17 April, watched by the devoted Mabel Every.

Gugliemo Marconi, the inventor of wireless telegraphy, was a passenger on what proved to be *Lusitania*'s last westbound voyage. One day out of Liverpool, when the liner was off the south coast of Ireland, he noticed a sudden increase in her speed. He was told that a lookout had sighted a submarine and that Turner had rung down for full speed ahead to get her out of the vicinity of the predator without any delay. The voyage passed without further incident and *Lusitania* docked in New York on schedule on 24 April. A detachment of Pinkerton security guards was stationed on the Cunard pier to ensure tight security. During the week the mighty ship was berthed in New York, Turner was able to take one evening off and go to the theatre to see his niece Mercedes Desmore, a successful actress who was appearing in a play called *The Lie* and take her to dinner. An article in the *New York Times* had described her: '. . . as a talented actress, possessed of much beauty and that . . . elusive attribute, personality. Miss Desmore is a niece of Capt. Turner of the *Lusitania,* one of the best known masters of the ocean liners sailing from New York.'[1]

By April 1915, the German community in New York was becoming increasingly active in its opposition to the Allied purchasing campaign. The German military and naval attachés in Washington, Captains Franz von Papen and Karl Boy-Ed, were actively involved in counter measures ranging from industrial espionage to setting up front companies to buy forward machine tools needed for manufacturing munitions and finished components on the British shopping list. They worked closely with the German community, particularly with the local representatives of the two large shipping lines, who had been left in charge of the liners laid up in Hoboken and had plenty of time to spy on Allied shipping and were well-informed of the volume of war materiel being shipped on passenger liners. The activities of both warring factions had not gone unnoticed in Washington and the Justice Department had sent a number of their Special Agents, the forerunners of the FBI, to keep a wary eye on what was going on in the New York docks. The agents were fairly tolerant of the British as Captain Gaunt was careful to stay within the limits of the law and pass on to them the information his intelligence network was collecting on the activities of the German service attachés. The Justice Department already suspected that Von Papen and Boy-Ed were involved in industrial espionage and was considering recommending their expulsion.

On 21 April, George Viereck, the editor and publisher of a pro-German newspaper *The Fatherland,* convened what he called his propaganda cabinet, made up of leading members of the German community in New York. Viereck and another cabinet member, Dr Bernard Dernburg, were undercover intelligence agents who enjoyed the tacit support of the embassy in Washington, which was also heavily subsidising *The Fatherland.* Dernburg was a former banker and minister of the colonies who had been sent to America at the start of the war to take charge of propaganda. They were worried that the sinking of any large British liner, with inevitable loss of American life, might endanger relations between Germany and America or, even worse, lead to war, a situation which was clearly not in their interests. They were concerned by the failure of the Wilson administration to ban or even to discourage American citizens from sailing on allied ships, although members of the German-American community had lobbied Bryan and several congressmen to institute such a ban.

The cabinet decided on a more aggressive approach, the placing of advertisements designed to dissuade American passengers from sailing on British ships, which should ideally be timed to coincide with the departure of the next large liner. They made sure of their ground by gaining Bernstorff's support. He agreed the copy and decided that the advertisement should be published in the embassy's name and appear on Saturday 24 April. The advertising agent retained by the embassy was unable to secure space in a number of New York papers and its appearance was delayed until the next Saturday, 1 May, the day that *Lusitania* was due to sail for Liverpool. It was placed in seven morning papers in New York, two in Philadelphia and one in Boston. In several papers, it appeared next to Cunard's regular advertisement. In view of the resultant controversy, it should be noted that the advertisement was not specifically aimed at *Lusitania* passengers but at all travellers. It was repeated on 8 May and a third booking on 15 May was cancelled following the hostile public reaction to the news of the sinking. The published copy read:

NOTICE!

TRAVELLERS intending to embark on the Atlantic voyage are reminded that a state of war exists between Germany and her allies and Great Britain and her allies; that the zone of war includes the waters adjacent to the British Isles; that in accordance with formal notice given by the Imperial German Government, vessels flying the flag of Great Britain, or of any of her allies, are liable to destruction in those waters and that travellers sailing in the war zone on ships of Great Britain or her allies do so at their own risk.

IMPERIAL GERMAN EMBASSY
WASHINGTON, D.C., APRIL 22 1915

The first serious breach of cruiser rules had occurred on 27 March 1915. The Elder Dempster liner *Falaba*, bound from Liverpool for West Africa, ignored *U-28*'s orders to stop before the U-boat commander eventually forced her to heave to and gave her passengers and crew only five minutes to take to the boats. Before this process could be completed a British trawler appeared and the U-boat promptly torpedoed the liner. She was evidently carrying a cargo of high explosives which blew up and *Falaba* sank immediately with the loss of 104 out of the 250 people aboard. An American mining engineer, Leon Thresher, was among the dead and the media coverage was distinctly unfavourable. Washington's initial reaction was equally furious but at this point a serious difference of opinion occurred inside the administration between Lansing, who wanted to take a hard line, and his superior, the Secretary of State, William Jennings Bryan.

Bryan had unsuccessfully run for President on three occasions on a populist ticket. Wilson owed him a considerable political debt for switching his support to him during the convention. Wilson's most recent biographer maintains that although Bryan's appointment was a political necessity, he was manifestly unfit for the job.[2] He was a pacifist, who did not share his colleagues' pro-Allied sympathies and he detested Wall Street and big business and their lucrative involvement in the Allied purchasing effort. Bryan did not always reason logically and he does not seem to have grasped the essential difference between the British and German blockades. Whilst the British merely confiscated American property, causing only monetary loss for which compensation was normally offered, the German departure from cruiser rules would inevitably lead to the loss of American life, of which *Falaba* was only the first incidence. He persuaded the President that *Falaba*'s captain was responsible for the loss of life by virtue of his initial resistance and that no diplomatic action should be taken against Germany. Wilson had significantly retreated from his principle that the German government should be held to strict accountability.

American vessels had come under German attack for the first time at the end of April. The freighter *Cushing* was bombed by a seaplane in the North Sea, fortunately escaping without damage, and the tanker *Gulflight*, bound from Port Arthur, Texas, to Rouen was torpedoed by *U-30* without any warning off the Scilly Isles. She was, however, being escorted by two British patrol boats and would thus have been a legitimate target had she been British-registered. *U-30*'s commander, Von Rosenberg, justified his action by claiming that he had not at first noticed that *Gulflight* was flying the Stars and Stripes and that when he discovered her nationality he broke off, enabling his prey to reach port. However, during his attack, two of her crew jumped overboard and were drowned and later that day her captain suffered a fatal heart attack. During his voyage, Rosenberg had ordered six other ships to stop before attacking them and his explanation seems credible.

U-30 was one of three submarines which had been ordered to sea on 25 April by Korvettenkapitan Hermann Bauer, the Fuhrer der Unterseeboote, or senior officer commanding the U-boats. They had specific instructions to attack merchant ships, warships and troop transports. *U-30* was to take up station at the western end of the English Channel, *U-20* was to patrol the Irish Sea and Liverpool Bay, and *U-27* the approaches to the Bristol Channel. They were, however, subject to an instruction issued by the Kaiser on 18 April, which reiterated the prohibition of attacks on neutral shipping. This had resulted from a stern protest made by the Dutch government to the foreign office in Berlin about the sinking a week earlier of the freighter *Katwijk* outward bound for Baltimore, in a channel which the Germans had declared to be safe. *U-20*, commanded by Kapitanleutnant Walter Schwieger, was delayed by repairs and did not sail from the submarine base at Emden until 30 April, five days after her sisters, and the day before *Lusitania* left New York.

*   *   *

Lusitania was moored with the Cunard pier to starboard and lighters clustered along her port side refuelling her coal bunkers and carrying cargo and provisions. Loading the big liner was a tedious and protracted affair, whose supervision fell on the shoulders of the hard-pressed Staff Captain Anderson and his complement of seamen, many of whom were inexperienced. *Lusitania* had not been designed as a cargo-liner and only one per cent of her enclosed space was allocated for mail and cargo. She was not well-equipped to handle the vast increase in cargo which she now had to carry, and though the Admiralty had greatly expanded her cargo space to include much of the forward third-class accommodation on D, E and F decks, no provision had been made for direct cargo access to this space. Many items, including those bought alongside by lighter, had to be hoisted aboard, either by *Lusitania*'s main booms or by the cranes located on the boat deck, which had originally been designed for baggage handling. The cargo had then to be man-handled down several decks to the stowage areas designated by Anderson, who was responsible for ensuring that the liner was properly trimmed before sailing. It is not surprising that this arduous task exacerbated the crew's poor morale which the local German agents had already detected and gleefully reported to their superiors. To add to Anderson's woes, a number of seamen jumped ship.

Virtually all *Lusitania*'s cargo carried on her last voyage, including a large quantity of foodstuffs, was contraband within the strict terms of the law. Allegations that the manifest had been altered to conceal the true nature of many items of her cargo have circulated ever since she was sunk and some writers have even questioned the consignment by eight different shippers of a total of 4,859 boxes of cheese. At this distance in time it is virtually impossible to verify these assertions and it is worth remembering that the German propaganda machine was understandably active in spreading these claims in their campaign to justify the torpedoing. The most obvious military cargo consisted of 4,200 cases of rifle ammunition (1,000 rounds per case) weighing 173 tons, consigned by the Remington Small Arms Co to the Woolwich Arsenal, and 1,248 cases of 3-inch shrapnel shells (four shells per case) totalling 51 tons, together with 18 cases of fuses, supplied by Bethlehem Steel. Under American regulations, these munitions were legal cargo on passenger liners. *Lusitania* also carried 184 cases of accoutrements (ie haversacks and pouches) consigned to Booth & Co, part of the War Office contract which George Booth had ordered during his visit to the US. The manifest also recorded some 50 barrels and 94 cases of aluminium powder, extensively used in the production of nitrate-based explosives, and 400 cases of machine tools and components, including castings, forgings, brass rods, sheet brass, and copper tubing, almost certainly destined for the munitions effort.[3] By a strange irony, an accumulation of British legal documents relating to the loss of *Titanic*, which had been sent to New York for the recently concluded liability trial before the same Judge Mayer, who would later preside over the similar case over the sinking of *Lusitania*, were being shipped back to London on the Cunarder.

A consignment of 33 cases and 282 bales of furs has aroused suspicion and some commentators have alleged that it may not have been what it claimed to be. The shipper, Alfred Fraser, was an unsavoury character and a flagrant profiteer. In October 1914, he had been awarded a War Office contract to supply 30,000 sheepskin-lined leather jackets at 37 shillings each, a quantity later increased to 100,000. He had purchased the jackets in

Boston for only 25 shillings each. He was, however, unable to finance the second contract for 70,000 jackets and turned to the War Office for assistance. During his visit to America, George Booth was asked to investigate the second contract, which he was able to renegotiate on much more reasonable terms. Although Fraser was by then in serious financial difficulties, he was allowed to make further purchases of war supplies as a government agent under the strict control of Captain Gaunt. However unsavoury he may have been, he had some connection with the fur trade and it could reasonably be assumed that this consignment was, indeed, correctly listed in the manifest.[4]

Lusitania's manifest also included 205 barrels of oysters consigned by the South Norwalk Oyster Co of Norwalk, Connecticut, to an address in Liverpool. This shipment raises a number of questions. Oysters are a highly perishable commodity. Their shelf-life from the time they are harvested, even if they are packed in ice and stored in a refrigerated compartment, is only twelve days. To allow for packing, transport to the Cunard pier and loading aboard the liner, a process which as we note below, ,was completed on the evening of 30 April, the latest date on which this particular consignment could have been harvested was on the previous day, 29 April. *Lusitania* was due to dock in Liverpool on Saturday 8 May and the process of unloading (assuming that perishable items got priority), customs clearance and distribution to the consignee and then to point of sale, at hotels, restaurants and fishmongers, would have taken a further two days to Monday 10 May, allowing for the intervening Sunday. By this time eleven days would have elapsed since the oysters had been harvested and only one day's shelf-life would have been left. The whole process does not seem to be commercially viable. Two other points can usefully be made. In 1915 England was well-stocked with flourishing oyster beds, at Colchester, Whitstable and elsewhere and sending New England oysters to England was akin to sending coals to Newcastle. Oysters were then a luxury food, eaten only by discerning, moneyed consumers who insisted on them being fresh and only ate oysters in those months with an 'R' in their name. May is not one of them. The suspicion lingers that the oysters were not what they seemed to be.

The process of refuelling and loading cargo was not finally completed until around 9pm on 30 April. The interim manifests were delivered to the port authorities at 4pm that afternoon and *Lusitania* was given clearance to sail at 10am on the following day.

Anderson had been so fully occupied supervising the loading of the cargo, with less than the normal complement of seamen available, that he had almost certainly been unable to institute and oversee crew lifeboat drill as required by regulation.

This would have been a difficult if not an impossible task given the number of lighters which tied up alongside the liner's port beam within hours of her arrival, the last of which did not leave until after dusk on 30 April. Nevertheless, Anderson signed a certificate to the effect that all boats had been lowered and their crews had practiced the necessary drills including operating the davits. Although *Lusitania* would carry a crew of 694 on her last voyage, she only had 45 seamen, many of whom were inexperienced, and among whom were two brothers named Morton who had signed on solely to obtain passage back to Britain. This number was to prove critical as there was less than one seaman available per lifeboat, forcing Anderson to supplement them from the ranks of the stewards and stokers.

When the embassy's advertisement appeared in the morning papers on 1 May, it immediately created a media sensation. Official opinion in Washington took a dismissive view of the advertisement. *The Times* correspondent reported: 'It is generally pointed out that the manoeuvre was an ill-timed and exceedingly impertinent effort . . . to advertise German frightfulness, and . . . further the efforts of German propagandists . . . by rubbing in the inconvenience to Americans of the indefinite continuance of hostilities. That the effort will fail is a foregone conclusion'.[5] On the same day the *New York Tribune* noted in a leader: 'The German submarine "blockade" must be in a bad way when its existence had to be called to the notice of the public . . . through newspaper advertisements . . .'. It decried the advertisement as:

> that amazing notice to the world that German submarine commanders would be instructed to disregard all existing international law and torpedo enemy and even neutral merchantmen on sight . . . We can think of no reason for such a publicity campaign here except that the German submarines have not lived up to the expectations of the Kaiser and Grand Admiral Von Tirpitz . . . They have not shut British and Irish ports . . . The vessels torpedoed constitute less than 1 per cent of the total shipping passing through the German war zone. No big passenger steamer has yet been sunk.[6]

Captain Gaunt did not share this complacent view. He well understood the advertisement's sinister implications and immediately cabled it to the naval intelligence division at the Admiralty. For some reason, the normally alert Charles Sumner did not inform Alfred Booth, who first read of it in the British newspapers. A newsreel crew and a crowd of reporters arrived at Pier 54 as the first passengers were boarding. *Lusitania*'s masters-at-arms refused them permission to go on board. Sumner, hastily summoned, gave an impromptu press conference. Asked to comment on the advertisemement's implicit warning, he responded that the liner's speed was such that no submarine could catch her. His statement did not appease the reporters and he eventually cleared all but two agency representatives and the newsreel crew off the pier so as to permit the passengers to board unhindered by the press.

In a bid to increase load-factor Cunard had recently cut passenger rates. As a result, and with the onset of spring, bookings had risen and *Lusitania* would carry more passengers than on her previous wartime voyages: 291 in saloon- or first-class, 601, including a large number of young children, in second or cabin and only 373 in third class, constituting a total of 1,265 together with a crew of 694. One saloon-class passenger, A B Cross, a planter from Malaya, later wrote: 'I was astounded to find the ship full of rank, fashion and wealth'.[7] The passenger list was indeed a distinguished one. Alfred Gwynne Vanderbilt, head of one of America's richest and most prominent families and the great-grandson of the famous Commodore, was well known in Britain and America for his skill as a driver of four-in-hand coaches. A restless man, he was in some ways the forerunner of today's jet traveller, once making seven transatlantic crossings in a single year. On one of his visits to London, with the cool courage he later displayed after *Lusitania* was torpedoed, he had rescued one Mary O'Brien, whose horse had run away with her in Rotten Row, by grabbing the horse's reins and bringing it to a stop. Mary had been the mistress of a Latin American diplomat and Vanderbilt, estranged from his first wife, set her up in a flat in London. Pressured by his family, he married for a second time and the bereft Mary took poison. Edwardian society, normally tolerant of the goings-on of the rich and powerful, was outraged and Vanderbilt found himself ostracised for some time afterwards.[8]

Charles Frohman, the theatrical impresario, holder of the US rights to *Peter Pan*, was sardonically known as the Napoleon of Drama. The arts were also represented by the Parisian actress Rita Jollivet and the playwright Charles Klein, whose play *Potash and Pearlmutter* was one of the current hits of the London theatre. Elbert Hubbard, author and publisher of the magazine *The Philistine*, accompanied by his wife, was crossing the Atlantic to interview the Kaiser. George Crompton, a partner in Booth & Co, who ran their extensive tanning business in Philadelphia, boarded with his wife, six children and a nanny.

Among the British passengers were Charles Bowring, head of his family firm of Lloyd's brokers, Alexander Campbell, general manager of the Scotch whisky distillers, John Dewar & Sons, Father Basil Maturin, the Irish scholar, Roman Catholic chaplain to Oxford University and a famous preacher, the Antarctic explorer Commander Foster Stackhouse, and the Welsh industrialist and mine-owner D A Thomas, returning from a business trip to the US. With him was his daughter, Margaret Lady Mackworth, a militant suffragette, who had once been arrested for planting a bomb in a mailbox. Sir Hugh Lane, Director of the National Gallery of Ireland, had been acting as an expert witness for an insurance company in a case in which works of art had been damaged in transit to the United States. The screen designer at the Boston Opera House, Oliver Bernard, was returning to Britain in an attempt to enlist in the forces.

A number of passengers had regularly sailed on *Lusitania*, among them C T Hill from Richmond, Virginia, a director of British-American Tobacco; and Mrs George Washington Stephens from Montreal, the widow of a former Canadian cabinet minister. With her on this voyage was her grandson, John, aged eight, a lady's maid and a nurse. She was taking her grandson to see his father, who was ill in a London hospital, where her son-in-law, Hamilton Gault, who had raised the Canadian regiment, The Princess Patricia's Light Infantry, was also recovering from wounds received in France.[9] The Bostonian bookseller, Charles Lauriat, was making his twenty-third transatlantic crossing but his first on *Lusitania*. In the past he had preferred to take passage on a smaller and slower boat as he always enjoyed the voyage but on this occasion he wanted to make a quick business trip. Later that year he wrote a book of his experiences entitled *The Lusitania's Last Voyage*.

The liner also carried a contingent of doctors and nurses who had volunteered for duty in military hospitals in France and Belgium. Among them were Surgeon-Major Warren Pearl, accompanied by his wife, four children and two nannies; and Dr Howard Fisher, brother of a former Secretary of the Interior.

Shortly before the liner sailed, the valiant Belgian, Marie Depage, one of the most distinguished of her passengers, came aboard. She was the wife of Antoine Depage, a leading light in the Belgian Red Cross and later its president, who was then the director of the Hospital L'Ocean, run by the Red Cross at La Panne in the 20 square miles of free Belgium behind the flooded Yser River which King Albert and his army were grimly defending against the formidable might of Imperial Germany. Marie Depage had been involved in managing the school for nurses in Brussels, working closely with Edith Cavell, soon to be martyred. The two Depages, together with their eldest son as stretcher-bearer, had manned an ambulance sent by the Red Cross to Constantinople in the Balkan War of 1912. Marie Depage had come to America in January 1915 on a lecture tour to raise funds for the Belgian Red Cross and her husband's hospital, sponsored by the American Red Cross and the Hoover Relief Committee. Her tour had proved an overwhelming success and she had secured over $100,000 in cash and a further $50,000 in medical supplies. It was largely through her efforts that so many American doctors and nurses had volunteered for war service. Marie Depage had been booked on the Red Star liner *Lapland,* due to sail the day before *Lusitania.* At the last minute she had decided to address one more meeting on the afternoon of 30 April and had transferred her booking to the mighty ship.[10]

Lusitania's departure was delayed for some two-and-a-half hours by a last-minute decision by the Admiralty to commandeer the Anchor Lines steamer *Cameronia* as a troopship, thus necessitating the transfer of her passengers and their baggage to the liner. While this was in progress, Turner received his final sailing orders from the British Consul-General, Sir Courtenay Bennett, who was also acting as senior naval officer in New York. He was surprised to find that no course instructions had been sent and he decided, not unreasonably, that he should follow a similar course to that he had taken on his previous voyage. The procedure by which Bennett, a diplomat without any naval experience, was acting in this capacity is obviously open to criticism.

The German advertisement had little effect on *Lusitania*'s passengers. Lauriat wrote: 'I gave the notice no serious thought. No idea of cancelling the trip occurred to me. I did not sail with a feeling of defiance towards the Embassy, either for the notice or for any action that might follow; for I admit that I did not think that any human being, with a drop of red blood in his veins . . .

could issue an order to sink a passenger steamer without at least giving the women and children a chance to get away.'[11] Alfred Vanderbilt expressed the conventional wisdom that the Germans would never dare attack the ship. The notice might have had a greater impact if it had been published earlier in the week and it seems that only five passengers, a Mr and Mrs Leeds, a Mr and Mrs Drexel and an unnamed American clergyman, actually cancelled their reservations and transferred to the IMM liner *City of New York*, due to sail for Liverpool later the same day. She had been built at Clydebank in 1888, the first Atlantic liner with twin screws, and was rather unkindly described as 'an old tub'. She could offer neither *Lusitania*'s amenities nor the standards of service for which Cunard was well known and which the line seems to have been able to maintain even in wartime.

Telegrams reading 'HAVE IT ON DEFINITE AUTHORITY THE LUSITANIA IS TO BE TORPEDOED. YOU HAD BETTER CANCEL PASSAGE IMMEDIATELY' and variously signed John Smith or George Jones were received by Alfred Vanderbilt amongst others. They were all ignored and were later found to be hoaxes.[12] Most passengers willingly accepted Cunard's reasoning that *Lusitania*'s speed would enable her to outrun any U-boat. Frohman, Bernard, Lauriat and Fisher, among others, had chosen to sail on her precisely because of her speed. At least three people, John McFadden, a cotton broker from Philadelphia, and Edward Bowen, a Bostonian shoe manufacturer and his wife, had premonitions of disaster and cancelled their reservations, in McFadden's case as early as March. According to Bowen, a feeling had grown on him only the day before the liner was due to sail that a terrible fate awaited her.[13] Three others, an English actress, her mother and her young son, had an extraordinary escape. On the night before *Lusitania* sailed, their friends held a farewell party at which the mother became drunk and passed out. She was still out cold next morning when the cab arrived to take the family to the pier and they had to miss the ship.[14]

Shortly before 12.30pm local time, *Lusitania*, all her ensigns and house flags flying, her passengers crowding vantage points on deck, made ready to sail from New York for the 101st and, as it proved, the last time. As the traditional call 'All ashore that's going ashore' rang round her decks, Sumner wished Turner *bon voyage* and was the last man down the gangway. The departure of a mighty ship on a transatlantic voyage is always a moving spectacle. One third-class passenger, Edith Williams, nine years old at the time, vividly remembered the excitement of the sailing, the huge crowd watching ashore and the ship's band playing. Once the lines were cast off, Turner telegraphed down to the engine room for Slow Astern and *Lusitania*'s huge, high-tensile brass propellers began to turn. As the band broke into 'Auld Lang Syne', three tugs helped her out of her berth into the Hudson and pushed her bows to starboard until they pointed downstream. With a great farewell blast from her siren, the mighty ship was on her way. The newsreel crew atop the Cunard pier recorded her departure for posterity. Their film shows her steaming down river, past the unmistakable silhouette of the giant three-funnelled HAPAG liner *Vaterland*, laid up at Hoboken.

As *Lusitania* passed through the Verrazano Narrows separating New York and New Jersey, her two masters-at-arms were making their customary inspection of the ship to ensure that she was not carrying any stowaways. They discovered three men, neither crew nor passengers, one of them carrying a camera, hiding in a pantry on the shelter deck. They promptly locked the intruders up and sent for Anderson, who confiscated the camera and had them confined in the ship's brig. Turner decided to take them to Liverpool for interrogation. As the trio went down with the ship, their identities will never be known but it is likely that they were German agents, their mission being to discover evidence that *Lusitania* was armed. They had presumably managed to slip past security at the Cunard pier but for some reason had failed to go ashore before the liner sailed.

Outside the three-mile limit, Turner stopped engines close to the former Cunarder *Caronia*, now in naval service as an armed merchant cruiser. With other British cruisers her mission was to guard the mouth of the Hudson to prevent any of the laid up German liners escaping. American neutrality rules precluded her from entering territorial waters. James Bisset, later to command both *Queen Mary* and *Queen Elizabeth*, was then serving on *Caronia* and wrote in his biography *Commodore*:

> . . . on the bridge of *Lusitania* I could see her Master, Captain Will Turner, and his Staff Captain, Jock Anderson. I knew them both well, having served under them as Junior Third Officer in the old champion trans-Atlantic liner *Umbria* seven years before . . . He and Jock Anderson both came briefly to the port wing of the bridge to wave their greetings to former shipmates in *Caronia*. Then through the swirling mist-veils I saw the *Lucy*'s Second Officer, Percy Hefford. He

was a special friend of mine as we had served together as First and Second Mates in an old rattletrap tramp SS *Nether Holme* before either of us had joined the Cunard service. That had been in 1906, the year *Lusitania* had been launched on the Clyde. It had been Percy Hefford's dream of ambition then to serve some day on the *Lusitania*. Now there he was. We semaphored to each other with our arms – Cheerio! Good Bye! Good voyage! Good Luck![15]

Twenty years later, Oliver Bernard described this encounter in his biography *Cocksparrow*.

Soon after lunch, Sandy Hook was abaft and the pilot had said goodbye. Almost before there had been time to realise that the Atlantic had opened out, passengers got a glimpse of . . . *Caronia*. Heaving against the swell, her silhouette . . . shows she is now armed to the teeth: a cutter drops away from her side, twelve oars grow more distinct and arrive at the overhanging counter . . . of the giant liner which has now heaved to. . . . An officer climbs aboard . . . The cutter makes off again, a quiver from below and . . . *Lusitania* continues her voyage.'[16]

The officer took back with him a package containing the camera and slides and a report on the incident of the detained agents addressed to Captain Gaunt in Washington, to be delivered into New York by the next westbound British ship. These formalities completed, Turner hauled down his flags, telegraphed for Full Speed Ahead and set course for Liverpool. Someone aboard *Caronia* took the last photograph of *Lusitania* proudly steaming away eastbound though with no smoke issuing from her fourth funnel.

*   *   *

KapitanLeutnant Walther Schwieger, commanding *U-20*, was a tall fair-haired man of thirty, with blue eyes and sharply chiseled features. He had joined the navy as a cadet in 1903 and had transferred to the U-boat service in 1911, taking over command of *U-20* in December 1914. *U-20*, completed in 1913, displaced 650 tons and was equipped with a single 8.8m (3.5in) gun and four torpedo tubes, carrying seven torpedoes. A contemporary, Admiral Werner Furbringer, remembered him as a commander of exceptional ability, intellectually quick and with a noticeable sense of humour. He enjoyed the admiration and loyalty of his crew and he ran a happy ship, which was not always easy in the

cramped conditions and often fetid atmosphere of a small submarine. He was not prepared to take the same risks as some of his
contemporaries like Rosenberg and the safety of his boat and his
crew came first. He was ready to attack merchant ships without
warning, including those whom he suspected were falsely flying
neutral colours. Earlier in 1915 he had torpedoed the hospital
ship *Asturias* although she was painted white and was displaying
a prominent red cross on her hull in accordance with international regulations. Fortunately, *Asturias* made port and suffered
no serious casualties. On this voyage he was assisted by a pilot
named Lanz whose function was to identify the nationality of
potential targets. Like other U-boat commanders, Schwieger was
sceptical of the effectiveness of his torpedoes and preferred
wherever possible to surface and sink his victims by gunfire. He
was also wary of destroyers, regarding them as his most serious
adversaries.

On 2 May, three days out of Emden, Schwieger was passing
through the straits between the Orkney and Shetland islands,
when he encountered several British destroyers. As they were
steaming in a sweeping pattern in line abreast, they were clearly
looking for submarines. He was forced to submerge and travelled almost fifty miles before he could safely surface. He noted
that if he had been confronted with one more destroyer, he
could not have slipped past the British screen as his batteries
urgently needed recharging. He thus came close to having to
return to Emden, his mission aborted. On the following day he
had fired a torpedo at a 2,000-ton ship flying Danish colours
whom he suspected of being British. On 4 May he fired at a ship
flying the Swedish flag. On both occasions his torpedoes either
missed or failed to detonate. He cleared Fastnet around 2pm on
5 May and that evening he encountered the schooner *Earl of
Lathom* (132 tons) in ballast bound for Limerick, about twelve
miles south of the Old Head of Kinsale. He surfaced and
ordered the crew to take to their boats and sank the schooner by
gunfire. *Lathom* was the only ship out of the seven which he
attacked on that voyage to whom he gave any warning. At
8.50pm when he was off Daunt's Rock at the entrance to
Queenstown harbour he attacked a ship which he described as
flying Norwegian colours and once again his torpedo missed. In
fact, his intended prey was the British-registered *Cayo Romano*.[17]
Her officers must have seen the track of the torpedo as they noti-
fied the the Navy of the attack when the ship arrived at

Queenstown later that evening. Before midnight the news of both incidents had been passed on to the Admiralty. The Naval War Staff was thus fully aware that a U-boat was operating less than twenty miles from Queenstown on the main shipping lanes between North America and Britain and directly in the path of *Lusitania*, then still some 800 miles west of Fastnet.

Fog came down during the night and Schwieger headed out to sea, continuing his voyage eastwards. On the following morning, 6 May, he was cruising thirteen miles southeast of the Coningbeg lightship, which guarded the western entrance to the St George's Channel between Ireland and Wales, the sea lane which led to Liverpool. As the fog started to lift, Schwieger sighted the steamer *Candidate* (5,858 tons) of the Harrison Line out of Liverpool, bound for Kingston, Jamaica, and New Orleans. The researcher, John Light, who spent twenty-five years studying the history of *Lusitania*, alleged that *Candidate*'s boiler room crew had been court-martialled and shot for refusing to continue at their posts after the ship had been hit by gunfire from *U-20*. Light's assertion is at the best dubious.

Schwieger was on the surface when he sighted the cargo liner and opened fire with his deck gun, hitting her twice before she managed briefly to disappear back into the fog. In the words of the German records, *Candidate*'s captain, A B Sandiford, on being fired upon immediately: 'altered course and made a spirited attempt to escape under shell-fire'. This is hardly the action of a mutinous crew.[18] Sandiford was following an Admiralty instruction that no merchant ship should tamely surrender to a submarine but should do her utmost to escape and, if pursued by a U-boat on the surface, keep stern on towards her. At about 11am Central European Time (CET), she had emerged from the fog and Schwieger noted that the vessel was stern on to *U-20*, thus minimizing the risk of a torpedo hit. He continued firing on the cargo liner, hitting her twice, once on her bridge, after which Sandiford gave the order to abandon ship. Schwieger let the crew take to the boats before firing a torpedo which struck *Candidate* in her engine room. Although she settled by the stern she showed no sign that she was going to sink, forcing Schwieger once again to open fire. She took many shots at the waterline before finally sinking in Lat 51 50N Long 6 30W or thirteen miles southeast of Coningbeg. At about 3pm a naval auxiliary patrol boat rescued forty-four members of her crew and landed them at the Welsh port of Milford Haven at 3am on the morning of 7 May.[19]

Around 11.40am (CET) Schwieger sighted the White Star liner *Arabic* which was steaming too fast for him to intercept and which soon disappeared into a fogbank. Two hours later he torpedoed another Harrison cargo liner *Centurion* (5,945 tons), outward bound for South Africa, seventeen miles southeast of Coningbeg. Her crew abandoned ship without any loss of life. She too stayed afloat and Schwieger had to fire a second torpedo to finish her off. *Centurion* must have been a well-built ship as even then she took over an hour to go down, sinking in Lat 51 47 N Long 6 27 W. After ten hours in the boats her crew was picked up by the trawler *Fleswick* and landed at Rosslare on the Irish side of St George's Channel early the following morning by which time both the Admiralty and the Navy at Queenstown were aware of the fate of the two cargo liners. The news had leaked out and the Liverpool newspapers reported the loss of both ships in their morning editions on 7 May.[20]

Once *Centurion* had finally gone down, Schwieger made a detailed appreciation of his situation in his war diary:

> Thick fog. Dived to 24 metres. Course 240 degrees in order to keep out at sea. Decided not to proceed further towards Liverpool for the following reasons:
>
> (1) In view of the thick fog of the last two days, the lack of wind and the state of the barometer, there is no expectation of clearer weather in the next few days.
> (2) Timely sighting of the expected strong enemy patrols of armed trawlers and *destroyers* [author's emphasis] in St. George's Channel and the Irish Sea is not possible in thick weather; therefore continual danger necessitating submerged passage.
> (3) Surface action against transports leaving Liverpool impossible except in clear weather at night, for the reason that escorting destroyers cannot be sighted in time. Moreover it must be assumed that transports leave Liverpool at night and are escorted.
> (4) Passage to St. George's Channel has already consumed so much fuel oil that a return from Liverpool southward around Ireland would no longer be possible. I shall commence return passage when down to two-fifths fuel, avoiding the North Channel [between Ireland and Scotland] if at all possible because of the type of patrolling experienced there by *U-20* on her previous operation.
> (5) There are only 3 torpedoes left of which it is my intention to conserve, if possible, two for the return passage.

(6) Have therefore decided to remain to the south of the entrance to the Bristol Channel and attack steamers until down to two-fifths fuel, especially as there are greater attacking opportunities with less opposition than in the Irish Sea off Liverpool.[21]

Drawing on his previous experience, Schwieger had correctly appreciated the low priority and insufficient naval resources allocated by the Admiralty to the waters south of Ireland – an area which was rapidly becoming Britain's maritime Achilles heel. As darkness fell the fog set in once more; Schwieger, who was still cruising in the vicinity of Coningbeg, decided to 'submerge to twenty-four metres and overnight head for the open sea . . . to recharge my batteries far from the lightship'. While he was recharging he steered west towards the Old Head of Kinsale, an excellent location to find another target.

*   *   *

On board *Lusitania*, the voyage had passed pleasantly with calm seas and blue skies, and the war that was raging in Europe must have seemed thousands of miles away. Some of the more observant passengers were concerned to note the perfunctory nature of the crew's lifeboat drills, the failure to hold any passenger lifeboat musters and the absence of any posted information directing passengers how to reach their boat stations. Oliver Bernard, who had once served at sea, noticed that the same two boats, one port side and one starboard side, were always used in the crew drills. He doubted whether the crews were competent to lower the boats satisfactorily, a task he knew from his own experience to require both detailed training and considerable skill, even in calm seas.[22]

Several saloon-class passengers expressed their worries on this score to Captain Turner, who sought to reassure them by reiterating *Lusitania*'s speed and ability to outrun any U-boat. He added that in any emergency the liner was more than adequately equipped with lifeboats and passengers could rely on the crew who would allocate them a place in a boat. A B Cross wrote: 'Of course I thought that there was a sporting chance that we might not get to Liverpool, but one must take chances nowadays . . . From the very first the ship's people asseverated that we ran no danger, that we would run away from any submarine, or ram her, and so on, so that the idea came to be regarded as a mild joke for lunch and dinner tables.'[23]

On the morning of 6 May *Lusitania* entered the war zone and Turner effected Admiralty instructions to maintain radio silence, to darken ship and to swing out the lifeboats, although they were not lowered to the rails. Saloon-class passengers were sternly ordered not to smoke cigars on deck after nightfall. At dawn on the following day, 7 May, the number of lookouts were doubled. Two were stationed in the bows above the forecastle and two quartermasters were positioned on the bridge in addition to the two officers of the watch and the two lookouts in the crow's nest. The instructions given to the lookouts do not seem to have been sufficiently specific as the deposition of one crew member for the Mayer trial in New York would indicate. When he was asked to describe his orders, Frank Hennessy, port lookout in the crow's nest, replied: 'to keep a good lookout and report anything we could see, even if it was a broom handle'.[24] In hindsight he might have been better briefed to look not for inanimate objects but for the tell-tale spray from a periscope or the track of a torpedo.

At 7.52pm on 6 May, Turner received a signal from Vice-Admiral Sir Charles Coke, Vice-Admiral Queenstown, clearly concerned about the implications of *U-20* operating in such a busy sea lane. It was addressed to all British ships in the area and read: submarines active off the south coast of Ireland. Fifteen minutes later a second signal, sent by the Admiralty to all British ships, was received. Parts of this signal were relevant to *Lusitania*. Captains were reminded to avoid headlands, pass harbours at full speed and steer a mid-channel course, and those bound for Liverpool were instructed to take on a pilot at the Mersey Bar, a shoal which guarded the entrance to the estuary.

Another message was received aboard the ship that evening. It was addressed to Alfred Vanderbilt, who seems to have had a roaming eye: 'Hope you have safe crossing looking forward very much seeing you soon. May Barwell.' Later in the evening Turner attended the ship's concert, a popular feature of every voyage and one of the few social events which he found enjoyable. Addressing the passengers, he was reassuring, stating that on the next day he would steam at full speed so as to arrive in Liverpool on time. As we shall see, Turner's message was misleading. After the concert, whose highlight was an performance by the ever-popular Welsh Chorus, Turner retired for the night leaving Chief Officer Piper in charge on the bridge. In the public rooms social life was in full swing and an argument over a game of cards in the saloon-class smoking room deteriorated into fisticuffs.

CHAPTER 6

The Titans of the Admiralty

Before sailing, Turner had been asked by C T Hill whether there was any danger and was anything being done about it. He admitted that there always was a danger, adding that '. . . the best guarantees of your safety are *Lusitania* herself and that . . . whenever there is danger your safety is in the hands of the Royal Navy'.[1] Some passengers echoed the Captain. The distiller, Campbell, declared that: 'The *Lusitania* can run away from any submarine the Germans have got and the British Admiralty will see that she is looked after when she arrives in striking distance of the Irish Coast.'[2] They were happily unaware of a U-boat's ability to lie undetected in wait for its prey. Their confidence and peace of mind would have been further shaken had they known of the serious problems inside the Admiralty in May 1915 and the breakdown of the relationship between its political and service heads, Churchill and Fisher.

Lord Hailsham, who knew many British statesmen and who served in Churchill's 1940-45 Government, once remarked that although he considered him to be by far the greatest British political figure of the twentieth century, he displayed some of the characteristics of the Athenian politician and general Alcibiades. Although he was an effective military commander and a man of great charm and outstanding ability, many classical historians regard Alcibiades as being principally motivated by personal ambition and opportunism. They note that during that the Peloponnesian War (431-404 BC) he twice switched sides from Athens to Sparta.[3]

In May 1915, many of Churchill's contemporaries would have agreed with Hailsham's assessment. If President Wilson's father had doted on him, Churchill's had derided and ignored him. The only person who had shown him any affection as a boy was his nanny, Anne Everest. His father, Lord Randolph Churchill, had enjoyed a meteoric career, becoming Chancellor of the Exchequer in Lord Salisbury's second government at the age of thirty-seven. Within months he had destroyed himself by resigning over the army estimates. Salisbury quietly accepted his resignation and he never held office again. His health broke and he died a failure at forty-five. Remarkably, Churchill had returned his father's contempt with adoration and had dreamed of entering politics at his side. Although this ambition was never to be realised, he remained utterly determined to show his worth as a major public figure. Like many driven men with an objective to achieve, he seldom worried about making enemies.

Churchill had served in the 4th Hussars, a fashionable cavalry regiment – the author's grandfather was his commanding officer for most of his service – and had won a considerable reputation as a war correspondent. He had entered Parliament in 1900 as a Conservative and quickly fell out with the party leadership whom he vigorously assailed. In 1904 he switched parties and joined the Liberals. Eighteen months later the Liberal party won a landslide victory in a general election and he was appointed Under-Secretary for the Colonies in the new Government. When Asquith became Prime Minister in April 1908 he promoted Churchill to the Cabinet as President of the Board of Trade. At thirty-three, he was the youngest cabinet minister since William Pitt more than a century earlier. Such a spectacular rise does not make for popularity. Conservatives saw him as a renegade whilst Liberals mistrusted him as an opportunist with no fixed political principles who had jumped parties expressly to secure office.

Before his appointment to the Admiralty in 1911, Churchill had been a vocal opponent of increased naval expenditures. As First Lord he took a completely different view and his evident delight in successfully piloting ever larger naval estimates through the House of Commons had alienated many Liberal MPs, who were traditionally opposed to increases in military budgets. He had not only offended the backbenchers. The naval historian Arthur Marder wrote: '. . . he inspired such a profound mistrust among his Cabinet colleagues, mainly on account of his flamboyance, excessive self-confidence and vaulting ambition . . . that few of them were prepared to lift a finger to keep him in office.'[4] In particular, his charisma cut no ice with the Conservative leader, Andrew Bonar Law. Law was a completely different personality to the mercurial Churchill, a dour Ulsterman and teetotaller, who had been a successful businessman before turning to politics when he was already past forty.

For all his faults, Churchill was an energetic and effective First Lord, who had achieved much for the Navy. He never hesitated to make himself unpopular if he thought it necessary and he had frequently ridden roughshod over the Sea Lords. His habitual interference in operations, to the extent of sending telegrams to fleet commanders over the heads of the First Sea Lord and the Naval War Staff, was bitterly resented in the service.

Fisher was an equally controversial figure. Without the far-reaching reforms which he had rammed through remorselessly during his earlier term of office as First Sea Lord, the Royal Navy would have been in a much worse shape to conduct a war at sea against the Kriegsmarine. He was supported at the Admiralty by another former First Sea Lord, Sir Arthur Wilson, known to his contemporaries as Tug and affectionately nicknamed Old 'Ard 'Art on the lower deck, who had volunteered to serve in an un-official capacity, and by the chief of the war staff, Vice-Admiral Henry Oliver.

Fisher's reforms had, however, been achieved at a high price – a bitter quarrel with Admiral Lord Charles Beresford, then com-mander-in-chief of the Channel Fleet, which had led to the lat-ter's dismissal from his command and enforced retirement. The feud between the two admirals had split the Navy into two mutu-ally antagonistic factions, with pro-Fisher officers sarcastically called the 'Fishpond'. Charlie B, as he was widely known, had a considerable following both in the service, especially on the lower deck, and with public opinion. He had never forgiven Fisher for his forcible retirement. He was a remorseless enemy with a well-developed talent for intrigue and as long as Churchill and Fisher held power at the Admiralty, he was determined to be its most virulent critic. Beresford had entered Parliament as Conservative MP for the great naval city of Portsmouth. He had soon become the de facto leader of the retired naval and army officers who formed an influential group on the Tory back-benches and who in were in some respects Churchill's most relentless critics.

The gloomy succession of naval setbacks had continued through the winter of 1914/15. It was broken only by Admiral Sturdee's victory over Von Spee's squadron at the Battle of the Falkland Islands in December, which avenged Spee's destruction of Admiral Cradock's force at Coronel a month earlier. Public opinion had been exasperated and Churchill's standing weak-ened by the bombardment of the east coast towns of Scarborough, Whitby and Hartlepool by Admiral Hipper's battlecruisers on 16 December, apparently unopposed by the Navy. One hundred and twenty-two people were killed and over four hundred wounded. In reality, Hipper had only narrowly escaped an encounter with a larger British force, who had been hindered by poor leadership and a succession of communication errors.

As a defence minister in both world wars, Churchill, restless, imaginative and energetic, generated a constant stream of ideas for prosecuting war on the enemy. After Turkey entered the war, he had conceived the bold but flawed scheme to force the passage of the Dardanelles and bombard Constantinople with the objective of compelling Turkey to surrender and opening up an all-weather supply route to Russia. As Britain was finding it difficult to provide adequate supplies for its ever-growing army in France, despite the extensive purchasing programme in the US, and as the formidable Turks would have simply abandoned their capital and continued the war inland, the inherent unreality of his grand design, now known to history as Gallipoli, becomes evident. Nevertheless, with Asquith's support, Churchill succeeded in railroading the concept through Cabinet. Fisher's attitude to the plan had waxed and waned but by March 1915, mindful of Nelson's dictum that ships cannot fight forts, he had concluded that the Dardanelles could not be forced by seapower alone. Although he was supported by his fellow Sea Lords, Churchill overrode him. The old admiral was to be proved correct for the naval assault on 18 March was an unmitigated disaster. The Allied warships ran into an undetected minefield, three battleships were sunk and the battlecruiser *Inflexible* seriously damaged. Two more French battleships were repeatedly hit by gunfire. In all, 650 sailors were lost and the attempt to force the narrows by ships alone was never renewed.

On 25 April, Allied troops landed on the Gallipoli peninsula and ran into heavy Turkish fire from well-prepared defensive positions. Casualties were heavy and the campaign quickly bogged down into stalemate as the Allies were never able to gain control over the commanding heights which would have enabled the fleet to pass safely through the narrows. Worse still, the Navy was now confronted with the serious logistical problem of supplying the armies by sea over open beaches from bases fifty miles away and had, at the same time to continue to provide artillery support. This operation was inherently risky as by the end of April naval intelligence knew that German submarines were being sent to the area. This threat entailed the reinforcement of the Allied naval presence to which Fisher was deeply opposed as the additional ships would have to be found from the fleet in home waters, thus undermining its crucial superiority over the German High Seas Fleet.

Their fundamental disagreements over the Dardanelles fatally damaged the already deteriorating relationship between Churchill and Fisher and by the beginning of May they were barely on speaking terms. Assailed by critics across the entire political spectrum, Churchill was becoming increasingly isolated, relying for his survival on Asquith's continued support.

Twice during the winter Fisher had attempted to resign but each time Churchill and Asquith had thwarted him. The public relations value of retaining the old admiral, hugely popular in the country, was too great to allow him to retire. By the spring of 1915 Fisher was a tired man, worn down by the incessant arguments with his political chief, a man more than thirty years his junior. The strain of his post in wartime conditions was becoming too much for a man in his mid-seventies and his colossal ego was showing clear signs of declining into paranoia. He became obsessive about the Dardanelles, increasingly regarding it as a black hole which was going to swallow up his beloved navy which he had served with such ability and devotion for sixty years. This preoccupation grew to the extent that he had little time to spend on other operational areas not least of which was the growing U-boat threat. One astute observer inside the Admiralty, Captain Reginald 'Blinker' Hall, the Director of Naval Intelligence, who saw Fisher daily, considered that, by May 1915, he was in no fit state to stay on as First Sea Lord.

As chief of the Naval War Staff, Oliver's most important subordinates included Rear-Admiral Thomas Jackson, director of operations, Captain Richard Webb, director of the Admiralty's trade division, responsible for liaison with merchant shipping, and Hall. The latter, blinking incessantly (thus his nickname) and exuding vitality and confidence, bore a remarkable resemblance to Mr Punch and was one of the most prominent figures of the war. He had a great talent for intelligence work and under his inspired leadership, the naval intelligence division became hugely successful.

*   *   *

In December 1914, the coasts of Britain had been divided into a number of area commands, each headed by an admiral designated as senior naval officer or SNO for short. Admiral Coke, Vice-Admiral Queenstown, was responsible for Irish waters. In May 1915 he had under his command the 11th Cruiser Squadron, comprising four obsolete cruisers and seventeen small vessels, yachts and fishing boats, of the so-called auxiliary patrol, a force which became derisively known elsewhere in the service as 'the Gilbert and Sullivan Navy'. Apart from the cruisers, only a few of these vessels were fitted with wireless and the heaviest armament was a 12-pounder mounted on a yacht. Coke had no authority over any other warships. The resources at his disposal and the restrictions on his authority imposed on him by the Admiralty were clearly inadequate for the effective protection of these vital sealanes through which passed virtually all the transatlantic traffic inward bound for British ports.

On 5 May, two days before *Lusitania* was sunk, Churchill left for Paris. He was not to return for five days. After his departure, with Fisher absorbed with the Dardanelles to the virtual exclusion of any other matter and Oliver immersed in paperwork, a strange lethargy crept over the Admiralty. Churchill had been to France several times that spring to visit the commander-in-chief of the British expeditionary force, Sir John French. Westminster and Whitehall gossips inferred that Churchill, realising that there would not be another Trafalgar on his watch, was planning to leave the Admiralty and seek glory by returning to the army and taking a high command on the western front. To achieve this ambition he would need French's support. These visits had left him open to criticism from King George V, Fisher, who considered them unnecessary, and Churchill's wife Clementine, who sometimes gave the impression of being more worldly wise than her husband. He brushed all these protests aside.

This particular visit was, however, entirely justifiable. Ten days earlier, Britain and France had signed the secret Treaty of London with Italy which required that country to join the war on the side of the Allies within thirty days. Churchill was due to meet his French and Italian opposite numbers in Paris to conclude a convention governing the use of the Italian navy in the Mediterranean. Important though this agreement was, once it had been signed, he might have been wise to have returned to the Admiralty post-haste, in view of his escalating disagreement with Fisher. Once he had learnt of the disaster which had overtaken *Lusitania* he laid himself very open to criticism for tarrying in France on matters which had no connection with Admiralty business.

Churchill's authorised biographer, Martin Gilbert, records a bizarre event which occurred during his absence and which vividly highlights Fisher's declining mental capacity:

> When Churchill left for France on 5th May, the responsibility for the daily conduct of Admiralty affairs had fallen on Fisher . . . the responsibility agitated him. In an effort to soothe him Clementine Churchill invited him to luncheon at Admiralty House. All went well and the Admiral departed in a cheerful mood . . . some moments later she found him still lurking in the corridor. 'What is it?' she asked. 'You are a foolish woman' he replied 'All the time you think Winston's with Sir John French he is in Paris with his mistress.' Clementine Churchill was stunned by such a wounding remark. It was for her a sure sign that Fisher's mind was unbalanced. She reported all this to her husband on his return, fearing that Fisher might break down . . . she later recalled that the Admiral was as nervous as a kitten.[5]

The remark was all the more wounding for being totally unwarranted. Churchill's many detractors in his lifetime and the revisionist historians since his death, even the acerbic John Charmley, have never accused him of philandering. Fisher seems to have picked up and misunderstood some idle chatter among the civil servants in Churchill's private office, who would jokingly refer to his visits to France as 'jaunts to see the French mistress'.

CHAPTER 7

The Seventh Day of May

Eternal Father, strong to save, whose arm hath bound the restless wave,
Who bidds't the mighty ocean deep, its own appointed limits keep,
Oh hear us, when we cry to thee for those in peril on the sea
THE SEAMAN'S HYMN

At around 5am on 7 May *Lusitania* passed HMS *Partridge* one of Coke's patrol boats, some 120 miles west-southwest of Fastnet. Before dawn she ran into thick fog and when Turner came on to the bridge at 8am, visibility was down to only thirty yards. He reduced speed to 15 knots and ordered the liner's foghorn to be sounded. Oliver Bernard had an early breakfast and then went on deck. He found himself increasingly irritated by the constant wail of the foghorn, which he felt was unnecessarily advertising the presence of the great liner to any submarine which might be lying in wait for her. In reality, the sound of a foghorn is non-directional, a fundamental characteristic of low frequency sound, and it is thus almost impossible to accurately locate the position of a foghorn simply by listening to it; submarine commanders often preferred to submerge below periscope depth during fog so as to avoid the possibility of being accidentally rammed. One hundred miles to the east, *U-20* was on the surface, recharging her batteries, as Schwieger cruised west towards the Old Head.

Churchill left Paris, having concluded his negotiations with the Italians, and drove to Sir John French's HQ at St Omer in the Pas-de-Calais. French had invited him, and a number of other guests, to witness the start of his new offensive at Aubers Ridge in Flanders, set for the following Sunday, 9 May, on which he had placed high hopes. In London, Colonel House, President Wilson's envoy, who had crossed on *Lusitania* three months before, drove with the Foreign Secretary, Sir Edward Grey, to Kew Gardens. As they walked in the gardens, enjoying the superb spring weather, Grey spoke of the possibility of an ocean liner carrying American passengers being sunk. House replied tersely: 'I told him if this was done I believe that a flame of indignation would sweep the United States which would probably carry us into war.' House then called on King George V at Buckingham Palace. He wrote that: 'We fell to talking, strangely enough, of the possibility of Germany sinking a Transatlantic liner. Suppose, the King said, that they sink *Lusitania* with American passengers aboard . . .'[1]

Alfred Booth had learnt of the sinking of *Candidate* and *Centurion* and arrived at Cunard's offices on the Liverpool water-front a worried man. Concerned for *Lusitania*'s safety, he paid a call on Admiral Stileman, the SNO at Liverpool, demanding that Turner be specifically warned of the dangers lying directly in his course. The outcome of this meeting is unclear. Alfred apparently telephoned his cousin George telling him that Stileman had given him to understand that the liner was to be diverted to Queenstown. In fact, it was the Admiralty, not Stileman, who had the authority to issue instructions to Turner or, for that matter, any other master. Alfred Booth was later to maintain that the necessary instructions had been agreed but were never implemented. For his part George then sent a cable to the Cunard office at Queenstown addressed to his partner, Paul Crompton, instructing him and his family to leave the liner there and continue their journey by rail and ferry.

Around 11am, *Lusitania* emerged from the fog into a magnificent spring morning. There was not a breath of wind. The sea was as calm as the proverbial millpond, sparkling in the sunlight. An hour later she made landfall, sighting the cape of Brow Head and clearing Fastnet by 18½ miles – a wider margin than on any of her eight previous wartime voyages. On her peacetime course she would have passed no more than two miles from the rock. The green fields of County Cork were clearly visible twenty miles away to port and passengers flocked on deck to enjoy the perfect weather and their first sight of land since the shores of Long Island and Connecticut. Turner increased speed to 18 knots, three knots slower than the liner's top speed. He had chosen this speed as he was faced with the obstacle of the Mersey Bar, a sandbank which guarded the entry to the port of Liverpool. A ship of *Lusitania*'s draft could only cross this barrier three hours either side of high tide at 6.53am on 8 May.[2] Turner was anxious to avoid arriving at the bar before 4am, the earliest time when there would be sufficient depth of water to allow him to traverse the sandbank safely. He was well aware that the ship would be exceptionally vulnerable to a submarine attack if she had to wait outside the bar and he had determined that he would not even risk stopping for a pilot, as Admiralty instructions required, and that he would take the liner over the bar himself in line with a discretion permitted him by Cunard.

At 11.02am a one-word coded signal Questor was received from the Navy at Queenstown. Eight minutes later Turner replied Westrona. As sinister implications have been read into this perfectly explicable exchange of signals, it should be pointed out that Questor and Westrona were respectively code for 'What code are you using?' and '1st Edition MV or Merchant Navy Code'. Turner's anxiety was increased, however, by the arrival of the first of two further Admiralty signals sent via Queenstown, received at 11.52am: 'Submarines active in southern part of Irish Channel, last heard of 20 miles south of Coningbeg Light vessel'. The Admiralty had instructed Admiral Coke 'Make certain *Lusitania* gets this'. It is possible that this signal was sent in reaction to the urgent representations Booth had made to Admiral Stileman at their meeting earlier that morning. This information put Turner in a quandary as it indicated that a submarine was lurking directly in his course and close to the entrance to St George's Channel. He was not to know that this information, based on the sinkings of *Candidate* and *Centurion*, the latter almost twenty-four hours earlier, was completely out of date. The second signal, received at 1pm, read 'Submarine five miles south of Cape Clear proceeding west when sighted at 10.00a.m.' This information was totally inaccurate but as *Lusitania* had already passed Cape Clear without incident Turner may well have been lured into a sense of false security. Indeed he told third officer Bestic with evident relief that at least one submarine was now behind him.

At 10am CET, Schwieger finally decided to start his return journey. An hour later, as the fog was clearing, he sighted a trawler which he took to be one of Coke's patrol boats. He submerged first to a depth of 11 metres and thirty minutes later to 24 metres, writing in the war diary: 'I will go to 11 metres again at one o'clock' (noon local time). The diary continues: '1150. A ship with powerful engines is passing over the boat. When the boat rises to 11 meters . . . it turns out that the vessel which passed over the *U-20* is an English warship; old small cruiser . . . with 2 masts 2 stacks.' (This was HMS *Juno*, flagship of the 11th Cruiser Squadron, commanded by Rear-Admiral Horace Hood, returning from patrol to her base at Queenstown.) '1215 Travel after the cruiser to be able to attack it when changing course. The cruiser runs a zigzag course at high speed and presently passes out of sight in the direction of Queenstown.' (*Juno*'s top speed was 19 knots and *U-20*'s submerged speed was only 9 knots. The normally alert Schwieger had on this instance been caught unawares and was thus unable to catch up with the cruiser.) Finding himself alone on the sea he surfaced and blew out his bow tanks.

At 12.40pm, Turner steered *Lusitania* 30 degrees to port, making a course north 63 east, the first of two fateful course alterations. A number of different explanations have been advanced for this decision, including the improbable theory that he had accidentally responded to a signal sent by Coke to one of his ships which, due to some oversight, had the same call sign as the liner, instructing her to return to port, and was diverting to Queenstown. Testifying in the closed sessions of the Mersey inquiry, Turner advanced two reasons for changing course, both of which are plausible. First he needed to get a fix on his position after his transatlantic crossing, as required under Board of Trade regulations. Secondly, he was influenced by the signal advising him that submarines were operating 20 miles south of Coningbeg. By 1.40pm the Old Head of Kinsale was in sight and Turner altered course to starboard, resuming his previous course of south 87 east, effectively steering parallel to the coast, but approximately nine nautical miles closer inshore. He then instructed Bestic to take a four-point bearing, thus giving him an exact fix on his position. Between these two changes of direction, several passengers noted that the liner was steering what they described as a serpentine course. During the time a large ship takes to steady onto a new course, its helmsman has to make a continuous series of rudder turns to counter yaw. This results in an uneven pattern of the wake which is not significant but which a layman might wrongly interpret. Turner's turn to starboard took him away from Queenstown and contradicts the theory that he had been diverted there from Liverpool.

Schwieger wrote in his log (using Central European Time, one hour ahead of GMT).

13.45. Excellent visibility, very fine weather. Therefore surface and continue passage; waiting off the Queenstown Banks seems unrewarding.
14.20. Saw smoke on the horizon. Sight dead ahead 4 stacks and 2 masts of a steamer steering on a parallel course to us [coming from

the SSW towards Galley Head]. Ship identified as a large passenger steamer.

1425. Dive to periscope depth [11 metres] and proceed at high speed on intercepting course toward steamer in the hope that the steamer will alter course to starboard along the Irish Coast. At 1440 the steamer turns to starboard and sets course for Queenstown, permitting an approach for a shot. Proceed at high speed until 1500 in order to gain bearing.

Schwieger and his pilot Lanz knew full well that the ship which they were now hunting was British as no large four-stack liner was in service with any neutral merchant navy. *Lusitania's* silhouette was almost unique and on 7 May she was, as it happened, the only one of the five British four-stack liners at sea. *Mauretania* and *Aquitania* were laid up in the Mersey and the White Star Line's *Olympic* and the uncompleted *Britannic* in Belfast Lough. After the war, a fellow U-boat captain, Kiesewalter, confirmed that Schwieger did not know the exact identity of his target before he fired at her. He could safely believe that he was acting in line with Bauer's instructions and he may well have concluded that his prey was serving as a troopship. His statement that his target was making for Queenstown was incorrect for, as we have already noted, the change of course at 1.40pm took her away from the port. He correctly implies that if she had maintained her previous course of north 63 east (ie towards Queenstown) he would never have got within range. His initial sighting of *Lusitania* had been early enough to permit him to take up the bow-on position for a shot preferred by U-boat captains. His log describes her sinking vividly if coldly.

1510. Clean bow-shot from 700 metres. (torpedo set for 3 metres depth, inclination 90 degrees, estimated speed 22 knots [Here he over-estimates the liner's speed] Torpedo hits starboard side close abaft the bridge, [it was actually further back] followed by a very unusually large explosion with a violent emission of smoke, far above the foremost funnel. In addition to the explosion of the torpedo there must have been a second one (boiler or coal or powder). The superstructure above the point of impact and the bridge are torn apart, fire breaks out, a thick cloud of smoke envelopes the upper bridge. The ship stops at once and very quickly takes on a heavy list to starboard, at the same time starting to sink by the bows. She looks as if she will quickly capsize. Great confusion reigns on board; boats are cleared away and some of them lowered into the water. Apparently considerable panic; several boats, fully laden, are hurriedly lowered, bow or stern first and at once fill with water. Owing to the list fewer boats can be cleared away on the port side than on the starboard side. The ship blows off steam; forward the name *Lusitania* in gold letters is visible. Funnels painted black, no flag set astern. Her speed was 20 knots.

1525. As it appears that the steamer can only remain afloat for a short time longer, dive to 24 metres and proceed out to sea. Also I could not have fired a second torpedo into this mass of people struggling to save their lives.

1615. Come up to periscope depth and take a look around. In the distance astern a number of lifeboats; of the *Lusitania* nothing more can be seen. From the wreck the Old Head of Kinsale bears 358 degrees 14 miles. Wreck lies in 90 metres of water. (Distance from Queenstown 27 miles) position 51 degrees 22'6N 8 degrees 31'W. The land and lighthouse very clearly visible.

Then Schwieger set course for Fastnet and his voyage back to Germany.

*   *   *

On board *Lusitania* many passengers were finishing lunch and others were on deck or had gone to their cabins for an afternoon rest. The first lookout to spot the torpedo was the eighteen-year-old Leslie Morton, the former apprentice on a sailing ship who had signed on in New York. He was acting as starboard lookout on the forecastle head and noticed a streak of foam heading for the ship some 500 yards away. His first reaction was to tell his fellow-lookout that they had got them this time. Precious seconds had been lost before he hailed the bridge shouting through his megaphone 'Torpedoes coming on the starboard side'. He did not wait for an acknowledgment and then sped below to warn his brother who was off watch at the time. It is doubtful whether his warning reached the bridge.

Thomas Quinn, a steward and a former AB in the Navy, who was acting as lookout in the crow's nest, was an older man than Morton. He does not seem to have been particularly observant as, by his own admission, he did not see the torpedo until it was only 200 yards away. His call was received on the bridge but it was by then too late to take the evasive action which could have saved the ship. Turner had briefly left the bridge and was in his day cabin one deck below when Quinn's message was finally received. He returned just as the torpedo struck, immediately followed by two almost instantaneous explosions. From the moment she was hit the liner developed a 15-degree list to starboard, a list which rapidly became more serious as thousands of tons of water flooded into the breach in her side, eventually reaching 22 degrees. In only eighteen minutes she was to sink.

Oliver Bernard had lunched in the Verandah Café on the boat deck, a popular venue in good weather, and was leaning on the starboard rail just aft of the café when a movement in the water, less than 100 yards from the ship, caught his eye. He instinctively realised that he had seen the track of a torpedo and braced himself for what would follow. As the torpedo hit, the ship trembled and almost instantly he heard 'a terrific explosion ... then a sullen rumble in the bowels of the liner.'[3] From his vantage point on the rail, he saw a huge column of water and debris shoot from the vents into the air high above the liner's superstructure and then come crashing down on the deck ahead of him, ripping No 5 lifeboat, the third starboard boat, from its davits. A bell-boy, William Holton, noticed the lifeboat, apparently undamaged, floating in the sinking liner's wake. James Brooks, a saloon-class passenger from Bridgeport, Connecticut, who had been on deck close to where the torpedo struck, experienced the ferocity of the blast: 'There was a dull explosion and a quantity of debris and water was flung into the air beside the bridge. The waterspout knocked me down by the Marconi office. This explosion was followed soon after by a second rumbling explosion entirely different from the first . . .'. Charles Lauriat, on the port deck when the torpedo struck, thought that '. . . the shock of the impact was not severe: it was a heavy, rather muffled sound . . . a second explosion quickly followed'.[4] He correctly decided that this was not caused by a second torpedo 'for the sound was quite different; it was more likely a boiler'. Other passengers compared the explosion to 'a clip of lightning and a peal of thunder' or to 'a blow from a great hammer'. One American passenger told the Mayer inquiry in New York that it was 'a terrific explosion, like you would hear in a subway'. Passengers, who were further away from the point of impact, formed a less dramatic impression of the explosion and described it 'as relatively light like . . . the banging of a door'.

Within three minutes, all power was lost as the liner's generators failed. The duty wireless operator, McCormick, had to switch to his emergency batteries to continue sending out his SOS: 'Come at once. Strong list. Position 10 miles south Kinsale', which he had first transmitted at 2.11pm. D A Thomas and his daughter, Margaret, had a narrow escape from the fate that doomed anyone trapped in the now-useless lifts. They had just left the dining-room and were just about to enter the lift when they heard the explosion. Intuitively they turned back and like so many passengers set off to go below to their cabins to get their lifebelts, which, in a torpedoed liner, was a risky venture. (Six months later when the troopship *Persia* was torpedoed, an Indian Army Captain, Owen Gough, mustered on deck and then went below to retrieve his sword. He was never seen again.)

In his report Lord Mersey correctly noted the absence of panic on the stricken liner. The situation on deck could, however, be called confused, even chaotic. Orders and counter-orders were issued from the bridge. At first, Turner refused to order the boats to be lowered as the ship was still under way and later ordered those in the boats to get back on deck as he considered them, especially those on the port side, to be unlaunchable. Survivors' accounts tell of a breakdown of discipline and note that few officers could be seen directing the evacuation. The inadequate, almost risible, training of seamen in boat drill, the absence of any practice passenger musters and the failure to instruct passengers to carry their lifebelts with them at all times or even how to wear them, all combined together to produce a hideous dividend. Charles Lauriat reckoned that fewer than half of those passengers who were wearing lifebelts had put them on correctly. On the port side the liner's heavy list swung the boats inboard, making it impossible to successfully launch them. Only two port-side boats reached the water but each was so badly shredded by contact with the rivets as they bumped down the ship's side that they sank immediately and decanted their occupants into the sea.

A tragedy within a tragedy took place at the No 18 boat station on the port side. The crew member in charge had decided to keep the passengers in the boat until the water level reached the deck and then cut the falls so that the boat could float free. A saloon-class passenger named Isaac Lehmann, who had evidently passed a sleepless night, lost his head and pulled a revolver at the crew, forcing them to start lowering the falls. This ill-considered action resulted in the boat, which weighed five tons, swinging inboard and cutting a swathe through the throng of passengers waiting on deck. By his own account, Lehmann, who escaped this needless calamity with a broken leg and survived, saw thirty people killed or wounded.[5] On the starboard side, launching was easier but the inexperience of the seamen resulted in their losing control over the lowering of a number of boats, notably No 17, which tipped up throwing its occupants into the sea. Two others went down with the ship, held fast either by the falls or by the snubbing chain which no one knew how to release. By heroic improvisation, six of the remaining starboard boats managed to get free of the ship and reached port. The collapsible lifeboats installed after the loss of *Titanic* proved to be an almost total failure. There was not enough time to recover any of the falls so as to assemble them for launching and all that the crew could do was to free them from the chocks which held them in place so that they could float off. Survivors complained that they were corroded and short of equipment such as rowlocks and oars although in some cases these deficiencies could have been caused by the manner in which they floated free from the sinking liner.

There were those on deck who behaved badly like Lehmann or the black gang of stokers who were released from duty after power had been lost and who were accused by some survivors of rushing the lifeboats. There were many more who in those terrible minutes of adversity behaved exceedingly well and some who doubtless thought themselves to be quite ordinary who did the most extraordinary things to help their fellows. By all accounts the stewards and stewardesses performed heroically, going to great lengths to find lifebelts for passengers and to ensure that they were being worn correctly. Although he could not swim, Alfred Vanderbilt, the richest man aboard, gave his lifebelt to a woman passenger, Alice Middleton. A survivor noted that 'Vanderbilt was utterly unperturbed. He stood there, the personification of sportsmanlike coolness. In my eyes, he was the figure of a gentleman waiting for a train'.[6] Charles Frohman stood calmly on deck, telling Warren Pearl and Rita Jolivet as they helped her into a lifeboat: 'Why fear death. It is the most beautiful adventure in life.'[7]

Alice Lines, the English nanny to two of Warren Pearl's four children, Stewart, aged five and the baby Audrey, only three months old, was in their cabin on E deck when the torpedo hit. She was determined to get her charges up on deck without delay. Without a lifebelt, with the baby wrapped in a scarf round her neck and with the boy clinging on to her skirt, she fought her way through the confusion and the darkness up three decks to the boat deck. Twice she was knocked down in the crush and twice she managed to keep hold of the children and picked herself up. She could not recall seeing any sailors on deck and two passengers found places for her and the children in a lifeboat, which was safely lowered. Except for a few bruises they escaped injury. Her quick thinking and determination had saved her and the two children who had been entrusted to her care.

Lusitania sank at 2.28pm, less than twenty minutes after she had been torpedoed. For a few minutes, until it subsided, a seething mass of water marked the spot where she had foundered. Hundreds were still on deck when the liner went down, throwing them into the sea, and some were sucked down with her. The avalanche of deckchairs, lockers, spars, posts and other flotsam, which cascaded into the sea as the liner foundered, added to the hazards for passengers; inanimate objects suddenly become lethal projectiles which could maim and kill. Many of those who succeeded in getting clear found that their ordeal was only just starting. As a result of the rapidity with which *Lusitania* had gone down, the poor handling of the lifeboats and the mortal damage to those on the port side, many passengers and members of the crew had to survive in the cold waters of the Irish Sea for several hours before they could be rescued. In the main it was the determined, the fit and the fortunate who emerged unscathed. Mrs Henry Adams succeeded in reaching an overturned collapsible to which about twenty people were clinging. She ascribed her survival to her gymnastic training which enabled her to climb hand over hand on to the boat's keel and thus keep her in relative safety above water while the others found it difficult to cling on. Of the twenty only about six held on long enough to be rescued.[8] In two aspects, the survivors were fortunate. Had the sea been rough and the temperature of the water less than 55 degrees Fahrenheit, as recorded by HMS *Juno*'s log at noon that day, the death toll would inevitably have been higher.[9]

The planter A B Cross wrote that 'I had formulated no plan of campaign except a vague notion that if anything happened I would go right out and not wait to pick up anything; this I did and it probably saved my life. I stood for orders and endeavoured to assist some members of the crew in freeing boats from tackle but so far as I can remember the pulleys were rusty or the ropes had not been greased'. He eventually found himself a place on one of the port-side boats which fell into the sea and broke up. He managed to cling to some flotsam and survived.[10]

Oliver Bernard, like Vanderbilt a non-swimmer, had remained on the boat deck as the liner slipped ever deeper into the sea until he could slide into a lifeboat which was still secured to the ship by her falls. He joined its other occupants in a frantic but fortunately successful effort to cut the boat free. Only moments later and as the boat drifted aft, he watched *Lusitania*'s death throes. In her last seconds he noticed that her funnels were at an angle of almost 45 degrees, and his boat narrowly missed being struck by No 4 funnel as it fell into the sea. He saw a passenger, Margaret Gwyer, being sucked into the third funnel. She was almost immediately blown back into the sea, covered in soot, as an inrush of water into No 3 boiler room in the ship's last moments forced a powerful draught of steam up the funnel. He was long to remember the look of abject terror on her face. Another survivor, William Pierpoint, was also sucked into the funnel and he too was almost immediately blown out.

As Bernard wrote later:

> In a twinkling of an eye the monster vessel disappeared. What I saw in the water was . . . one long scene of agony . . . floating debris on all sides, and men, women and children clinging for dear life to deck chairs and rafts. There were such desperate struggles as I will never forget. Many were entangled between chairs, rafts and upturned boats. One by one they seemed to fall off and give up . . . One poor wretch was struck by the oar which I was sharing with a steward . . . he seized and clung to the oar like grim death until we were able to drag him into the boat . . . we saw a woman floating quite near us. Her face was just visible above the water and her mouth was covered with froth.[11]

Bernard and his companions pulled her aboard but she died within a few minutes. A week later the *Illustrated London News* published his vivid ink-wash drawings of *Lusitania*'s last minutes.

Lauriat had been brought up by his father to have no fear of the sea and he knew how to put a lifejacket on. He wrote:

> I didn't care to get into a lifeboat. I was perfectly willing to take my chance in the water but as I returned to the for'rard part of the [starboard] deck I found a sight that simply demanded action on my part. I found myself opposite the stern of a boat, into which had climbed about thirty-five people, principally women and children.

As it was still connected to its davits, he jumped into the boat to assist in freeing it. Before the bow davit could be cleared the boat started to sink and Lauriat was forced to jump into the sea, followed by only three or four of its other occupants. He was then struck by the liner's wireless aerial which pushed him under water but he managed to shake it off. From the water he watched *Lusitania* founder, and the lifeboat from which he had just escaped being pulled down with her. Lauriat noted that 'there was very little vortex: . . . rather a shooting out from the ship'. He ascribed the lack of suction to what he took to be a further boiler room explosion in the ship's dying moments. He vividly recalled '. . . a deep lingering moan that rose, and which lasted for many moments after the ship disappeared. They who were lost seemed to be calling from the very depths'. Lauriat had heard the siren song of the shipwreck, that strange phenomenon which has been noted by survivors of other sea disasters. As it faded away, it was succeeded by an awesome silence – the silence of death. In one lifeboat a third-class passenger, Elizabeth Duckworth, found herself reciting the 23rd Psalm, repeating time and again its great words of faith and comfort: 'Yea, though I walk through the valley of the shadow of death, I will fear no evil, for Thou art with me.'[12]

*   *   *

Turner was washed off the bridge into the water by his dying ship. He floated in the sea for nearly three hours until he was rescued by one of the lifeboats. Third Officer Bestic, who had been trying to cope with the difficulty of launching the port-side boats and who was not wearing a lifebelt, was also swept off the deck and managed to swim to one of the collapsibles. First Officer Arthur Rowland Jones had been lunching in the saloon-class dining-room on D deck when the torpedo hit.[13] With some difficulty he forced his way up to the boat deck, where he took charge of loading the starboard boats, particularly Nos 13 and 15. He got No 13 away safely with some sixty-five people and then turned his attention to No 15 which he lowered with almost eighty on board. By this time the deck was level with the sea and he slid down the falls into the boat. The lines were cut in the nick of time only for Jones and his company to encounter a new peril. The liner's wireless antenna fell across the boat and threatened to pull her down. Fortunately, it snapped and the boat survived. He came across a near-empty boat, promptly transferring a boat's crew made up of the bosun's mate, the assistant purser and a number of stewards together with forty passengers.

With two boats under his command, Jones rowed back towards the site of the wreck where they picked up a large number of passengers. He had spotted a trawler, *Bluebell,* and rowed over towards her. Once he had passed his passengers over, he once again started back towards the site of the wreck. After some two miles he found a leaking collapsible with a small group of injured or distressed passengers whom he took on board. James Baker, a saloon-class passenger, who later gave evidence before the Mersey inquiry, was amongst those whom Jones had rescued from the collapsible. Baker, who had been on the liner's starboard boat deck, helping to launch collapsibles, told reporters:

> Before many minutes had passed the water was coming right over the upper deck and I thought it was time to quit. I jumped overboard, swam about and found a couple of spars, which were useful in supporting me in the sea. Another man swam up to me, and he, too, was able to keep above water with the help of the spars. At the end of an hour they picked us up on one of the rafts, though this was partly smashed in, and we were glad when the first mate's [*sic*] boat found us, and took us to a trawler.[14]

Shortly afterwards Jones transferred the group whom he had rescued from the collapsible to a trawler. The admirable First Officer continued his efforts pulling twelve more people out of the water, including two women who died in his boat. It was now almost 8pm and he had discovered that the boat had no provisions and its water casks were empty. His crew, who had done so well, had now been rowing for more than five hours and were showing clear signs of exhaustion and dehydration. He went alongside the tender *Flying Fox* and put his crew and passengers aboard her. Jones and those whom he had rescued from the sea finally reached Queenstown at around 11pm.

Leslie Morton, the eighteen-year-old lookout, who had abandoned his station before his shouted message had been acknowledged by the bridge, did much to atone for this error. Morton was allotted to No 13 boat on the starboard side which as we have seen was successfully launched. He declined a place in the boat so as to find more room for passengers. Morton jumped into the water and with another seaman, named Parry, he managed to reach an empty collapsible where they were joined by Charles Lauriat and James Brooks. Between them they ripped off its canvas cover with their knives and not without difficulty succeeded in raising its sides thus making it reasonably seaworthy. Although they could find no oars on board, they were able to collect enough floating in the water to enable them to row the boat, and at the same sime picked up between fifty and sixty survivors. Lauriat recounted that among the passengers whom they rescued was Margaret Gwyer who had been blown out of No 3 funnel, covered in soot. At first sight he thought she was black. He wrote: 'Most of her clothes had been blown away and there wasn't a white spot on her except her teeth and the whites of her eyes. Marvellous to say she wasn't hurt and proved a great help in cheering us all by her bright talk.'

They rowed out towards the fishing boat they saw some five miles off, to whom they handed over the rescued passengers. Lauriat noted that 'aboard the fisherman I witnessed one of the most affecting scenes of all . . . the husband of the temporary negress we picked up was aboard . . . as we approached she recognized and called to him: but he stood at the rail with a perfectly blank expression on his face. Not until we were directly alongside and . . . he could look the woman squarely in the face did he realise that his wife had been given back to him'. After about an hour, Lauriat and his fellow-survivors, some eighty in all, were transferred to the paddle-steamer, *Flying Fish*, another of the tenders which normally carried passengers and cargo to and from the ocean liners when they put in at Queenstown. *Flying Fish* docked at 9.15pm. On the quay, Lauriat found the American Consul, Wesley Frost, busily engaged in helping those of his fellow-countrymen and women who had survived the disaster.

Morton and Parry turned back and rescued some twenty or thirty more survivors from a lifeboat which appeared to be sinking. They were eventually picked up by the minesweeper *Indian Empire*, which arrived at Queenstown some fifteen minutes after *Flying Fish*. Morton was later awarded a medal by King George V for his lifesaving efforts.[15] In view of the criticism which has been directed against *Lusitania*'s officers and crew, it is fitting to record that Jones, Morton and Parry had between them brought over two hundred people to safety, almost one in three of all those who survived this tragedy.

While he was stalking his prey, Schwieger had noted the total absence of any other shipping in the vicinity of the liner. With the exception of the fishing boats *Bluebell* and *Wanderer*, there were no rescue ships close at hand, a circumstance which undoubtedly served to increase the loss of life. By the time *Wanderer* arrived at the scene of the wreck, her crew found many survivors floating in a sea strewn with all kinds of flotsam and a number of bodies. As skipper Ball wrote to *Wanderer*'s owner, Charles Morrison:

> We had rather an exciting experience on Friday afternoon at about 2.30p.m., we were coming in with about 800 mackerel, the wind light and ahead. We put off to sea again for another shot rather than lose the night. When we were six or seven miles off the Old Head we saw the *Lusitania* sink after being hit by a submarine about three miles SSW outside of us.
>
> We made straight for the scene of the disaster. We picked up the first boats a quarter of a mile inside of where she sunk and there we got four boat loads put aboard us. We couldn't take any more as we had 160 men, women and children. In addition we had two boats in tow, full of passengers. [Among the survivors in the boats was D A Thomas.]
>
> We were the only boat there for two hours. Then the patrol boats came from Queenstown . . . we took them to within two miles off the Old Head . . . The tug boat the *Flying Fish* from Queenstown then came up and took them from us . . . it was an awful sight to see her sinking and to see the plight of these people. I cannot describe it to you in writing.

As she waited for larger rescue ships to arrive, the fishing boat was so heavily overloaded that she was lying dangerously low in the water. James Brooks, who was one of those she rescued later wrote that he 'even had to sit with my leg hanging over the side because there was no room inside'. The crew generously gave the survivors their spare clothes, brewed many mugs of tea and even dispensed their stock of whisky, as well as strapping up many broken limbs. Later that year, the gallant efforts of *Wanderer*'s skipper and crew in bringing to safety almost three hundred survivors were recognised. In a ceremony on the historic Tynwald, the home of the Manx Parliament, the Manchester Manx Society presented skipper Ball with a silver medal and the six members of his crew, including his son Stanley, with bronze medals, marked '*Lusitania* rescue 7 May 1915'.[16]

At about 2.30pm, the Rev William Forde, the Secretary of the Courtmacsherry lifeboat, received the news that a large liner was sinking some miles off the Seven Heads. He hurried to the lifeboat station at Barry's Point some two miles south of the village where he met a breathless Tim Keohane and his twelve-man crew. The Courtmacsherry lifeboat *Kezia Gwilt* was launched at 3pm, Forde and a neighbouring farmer, a Mr Longfield, accompanying them. In an epic effort, and in the highest traditions of their service, Keohane and his crew rowed for some fourteen miles to reach the spot where the liner had gone down. Reporting to the Royal National Lifeboat Institution on the following day, Forde wrote:

> We had no wind so had to pull the whole distance. On way to wreck we met a ship's boat crowded with people, who informed us that the *Lusitania* had gone down. We did everything in our power to reach the place but it took us at least three and a half hours of hard pulling to get there only in time to pick up dead bodies.

Forde voiced the frustration of these devoted men.

> Everything that was possible to do was done by the crew to reach the wreck in time to save life but as we had no wind it took us a long time to pull out from the boathouse. If we had wind or any motor power we would have been among the first on the scene. It was a harrowing sight to witness, the sea was strewn with bodies floating about, some with lifebelts on, some holding on to pieces of rafts, all dead. I deeply regret it was not in our power to have been in time to save some.

Kezia Gwilt, joined by the Queenstown lifeboat which had been towed out by a trawler, remained on the scene, engaged in the doleful task of picking up bodies, until about 8.40pm when they set off for home, being towed by a drifter for part of the way. She eventually reached the boathouse at about 1am, having been at sea for ten hours.[17]

As soon as he received *Lusitania*'s SOS, Admiral Coke ordered every available ship under his command, including the cruiser HMS *Juno* and three equally ancient torpedo boats together with the trawlers *Warrior* and *Stormcock* and the patrol boats, to sea to rescue survivors. A number of fishing boats from Queenstown and Kinsale joined them. It was almost two hours before the first rescuers reached the scene and the apparent delay in organising the rescue needs explanation. The liner had sunk about twenty-five miles from Queenstown. Many crew members were ashore and had to be rounded up at short notice and steam had to be raised. The calm conditions made it almost impossible for sailing boats to reach the scene. A false allegation has been made that *Juno* had turned back within sight of survivors struggling in the water. *Juno* had had dropped anchor at Queenstown at about 2.15pm and although Admiralty regulations forbade the use of warships for rescue work after submarine attacks, Coke had ordered her to sea and she was under way by 3pm. As she reached Ronan's Point, at the entry to Queenstown Harbour, some twenty miles from the site of the sinking at 3.40pm, he recalled her. He had by then learnt that the liner had sunk. Coke decided, with justification, that he could not expose the old cruiser to attack by an already triumphant U-boat and that he would therefore have to rely on his smaller vessels which U-boat commanders normally ignored. At 4.15pm Oliver, unaware that Coke had pre-empted him, ordered her recall by which time she was already approaching Queenstown.

Schwieger was meanwhile continuing his homeward voyage. At 5.08pm CET, almost two hours after he had sunk *Lusitania*, he sighted a freighter of about 7,000 tons making for Fastnet and fired one of his two stern torpedoes at her from 500 metres and at a favourable 90-degree angle. Although he described his prey as a Cunarder, she was in fact the tanker *Narrangansett* outward bound from Liverpool for Bayonne, New Jersey. The torpedo attack failed and the freighter steamed on, presumably unaware of its lucky escape.

As the evening wore on, Coke's rescue ships came back to Queenstown one by one bringing with them the quick and the dead. Wesley Frost vividly recorded his memories:

> We saw the ghastly procession of these rescue ships as they landed the living and the dead that night under the flaming gas torches along the Queenstown waterfront . . . ship after ship would come up out of the darkness . . . awaiting their turn in the cloudy night to discharge bruised and shuddering women, cripples and half-clothed men and wide eyed little children.[18]

On the quays were waiting doctors, nurses and priests on their mission of comfort and a huge throng of the people of Queenstown, who, like all seafaring communities, knew the vagaries of the ocean all too well, united in an impressive effort to help those who had found themselves in peril on the sea. Men acted as stretcher-bearers or supported the walking wounded while women proffered blankets, cups of tea and bowls of hot soup or just a helping hand. Cunard's local manager, Jerome Murphy, and his staff worked prodigies to find accommodation for the survivors. Once the hotels and boarding houses were full, many residents welcomed them into their homes, however humble, and lent them clothes.

Among the exhibits in the Cobh Heritage Centre is a letter from one survivor, Winifred Hall from Cheshire, to the family who had taken her into their home: 'Neither I am sure will we ever forget the wondrous kindness shown us who survived that awful experience by the people of Queenstown. Dear Mrs. Swinton, words fail me to try and thank you'. Contradicting accusations made at the Mersey Inquiry that Cunard had ignored survivors, Mrs Hall wrote that 'Officials from Cunard met us at Holyhead and took care of us in every way.'[19] Charles Lauriat noted that 'the street in Queenstown was filled with people ready to do anything in their power to relieve our sufferings . . . I never saw anything more spontaneous or genuine or more freely given than the Irish hospitality of Queenstown'. With some fellow-survivors who had been on the same collapsible, he found accommodation at a pub grandly known as the Imperial Bar. The landlady gave them welcome glasses of Irish whiskey and when he woke in the morning he found that she had dried his and his companions' clothes before a fire she had kept going all night.[20]

Throughout the night, the police, Coke's officers and the indefatigable Murphy and Frost continued with the thankless task of listing the living and attempting to identify the dead. Frost described how the 'piles of corpses like cordwood began to appear among the paint kegs and coils of rope on the shadowy old wharves'. The *Cork Examiner* wrote of 'the heart-rending spectacle of the landing of the dead to the number of 131'.[21] As they worked on, the scale of the disaster came ever more apparent. Once the last rescue ship had docked and every survivor landed, the final toll could be calculated.

Lusitania had departed America with 1,962 people on board; 1,265 passengers, 694 crew and the three hapless agents, confined in the brig. Only 474 passengers and 290 crew had survived.[22] In contrast to *Titanic,* where the death toll had been heaviest among third-class passengers, only a quarter of whom had escaped, the loss of life was spread almost evenly between saloon, cabin and third class. A higher proportion of the crew had survived than had of the passengers, giving some credence to the belief that the black gangs had helped themselves to positions in the boats at the expense of passengers. Many passengers who had been decanted into the water in the liner's death throes had perished from hypothermia before they could be rescued. More were to die on the voyage back to Queenstown before they could reach medical help.

Lauriat noticed that many passengers had shed clothes before going into the sea which could only have rendered them more susceptible to the colder temperature as the evening wore on. The children proved especially vulnerable to exposure and of those who were one year old and more, only thirty-one out of ninety survived. Audrey Pearl was one of only five out of thirty-nine babies, less than a year old, to be rescued. The youngest survivor, Billy Doherty from Long Island, was but two months old. Sadly, only nine of the twenty-five stewardesses, who had performed so well on the decks of the sinking liner, survived. Apart from Turner, only three of *Lusitania*'s deck officers, Jones, Bestic and Third Officer Lewis were rescued. During the voyage, Jock Anderson was said to have remarked to Turner that he felt a strong presentiment of death, a premonition which had proved to be only too well founded. He was last seen helping passengers on the port side of the boat deck. Second Officer Simon Hefford had gone down with the ship on whom it had been his career ambition to serve. Gone too were Chief Engineer Bryce, purser McCubbin and Surgeon McDermott. McCubbin had been on his last voyage before retiring and McDermott had been standing in for the liner's usual surgeon, John Pointon, who was on sick leave. Some writers have wrongly suggested that Archie Bryce had been killed when on an inspection tour of the forward boiler rooms. This can be refuted as Second Engineer Andrew Cockburn told Mersey that he had conferred with Bryce in the engine room after the second explosion.

The greatest single tragedy of *Lusitania* was the fate of the Crompton family. Paul Crompton, his wife, all six of their children and their nursemaid, Dorothy Allen, had perished. Mrs Stephens, her grandson and their two servants were all lost. Other families were rent asunder. Arthur Adams and his son Mcmillan had been thrown into the water from boat No 19 and lost touch with each other. The father died, the son lived. William Hodges of Philadelphia survived; his wife and two sons, aged eight and five died. Mrs Henry Adams, gymnast and honeymooner, lost her husband. Edith Williams and her five-year-old sister Florence had become separated from their mother and four siblings in the liner's last minutes and the two girls were swept into the sea. Edith held grimly onto her sister's hand but Florence's grasp weakened in the seething waters and eventually she slipped away. For years afterwards Edith could hardly bear to be touched on her left hand. She clung on the skirt of another survivor and was eventually hauled to safety on a lifeboat. When she reached Queenstown she found that she and her brother Edward, aged seven, were the only family survivors.

Warren Pearl and his wife were rescued and were reunited with the determined Audrey Lines and their two children whom she had brought to safety. He told the *New York Sun* that:

> I saw no sign of panic. I did not know whether my wife or children were safe until I got ashore after three hours in the water during which time I floated with the greatest of ease in my life belt. When I reached the land I found my wife suffering from a broken arm. I soon found two of my children and brought them to her. Two were gone but I thank God that so many of my family were saved especially when I recall that whole families have perished.

Admiral Coke offered the Pearl family the hospitality of Admiralty House where they stayed for three weeks while they searched for their second nanny, Greta Lorenzen, and their other two children. Sadly they were never seen again.[23]

A swathe had been cut through the notables on the passenger list. Vanderbilt, Frohman, Hubbard and his wife, Klein, Hugh Lane, Stackhouse and Maturin had been lost. Tragically, the indefatigable Marie Depage had paid with her life for her devotion to her embattled country. Dr James Houghton, one of the doctors bound for Belgium, described how he met her on the boat deck, where, professional to the core, she had been bandaging the hand of a passenger who had injured it while assisting in launching a lifeboat:

> I saw that the time had come to leave the ship – now well down by her head. I said to Madame Depage that we had better jump overboard and trust to be picked up by one of the rafts or lifeboats. This we both did and as I struck the water my head came into violent contact with a piece of wreckage, which stunned me and I commenced to sink. Happily I came to the surface again and struck out for a raft . . . My first thought was to . . . save Madame Depage, but no trace of her was to be seen and I can only conclude that she was drowned.[24]

Oliver Bernard was one of the many survivors who had found it difficult to sleep on the night of the tragedy. As dawn approached, he rose and walked the streets, watching the scenes as Queenstown dealt with the after effects. Visiting the makeshift morgues, he saw 'a heap of what looked like battered, bruised, broken dolls laid aside as factory refuse might be'. In this macabre setting, one which he could never forget, other survivors were engaged in the heartbreaking task of searching for their lost relatives. To his artist's eye 'the most appalling impression this experience left . . . was in death all human beings were alike, shapeless inanimate clay . . . death masks would have revealed . . . nothing but a horrible, lifeless uniformity'. In the second of these morgues, a flash of sunlight, breaking through the grime of the windows, lit upon gold braid and Bernard found the body of Jock Anderson, his features so bloated as to be almost unrecognisable. He concluded that *Lusitania's* Staff Captain had stuck to his post to the end and had not drowned without a hard struggle. In another morgue he came across one of the tragedy's best-known victims: 'poor Charles Frohman alone was undisfigured: he must have died without protest before the sea could do its worst'.[25]

The Times correspondent in Queenstown recorded the full horror of the scene in the three mortuaries, including the town's market hall:

> . . . a small bare chamber . . . filled with as many victims of the nameless submarine as it can hold. Men and women have been passing down the files of dead all day long seeking relatives and friends who, they feared, were among the missing. Human emotion has at times reached breaking point. The dead lay as they were found, in the clothing in which they were taken from the water. Their faces still bore the expression with which each one of these cruelly slain men, women and children had met death. For there were several children in the chamber of death . . . Men broke down when they looked upon a young mother, lying there with her baby . . . folded in her protective arms. Nearby were two baby twins . . . a sailor, who was found with a body of a little child strapped to his shoulders. Two children, who went down together with their arms around each other, were still folded firmly together . . . Some of the dead wore expressions of terror . . . others were calm and beautiful. There have been heart-rending recognitions and there have been steps that turned away to come again on the morrow.'

Moved to anger at these tragic sights, neither *The Times* correspondent nor the people of Queenstown had any illusion as to who was to blame.

> And with the solemn panoply of death, there is nothing to suggest . . . that this spectacle had even a remote connection with civilised warfare . . . these poor souls were unarmed and helpless when they went to their death. So it is that Queenstown is seething with the fury of men who ask themselves what they can do to make the Germans answerable for this appalling crime.[26]

For many years afterwards, an American saloon-class survivor, Dwight Harris, would relate how he had taken the precaution of ordering a specially-designed lifejacket from the well-known New York sporting outfitters, Abercrombie & Fitch, before he sailed. The lifejacket was fitted with several pockets for carrying valuables and the prudent Harris wore it from the time *Lusitania* entered the danger zone, with his wife Eileen's jewelry stowed in one of its secure pockets. He described how he had been on deck and had seen the torpedo strike. With some presence of mind, he rushed down to his cabin and collected a couple of books and his toothbrush, before returning to the deck and seeing Eileen into a lifeboat. He went into the sea, and supported by his lifejacket floated comfortably until he was picked up by one of the rescue boats. When Eileen Harris reached Queenstown, she asked to be directed to the best hotel, where she knew that she would find her husband and, just as she expected, there he was waiting for her.[27] Another saloon-class passenger, Harold Boulton, recounted that for ten or twelve years after the disaster, he would wake from a nightmare in which he was being sucked down into the depths by the sinking liner to find that he was standing on his bed with his arms flailing above his head as if he was desperately clawing his way upward in a subconscious effort to avoid being drowned.

Among others who had escaped were D A Thomas and his daughter Margaret. With the water almost level with the deck, he saw a woman passenger with a small child hesitating about getting into a lifeboat. He shoved them both into the boat before jumping in it himself just before the liner foundered. Margaret Mackworth felt herself go down with the ship. Fortunately for herself, she was wearing a lifebelt which brought her up to the surface and kept her afloat when, after some time in the water, she passed out. When she came to, she was in the captain's cabin on board the trawler *Bluebell*, together with a crowd of survivors. She listened to a woman launch into a tirade, claiming that there had been no organisation or discipline on the sinking liner. She realised that this was clearly aimed at another survivor and then she recognised a despondent Turner, hunched in a blanket in a corner of the cabin. Reunited with her father in Queenstown, she shared with him a moment of accidental humour. A sub-editor in a Welsh newspaper had devised an artless headline:

GREAT NATIONAL DISASTER
D A Thomas Saved[28]

CHAPTER 8

Reaction

On the evening of 7 May, Walter Hines Page, American ambassador in London, was giving a dinner party in honour of Colonel House. As his guests were assembling, the ambassador received a telegram from Consul Frost setting out the full extent of the tragedy and forecasting a death toll of over a thousand, including a hundred Americans. After a hurried discussion with his wife, he decided that the dinner should go ahead. It was a melancholy affair. From time to time the embassy butler entered the dining-room bearing more messages of bad news. The loss of *Lusitania* dominated the conversation with Page and House both asserting that the sinking would lead to early American entry into the war. Page's opposite number in Berlin, Gerard, took the same view, even ordering a special train to stand by to take the embassy staff out of the country.

A heavy gloom settled over the Admiralty as Coke's signals came in from Queenstown. Fisher, who started his working day early, went home for dinner as was his habit, leaving Oliver in charge. The chief of the war staff sent for Captain Webb, director of the trade division, and the two men sat well into the night assessing the disturbing implications of the latest in the long string of failures and disasters which had taken place on the Navy's watch. Whilst other sinkings had only involved naval loss of life, the loss of *Lusitania* entailed heavy civilian casualties. The death toll among her American passengers was an even more ominous factor. The need for a rapid investigation was only too obvious and Oliver asked Webb to prepare a report with the minimum of delay setting out exactly why the great liner had met her doom and, more importantly from the embattled Navy's point of view, who was to blame. When Webb left, the Admiralty's workhorse turned back to the pressing volume of paperwork which kept him occupied for up to eighteen hours a day.

Woodrow Wilson heard the news as he was about to leave the White House for a round of golf. In March 1915, Cary Grayson, the President's doctor and regular golfing partner, had introduced him to Edith Mary Galt, the vivacious widow of a

99

Washington businessman, then in her early forties. From their first meeting, they were strongly attracted to each other. On 4 May, three days before *Lusitania* was sunk, Wilson impulsively proposed to her. In accord with the conventions, Edith Galt declined him on the reasonable grounds that they had known each other for only two months and that Ellen Wilson had been dead for less than a year. Wilson was too overwrought to understand the reasons for her refusal. When the news of the tragedy reached him, the anguish which he felt at the heavy loss of life added to his existing emotional turmoil.

Cancelling his game, he retreated to his office where he sat alone to await more detailed reports. As the afternoon wore on the skies clouded over and a steady drizzle set in. Shortly after 8pm he was told that the death toll was expected to be more than a thousand, and in the words of one of his biographers: 'the President leapt to his feet and before his Secret Service agents realised what had happened, he strode out . . . into the rainy twilight. For an hour he walked the streets of Washington, alone with his responsibility and with the terrible visions of suffering and death.'[1]

Bernstorff learnt of the sinking when he arrived in New York on one of his regular visits to the city's German-American community. He was besieged in his hotel by a crowd of reporters, to whom he had no desire to talk. They pursued him all the way to Penn Station where he caught an early morning train back to Washington to deal with the sinister implications of the tragedy.[2] The news reached Wall Street towards the end of the trading day and the market reacted strongly. It too expected war and prices dropped like the proverbial stone. By the end of the day the Dow Jones Index had fallen by 4.5 per cent. In 1915 the market was open on Saturdays and on 8 May it dropped by a further 3.5 per cent, making a total fall over the two days of over 8 per cent.

As the news spread a bitter feeling of anger erupted against Germany and everything German, stronger even than the reaction to the atrocities in Belgium the previous autumn. The disaster was most strongly felt in *Lusitania*'s home port of Liverpool, where the loss of life was to be most concentrated. The liner had been a symbol of pride to the whole city, their own beloved Lucy. Taking their children to see the mighty ship come and go from the Mersey was a favourite family outing. Other liners might have been larger, newer and more luxurious but in the minds of the people of Liverpool she was the undoubted empress of the North Atlantic, superior to any of her contemporaries. Now people muttered to each other that the accursed Germans had sunk their ship and had killed four hundred members of her crew, most of them fellow-Liverpudlians. Trouble had been brewing even before the special train bringing the survivors of the crew arrived at Lime Street Station early on the morning of 9 May. *The Times* correspondent graphically described the scenes at the station.

> Even at that hour there was a big crowd . . . to meet the survivors. They were the same people I had seen last night waiting and weeping before the windows of the Cunard offices in which were shown the names of rescued passengers and crew as they were telegraphed from Queenstown. For the most part they were women and girls, the mothers, wives, sisters and sweethearts of the crew . . . they kept vigil through the night and hungrily scanned each fresh bulletin. Now and then a piercing cry was heard 'He's saved' three or four women would rush away to spread the good news in their neighbourhood. The scenes at Lime St. Station were even more poignant. Shortly after 6 o'clock the train came in with 200 of the crew . . . a few petty officers, . . . engineers, stewards, firemen, seamen, trimmers, watchmen, waiters and messenger boys . . . what was most curious was the contrast between their stoical unconcern, and the tear-stained faces of the throng of women and girls by whom they were immediately surrounded.
>
> I saw one elderly woman with her shawl hanging from her shoulders and her gray hair in disarray advancing slowly through the crowd calling out ' Is Dan Daly among ye? Dan Daly the fireman?'. She was a mother seeking distractedly for her son. Clutching by the arm each member of the crew she would moaningly ask whether he did not know Dan Daly the fireman but none of them knew him. At last she came upon a fireman who did know and I heard the decisive answer which shattered her hopes. 'Dan is gone, Ma'am. He was down below at the time'. Throwing her hands up with a gesture of despair the mother turned aside to lean over a packing case for support while she wailed and wailed in sorrow.[3]

As the day wore on, tension, bred from what *The Times* correspondent described as the lethal emotions of grief and fury, simmered and as night fell it exploded.[4] Riots broke out in several parts of the city and across the Mersey in Birkenhead, continuing throughout the next day. Mobs of up to 3,000 people, among them crew members and the relatives of some of those who had died, directed their anger at German-owned shops, mostly pork-butchers, some of whom had been in business in the city for two generations. They were even joined by some seamen from American ships which had docked after *Lusitania* had been sunk. One American sailor told the *New York Times* that he had joined a crowd who were attacking a cutlery shop in Scotland Road. He gleefully admitted to picking up a brick and heaving it thorough a window. Within a few minutes the shop was wrecked and its owner's furniture thrown out into the street. He went down the road with the mob and took part in smashing four more German shops.

The situation in the Everton district of the city became so bad that a posse of about fifty police, clearly caught off guard, had great difficulty in restoring order. About twenty arrests were made and the police were badly jostled by angry rioters trying to release those who had been taken into custody. On the following day all public houses were closed and the police were forced to invoke the Defence of the Realm Act and order the internment of all German and Austrian citizens as a protective measure. Even those who had been naturalised were advised to leave the city. Anti-German riots erupted in many parts of London, in Newcastle and in cities as far away as Victoria, British Columbia, where the German club was wrecked and the mayor was called out to read the Riot Act. An unfortunate German was rolled in the mud by angry butchers at Smithfield and had to be rescued by the police. On the stock exchange anyone of German origin was boycotted. Workers downed tools in a textile factory in Bradford and at Swan Hunter's shipyard on Tyneside, where *Mauretania* had been built, and refused to return to the job until German- and Austrian-born employees had been given their tickets. Schwieger had not only sunk a mighty liner, he had, in the words of one historian, let loose 'the dark well of aggressiveness that lies within human nature and finds release in the pleasurable adrenalin surge that comes from violence, risk and danger'.[5]

In the Cunard building, Alfred Booth with his directors and senior managers and the line's solicitors, Hill Dickinson, were in almost constant session, dealing with the aftermath of the disaster and the myriad ensuing human problems. On the day after the sinking he cabled Sumner: 'we are all at one in our feelings with regard to this terrible disaster to *Lusitania* and it is quite hopeless to put anything in writing. My own personal loss is very great. The loss of life appears to have been appallingly great as the time was so short'.[6] He was referring to the loss of Paul Crompton and his entire family and he was clearly suffering from considerable stress. On the next day he had the sad duty of telegraphing the confirmation of their deaths to his cousin George. *Lusitania* had been fully insured by the Liverpool & London War Risks Association, a mutual company, which had been established by a number of leading shipowners including Cunard and which was managed by Hill Dickinson. The risk on the liner had effectively been reinsured by the Government under its agreements with the various war risk associations. On the day after the sinking, the association confirmed that the liner had been fully covered and that compensation would be paid to wounded crew members and to the relatives of the dead.

At about the same hour as the train bringing survivors of the crew arrived in Liverpool, the first of the night trains from the Irish ferry terminal at Holyhead steamed into London's Euston Station carrying rescued passengers. Ambassador Page, who had come to Euston to welcome American survivors and provide any support which they might need, was among the large crowd on the platform, many of them waiting to greet their relatives and friends and others hoping against hope for news of the missing. *The Times* correspondent noted that the survivors,

> were weary and showed in their faces the strain of the terrible experience through which they had passed. A man who was dressed in tweeds and without a hat, who was greeted by Dr. Page, who would not speak to [the] press . . . of the disaster . . . 'don't ask me about it' he said 'I wouldn't talk for a guinea a minute' . . . Two white-faced boys, in the care of a porter from the Euston Hotel, walked down the platform with their eyes directed upon the ground. They looked at no one and never spoke. The greater number of the passengers travelled by the second train – the Irish Mail. Among them the people on the platform found their friends. Relatives embraced each other with fervour and gratitude. Several survivors had kept their belts . . . and one said dryly 'That tells the story'. On the side of the belt he had written 'R.M.S. *Lusitania*, May 7th 1915. Off Ireland. Torpedoed 2.15 p.m.' He said he would keep the belt all his life.
>
> The reunions provided the happy side of the picture. The tragedy of it all was brought back by the women without hope. They passed from group to group, and always they asked the same question. 'Were you on the *Lusitania*? Did you see Mr. ———? Have you heard anything of him?' Congratulations were checked for a moment by these pathetic interruptions . . .[7]

Page soon saw a familiar face: Charles Lauriat. Before Wilson had appointed him to the London embassy, Page had been the publisher and editor of the prestigious *Atlantic Monthly* and he had known the Lauriat family through literary connections. As it was a Sunday there were no early morning suburban rail services and Lauriat's London representative had walked nine miles to Euston to welcome him and take him to his home. After a traditional English Sunday lunch of roast beef and Yorkshire pudding, a weary Lauriat went to bed and slept the sleep of the saved, not waking until the next morning.

German embassies and wire services in neutral countries speedily picked up the news and passed it on to Berlin where it was received with unrestrained satisfaction. Press reports inaccurately described *Lusitania* as a fully-armed cruiser. Little or no sympathy was expressed for the plight of the passengers and the sinking was generally hailed as a great success for the U-boat service. The reaction of the *Kolnische Volkszeitung*, which supported the allegedly moderate Catholic Centre Party, a direct forebear of the present-day CDU, exemplified the triumphant and insensitive tone adopted by the German press:

> The sinking of the *Lusitania* is a success of our submarines which must be placed beside the greatest achievement of this naval war. The sinking of the giant English steamship is a success of moral significance which is still greater than material success. With joyful pride we contemplate this latest deed of our Navy. It will not be the last. The English wish to abandon the German people to death by starvation. We are more humane. We simply sank an English ship with passengers who at their own risk ... entered the zone of operations.[8]

The Austrian press was remarkably restrained, for the most part reporting the disaster without comment. The Viennese *Neue Freie Presse* was an exception, noting in one sentence that the catastrophe could hardly have happened without the greatest loss of life and in the next gloating over the success of their ally's navy. Throughout Britain and America, the press reacted with dismay and outrage, castigating Imperial Germany. *The Times* denounced the sinking as 'wholesale murder'. The *New York Herald* thundered that 'even the rattlesnake gives warning before striking'. The *New York Times*, voice of the east coast establishment, was even more outspoken, concluding that 'if this [sinking] is to be accepted as a true manifestation of the German spirit then all neutral nations are on notice that the complete defeat of Germany and the eradication of its military spirit are essential to their peace and safety'. In a further editorial it argued that Germany was now an outlaw, declaring that;

> it had snapped its fingers at the laws of war as at the law of morality when she did this deed of blood. We know now how she makes war . . . Had we known on August 1st what is now so painfully clear . . . we should have taken a different course. We passed over in silence the lawless violence visited on Belgium . . . We should have protested . . . and shown less forbearance in the cases of the . . . *Cushing*, the *Gulflight* and the *Falaba* . . . The time for protest has passed. It becomes our duty as a nation to demand of Germany to find means to carry on her war without putting our citizens to death . . . It may be said that in this demand we should call upon Germany to surrender the right to fight her own enemy in her own way. It is precisely that. Her own way is that tigerish ferocity which neither neutrals or enemies believed her capable.

In neutral countries, some newspapers, whose editors either sympathised with Germany or felt the need not to antagonise her, were restrained. Pope Benedict XV saw no reason for restraint and sent a cable to the Kaiser, deploring his inhuman methods. Most of the neutral media, from the Vatican's official organ *Osservatore Romano*, taking its line from the Pontiff, to the *La Prensa* of Buenos Aires, was as critical as their Allied counterparts. The sinking was strongly condemned by the Italian press, even by those who advocated continued neutrality. The Milanese *Corriere Della Sera* wrote: 'This enormous brutality passes all limits by far. We must go far back in time to find such a total suppression of humanity. Germany thinks to terrify the universe by filling it with as much blood as it is possible to spill.' The Milanese *Secolo* noted that the sinking, added to their blind destruction of lives and property, placed the Germans beyond all law. The local *Times* correspondent reported that 'the . . . disaster was decried in the streets of Milan in terms unthinkable a few weeks ago' and that it had led to 'a tremendous outburst of indignation'. In Scandinavia the reaction was equally hostile. Even in Sweden, traditionally close to Germany, the press and public opinion were outraged. The Social Democrat Prime Minister, Hjalmar Branting, was particularly forthright, stating that even if *Lusitania* carried contraband, it did not constitute a right for a German war vessel to sink her. The *Nya Dagligt Allehanda* of Stockholm, echoing a widely-held view, declared that 'a cry of horror and indignation will be sent up by the civilised world at the sinking . . . This is an unpardonable crime against humanity'. A similar point was made by the *De Telegraaf* of Amsterdam, which called the sinking a premeditated crime and noted 'the spontaneous . . . protest of the entire civilised world from which Germany has separated itself'. Spanish society, hitherto sympathetic to Germany, was profoundly shocked by the wholesale drowning of neutral citizens and women and children.[9]

*   *   *

The first of the inquiries took place on the day following the tragedy. Fishing boats from both Queenstown and Kinsale had come to the rescue of survivors. The latter town jealously guarded its ancient privileges as an independent authority. When he discovered that five bodies had been landed there by Kinsale boats, the town's coroner, John Horgan, a local solicitor whose family were close allies of John Redmond, the leader of the parliamentary wing of the Irish Nationalist Party, moved speedily to convene an inquest. He went over to Queenstown on the morning of 8 May and subpoenaed Turner and a number of survivors to appear before him. Shrewdly suspecting that higher authority might forestall him, he opened hearings that afternoon in the historic Market House of Kinsale before a coroner's jury of local merchants and fishermen. In his memoirs Horgan described Turner, who appeared before him on the morning of 10 May, as 'clad in a badly-fitting old suit . . . suffering from the strain of his experience'. Despite his mental condition, with no lawyers on hand to coach or restrain him as in the later proceedings, Turner gave evidence in a confident manner. He convincingly answered questions on the navigation of the liner, including her speed, her course and whether she was zig-zagging.

In the light of the subsequent controversy, Turner's response to questioning on whether the liner should have been escorted is enlightening.

Jury foreman: In the face of the warnings at New York that the *Lusitania* would be torpedoed, did you make an application to the Admiralty for an escort?

Turner: No, I left that to them. It is their business, not mine. I simply had to carry out my orders to go – and I would do it again.

Horgan: I am very glad to hear you say so, Captain.

106

It was only when Horgan condoled with him and with Cunard on the loss of his ship that, clearly overwrought, he collapsed in tears.

After local doctors had testified that the victims had died from immersion or exposure, what would now be called hypothermia, Horgan quickly concluded the inquest. In his instructions to the jury he pointedly and correctly advised them that 'as to the warning in American papers, it had no more legal or valid effect than that of an assassin who sent an anonymous letter to his intended victim'. (This point was later to be made by other legal luminaries.) The jury brought in the ringing verdict: 'this appalling crime was contrary to international law and the conventions of all civilised nations, and we therefore charge the officers of the submarine and the German Emperor and the Government of Germany, under whose orders they acted, of wilful and wholesale murder.'

Within hours the verdict of the Kinsale jury was flashed round the world. Half an hour after it had been reached, Horgan's suspicions about higher authority were realised. Thirty years later he wrote in his memoirs that 'my friend Harry Wynne, the Crown Solicitor for County Cork, arrived with instructions from the Admiralty to stop the inquest and prevent Captain Turner from giving evidence'. He added sarcastically that 'That august body were, however, as belated on this occasion as they had been in protecting *Lusitania* against attack'. Horgan was, however, exaggerating. The Admiralty had certainly been slow to react to the Kinsale inquest but their anxiety arose from a desire not so much to cover up the sinking but rather to prevent any security leak which might have assisted the Germans. In a rather belated cable, sent at 10.56am on 10 May, Graham Greene had merely requested Sir Matthew Nathan, the senior civil servant at the Irish Office in Dublin, to ensure that the Admiralty's instructions for the guidance of merchant ships in evading submarines would not be mentioned at the inquest.[10] Moved by the tragedy and realising how vulnerable were those who ventured on the seas, Horgan would devote much of his time to serving as a reserve officer in the Coastguard.[11]

On that same day Queenstown, with its shops and businesses closed and curtains and blinds of private homes drawn as a mark of respect, buried 140 of the dead of *Lusitania*. The Bishop of Cork, Dr Brown, conducted a requiem mass in the Victorian Gothic St Coleman's Cathedral which dominates the town's skyline, and which was attended by Admiral Coke and other civil and military dignitaries. For almost three hours after the service, a succession of funeral processions, escorted by sailors and soldiers and preceded by military bands playing the 'Dead March in *Saul*' and Chopin's 'Funeral March', wound their way through the streets, lined with onlookers, their heads bowed, to the old cemetery, which lies in a valley by the road to Cork. Twenty-five of the coffins were draped in the Stars and Stripes. After a short ecumenical service, seventy-six of the dead, who could not be identified, were buried in three mass graves. As each coffin was lowered into the ground, soldiers fired off a volley.[12]

For weeks afterwards, bodies of victims were washed ashore all over the south coast of Ireland. One of them, Captain James Miller, an officer in the US coast and geodetic survey, was found as far away as Galway. Among the bodies who were recovered were those of Father Maturin, Marie Depage and Mrs Stephens. Her son-in-law went to Queenstown for the grim task of identifying her body which he found lying in a mortuary surrounded by many others. There were no indications that she had drowned and her son-in-law concluded that she had probably suffered a fatal heart attack on going into the water. She had been carrying a jewellery bag containing a long string of pearls which was returned to her family and which now belong to her great-granddaughter. A grieving Antoine Depage arrived to identify Marie and to take her back to Belgium where she was buried with military honours in the sand dunes at La Panne, close by the hospital which she had served with unswerving dedication. One week after the sinking, Jock Anderson was laid to rest in Liverpool, his funeral service attended by a vast throng from the city's shipping community. Father Maturin, who would have preferred to have been buried in a simple country church, was given a solemn requiem mass in the Brompton Oratory in London. On 24 May, *City of New York* returned home bringing with her a number of the American dead, among them Charles Frohman. On the following day Fifth Avenue came to a stop for his funeral service at Temple Emmanuel as thousands of New Yorkers, led by actors and actresses, authors and theatre managers, paid their last respects to the great impresario. On his casket lay a single bouquet of violets from the actress Maude Adams, to whom many people suspected he was secretly married. On 16 June, nearly six weeks after the tragedy, the last victim, A S Witherbee, a four-year-old boy from New York, was buried in the cemetery at

Queenstown.[13] The bodies of nine hundred of *Lusitania*'s passengers and crew, among them Alfred Vanderbilt and young John Stephens, were never found. Mrs Stephens was fated never to be buried on land. Her coffin was being returned to Canada on the liner *Arabic* which was torpedoed the following August.

*   *   *

The almost universal reaction to the sinking and to the subsequent German crowing over Schwieger's achievement was well expressed by the former British Liberal Prime Minister, Lord Rosebery, in a letter to *The Times*, published three days after the tragedy. He wrote:

> There are one or two points to be noted with regard to this infamy. [Rosebery penned the same word which twenty-six years later Franklin Roosevelt used to describe Pearl Harbor]. The moral degradation of a nation that can hail such victory and rejoice over it . . .The mental degradation of a nation which can offer warning as an excuse for massacre. It is constantly proved in humbler cases of homicide that the murderer declared 'I'll do for him' but that has never saved the culprit from the gallows . . . The stupidity of it. Never has that much clarioned saying 'it is worse than a crime; it is a blunder' been more fully exemplified. It is intended to dismay our people. It will only rouse them to more furious effort. It is intended to alarm neutrals, whom it will only alienate and incense. And all this to secure without any possible competition the title of the enemy of the human race and the horror of the civilised world.[14]

Rosebery's perception of the international reaction to the sinking was to prove correct. The same point was to be made forcibly by Ballin. He wrote to the Foreign Minister, Gottlieb von Jagow:

> As I have learned from the States, people are very disturbed in America by the torpedoing of the *Lusitania* and their mood will not be completely reflected in the official note which will arrive here soon. . . . I think it unfortunate . . . if we officially justify our submarine action in the light of the depravity of the English and of starving German women and children. I consider it a mistake to present the use of submarines as retaliation since we thereby admit that this form of military operation is illegal in international law . . . it is not in our interests to denounce the illegality of other countries actions, as we did in Wednesday's note to the neutrals . . . I believe that we would do well to emphasize that our strategy is based on the *novelty* of the weapon.[15]

The normally bellicose German Consul-General in New York reported to Bernstorff that demonstrators in the streets of the city had expressed virulent anti-German feelings, adding that 'We have lost much sympathy.' Jacob Schiff, the highly respected head of the Wall Street firm of Kuhn, Loeb had been born in Germany and was widely thought to be pro-German. Two years later, he wrote:

> But ever since the sinking of the *Lusitania* and the subsequent ruth-less and inhuman acts of the German Government, my attitude has undergone a thorough change, and I only hope that before very long Great Britain and France will be able to force a peace which will prevent the return of conditions that have brought upon the world the present ghastly situation.[16]

Matters were made worse by inflammatory statements by two senior representatives of the German government. The military attaché, Franz von Papen, reacted with considerable disregard for accuracy: 'Germany was forced into the war and forced to keep on fighting. It was criminal of the British Government to allow Cunard to carry passengers on a ship transporting explosives and munitions. You read of 1000 Germans being killed and pass it over without qualm. This will bring it [the reality of war] home.'[17] Dernburg, described by the New York Sun as 'that un-official mouthpiece whose words are grating on the Washington ear' told a meeting in Cleveland that Germany had the undoubted right to sink contraband runners without warning and that the American flag would not offer them any protection. This statement was a complete travesty of the cruiser rules and of the Kaiser's instruction that neutral shipping should not be attacked. An angry Bernstorff promptly sent Dernburg home before he could do any more damage or the authorities could expel him.[18]

Deeply depressed by the tragedy, Wilson spent most of the next three days in the White House drafting a sternly-worded protest to the German government. On the evening of 10 May he went to Philadelphia to address a meeting of recently naturalised citizens in what became known as 'the too proud to fight' speech. Departing from his prepared text, he made these off-the-cuff remarks which he immediately regretted.

> The example of America must be a special example . . . not merely of peace because it will not fight but of peace because peace is the healing and elevating influence of the world and strife is not. There

is such a thing as a man being too proud to fight. There is such thing as a nation being so right that it does not need to convince others that it is right.

These remarks were the unalloyed language of appeasement and have been described as one of the biggest errors of his presidency.[19] Wilson's lapse is more explicable in the light of his emotional state after Edith Galt's rejection of his proposal. On the following day he confessed ruefully to Mrs Galt that 'I just do not know what I said in Philadelphia. My heart was in a whirl'.[20] The press was bitterly critical and the President found himself at odds with his Cabinet and with public opinion. The speech was badly received in Britain, the author John Buchan noting that it had an ugly air of cant. Although Wilson quickly sent out a press release stating that his words did not reflect the policy of the administration, the damage had been done and contradictory signals had been sent to Berlin.

$$* \qquad * \qquad *$$

Schwieger was rounding the coasts of Ireland and Scotland on his return voyage, with one torpedo left. At 8pm on 9 May he sighted a three-masted barque, *Simetra*, in ballast and en route from Bergen to New Orleans but carrying no colours. When he ordered *Simetra* to heave to, she hoisted the Norwegian flag. He summoned her captain on board *U-20* and let him go when he found his papers were in order. He encountered two other ships both flying Norwegian colours and took no action against them. On the following day, 10 May, shrewdly calculating that the Royal Navy, bent on avenging the loss of *Lusitania*, would spare no effort in hunting him down, Schweiger wisely took a longer way round, passing to the north of the Shetlands, putting a greater distance between his submarine and the naval base at Scapa Flow. He had indeed been sighted off the island of Lewis at 1am that morning. Oliver ordered Jellicoe to make every effort to intercept and sink him when he was off Orkney.[21] On the morning of 12 May, Schwieger re-established radio contact with the naval station on Heligoland, reporting that he had sunk one sailing vessel, two steamers and *Lusitania*. In a further signal he noted that he had only used one torpedo to sink the liner. His news elicited an immediate reply from the C-in-C of the High Seas Fleet, Admiral Von Pohl: 'My highest appreciation of commander and crew for success achieved of which the High Seas Fleet is so proud and my congratulations on their return.'

Schwieger was also ordered to proceed not to his base port of Emden but to Fleet HQ at Wilhelmshaven. After *U-20* came alongside at 11.30am CET on the morning of 13 May, Schweiger was surprised to discover that he received a rather cool reception in some quarters despite Von Pohl's congratulatory signal. In the six days since he had torpedoed *Lusitania,* hostile world reaction, not least the Pope's condemnation, had affected the Kaiser, always a weather vane, and Admiral Muller, the chief of his naval cabinet. The Imperial Chancellor, Bethmann-Hollweg, and the Foreign Office, whose ambassadors had borne the brunt of neutral criticism, had also concluded that the sinking of the great liner had been a blunder of the first magnitude. Wilhelm actually reprimanded Schwieger for torpedoing the liner, a censure which was bitterly resented in the submarine command. In an interview with the London *Sunday Express* in 1929, a surviving U-boat captain, Max Valentiner, who, as commander of *U-38* had sunk the liner *Ancona* in November 1915, and had been a close friend of Schwieger, said that the latter had been appalled by the loss of life. (He confirmed that Schwieger had gone below periscope depth and left the scene before she sank.)[22]

CHAPTER 9

How are the Mighty Fallen

Churchill did not return to the Admiralty until late on the morning of Monday 10 May. On the previous day, he had witnessed the start of French's offensive at Aubers Ridge, which, like so many of the big pushes on the Western Front, had failed to achieve any of its objectives. By the time he had reached London, the Government had already appointed Lord Mersey to preside over a Board of Trade inquiry into the loss of *Lusitania*.

Whilst the British press had fulminated against Imperial Germany for torpedoing *Lusitania* and for the resultant loss of civilian life, some leader writers had already questioned the extent of the Admiralty's responsibility for the loss. On the day after the sinking the Liverpool *Daily Post* had inquired how a large liner had come to be such an easy target. In their lead editorial on 10 May, which was highly critical of the Admiralty, the conservative *Morning Post* had pointedly asked why one of Britain's greatest ocean liners had not been protected, particularly in a vulnerable area like the approaches to Queenstown.

In a lengthy dispatch in that morning's issue, the paper's Washington correspondent had included a paragraph headed 'Anger against England'.

> Coupled with the American horror of German barbarity is intense indignation at the supineness or incompetence of the British Government in permitting the *Lusitania* to enter the danger zone without adequate protection . . . in view of the warning given by the German Embassy . . . extra precautions should have been taken to safeguard the vessel. The public asks why the vessel was not convoyed, why she was allowed to approach the coast of Ireland without an escort . . . why the only protection afforded her was the vigilance of merchant seamen . . . Nothing has so shaken American confidence in British naval supremacy as this revelation of indifference or mismanagement that permitted the *Lusitania* to sail into a German trap.'[1]

As American opinion clearly held the Admiralty, rather than Cunard, to blame for the liner's loss, the Government had a

113

major damage-control problem on their hands. Churchill's private office thus had every reason to be uneasy and they were expecting trouble at question time in the House of Commons that afternoon. The House was full when he took his place on the ministerial front bench, sandwiched between Asquith and Lloyd George and facing Bonar Law and his principal colleagues.

The impressive bulldog figure of Admiral Lord Charles Beresford rose from the Conservative backbenches to ask a veritable broadside of questions about the sunken liner. What was her speed? Was she standing in for the Old Head of Kinsale? Was there a patrol in the locality? If not where was the nearest patrol? Were all points of departure made by homeward bound vessels adequately patrolled? Had the Admiralty received the warning given to passengers? Beresford was followed by two other Conservative MPs, Donald Macmaster, member for Chertsey, a Canadian-born lawyer, who was later to represent the Canadian Government at the Mersey inquiry and Robert Houston, a Liverpool shipowner and member for the West Toxteth division of the city. Macmaster expanded Beresford's final point and inquired as to 'what steps had been taken to safeguard *Lusitania* in the light of the fact that the German Ambassador in Washington had issued a . . . notice that the vessel would be attacked during the voyage and that passengers must run the risk of the journey?' (The threats made in the advertisement had not in fact been specifically directed at *Lusitania* but rather at all Allied liners.)

Houston asked Churchill if he had been aware that submarines had for some time been active in the seas around Ireland and that two Liverpool liners (referring to *Candidate* and *Centurion*) had been torpedoed on the previous Thursday. He continued: 'Was he [Churchill] aware that the Admiralty had provided destroyers to meet steamers off the South Coast of Ireland which were carrying horses on government account from the United States and convoy them to Liverpool?' He concluded by asking 'what arrangements, if any, had been made by the Admiralty to protect or convoy *Lusitania* to Liverpool?'

Churchill was an experienced hand at the dispatch box and dodged the more difficult questions by invoking national security and by reference to the recently announced Mersey inquiry, stating that he did not want to throw blame on the Captain of *Lusitania* before a full investigation had been held. He told the House, quite correctly, that the resources at his disposal did not enable him to supply destroyer escorts for merchant or passenger ships, more than two hundred of which, on average, arrived or departed safely every day. Understandably, he did not mention that the number of destroyers in home waters had been depleted by the demands of his brainchild, the Dardanelles expedition.

At this stage, Bonar Law, who had hitherto stayed silent, keeping a wary eye on the activities of his backbenchers, intervened:

Law: May I ask the Rt Hon Gentleman whether any answer was received to the instruction sent to the captain of *Lusitania* so as to make sure he received them?

Churchill: Both messages were acknowledged and the second message was acknowledged shortly before the end.

A succession of supplementary questions now rained down on the Prime Minister and the First Lord

Houston: The Rt Hon Gentleman has not answered my question with regard to the convoying of ships carrying horses to Liverpool.

Churchill: I do not remember the actual cases. We do sometimes attempt . . . to provide escorts for vessels carrying troops, munitions . . . and cargoes vitally needed . . . our principle is that the merchant traffic must look after itself . . . shocking exceptions like this ought not to divert the attention of the House, or the world . . . from the main fact that almost the entire trade of these islands is being carried on without appreciable loss.

Beresford: May I ask . . . the Rt Hon Gentleman that I wrote him a letter on 15 April giving him warnings of the perils which met the *Lusitania* and making certain proposals with regard to avoiding them . . . why were they unheeded?

Asquith: They were heeded.

Churchill: . . . the letter of the Noble Lord [Beresford] was carefully studied . . . far from being unheeded, a great many measures which he advocated . . . have already been applied on the largest possible scale by the Admiralty.

Churchill's reply was disingenuous and was aimed at Beresford's major weakness, his all-consuming vanity. He had recently told Asquith that Beresford was an old clown on whose ideas he was not going to waste any time!

The persistent Houston was not going to be swept aside:

Is the Rt Hon Gentleman not aware that in February, when the submarine danger was not nearly as pressing as it is now, the steamship *Hydaspes*, bringing horses from New Orleans, was met on the south coast of Ireland and convoyed to Liverpool by the destroyers HMS *Loyal* and HMS *Legion* and a similar course was taken with regard to the steamer *Armenian* which was also carrying horses?

Churchill: I think I cannot contravert that statement.

Macmaster: May I ask whether any provision . . . was made to safe-guard this ship, in view of . . . the threat . . . made of her destruction?

Churchill: I have stated that two warnings were sent to the vessel, together with directions as to her course . . . If the Hon member asks if a special escort was sent out my reply is 'no'.[2]

In the light of the subsequent controversy, it should be noted that during question time Churchill had twice categorically stated that two specific warnings had been sent to *Lusitania.* His answers were no doubt based on the detailed briefing he had been given on his return to the Admiralty by his private office, who had in turn been briefed by the naval war staff. This interpretation was clearly correct as the two earlier signals received by Turner on the evening of 6 May were of a general nature addressed to all British merchant ships in the war zone.

Beresford and his allies had set out to demonstrate that the Admiralty was inept and complacent about submarine warfare. Churchill's statement can have done little if anything to allay their presumption. Houston had succeeded in ambushing Churchill and extracting the unfortunate implication that the Admiralty was more concerned with the safety of horses than it was with that of men, women and children. All in all, the First Lord had passed an uncomfortable afternoon.

A week later, Houston returned to the attack, clearly implying that the Admiralty had been negligent and querying the disposi-tions of warships in the Western Approaches at the time of the sinking, introducing an allegation which has been repeated on several occasions by later commentators. He asked Churchill why a number of modern 'L' class destroyers and other patrol vessels based at Milford Haven, some five hours sailing from the Old Head, were not deployed to escort *Lusitania,* noting that on 6 May a ship carrying horses to Liverpool had been warned by the navy of the presence of a submarine off the Irish coast. One of Churchill's junior ministers, J J Macnamara, stonewalled the question, telling Houston that he had nothing to add to the reply which the First Lord had given on 10 May.[3]

On 12 May, it was the Prime Minister's turn to appear at question time. Lord Robert Cecil, son of the great Lord Salisbury and pillar of the Tory establishment, asked Asquith what government duties Churchill had been carrying out at the Front. The Prime Minister replied that he had visited Paris on important government business, adding obliquely that he had spent Saturday and Sunday at French's HQ. Cecil riposted with a lethal supplementary which elicited the damaging admission that Churchill had not been discharging any government business during his visit to the front. This revelation did not go down well with the House. Asquith would have been well-advised to have said no more but he essayed an unsuccessful effort in damage control, noting that since the outbreak of war Churchill had spent less than two weeks away from the Admiralty. In every part of the House, this news was received with incredulity. The fallout from the sinking and his failure to return to London immediately he had learnt of the disaster had further eroded Churchill's standing but whether the loss of the liner would have proved fatal to his position at the Admiralty is moot. Before the week was out two more crises, which had long been simmering, were to assail Asquith and his Government.

On the night of 12 May, the destroyer *Muanvent*, commanded by KapitanLeutnant Rudolf Firle, seconded from the Kriegsmarine to the Turkish navy, slipped through the narrows of the Dardanelles at night and torpedoed the old battleship HMS *Goliath* at an unprotected anchorage. She listed heavily, due to asymmetrical flooding, and then capsized, 570 of her crew going down with her.

At this inauspicious moment Captain Webb delivered his reports to his superiors at the Admiralty. The first dealt with the possibility of a security leak inside Cunard's New York office and the second with Turner's navigation of his ship. Richard Webb was a particularly private man, even for a naval officer, and little seems to be known of him. He eventually retired as a full admiral but he never held any of the main sea commands. In March and April 1917 he strenuously resisted the introduction of convoy, as did Jellicoe, by then First Sea Lord, and Oliver. This would suggest that he was neither an innovator nor a man who would readily use initiative. One might reasonably assume that he was devoted to the service and bitterly disappointed by the succession of setbacks which it had suffered since the outbreak of war. With detailed circumstantial evidence which could be used against

Turner, he doubtless felt a powerful temptation to cast the Captain in the role of scapegoat and thus exonerate the Navy from blame for this latest disaster. Webb was in a marginal position in the war staff hierarchy and given the prevailing centralisation it is probable that he had discussed and cleared his report in detail with Oliver in advance.

The state of Cunard security in New York had been a constant worry to Captain Gaunt, British naval attaché in Washington. As we have seen, German agents had succeeded in penetrating the screen round the liner and boarding her on the morning of her departure. Gaunt disliked Sumner, Cunard's manager in New York, intensely and had doubted the integrity of several managers in Cunard's New York catering and customer-service departments. When these were being reorganised some ten years earlier, Cunard had sensibly recruited experienced executives, most of them German-Americans, from HAPAG and NDL. The presence of these managers had caused concern before and, in December 1914, Graham Greene had virtually ordered Alfred Booth to dismiss the head of catering, one Ernest Farnham or Fahrenheim, a naturalised German with some eight years service with Cunard. On this occasion Booth vigorously defended his staff and transferred only one manager, named Winter, out of New York. He wrote to Sumner: 'I was convinced of the devotion of the Cunard Line staff working in furtherance of the cause of the allies. You might sometimes be inclined to growl but nevertheless you delivered the goods.'[4] There was little contact between the catering and customer-service departments and the line's operating staff. Turner was renowned for being uncommunicative and it will be remembered that he had received no instructions before sailing. No evidence could be found to support the assertion that anyone in New York had disclosed the liner's course and the accusation seems to be nothing more than a red herring. Nevertheless, Graham Greene, quoting from a schedule in the 1903 agreement which stated that no foreigner was to be employed as a 'principal officer' of the company, was so concerned that he summoned Booth and Sir Norman Hill, the senior partner of Hill Dickinson, Cunard's solicitors, to see him on two days notice. Booth agreed to send one of his senior captains, John Charles, a former master of *Lusitania*, to New York to back up Sumner.

The second, and more important, report was compiled from Turner's debriefing by Admiral Coke's staff. Coke, understandably anxious to distance himself from any blame for the tragedy, had told the service attachés sent by ambassador Page to Queenstown to assist American passengers that he was surprised that Turner had come so close inshore. Webb based his findings almost entirely on a signal sent by Coke to the Admiralty at 12.39pm on 8 May which read 'Ship was proceeding along the usual trade route – had received warnings on the 6th and 7th to give headlands a wide berth and steer a mid-channel course. Strong evidence of reduced speed.'[5] This signal enabled Webb to report that Turner had disregarded a series of Admiralty instructions in his possession, directing him to steer a mid-channel course, avoid headlands, maintain maximum speed and zigzag, and had ignored warnings that submarines were active off the Irish south coast. His final paragraphs constituted, at first sight, a damning attack on Turner:

> Further, when he was approaching the Irish Coast there was no need for him to have come into the land. It was within his power to raise steam for a higher speed, to have kept well out to sea and to have made St. George's Channel on a northerly course after dark.
>
> The Master, therefore, had several alternatives to the course and speed at which he should proceed through the dangerous area, in which, as he had been informed, submarines had been active. Instead of this, he proceeded along the usual trade route at a speed three-quarters of what he was able to get out of his vessel. He thus kept his valuable vessel for an unnecessary length of time in the area where she was most liable to attack, inviting disaster.[6]

In his zeal to clear the Admiralty of any responsibility for the loss and place it firmly on Turner, Webb had been somewhat economical with the actuality. As he must have known, *Lusitania*'s top speed with three boiler rooms operational was 21 knots and she had been steaming at 18 knots when she was torpedoed; 18 is not three-quarters of 21. He did not mention that Turner had steered what could be reasonably described as a mid-channel course until he changed course 30 degrees to port at 12.40pm and he did no provide any reason for this change. There are some odd featur about this report. It comprises only two pages of printed foolsca starting with some rather selective excerpts taken from Admira warnings dating back to the previous November. It was dated May, only one day after the sinking, which hardly provided su cient time to compile an entirely objective accident report.

On 13 May, Webb officially submitted his reports to Oliver, w signed them and sent them to the First Sea Lord. Fisher ha

vengeful side to his character which had become more pronounced as he grew older. As one obituary noted: 'in later years
he tended to treat those . . . who found themselves in direct
antagonism with a hostility which left bitter feelings behind.'[7]
This trait was usually directed at the not inconsiderable number
of admirals with whom he had fallen out and those in the service
who had been connected with them. After his return to the
Admiralty he had told Oliver that Rear-Admiral Arthur Leveson,
then director of operations, was a traitor for no better reason
than he had once been Sir William May's Flag-Captain. Willy May
was a distinguished admiral who, as Third Sea Lord, had been a
party to and signatory of the 1903 Inverclyde-Selborne agreement but who had fallen out of favour during Fisher's earlier
term as First Sea Lord.[8]

Fisher's reaction on reading Webb was extreme, suggesting
that he was close to losing touch with reality. He angrily under-
lined Webb's subjective conclusion that 'the Master appears to
have displayed an almost inconceivable negligence and one is
forced to conclude that he is either utterly incompetent or he has
been got at by the Germans'. In his inimitable handwriting he
penned furiously in the margin of the report:

> as the Cunard company would not have employed an incompetent
> man, the certainty is absolute that Captain Turner is not a fool but a
> knave. I feel absolutely certain that Turner is a scoundrel and [has]
> been bribed. No seaman in his senses would have acted as he did. I
> hope that Captain Turner will be arrested *immediately* after the
> inquiry, *whatever* the verdict or finding might be.

Churchill was only marginally more magnanimous. He commented that 'I consider the Admiralty case against the Captain
should be pressed before Lord Mersey by a skilful counsel and
that Captain Webb should attend as witness, if not employed as
an assessor. We should pursue the Captain without check'.[9] Only
days earlier, he had told the House of Commons that he did not
wish to throw any blame on the Captain of *Lusitania* before the
ss had been fully investigated.

Sir John Colville, Churchill's Private Secretary during and after
Second World War, who knew him as well as any man, wrote
him that he hated vindictiveness above all things and recalled
saying that he could not endure a manhunt.[10] Yet here he
fully prepared to start a witch-hunt against Turner on the
is of what was essentially an interim and highly subjective
miralty report without waiting for the Mersey inquiry at which

120

the hapless captain would have the benefit of legal defence. The vituperative hostility which Fisher and Churchill displayed towards Turner might indicate that both men knew that the Admiralty case was by no means as solid as Webb had suggested. Churchill had another, more justifiable, motive for endorsing the decision to scapegoat Turner. He was determined to do nothing which might have alerted the Kriegsmarine to the fact that the Admiralty could read their codes. With security in mind any detailed discussion of the Navy's responsibility for the disaster had be rigorously avoided. It thus suited him to pin the blame on the unfortunate Captain.

On the morning of Friday 14 May *The Times* led with an article which created a media sensation, quickly dubbed the shells scandal. Under the byline of its military correspondent, Colonel Charles à Court Repington, *The Times* asserted that the failure at Aubers Ridge had been caused by a chronic shortage of heavy artillery shells. This shortage, about which French had consistently but unavailingly complained to Kitchener, reflected an even more serious problem. The War Office had proved unable to effectively organise British industry to provide the vastly increased demands of the army for every kind of materiel needed for a long war. Despite the success of the purchasing programme in America the main brunt of this effort had to be borne by manufacturing industry at home. *The Times* was then owned by Alfred Harmsworth, Lord Northcliffe, whose domination of the British press was of the same scale as that of Rupert Murdoch today. Northcliffe was closely allied with the opposition Conservative party and like his American contemporary, William Randolph Hearst, he had an immense ego and a huge appetite for power. He saw in this story the potential to bring down Asquith and his Government and increase his own influence.

Despite the gathering storm, Churchill had other pressing issues to settle. The torpedoing of HMS *Goliath* had caused severe repercussions inside and outside the Admiralty. As the fleet at the Dardanelles was even more vulnerable to attack than he had previously supposed, a worried Fisher reiterated his demand that HMS *Queen Elizabeth*, the Navy's newest and fastest battleship, be brought home without delay. On the afternoon of 14 May Churchill and Fisher met in an attempt to settle their differences and decide the changes to be made to the fleet. After a protracted discussion they eventually agreed to the replacement of *Queen Elizabeth* by two old battleships and to a number of other

ship movements. By the time they had finalised these arrangements, it was well into the evening and the old Admiral was
exhausted. Churchill said to him kindly: 'Now go home, Fisher,
and get a good night's sleep'. Once he had left, Churchill ill-
advisedly added two newly commissioned submarines to the list
of the ships earmarked for the Dardanelles. Nothing could have
been more guaranteed to ignite the old Admiral's latent paranoia. Churchill's private office and Fisher's naval assistant,
Captain T E Crease, were aghast at this decision. The First Lord
would not even listen to their protests.

When Fisher reached the Admiralty on the following morning,
15 May, and discovered Churchill's meddling, his reason finally
snapped. Crease always believed that the old Admiral never
entirely recovered from the stress of the Dardanelles and of the
feuding with Churchill. Without further ado he resigned, leaving
the Navy without a professional head in the middle of a war. He
went to ground in a room at the Charing Cross Hotel, refusing a
written instruction from Asquith: 'In the name of the King, I
order you to return to your post at once'. Unknown to either the
Prime Minister or the First Lord, the vengeful Fisher had sent a
coded message to Churchill's nemesis Bonar Law, thus exploding
the crisis at the Admiralty into the political arena. A strange link
ran between the sinking of *Lusitania* which had been running
contraband to assist the war effort, the War Office's ineptitude in
the field of logistics and the corrosive effect of the Dardanelles
on the Admiralty and its control of operations, notably the lack
of attention paid to the submarine menace.

Fisher's resignation sounded the death knell for Asquith's
Liberal Government. On the morning of Monday 17 May, Bonar
Law called on Lloyd George at the Treasury. Law is a strangely
underrated figure in British political history, whom his biographer Robert Blake was to call the Forgotten Prime Minister.
Despite their very different political views a friendship had grown
up between the two men. Law had for some time been chafing at
the restraints of the political truce which he had agreed with
Asquith nine months before. In essence, the truce obliged him to
support the Government and its policies without enabling him to
influence them. Once Lloyd George had confirmed the extent of
the disarray at the Admiralty, Law put his cards on the table. He
explained that the melancholy succession of losses and setbacks
and the revelations of operational and logistical shortcomings at
both the Admiralty and the War Office made it impossible for

him to continue the truce. In a tacit reference to Beresford and his allies, who had caused Churchill such trouble a week earlier with their persistent questioning about the loss of *Lusitania*, he told Lloyd George that he could not restrain his supporters any longer.

The two men quickly agreed that they could see no alternative to the formation of an all-party government to provide for more effective direction of the war. Law made it clear that the Conservative party would insist that Churchill had to be replaced at the Admiralty. Lloyd George asked Law to wait while he went to No 10 Downing Street to see the Prime Minister where he recounted his conversation with Law. Asquith had a reputation for being adverse to taking hard decisions but as Doctor Johnson had once famously remarked: 'There is nothing that concentrates a man's mind so wonderfully as the knowledge that he is to be hanged'. On this occasion he quickly realised that his Government's position was beyond redemption and that Churchill could not remain as First Lord. Bonar Law was called in and told that his terms had been accepted and the haggling over office began.[11]

Two days later, Fisher wrote to Asquith, demanding his reinstatement as First Sea Lord in terms so extreme that no Government could countenance them. He demanded Churchill's total exclusion from the Cabinet as well as complete authority over the war at sea. He made the impractical claim that he could guarantee the termination of the war and the total abolition of the submarine menace.[12] Less than ten days earlier as the professional chief of the service he had been unable to protect *Lusitania*. Asquith quite reasonably regarded the letter as proof positive that Fisher 'had gone off his nut' and quietly accepted his resignation. As Colonel Maurice Hankey, the Secretary to the Committee of Imperial Defence, sardonically noted: 'Jackie got megalomania and has done for himself'.[13] It was a pathetic end to a brilliant career.

Even in the middle of a war it took Asquith a week to form his new Government. The incoming Cabinet included eight Conservatives, among them Bonar Law, who became Colonial Secretary, the former Prime Minister, Arthur Balfour, who succeeded Churchill at the Admiralty and the distinguished lawyer, Sir Edward Carson, the new Attorney-General. As the Government's chief legal adviser, Carson was to play a prominent role in shaping the inquiry into the loss of *Lusitania*. Lord Robert Cecil, who had asked the lethal question about Churchill's visit to the front, became Under-Secretary at the Foreign Office.

Lucifer's fall from heaven cannot have been any more dramatic than that of Churchill from the commanding heights of the Admiralty to the sinecure post of Chancellor of the Duchy of Lancaster. A *Punch* cartoonist, forgetting that Churchill was the grandson of a duke and had sat in Parliament for Lancashire constituencies, depicted him standing outside the Admiralty, his bags packed and quizzically asking 'What is a Duchy and where is Lancaster?'[14] His demotion was a crushing blow, worse even, historians believe, than the defeat of his government in the general election of 1945. Six months later, frustrated by his exclusion from any influence over the course of the war, he resigned and rejoined the army in France.

Lloyd George left the Treasury to take over the new post of Minister of Munitions, with the objective of organising British industry on a footing where it could fully meet the ever-increasing materiel demands of the army, now greatly enlarged in size. One of his first acts was to co-opt George Booth's Push and Go Committee to provide the managerial expertise he sorely needed, Booth becoming the new Ministry's Deputy Director-General. Over the next year the ministry significantly boosted the output of British manufacturing industry.

The Navy did not benefit from the changes. The senior fleet commanders, Jellicoe, C-in-C of the Grand Fleet, and Beatty, Vice-Admiral Battlecruiser Force, both expressed their misgivings that Fisher's departure would deprive the Admiralty of energy and drive, the vital sparks which the service so sorely needed. Balfour had considerable knowledge of defence as well as many other qualities. Energy was not one of them. The new First Sea Lord, Sir Henry Jackson, an expert in the field of wireless telegraphy, was basically a desk admiral with a scientific background. His last seagoing appointment had been in 1910 when he had commanded a cruiser squadron in the Mediterranean. Neither man was to prove a success. Ironically, one of Balfour's first decisions called into question Churchill's assertion to the Commons that destroyers could not be spared to escort passenger liners. When Colonel House sailed from Liverpool on the American liner *St. Paul* on 5 June at the end of his mission, Balfour arranged that she be escorted through the war zone by two destroyers. With the tragic memory of *Lusitania* fresh in his mind, House felt embarrassed by this gesture especially as the Cunarder *Orduna* had sailed unescorted three hours earlier.

The new coalition Government, with an unwieldy cabinet nearly twenty strong, proved ineffectual in directing the war effort. Asquith had been an effective peacetime Prime Minister but he was now past his best and not well suited as a war leader. In December 1916 a cabinet revolt, led by Lloyd George and Bonar Law, forced his resignation. He was succeeded by Lloyd George, who headed a five-man war cabinet, including Bonar Law as Chancellor of the Exchequer, to run the war and mobilise every aspect of national life on a war footing as Lloyd George had done so successfully with manufacturing industry at the Ministry of Munitions. The new Prime Minister brought a number of technocrats, recruited from industry and academia, into the Government, among them the *Lusitania* survivor, D A Thomas, who became Food Controller. The control of merchant shipping, previously and unsatisfactorily split between the Admiralty and the Board of Trade, was entrusted to a newly created Ministry of Shipping, headed by a Glasgow shipowner, John Maclay. The future chairman of Cunard, Sir Percy Bates, who had been seconded to the Admiralty as Director of its transport division, became the new Ministry's Director-General of Commercial Services.

CHAPTER 10

Lord Mersey Inquires

With its political flanks covered and the media squared, at least for the moment, Asquith's new Government moved swiftly to institute damage-control. The shells scandal could be resolved by the superior management techniques harnessed by Lloyd George for the new Ministry of Munitions. The Dardanelles could be reduced to a sideshow and its sponsor, Churchill, had been demoted and increasingly excluded from any influence over strategic planning. Neither issue involved relations with a foreign country. In some ways, the fallout from the loss of *Lusitania* was the most intractable of the problems which it now faced and one which needed careful management. As the American purchasing programme and the financial support which had been negotiated with the Morgan Bank were of crucial importance in what was clearly going to be a long-drawn out war, it would be folly to endanger relations with Washington or antagonise American public opinion.

In large measure the Government's future lay in the experienced hands of the new Attorney-General, Sir Edward Carson, in this issue its chief risk-manager. Technically, Carson appeared on behalf of the Board of Trade and was instructed by their solicitor, Sir Ellis Cunliffe. Even in an era of remarkable legal personalities, Carson was noted for his formidable forensic talents. He was a man of striking presence, who, like Turner, had piercing blue eyes. He had first achieved public attention twenty years earlier as defence counsel in the action which Oscar Wilde had so disastrously brought against Lord Queensberry for calling him a 'somdomite [*sic*]'. His merciless cross-examination, an art in which he was a master, had led inexorably to Wilde's downfall. More recently Carson had attracted recognition (or notoriety) for his charismatic leadership of the Ulster Protestants in their bitter campaign against Home Rule for Ireland.

He was assisted by another formidable advocate, the new Solicitor-General, his fellow-Conservative, F E Smith. From a modest home in Birkenhead, F E had won a scholarship to Oxford, where he had honed his considerable debating skills in

126

the union. He had won his spurs as a lawyer on the northern circuit and in 1906 he was elected to Parliament from a Liverpool constituency. Within weeks he made a national reputation with a vigorous maiden speech in which he savaged the policies of the newly-elected Liberal Government. As a result of his eloquent performance in Parliament and despite their party differences, he became a firm friend of Churchill, who took a liking to the buccaneering side of Smith's character. Tall and saturnine, F E dominated any courtroom. With a steel trap mind and a sparkling wit, he could shred a witness and he habitually treated judges with scant respect. The crusty Mr Justice Darling, irritated almost beyond endurance, once asked F E what he thought he was on the bench for. F E's response was devastating: 'It is not for me, My Lord, to fathom the inscrutable workings of providence'. At one stage during the inquiry, he told Mersey that he did not intend to call all the passengers who had made statements on the basis that much of their evidence was repetitive. An acid discussion then ensued during which he descended to the sarcastic: 'There is nothing I would like better than to go on taking evidence if it will amuse your Lordship to hear passengers called.'[1]

Poor Captain Turner would be clay in the hands of two of the most forceful and relentless advocates in the land. But not defenceless. As soon as the Mersey inquiry had been announced, Cunard's Liverpool-based solicitors, Hill Dickinson, had made an astute move and retained Butler Aspinall as their lead counsel. Aspinall was widely recognised as the most able specialist shipping barrister practicing in London. He had plenty of experience of inquiries on both sides of the legal fence. He had appeared for the Board of Trade in the *Titanic* inquiry and for the shipping line in the loss of the Canadian Pacific liner *Empress of Ireland* in the St Lawrence, in both cases before Lord Mersey. His brief in defending Cunard was marked at the then colossal fee of 250 guineas with a refresher of 50 guineas per day. He was to be worth every penny to Cunard and Turner.

Carson and Smith had a clear objective in conducting the inquiry, the defence of the national interest, and as the Government's leading counsel they had wide powers to shape its course. The inquiry has been called a cover-up and described as a whitewash of Captain Turner. In reality it was a highly successful exercise in damage-control. In the interests of security, Carson had insisted, against every precedent, that all evidence relating to the navigation of the liner should be heard in camera, with only the Government and Cunard lawyers present. He also managed to keep the Admiralty at a safe distance from the inquiry. Churchill's suggestion that Captain Webb should give evidence was firmly scotched, probably by the astute Graham Greene. In the event, no Admiralty minister or civil servant and no naval officer, higher than the rank of Commander, appeared as a witness.

Carson succeeded in playing down the potentially dangerous issue of the cargo by placing in evidence a letter from Dudley Field Malone to Charles Sumner, which read: 'I have to state that all of the articles specified in the manifest of the *Lusitania* are permitted to be shipped on passenger vessels under the laws of the United States.'[2] As the Attorney-General well knew, this letter was disingenuous as the rifle ammunition on board, which was certainly contraband, could legally be carried on passenger liners under American law. In preparing his case, Carson had one involuntary but extremely helpful ally, Germany. Their crowing over their feat, their total insensitivity to the loss of life and the blatant misinformation emitted by their propaganda machine created an opportunity for him to heap the blame for the disaster on German shoulders, an opening which he was quick to exploit.

At 10am on 15 June, in the Central Hall in Westminster, Lord Mersey called the inquiry into the loss of *Lusitania* to order. Despite his estuarial title he had practiced at the commercial bar before becoming a judge and a certain lack of familiarity with shipping law sometimes became apparent. He had a ready wit and was known not to suffer fools gladly. During the *Titanic* inquiry, one witness, Alexander Carlisle, described a meeting at which he and Harold Sanderson, a director, and later chairman, of White Star Line, had remained silent: 'Mr. Sanderson and I were more or less dummies'. Mersey retorted: 'That has a certain verisimilitude'. He could also be overbearing. When George Little, *Lusitania*'s Third Engineer, was being questioned about the design of the ship's water-tight doors, he intervened rather testily: 'This gentleman is a Third Engineer. Do you think his answers are of any value on these abtruse points'. Mersey had served as a high court judge and as president of its divorce, admiralty and probate division before he became Commissioner of Wrecks in 1911 and he was rising seventy-five. His handling of the *Titanic* inquiry had aroused some criticism. One source described him as passive and another as an establishment man to the core.

The *Nautical Magazine*, the journal of the Merchant Service Officers Association, complained that 'Lord Mersey's judgement . . . is colourless, timid and cautious. We had expected more backbone in Lord Mersey'.[3] He was to be assisted by four assessors, Admiral Sir Frederick Inglefield and Lieutenant-Commander H J Hearn, a submariner, together with two merchant navy captains, David Davies and John Spedding. Inglefield was sixty-one and was about to retire. He had commanded a cruiser squadron and had served as Assistant Director of Naval Intelligence and Fourth Sea Lord, responsible for transport and supply. More recently he had been Admiral Commanding Reserves and Coastguards. Since mobilisation in August 1914 he had acted as Admiral, Coastal Patrols. Like Henry Oliver, Inglefield had supported Fisher in his quarrel with Lord Charles Beresford, and his papers include a number of letters from Fisher, full of his habitual caustic comments on other admirals.[4]

Before Mersey sat Carson, Smith and Aspinall with their junior counsel and instructing solicitors and eight other lawyers representing interested parties. Three of them were MPs – Donald Macmaster, acting for the Canadian Government, Thomas Scanlan, a fiery Irish Nationalist, representing some seventy-five passengers and Clem Edwards, a trade union lawyer, appearing for the National Union of Sailors and Firemen. Two other unions were represented by their general secretaries, Joseph Cotter for the cabin and catering staff and W L Marshall for the Marine Engineers Association. One barrister, G A Scott, acting for Alfred Vanderbilt's family, must have earned a comfortable fee for asking each witness whether they had seen the lost multi-millionaire. No witness could remember having seen Vanderbilt on the fatal day although one survivor recalled once having met him in the Knickerbocker Club in New York. The hall was crowded with many passengers and a large contingent of celebrities and diplomats, including several from the American embassy. The inquiry took a much shorter time than that into the loss of *Titanic* three years before. It heard evidence on five days between 15 June and 1 July including the two closed sessions.

Carson rose to deliver his opening statement. After quoting the American note rebutting the German claims which he styled as an invention, he alluded to events on the day of the sinking, repeating the conventional opinion that a second or even a third torpedo had been fired. Emphasising that there had been no warning, he denounced Imperial Germany in ringing tones:

the course adopted by the German Government was not only contrary to international law and the usages of war but was contrary to the dictates of civilisation and humanity; and to have sunk the passengers under these circumstances and under the conditions I have stated meant in the eye, not only of our law but of every other law that I know of in civilised countries, a deliberate attempt to murder the passengers on board that ship. . . . We know that there was a premeditated design to murder these people on board this ship . . . Everything points to that perfectly clearly . . .

In all, thirty-four witnesses, Turner and fifteen other members of the crew, fourteen passengers, including D A Thomas and the heroic Alice Lines, and four others, most notably Alfred Booth, were to testify.[5] Turner was the third witness to be called. He was one of those sea captains who seem to visibly shrink in stature the moment they set foot on dry land and he cut a poor figure under cross-examination. He was clearly suffering from a kind of delayed shock caused by the loss of his ship and of so many lives, including those of old friends and shipmates like Jock Anderson and Archie Bryce. He replied to an old friend in Boston, who had written a letter condoling with him on the loss: 'I am thankful to say that I have not felt any bad effects from my terrible experience but I grieve for all the poor innocent people who lost their lives and all those who are left to mourn their dead one's loss. Please excuse me saying any more because I hate to think or speak of it'.[6] To make matters worse, his estranged wife had chosen this moment to desert him and strangers had insulted him in the street.

Turner survived Carson's questioning without much difficulty, confirming the ship's speed when the torpedo struck and that he had been on the bridge at the time. Under interrogation by the union secretary, Joseph Cotter, he was forced on to the defensive.

Cotter: Were the crew of *Lusitania* proficient in handling boats in your estimation?
Turner: No, they were not.
Cotter: Were the stewards proficient in handling boats?
Turner: Just about the same as they are all are now, as ships' crews go now.
Cotter: Then your contention is that they are incompetent to handle boats?
Turner: They are competent enough – they want practice. They do not get practice enough and they do not get the experience.

Aspinall quickly showed his skill in damage control when he examined Turner. He established that Turner had thirty-two years service with Cunard and had held an extra master's certificate for eighteen and he deftly steered the Captain away from danger.

Aspinall: You told the gentleman who sits behind me [Cotter] that in your view the crew of the *Lusitania* were not proficient in handling boats. I want you to explain that a little. Is it your view that the modern ships, with their greasers and their stewards and their firemen, sometimes do not carry the old-fashioned sailor you knew of in the days of your youth?
Turner: That is the idea.
Aspinall: That is what you have in your mind?
Turner: That is it.
Aspinall: You are an old-fashioned sailor man.
Turner: That is right.
Aspinall: And you preferred the man of your youth.
Turner: Yes, and I prefer him yet.

Joseph Cotter firmly established the makeshift nature of *Lusitania*'s crew when he examined Alfred Booth, who followed Turner into the witness-box.

Cotter: Since the war broke out you had a different class of men on board the ships, I take it?
Booth: Yes, we have lost all our RNR [Royal Naval Reserve] and fleet reserve men.
Cotter: And you had to take the best you can get?
Booth: We had to take on the best we could get and train them as best we could in the time at our disposal.

Alfred Booth was a confident witness, giving detailed answers to Carson's questions. He gave a sanitised version of his dealings with Graham Greene, initially referring only to his decision to reduce the liner's achievable top speed by decommissioning No 4 boiler room to cut costs and thus allow one of the three fast Cunarders to continue on the North Atlantic route. Carson turned to the vital question of submarine attack and the warning advertisement published in the American press.

Carson: You told me . . . that the day after *Lusitania* sailed, you heard of the special threats by advertisement in America . . . to sink *Lusitania* . . . did you after that take any steps?
Booth: We were unable to communicate with the ship ourselves.

Mersey: Why not?

Booth: Because only the Admiralty could communicate with the ship.

Mersey: Could you not send a marconigram to the ship?

Booth: We could only ask the Admiralty to send a message for us.

Carson: Did you make any communication to the Admiralty?

Booth: Not at that time.

Carson: Not till after the accident, I think.

Booth: Not till the Friday morning.

Carson: Did your company give any special directions to your officers with reference to submarines?

Booth: We discussed the general form the danger would take with the individual captains . . . we could not venture to give specific instructions when in an emergency they would be in possession of facts which would not be in our possession, and we felt it would be very dangerous to attempt to give specific instructions when the circumstances might make these instructions absolutely dangerous to follow.

In response to further questioning by Carson, Booth continued :

> We discussed the general form the danger would take and the general methods whereby it could be best avoided . . . the question of closing the watertight doors when in the danger zone, swinging out the boats, seeing that all the ports were closed, seeing that everything was ready in the boats; and another point was the danger of stopping in the danger zone to pick up a pilot or stopping at the Mersey Bar to wait for the tide to rise.

He confirmed that these points had been discussed with Turner by Cunard's General Manager and that Admiralty suggestions (Carson's phrase) went direct to the Captains and were not usually copied to Cunard.

Carson now broached the vital question of *Lusitania*'s arrival at the Mersey, or as he called it the Liverpool, Bar.

Carson: Was the question of when the ship should arrive at the Bar at Liverpool settled by you . . . or how was it left?

Booth: That was left in this way. It was one of the points which we felt it necessary to make the Captain understand the importance of. *Lusitania* can only cross the Liverpool Bar at certain states of the tide and we warned the Captain that we did not think it would be safe for him to arrive off the Bar [if] he had to wait there, because that area had been infested with submarines and we thought it wiser to arrange his arrival, leaving him an absolutely free hand . . . that he could come in without stopping at all. The one definite instruction . . . was to authorise him to come up without a pilot.

Carson: On Friday morning, the 7th May . . . the day *Lusitania* was sunk, had you heard of certain ships being sunk in St George's Channel?

Booth: Yes. Two steamers of the Harrison Line; *Candidate* and *Centurion* They had been sunk the previous day.

Carson: Did you take steps to send a message to *Lusitania* to inform them on board of that fact. I suppose you went to the Admiralty?

Booth: We went to the Admiral or senior naval officer in Liverpool and asked him to send a message. We, of course, did not venture to send any message to the Captain as to how he should proceed, because the Admiralty might be doing that, or the Captain might know a great deal more about it than we did. We merely asked the Admiralty to convey the fact that these ships had been sunk.

Carson: But I think you are of opinion, having regard to the time you asked that should be done [*sic*] the information could not have arrived in time.

Booth: I think it did not arrive in time.

At this point Carson concluded his examination of Alfred Booth. The Chairman of Cunard had demonstrated the extent to which *Lusitania* was under direct Admiralty control when at sea and that whatever the Admiralty's reaction to the dangerous situation off the south coast of Ireland had been, he had correctly appreciated the hazard. The Admiralty's failure to implement his request that, as a matter of urgency, Captain Turner should be warned of the sinking of the two Harrison liners directly in his ship's path, should have made a positive impression on the inquiry. Whilst Carson was not anxious to dwell on any aspect of the sinking which could reflect unfavourably on the Admiralty, it is remarkable that neither Macmaster for the Canadian Government nor any of the lawyers representing passengers and unions ever cross-examined Booth on these matters. Mersey's passive attitude in conducting these inquiries is illustrated by his failure in the light of this evidence to demand that senior naval officers appear and testify on the Admiralty's control over *Lusitania* and their actions on 7 May, at least in the closed sessions.

Lusitania

After Booth had stood down, the inquiry heard testimony from surviving crew members, including First Officer Jones and the lookout Leslie Morton. The most significant evidence was supplied by the three surviving firemen from No 1 and No 2 boiler rooms, Thomas Madden, Frederick Davis and Eugene McDermott. All three had escaped by way of the ventilation shafts. The three firemen told of a huge rush of water into the boiler rooms, confirming that the impact of the exploding torpedo had breached the inner bulkhead dividing the bunker from the boiler room. Madden and Davis both testified that there had been an explosion on the starboard side of No 1 boiler room. The off-duty wireless operator, Robert Leith, gave evidence that he had been at lunch in the second-class dining-room towards the aft of the ship when she was hit.

Carson: Did you feel the shock?
Leith: I felt some shock or other and I thought it was a boiler room explosion.

He then described how he went immediately to the wireless cabin to help his assistant McCormick send out a succession of distress signals.

Carson: Now how were these messages sent out?
Leith: They were sent out both by the ship's power . . . three or four minutes after the torpedo struck the ship, the power section gave out and we had to fall back on the emergency section . . . inside the wireless cabin.

The two operators continued to send out their signals until the last possible moment. Leith told Carson that he had jumped into a lifeboat as *Lusitania* was going down.

The evidence given by the passengers described a state of confusion and a lack of direction on deck but no panic. One saloon-class passenger, James Baker, was closely examined on this point.

Carson: Do you desire to make any statement about the crew?
Baker: . . . I want to repeat that to me there appeared to be not a question of discipline but no competent men aboard.
Carson: Does that apply to the whole time?
Baker: No, only to the lowering of the boats and the advice to the passengers as regards lifebelts.

Carson returned to this subject at the end of his examination.

Carson: And the general purpose of your evidence is that there
was a want of general control and an absence of authority?
Baker: An absence of authority and of competent men at the falls.

Those who had been below at the time the torpedo hit told of the
difficulty in reaching the open deck due to the list and the darkness after the loss of electric power. Several witnesses paid tribute
to the stewards and stewardesses but stated that they could not
see any officers on deck. This implied criticism should be taken
in perspective. *Lusitania* had eight deck officers and two of these
had to stay on the bridge. With hundreds of passengers milling
about in the hectic confusion on deck it is not so surprising that
few of them encountered one of the six remaining officers in the
liner's last minutes. Alice Lines was examined by F E Smith and
stuck resolutely to her story that she had left the ship with the two
children in her care in a port-side boat. In an interview with the
Imperial War Museum many years later she insisted that her
assumption was correct. Despite Smith's remark to Mersey that
'this was the only boat, so far as I know, which got off from the
port side' the evidence is overwhelming that no port-side boat
was ever successfully launched. This point was confirmed at the
time by one of the surviving desk officers, A A Bestic.

Alice Lines was followed on to the stand by D A Thomas, the
most prominent witness to be called before the inquiry. Thomas
had been highly critical of the performance of the crew. He had
told the *Morning Post* two days after the sinking: 'There was no
question of bravery, of organisation or of discipline. There was
absolute panic and they crowded into the boats. There were
shouts of women and children first but there should have been a
few revolvers to enforce the order.'[7] Under examination by
Smith, he backed down from the rather extreme views he had
expressed to the newspaper, admitting that he had been out of
temper at the time.

Smith: Now I want to ask you about the crew of the *Lusitania* . . .
were you able to form an opinion as to the demeanour and
behaviour of the officers?
Thomas: Well, I really saw very few officers. I am not prepared to
swear that I saw an officer at all, but my impression was that the
officers behaved very well and the stewards and stewardesses
behaved . . . heroically.

Asked by Smith whether he had any other observation to make to
the court, he replied: '. . . I would say that there was no kind of

organization but there was certainly panic five or ten minutes after the ship was struck and I do not think the order of the captain "women and children first" was obeyed by a large number of the crew'.

Pressed further first by Smith and then by H W Wickham, one of the lawyers representing passengers, Thomas had to admit that he had not personally seen any women or children prevented from getting into the boats. He was the only witness to allege that there had been any panic on deck which he attributed to third-class passengers, an assertion which ran contrary to his statement that the second- and third-class passengers had behaved exceedingly well. Although his daughter Margaret Mackworth told *The Times* that she had seen no panic on deck, in her biography *This Was My World*, published in 1933, she related that she had watched third-class passengers rushing on to the boat deck and fighting their way into a lifeboat. She noted a clear lack of order with the strong blatantly pushing the weak aside.[8]

After Thomas had stood down, Smith suggested to Mersey that his allegations about the crew were based on hearsay evidence and should be disregarded. Thomas and his daughter cannot be described as reliable witnesses. It should be noted that the passengers' evidence was not always accurate, with one witness, Theodore Diamandis, alleging that he had seen a submarine to port of the sinking liner after the torpedo struck.

The union lawyer, Clem Edwards, smarting at his exclusion from the closed sessions, made a determined attempt to open up the question of *Lusitania*'s speed and navigation. He accused Cunard management of negligence and of putting profit ahead of people by cutting the liner's top speed from 25 to 21 knots. Joseph Cotter was not present at this session but, significantly, neither W L Marshall, for the engineer officers, nor any of the lawyers representing passengers backed Edwards up. Mersey reiterated his refusal to hear any testimony on navigation in open court. Aspinall rose to make what can only be called a robust and resonant defence of Cunard and Turner. He began by citing the clean bill of health which *Lusitania* had been given by the Board of Trade surveyors before she left Liverpool on 17 April and the precautions which Turner had effected when the liner had entered the war zone on the morning of 6 May. Turning to the vital question of the handling of the boats, he put forward an eloquent plea in justification of the crew.

My Lord, I submit that these men were not found wanting in this hour of need. We have it that the first consideration on the part of the officers and the master were the women and children. There is an abundance of evidence that is what came first, not only on the part of the captain, not only on the part of the officers and crew, but very probably on the part of the male passengers – women and children first: and if there was some slight confusion can it be unexpected? There was no panic. Of course, there was confusion, and . . . the steerage passengers, to some extent, as it were, rushed the ship, but women and children came first and if one may go on the end of this drama, this tragedy of the sea. What happened? As this great vessel goes down, where do we find the captain? Where would you expect to find him? On the bridge of his vessel. The time is short; the vessel has a list which means that practically all the boats on the port side were put out of action . . . in addition the ship never lost her headway. . . . when one remembers the height from which the boats have got to be lowered into the water . . . I submit that extremely good work was done by those men in handling the boats.

At this point Aspinall entered the defence that well-meaning passengers had hindered the launching, an assertion which was to be adopted almost word for word by Mersey in his judgement:

> There were mistakes with regards to the boats . . . it should be noted that . . . these mishaps mainly happened on the port side. Unfortunately the passengers I have no doubt actuated by the best wish in the world, wishful to save the lives of others and their own, took charge of certain of the boats on the port side . . . I submit that it is fairly certain that these boats met with catastrophe.

In so far as Lehmann's disastrous intervention at No 18 boat station is concerned, Aspinall's defence is totally convincing. He also made the valid point that those port-side boats which were successfully launched were leaking by the time they reached the water as a result of contact with the ship's side. He concluded his ringing defence of the crew by praising the eighteen-year-old Leslie Morton and his companion Parry for their valiant rescue efforts after the ship had gone down, a point to which Mersey was to refer in his judgment.

Aspinall then moved on to the controversial question of *Lusitania*'s speed and effectively demolished Edwards's claim of negligence:

> I submit, my Lord, that the Cunard Company have nothing to reproach themselves with for having sent their ship to sea . . . at a

reduced speed. They are, of course a business company: they are not philanthropists: they send their vessels to sea in the hope of making a profit . . . they came to the conclusion, as I submit they were rightly entitled to do, *having regard to the experience they had at the time* [author's italics] that it was safe and reasonable to drive her at a speed of 21 knots through the water.

He bolstered his defence of his clients with an extremely powerful argument:

In fact . . . she still . . . continues to be the fastest vessel crossing the Atlantic and . . . if it were wrong to send a ship to sea which would travel at only 21 knots it would be almost criminal for the other passenger steamers which happily are still safely crossing the Atlantic to continue to do so.

CHAPTER 11

In Camera

T he real meat of the Mersey proceedings can be found during the two closed sessions, held on the afternoon of the
first day of hearings, 15 June, when Turner gave evidence,
and again on 18 June which was taken up with submissions by
Aspinall for Cunard and Turner and by Smith for the Government.[1]

Carson read out to Turner a series of Admiralty instructions
issued between November 1914 and April 1915. In the first of
these, dated 3 November 1914, captains were told, *inter alia*, that:
'Remember that the enemy will never operate in sight of land if
he can possibly avoid it.' A later instruction dated 15 April
included the warning: 'German submarines appear to be
operating off prominent headlands and landfalls. Ships should
give prominent headlands a wide berth . . .' These warnings are,
of course, contradictory. A further directive issued on 22 March
stated that: '. . . vessels passing up the Irish or English Channels
should keep mid-channel course.' The Admiralty's failure to
attempt a precise definition of either 'wide berth' or 'mid-
channel' was to lead to some confusion during this phase of the
inquiry. Turner confirmed that he had received all these instructions and the Admiralty telegrams sent on the evening of 6 May
and the morning of 7 May.

Carson then started questioning Turner on the course of the
liner. The interchange showed Turner in a rather poor light, as if
he was bumbling and inarticulate.

Carson: What I want to ask you first is why, with all that information before you, did you come so close to Old Kinsale Head?
Turner: To get a fix. We were not quite sure what land it was; we
were so far off.

Confronted with this rather glib explanation, Carson began to
bully Turner.

Carson: Is that all you have to say. You say you were warned specially to avoid headlands and stay in mid-channel . . . do you
mean to say you had no idea where you were?

Turner: Yes I had an approximate idea but I wanted to be sure.

When Mersey intervened, Turner, recovering his pose, made an apt reply.

Turner: Well, my Lord, I do not navigate a ship on guesswork.
Mersey (missing the point): Why did you want to go groping about to try and find where land was?
Turner: So that I could get a proper course.

If Mersey had possessed some working knowledge of the principles of navigation, he might have known that a position taken by dead reckoning could produce an error of several miles. Although *Lusitania*'s bearings taken earlier on the morning of 7 May appear to have been accurate, Turner's decision to take a fix was in fact justified. It reflected his innate caution after many years of experience in command of passenger liners and of the waters in which he was sailing on the day of the disaster.

The Admiralty's failure to define precisely what they meant by 'mid-channel' or 'giving headlands a wide berth' resulted in both Carson and Turner making heavy weather of the proceedings. The Attorney-General went on in a somewhat caustic manner to probe Turner on what constituted a mid-channel course.

Carson: You do not suggest for a moment, do you, that when the torpedo struck . . . you were in mid-channel?'
Turner: It is practically what I call mid-channel. . . .
Mersey: Do you call that mid-channel?
Turner (assailed by the full force of the British legal establishment, made a spirited response): Yes, I should call that mid-channel, as a seafaring man.
Carson: Do you really call eight miles from land mid-channel? Do you not know perfectly well that what the Admiralty instructions were aiming at was that you should be further out from land than on the ordinary course.
Turner: So I was, considerably further out . . . We generally pass it [the Old Head] a mile off in ordinary circumstances and in fine weather.

Carson's next questions concerned Turner's decision to reduce speed, which Turner justified on the grounds that he did not wish to arrive at the Liverpool Bar before there was sufficient tide to allow him to cross without delay. He asked a leading question: 'Then there was nothing to prevent you, on the facts I have elicited, keeping in mid-channel and still arriving in proper time in Liverpool?' Turner could only say no. At this point Mersey once again intervened, his lack of familiarity with seamanship all too apparent. He told Turner that: 'I do not understand what you mean when you say you were coming in [to shore] because you wanted to navigate the ship safely. What danger was there in mid-channel?' Turner riposted with a highly valid defence: 'Well, my Lord, it might have come on a thick fog and I did not know exactly the proper position of the ship and two or three miles one way or the other might have put me ashore on either side of the channel . . . I wanted to know my proper position.'

Fog is, indeed, an occupational hazard to navigation off the south coast of Ireland in April or May. It will be recalled that Schwieger had been hampered by swirling and intermittent fog during his pursuit of the Harrison liners on the day before he sank *Lusitania*. In the report on his voyage which he added to his war diary, he complained about the prevalent fog, noting that it would have ruined the whole undertaking if it had lasted two more days. The fog had only lifted after 11am on 7 May and Turner had no way of knowing that it might not return at any moment particularly as the afternoon wore on and the temperature began to fall. Replying to further questions from Carson, Turner reiterated that he wanted to know his exact position adding that 'distances are very deceptive, particularly in clear weather'.

After a shaky start, he had weathered Carson's onslaught and Mersey's interruptions in a doughty fashion, presenting a remarkably coherent defence of his actions. When Carson turned his attention to zigzagging, he once again faltered badly, at least in the eyes of the Court.

Carson: Now tell me this. Did you zigzag the boat?
Turner: No. . . . I understood it was only when you saw a submarine that you should zigzag.

Carson read out the confidential Admiralty memorandum on the subject of zigzagging, which Turner had already confirmed that he had received:

> War experience has shown that fast steamers can considerably reduce the chance of a successful surprise attack by zigzagging, that is to say, altering course at short and irregular intervals, say ten minutes to half an hour. This course is almost invariably adopted by warships when cruising in an area known to be infested by

submarines. The under-water speed of a submarine is very low, and it is exceedingly difficult for her to get into a position to deliver an attack unless she can observe and predict the course of the ship attacked.

Carson read the directive three more times but although its wording seems clear, Turner continued to insist that he was not actually required to zigzag until he had sighted a submarine. A plea in mitigation of the Captain should now be entered. The directive had been issued by the Admiralty on 16 April, one day before *Lusitania* had left Liverpool on her last westbound voyage. Captain G C Frederick, second-in-command to Admiral Stileman, SNO Liverpool, later confirmed to the Admiralty that he had passed the instruction to Cunard before the liner had sailed. He added that he had had no contact with Turner during the time *Lusitania* was berthed in Liverpool between 11 and 17 April although he had briefed him before his first voyage as Captain in March. Frederick's testimony appears disingenuous.[2] An instruction prepared by Hill Dickinson for the use of Cunard's American counsel, Lucius Beer, stated that before sailing on *Lusitania*'s last westbound voyage, Turner had asked SNO Liverpool whether there were any special instructions for him and was told that there were none.

It seems clear that a serious breakdown in communications had taken place for which the Navy must bear much of the responsibility. The Admiralty's representatives in Liverpool were lax, to say the least, in failing to brief the Captain of a ship as important as *Lusitania* on a major new directive, particularly as she was under direct Admiralty control when she was at sea. Turner would have been preoccupied with the manifold tasks necessary in getting the liner ready for sailing, including on this occasion the replacement of lifesaving equipment following the Board of Trade surveyors' inspection. As he said later he could have papered his walls with Admiralty instructions and the directive's significance might have escaped him. When Aspinall rose to examine Turner, he took him once again through the Admiralty directive on zigzagging, asking him: 'What did you understand that to mean?' He reiterated that 'I understood it to mean that if I saw a submarine to get clear out of its way'. Aspinall coaxed him into admitting that he had misinterpreted the instruction.

The next issue to be examined was Turner's decision to come inshore. Aspinall established that *Lusitania* had been holding a course about twenty miles offshore until 12.40pm when Turner steered her sharply to port.

Aspinall: . . . at this time, if your evidence is right, you had information by wireless that in mid-channel were German submarines? . . . you hauled in here [ie inshore] for what purpose?

Turner: To get the distance off the land, to get a fix there.

Aspinall: What is your object in getting a fix?

Turner: For getting the position of the ship and then steering a course for Coningbeg. [The lightship, marking the entrance to St George's Channel between Ireland and Wales, the shipping lane leading to Liverpool.]

Aspinall: . . . if you achieved that object, would that enable you to determine with precision where your ship was?

Turner: Certainly.

Aspinall: Why . . . when you altered course, did you not alter out more . . . to bring you to mid-channel but were heading up to the north of mid-channel?

Turner: Because I wanted, in the first place to make Coningbeg, seeing we were twenty miles south of it. Then I thought it was safer close to the land in case we did get a submarine.

Later in his testimony, Turner confirmed that: 'I would not have gone closer than half-a-mile to Coningbeg . . .'

Aspinall went on: . . . you intended, in fact, to take your ship close up to Coningbeg; would that have been giving effect to the Admiralty . . . instruction to keep to mid-channel?

Turner: No, it would not.

Aspinall: Why did you, having knowledge of . . . Admiralty instructions . . . steer a course which . . . should take your ship so close to Coningbeg and not out into mid-channel?

Turner: Because there was a submarine in mid-channel, as I understood it, and I wanted to keep clear of him.

Aspinall: Is that what weighed with you at the time?

Turner: Yes.

Aspinall: Did you give the matter consideration?

Turner: Certainly I did.

Turner had not taken this decision alone. He had consulted his two senior officers, Anderson and Chief Officer Piper, both of whom had agreed with him. Unfortunately, neither man survived. Aspinall had also elucidated the existence of rocks and shoals inshore of the lightship and extending up St George's Channel.

In this adroit textbook examination of his client, Aspinall had successfully demonstrated the dilemma which Turner faced when confronted with the Admiralty telegram advising him that submarines had been seen twenty miles south of Coningbeg. The information that submarines lay in mid-channel directly ahead of him effectively forced Turner to change course and head inshore. The new course also necessitated the most precise navigation, dead reckoning not being sufficient, given the dangers which lay inshore and the possibility that fog might return. In making these submissions before Mersey, Aspinall had exposed the first flaws in the Admiralty's indictment of Turner.

His advocacy was not long in bearing fruit. When F E Smith re-examined Turner on his alteration of course, he was interrupted by Mersey, who suggested that Turner had been justified in changing direction as he knew that submarines were operating south of Coningbeg. Smith agreed, adding that: '. . . having regard to the telegram . . . I think he was justified in not obeying any pedantic instructions that he should adhere to mid-channel at that point.' In reviewing Captain Webb's report, Churchill had requested that the Admiralty case against Turner should be pressed before Lord Mersey by a skilful counsel. Yet here was one of the most skilful counsels in the land, and one of Churchill's closest friends to boot, in essence conceding a major point to Turner's counsel.

Smith was quick to counter-attack. Adopting the approach of a Monday morning quarterback, he pressed Turner to agree that he should have stood out further to sea, suggesting that this was a safer course.

Smith: All your warnings were that submarines were near the land, so that if you went out more into mid-channel, you had no reason to meet more submarines than when you are close to the headlands.
Turner: No.

This cryptic answer produced another of Mersey's interventions: 'when you go out far away from the land, do you expect to meet more submarines than when you are close to the headlands?'

Turner: I expect to find them in any distance within 100 miles or so off the land in these times. [In a signal to the War Staff after the sinking, Admiral Hood, commanding the cruiser squadron at Queenstown, had made exactly the same point, reporting

that his cruisers had already been forced to hunt for U-boats
up to 100 miles out to sea.]

Mersey concluded this line of inquiry by opining that it was safer
to get away from the land and asked Aspinall to explain Turner's
navigation. He went straight to the point, reiterating that after
Turner had made landfall: 'from that time onwards he is in
narrow waters . . . where there are rocks and shoals and places
where from time to time you meet with fog . . . therefore it is
highly important that you should have a landfall which will give
you your exact position on the water'. Aspinall again reminded
Mersey of the significance of the signal informing Turner that
submarines were operating in the middle of the channel through
which he would have to pass, thus forcing him to change course.

When the closed sessions resumed three days later, Mersey
began: 'Now, Mr. Aspinall, I have had a great deal of difficulty with
the Captain.' During the ensuing courtroom dialogue, Aspinall
admitted that the Captain was, undoubtedly, a bad witness,
although he may be an excellent navigator, adding: 'Well he was
confused, my Lord.' Mersey replied that: 'he may have been a bad
master during that voyage but I think he was telling the truth'.
With Smith's concurrence, Mersey readily agreed with Aspinall's
submission that Turner was an honest witness. Later in the session,
Aspinall pointed out to Mersey that in giving evidence Turner did
not always do full justice to his case and reminded him of the considerable physical and mental strain which Turner had gone
through, including the deaths of so many of his officers and crew.

He then began his summing up for Turner, dealing firstly with
the reduction in speed and then with the reasons for ordering
the change in course at 12.40pm, after receiving the signal that
submarines were south of Coningbeg. He noted that the Captain
had consulted his Staff Captain and Chief Officer, both of them
experienced navigators. His argument was forceful:

> . . . my submission is that there was no reckless disregard of this
> instruction [to maintain a mid-channel course]. He discussed the
> matter; he had present in his mind that the main thing was to avoid
> submarines, and that he had got general instructions, no doubt of
> very great value, which would give effect to that purpose . . . but he
> had got specific knowledge that when last seen the submarine dan-
> ger was . . . in the neighbourhood of mid-channel and under these
> circumstances he said to himself . . . although I fully recognise the
> utility of the general instructions, in the circumstances of this case, in

order to avoid that danger, he [Turner] made up his mind to go close to Coningbeg. My submission is that that was a proper judgment in view of what he had been told.

Aspinall's argument had got to the heart of the issue, reinforcing the point he had made during his examination of Turner. Mersey asked Aspinall whether he thought it wise to make for St George's Channel under the circumstances, setting up a lengthy dialogue. He revealed that his assessors had told him that if Turner was to enter the channel at all he would have been wise to steer as far north as possible. Mersey also conceded that 'the best thing he could have done having regard to the telegram which told him that there were submarines twenty miles south of Coningbeg was to make a move and get clear'. Aspinall pressed his case vigorously, defending Turner's decision to take an inshore course and implicitly warning against the dangers of hindsight which suggested that the more of the ground he was covering and the longer he remained at sea in that part of the ocean the more possible it was for the submarine to attack him.

Mersey: It is a question of prudence.

Aspinall: Yes ... he [Turner] must exercise good judgment. I mean ... we have the very great advantage of knowing so much now which was not known to him then; we are sitting on the matter in cool judgment, with the opportunity of looking at the charts and the circumstances under which we are dealing with it are not the circumstances under which the master would have an opportunity of dealing with it.

He turned to another weak point in the Admiralty's case, emphasising the vague way in which their directives were so often worded. He repeated Turner's reply ' What is a wide berth?' when Carson had read to him the instruction of 15 April: 'Ships should give prominent headlands a wide berth', and also noted the lack of definition in the signal of 22 March: '... Most important that vessels passing up the English or Irish Channels should keep a mid-channel course. He asked pointedly: 'I have been wondering ... what is the Irish Channel. Is it ... the water south of Ireland or is it the channel on the east coast of Ireland ... a glance at the chart shows that here is undoubtedly a channel there but it is very difficult indeed to say what is the channel and what is the mid-channel when dealing with the south coast of Ireland. The waters are extremely broad'. In fact, the nearest landfall is the Spanish province of Asturias, 700 miles to the south'.

As he reached the end of his submission, Aspinall broached a fundamental issue, answering a question which Mersey had raised earlier.

> Is it legitimate to override the Board of Trade regulations by an Admiralty instruction? . . . first of all, for the safe navigation of the ship she must be navigated so that she does not get on rocks or on the shore, secondly give effect to the Admiralty instructions so as to avoid the submarine menace. What a careful man ought to do . . . is, as far as he can, give effect to both but there may be special circumstances where it is impossible to give effect to both.

Aspinall adroitly reminded Mersey that if Turner had run his ship aground in fog he would have found himself in considerable trouble. Once again he hammered home the point that Turner had to ascertain his exact position by taking a fix.

Mersey: Your contention is . . . that in each case the Captain must use his judgment to see which is the overriding advice and direction.

Aspinall: Yes; and . . . while these instructions from the Admiralty are, of course, of great value, the Master always has to say . . . I have got the general instruction that I must keep in mid-channel, but if the Admiralty inform me by wireless that by going into mid-channel, I shall meet with dangers they are wishful that I should avoid, you leave out . . . the special instruction and he applies his mind to the special circumstances of the case.

Aspinall went on to stress the desirability of avoiding reducing speed in the approaches to the Mersey which had influenced Turner to steam at only 18 knots on the morning of 7 May. He made a powerful argument, quoting a letter from the London and Liverpool War Risks Association of which Cunard was a member, which stated: 'that from January 30th up to the present date we have regarded Liverpool Bay as a very dangerous area and we have issued most stringent instructions to Masters of all vessels . . . to avoid anchoring or reducing speed whilst making the entrances to the Mersey'. The letter listed five ships which had been attacked or sunk by U-boats in the Bay. Aspinall rested his case by submitting that: 'for the reasons I have indicated, Turner was not to blame for the loss of his ship, nor had he committed an error of judgment.'

Once again Smith counter-attacked: 'Here was a case in which *Lusitania* was sailing under wholly unprecedented circumstances from New York . . . we know that warnings of some kind had been issued and of which it is sufficient to say that no one aboard was unaware that . . . there might be an attack by submarines. Therefore the period of vigilance . . . and co-ordination of every step taken for . . . bringing the ship safely into harbour was that of the whole voyage and not any particular moment when the vessel was already off the coast of Ireland'. He emphasised his point by referring to the Admiralty warnings about submarine activity and sought to counter Aspinall's defence of Turner's decision to come inshore by quoting from a further signal which he stated had been sent to all British merchant ships on 7 May: 'Submarine areas should be avoided by keeping well off the land'.

Smith had unwittingly stepped on a hornet's nest. Mersey asked him pointedly to which telegram he was referring and where did it appear in the evidence. It quickly became clear that Mersey and Smith were reading different versions of the same Admiralty memorandum, headed *Lusitania*. Once again faulty staff work had let the Admiralty down. A clearly irritated Mersey summoned Sir Ellis Cunliffe, Solicitor to the Board of Trade, asking him: 'What is the meaning of it, Sir Ellis, do you know?' Cunliffe prevaricated, indicating that the version from which Smith was reading had been prepared for use if the entire case had been heard in open session. Mersey was not satisfied with this risible explanation and continued to press Cunliffe: 'Will you tell me which is the one which is an exact translation, the one Sir Frederick [Smith] has or this one?' Cunliffe was forced to confirm that Mersey was reading from the correct version. Aspinall and his instructing solicitors stoutly denied any knowledge of this telegram, which does not appear in a certified copy of the log of the signal traffic between *Lusitania* and the wireless station at Valentia on 7 May. The log covers a period from 7.30am on 6 May to the SOS she sent out at 2.11pm on 7 May after she was torpedoed.[3]

Seeing the danger, Smith quickly backed down and withdrew the controversial signal from evidence. The Solicitor-General was justifiably annoyed at the significant damage which had been done to his case and at being made to look foolish in front of a judge. What he must have said to the unfortunate Cunliffe after the inquiry rose should best be left to the imagination. Someone in the War Staff appears to have decided that their signals to masters of merchant ships were ambiguously worded and to have drafted what might be called a phantom signal. This directive

(Top) *Lusitania* on the slipway at Clydebank, shortly before she was launched in June 1906, showing her elegant lines and her port-side propellers. (Above) *Lusitania* in the fitting out basin. This wonderful view was obtained from the top of John Brown's 150-ton crane.

Opposite page
(Top) *Lusitania* steaming at speed.
(Middle) *Lusitania* arrives in New
York at the end of her maiden voyage, September 1907. (Bottom)
The last photograph of *Lusitania*,
taken from *Caronia* on 1 May 1915.
There is no smoke coming from
her aftermost funnel, evidence that
her No 4 boiler room was out of
commission.

(Right) Captain William Thomas
Turner as Commodore of the
Cunard Line. (Below) *Carmania* as
as an armed merchant cruiser in
Malta in 1915. Her 4.7in guns can
clearly be seen on her boat deck
and at her stern. She was the first
Cunarder to be equipped with
turbines and served as a test bed
for *Lusitania*.

Debris blowing up
through 4 decks

Column of water

YERANDAH CAFE

"THE EXPLOSION" 2.22 pm
Starboard Boat Deck

THE BEGINNING OF THE CATASTROPHE: THE EXPLOSION CAUSED BY THE TORPEDO
AS SEEN ON THE STARBOARD BOAT-DECK.

THE END OF THE CATASTROPHE: ONLY THE FUNNELS AND MASTS OF THE GREAT LINER ABOVE WATER
AS THE LAST BOAT LEAVES.

A series of five drawings of *Lusitania* sinking, by the survivor Oliver Bernard.
These appeared in the 15 May 1915 issue of the *London Illustrated News*.

iv

Debris flung aft

Explosion coming up through deck

White mountain of water thrown up

OLIVER P. BERNARD

A COWARDLY STAB IN THE SIDE BY AN UNSEEN ASSASSIN: THE "LUSITANIA" STRUCK
BY THE GERMAN SUBMARINE'S TORPEDO.

The last boat away from Starboard side just missing funnel. N°?

OLIVER P. BERNARD

THE LAST BOAT LEAVING THE STARBOARD SIDE OF THE SINKING LINER, AND JUST MISSING A FUNNEL:
THE END OF THE "LUSITANIA."

The great upheaval of water after the Lusitania went under

OLIVER P. BERNARD

"GONE." 2.30 pm

AFTER THE GIANT CUNARDER HAD DISAPPEARED BENEATH THE SURFACE: THE VORTEX CAUSED
AS THE "LUSITANIA" WENT UNDER.

(Top) 'The track of the *Lusitania*', an understandably emotive portrayal by W L Wyllie, painted not long after the event. (Above) A headstone of one of the mass graves of *Lusitania* victims in the Cobh cemetery, taken by the author in July 1997. The bouquet was placed in his memory by the family of the Fireman, John Ford, who was lost in the disaster.

Captain Turner, the day after the sinking, wearing a shrunken uniform and borrowed cap.

Henry Oliver as Admiral of the Fleet by G Blair Leighton, 1935. The portrait hangs in the Royal Navy's School of Maritime Operations, HMS *Dryad*, Southwick, Hampshire.

Winston Churchill as First Lord of the Admiralty, *c*1914.

Admiral of the Fleet Lord Fisher in the insignia of the Order of Merit, by William Strang 1908. This drawing forms part of a collection of drawings of holders of the order in the possession of HM the Queen.

(Above) Woodrow Wilson is greeted by the Mayor, Mr E W G Farley, on his arrival at Dover, 26 December 1918, the first occasion that a President of the United States had set foot on British soil.

Kaiser Wilhelm II, in the uniform of a Grossadmiral of the Kriegsmarine, conferring with Admirals von Tirpitz (centre) and Henning von Holtzendorff.

'Take up the Sword of Justice' by Bernard Partridge, an outstanding example of Allied propaganda generated after the sinking of *Lusitania*.

had thus been written after the event in more precise terms to remove any doubt as to the course the Admiralty was advising masters to steer. Whoever conceived this notion can have had little understanding of courtroom practice and in particular that Aspinall would object to the introduction of such dubious evidence, whose authenticity could easily be disproved.

The phantom signal also contradicted Churchill's statement to the House of Commons on 10 May that two warning telegrams had been sent to *Lusitania* on of 7 May, the first at 11.52am, regarding the submarines off Coningbeg and the second at 1pm, containing the erroneous report that a U-boat had been seen off Cape Clear heading west. Commander M H Anderson, attached to the trade division and the senior naval officer in attendance at the inquiry, was a qualified barrister, which makes this unforced error difficult to understand. He may possibly have objected to its inclusion in evidence only to be overruled by his superiors. It is even more difficult to understand why a presumably experienced government lawyer like Cunliffe should have been so careless in his preparation of the Admiralty's case.

The incident of the phantom signal had a decidedly jaundiced effect on the normally passive Mersey. Aspinall had already effectively demonstrated the fallacies in the Admiralty's allegations against Turner. Establishment judge he may have been but for a department of state to tamper with evidence was a serious matter, bordering on the unacceptable. He pointedly told counsel that he had to get at the truth and from that moment on he adopted a more critical approach towards the Admiralty's case.

Although the formidable Smith must have felt the case beginning to slip away from him, he continued to assail Turner. He insisted that Turner should have stood out to sea in response to the signal advising him of the presence of U-boats off Coningbeg and decried his decision to take a fix. In so doing he once again ignored the lack of accuracy inherent in navigation by dead reckoning and the consequent dangers which Turner would have faced in steaming up St George's Channel in darkness and possibly in fog. A somewhat testy Mersey reminded him of his earlier statement that the Board of Trade's objective was to get at the truth, specifically asking him: 'Is there anything which occurs to you which can be said in favour of the captain in the course that he followed?'

For the second time in the inquiry, Smith made what was in effect a statement in mitigation of Turner: 'I should lay stress on the extraordinary difficulties in which he found himself . . . and I should further remember that all the instructions which he received . . . were general . . . with the exception of the instruction with regard to the submarine which was eighty miles away at Coningbeg.' It was left to Aspinall to point out that *Lusitania* with her high silhouette did face risks in standing out to sea if, as reported, several submarines were off the lightship. After an exchange on legal procedure with Smith, Mersey, evidently apprehensive that further evidence might be adduced, adjourned the inquiry *sine die*.

His intuition proved well-founded as a bizarre intervention forced the reopening of the open hearings on 1 July. One survivor, Joseph Marichal, a French citizen and former army officer, had demanded to give evidence stating that he had important but unspecified information to present to the inquiry. He had been travelling with his pregnant wife and their three children, all of whom had survived, although his wife apparently had a miscarriage after the sinking. Compared with many other families, the Marichals had been remarkably fortunate. Marichal proved to be a highly unsatisfactory witness. He had submitted a claim to Cunard after the sinking for £1,050 for loss of personal effects and shock to his system. This was by far the largest claim presented at the time, most other claimants asking only for personal losses and out-of- pocket expenses.[4] He was less than frank in his evidence.[5]

Smith: You, I think, were Lecturer in Romance Languages at
   Queens University in Kingston, Ontario?
Marichal: That's right.
Smith: And I think you were returning to this country for a holi-
   day on the *Lusitania?*
Marichal: That's right.

If the Marichal family had been travelling on holiday, as he had stated under oath, it was an enforced one. Joseph Marichal had been engaged by Queens University as a Lecturer in October 1913. By the spring of 1915 he was seriously at odds with the University authorities. In March he wrote to them stating that he was prepared to sever his connection with the University if he received a full financial settlement. The authorities agreed and paid him the balance of his salary for the rest of the academic year. In the following month the full board of trustees tersely reported that: 'the services of Mr. Marichal be dispensed with.' It seems evident that Marichal had resigned to avoid being sacked and that the University was pleased to see the back of him.[6] Marichal also told Mersey that he had lost a child in the disaster although the casualty list does not confirm this. It seems that he was stretching the point of his wife's alleged miscarriage a little too far.

He told Smith that he had been lunching with his family in the second-class dining-room when the torpedo struck. The dining-room was several hundred feet aft of the point of impact which itself was well aft of the ship's cargo well. He asserted that the second explosion had been caused by the (non-explosive) rifle ammunition carried in the cargo blowing up. The theory that the second explosion was due to the ammunition is now discredited by marine architects and engineers. Replying to Mersey he suggested that: '. . . the second explosion might have been due primarily to the explosion of a torpedo but not to a torpedo alone. The nature of the explosion was similar to the rattling of a machine gun for a short time'.

Mersey: Do you suggest that a Maxim gun was discharged on the ship?

Marichal: No, my Lord, I suggest that the subsequent explosion of the torpedo caused the subsequent explosion of some ammunition and [citing his Army service] I have special experience of explosives.

Smith: Where did the sound of the explosion which you attribute to ammunition seem to come from – from what part of the ship?

Marichal: From underneath; the whole floor was shaken. The whole of the silver plate fell down, which it did not do in the first explosion and the ship at once took a very decided list.

Smith [clearly irritated by the witness]: You have not answered my question: From what part of the ship, forward, aft or amidships did the sound come?

Marichal: We were in the dining room and the only idea that we could form was that the whole floor was shaken.

Smith: Do you mean underneath the dining room?

Marichal: The whole floor of the dining room was shaken by the explosion. I could not form any idea as to . . . where the explosion took place.

Marichal had produced no details to support his allegation and Smith had forced him to contradict himself as to where he thought the explosion had taken place. A much more reliable witness, Robert Leith, the ship's senior wireless operator, who had been in the same dining-room at the time the torpedo hit, had testified that he had heard what he took to be a boiler-room explosion – a very different sound. The remainder of Marichal's evidence consisted of a long diatribe against Cunard, hotels in Queenstown and Dublin and the railway companies. He even complained about Cunard's decision to cut fares, snidely remarking that it would have been better to have attacked the passengers' pockets than their lives. Although the University had paid him the balance of his salary, he represented himself as being penniless. His testimony was directly opposed to the experience of other survivors, including Charles Lauriat and Winifred Hall, who had referred in glowing terms to the helpfulness and hospitality they had encountered in Queenstown.

Smith was followed by the union leader, Joseph Cotter, who had been in Queenstown on the night of the tragedy. Referring to Marichal's allegation that the Cunard office had not opened until 9am on the morning following the sinking, Cotter told Mersey that '. . . some of his [Marichal's] statements I do not want to go unchallenged'.

Cotter: Would it surprise you to know that that the officials of the Cunard company were working for two nights without leaving the office?

Marichal: Not for the comfort of the passengers.

Cotter: Would it surprise you to know that they were at the office for two nights?

Marichal: Not a bit if you say so.

Cotter: Because you said the office was not open until 9 o'clock.

Marichal: It was not open to passengers.

Cotter: I suggest to you that it was open to anybody any moment day or night?

Marichal: I say it was not correct.

Marichal was then questioned by Macmaster, counsel for the Canadian Government, who told him pointedly that his instructions were that the passengers were fairly well looked after following the disaster. His reply was weak: 'that was not my experience'. By this time Marichal had exasperated Mersey and every lawyer in the court. It was left to Butler Aspinall, on behalf of Cunard, to strip bare what was left of his credibility and expose him as a tawdry blackmailer. Aspinall produced a letter from Marichal to Alfred Booth, in which he had written: '. . . I must ask you to make some immediate allowance on account or else I will have the unpleasant duty to claim publicly and, in so doing, to produce evidence which will not be to the credit either of your Company or of the Admiralty.' When confronted with this he could only bluster. Mersey dismissed Marichal tersely in his report: 'I did not believe this gentleman. His demeanour was very unsatisfactory.'

After Marichal had been stood down, Mersey recalled Turner to the stand. By the end of June 1915, the German claim that a draft of Canadian troops had been aboard *Lusitania* had received wide currency and Mersey had asked P J Branson, a junior government Counsel: 'Is there the least pretence for saying that there were any troops aboard'. Branson replied: 'None that I know of: but Captain Turner is here, and one question will settle it'. He asked Turner directly: 'Were there any Canadian troops aboard?' Turner was equally forthright: 'None whatever.' Mersey repeated the question in broader terms: 'Were there any troops aboard?' Once again Turner replied : 'None whatever.'

Two days before the last of the open Mersey hearings, Admiral Inglefield, the Senior Naval Assessor, went to see Sir William Graham Greene at the Admiralty, to discuss the degree to which Turner should be condemned for having ignored his official instructions. He told Greene that Mersey privately believed that if he criticised Turner too heavily, he feared that the German government would seize the opportunity to justify the sinking of the liner. Inglefield was obliquely inferring that Mersey was not prepared to cast the hapless Turner in the role of scapegoat as the Admiralty wanted. Greene had many years of experience of Whitehall and, confronted with this unexpected problem, hurriedly consulted his opposite number at the Foreign Office, Sir Arthur Nicolson. The outcome was a masterpiece of establishment guidance, couched in the terms in which Whitehall mandarins customarily made decisions in the names of their ministers. According to the combined wisdom of the Admiralty and the Foreign Office, Turner could be censured but only on the grounds that he had omitted to follow suitable written instructions and that he had been properly informed of the presence of U-boats in the area in which he had been torpedoed. The mandarins concluded that this degree of censure would serve two desirable purposes, exonerating the Admiralty from any blame and denying Berlin any ammunition which they could use to justify their torpedoing of *Lusitania*.

Mersey announced his decision on 17 July. He followed the line taken by Carson in his opening address, placing the entire blame for the disaster on Germany. On the crucial subject of Turner's navigation, he acknowledged that: '. . . in some respects Turner did not follow the advice given to him but the question remains was his conduct [that] of a negligent or incompetent man . . . the advice given to him, although meant for his most serious and careful consideration, was not intended to deprive him of the right to exercise his skilled judgment in the difficult questions which arise from time to time in the navigation of his ship. His omission to follow the advice in all respects cannot be fairly attributed either to negligence or incompetence.'

In reaching this decision, Mersey referred to the guidance he had received from his assessors. Earlier commentators have suggested, seemingly without corroborative evidence, that Admiral Inglefield would have followed the Admiralty line and advised Mersey that Turner was to blame for the sinking. His papers include a copy of the questions prepared by the Board of Trade for Mersey and his assessors, which appear together with the court's answers, in the final report of the inquiry. Inglefield's copy, annotated in his handwriting, shows that he considered that the liner's position, course and speed before and at the time she was attacked was not proper in the circumstances (Question 9b). Question 20 asked: 'Was the loss of the *Lusitania* and/or the loss of life caused by the wrongful act or default of the Master of the *Lusitania* or does any blame attach to him for such loss?' Despite his response to question 9b, Inglefield wrote against this question – No blame.[7] This would seem to suggest that the advice given to Mersey by his assessors was unanimous. The two merchant navy captains would have probably accepted Aspinall's contention that the Admiralty directives did not overrule Turner's right to exercise his judgment in line with Board of Trade regulations. They would almost certainly have agreed with his decision to obtain an accurate reading of his position. They may also have advised Mersey that the Admiralty directives were not only vague and ambiguous but inadequate in the knowledge that three ships had been sunk off the south coast of Ireland during the previous forty-eight hours.

Aspinall's patient and effective advocacy had succeeded in persuading Mersey to clear Turner of blame. Although he was justified in declining the Admiralty's gambit that blame should be very prominently laid upon the Captain, and in concluding that there had been no explosion of the cargo, a finding which has been confirmed by Dr Robert Ballard's exploration of the wreck, in almost every other aspect Mersey's conclusions are highly unsatisfactory. The importance of preserving national security and preventing the hyperactive German propaganda machine from deriving any advantage from his verdict clearly took precedence over a comprehensive examination of the evidence. A number of American survivors including Warren Pearl, who had lost two of his children and their nanny, Dr Howard Fisher and Charles Lauriat and relatives of some victims, were profoundly critical of Mersey's conclusions. The British Government's insistence that the national interest took priority over other considerations cut little ice with them.

The articulate Lauriat included a critical analysis of the inquiry's findings in his book. In general terms his account has stood up well to the tests of time and subsequent discovery and focuses on several contentious points. In his report Mersey had suggested that the portholes were closed. In fact many had been left open. Lauriat had noticed that:

> the portholes on both sides of the [first class] dining room were open. I had special reason to notice this, as my seat was directly under an electric fan and several times . . . when the portholes were open and the fan going the draught was so strong that I had been obliged to request the steward to shut the fan off. This was the case this noon i.e. the day of the sinking.

In another section of his narrative he recounts how he went down to his stateroom on B deck to recover some documents. As he was returning to the boat deck he noticed a number of open portholes. Lauriat's criticism is well-founded and is confirmed by the accounts of other survivors.[8]

Lauriat strongly disagreed with Mersey's conclusion that the boats were in good order at the moment of the explosion and that the launching was carried out as well as the short time, the moving ship and the serious list would allow. Lauriat cites the lack of discipline and inexperience displayed by many of the crew, citing two instances when boats had been dropped some twenty feet into the water as a result of handling errors. He noted Mersey's comment that 'since the commencement of the war, the Cunard Company had lost all its fleet reserve and naval reserve men and that the managers had had to take on the best men they could get and to train them as well as might be in the time at their disposal.' From this he drew the reasonable inference that a makeshift crew could not be trained in a few weeks to the standard where, in Mersey's words, they could deal with a major disaster 'with skill and judgment'. At first sight, Mersey's conclusion seems extraordinary given Turner's frank admission that *Lusitania*'s crew were not proficient in handling boats and James Baker's evidence that there had been a lack of competent seamen. It becomes more explicable in the light of his determination to avoid giving the Germans too much evidence of the crew's errors and shortcomings, thus denying them any ammunition with which they could deflect hostile world opinion.

Lauriat was critical of the inquiry's failure to properly investigate the condition of the collapsible boats which had in the event proved to be both impractical and badly maintained. He could also have criticised the lack of any crew training in their handling. On two further points Lauriat's censure of the report is less valid. He dismissed the conclusion that: 'the reduction of ... speed was of no significance'. This view was widely held at the time but a fuller examination of the part the liner's speed played in the tragedy will be found in the chapter *The Reasons Why*. On this point the author would agree with Lord Mersey. Lauriat sharply disagreed with Mersey's conclusion that the passengers' efforts to assist in launching the boats were well-meant but probably disastrous. His annoyance with this conclusion is perfectly understandable, given his valiant efforts to assist its crew's attempt to free one of the boats from its davits and his commendable performance in the collapsible. However, he left the liner from its starboard side while Mersey's criticisms related to the attempts to launch the port side boats. Lehmann's interference with the crew of boat No 18 certainly had disastrous results although this incident was not directly addressed in any of the sessions. To this extent Mersey's conclusion is not entirely unjustified.

The most unsatisfactory aspect of Mersey's report was its failure to address any of the technical issues. Where had the torpedo struck? Why had *Lusitania* developed such a heavy list to starboard? Why had the electric power been lost? Why had the liner sunk so quickly? The supercilious Mersey had doubted that the Third Engineer, George Little, could provide any worthwhile information to his inquiry. How much less could mere firemen contribute? Madden, Davis and McDermott had testified that the ship was taking in water in both No 1 and No 2 boiler rooms and

Madden and Davis had affirmed that an explosion had occurred on the starboard side of No 1. The examination of the engineers and boiler room staff was perfunctory and often left to junior counsel and their evidence was totally ignored. Mersey decided that *Lusitania* had been hit by two torpedoes. Eyebrows must have been raised at the Admiralty by this judicial opinion. Through its decrypts of the German signals, the War Staff was perfectly well aware that Schwieger had used only one torpedo to sink *Lusitania*.

In November 1915 the *New York Times* carried a front-page interview with Turner, who was then in command of the freighter *Ultonia*, which was loading cargo in Quebec.[9] His commentary tallies with his evidence to the Mersey inquiry, except for one important detail. His reaction to the German advertisement was in line with the conventional wisdom. '. . . When . . . I read the warning which had been issued to the traveling public by the German Embassy . . . I did not believe that the threat of torpedoing the *Lusitania* would be carried out by the submarine commanders . . . but I decided to take every precaution possible in case of accident.' Within the parameters of the information at his disposal and as no large liner had yet been attacked by a U-boat this statement is not unjustified.

Turner told the *Times* that: 'he was actuated by a desire to clear the reputation of his officers and men who survived and also the memory of those who died.' He showed commendable, if somewhat misplaced, loyalty to his seamen, claiming that although he had a scratch crew '. . . they were about as good as most sailors who go to sea nowadays'. He denied that they were green and did not know their duties. In stating that: 'the old-fashioned able seaman, who could knot, reef, splice and steer disappeared with the sailing ship . . .' Turner repeated almost word-for-word his response to a question from Aspinall during the inquiry after his admission under cross-examination by Joseph Cotter that his crew were not proficient in handling the lifeboats. In the interview Turner asserted that all hands were well-drilled in their duties regarding the lifeboats, thus contradicting the statement he had made under oath, as well as ample survivor testimony. He might have been better to have pointed out in mitigation that the liner's heavy list had made the crew's task extremely difficult and the rapidity with which she sank had resulted in a heavy loss of life. On other aspects Turner was on stronger ground, particularly in praising the performance of the stewards and stewardesses.

He was clearly on the defensive about the many portholes which had been left open on the day of the sinking. Charles Lauriat had drawn attention to this issue in his book *The Lusitania's Last Voyage* which had been published at about the time of this interview. Turner revealed that on the morning of 6 May he had ordered all portholes closed up to B deck and that, later that morning, the liner's chief steward, Frederick Jones, had reported to him that his instruction had been implemented. He added that 'if any portholes in the staterooms had been opened later, it was done by the passengers themselves'. In hindsight, passengers should have been directly instructed to keep them closed but Turner and Anderson were both extremely reluctant to issue orders to them and indeed had little control over them. Indeed, there were only two references to open portholes during the Mersey inquiry and neither Turner nor Jones had been questioned on the issue. Francis Jenkins, a saloon-class passenger, testified that he had momentarily grabbed hold of an open porthole after he had gone into the sea. First Officer Arthur Rowland Jones, who had been lunching in the saloon-class dining-room when the torpedo hit, stated that he had immediately ordered the dining-room portholes to be closed but he could not confirm whether he had seen any that were open. Turner was implying that the portholes were closed in the liner's public areas, an assumption which was plainly incorrect. However, the glass in some of the portholes might have been destroyed in the initial explosion.

Portholes are an inherent threat to the safety of a ship and were thus never fitted to warships below their watertight decks. When *Lusitania* was designed, the technology of forced draught ventilation had not been developed and the only effective method of ventilating a large passenger liner was to cut a substantial number of portholes in its side as any photograph of contemporary ships will illustrate. In retrospect, they were installed far too close to the waterline and passengers and some crew members had a tendency to open and leave open portholes both in cabins and in public rooms so as to circulate fresh air. The degree of risk which open portholes posed to ships' safety does not appear to have been fully appreciated until the Second World War and regulations requiring their closure were not regularly enforced. This might explain why *Lusitania*'s cabin stewards were not told to shut any portholes which they found open and why a progressive and unauthorised relaxation of Turner's order seems to have taken place.

In 1916 a grateful Asquith created Mersey a viscount, raising him one rank in the peerage, and made Alfred Booth a baronet. In June 1919, in response to a question in the House of Commons by Commander Carlyon Bellairs, a Conservative MP, the Admiralty raised no objection to publishing the proceedings of the closed sessions.[10] With the end of the war the previous objections on the grounds of national security no longer held good. No one who had been directly concerned with the case was still serving at the Admiralty. Churchill was at the war office, Oliver held a sea command and Webb, now a rear-admiral, was serving as assistant high commissioner in Turkey. In July 1917, Graham Greene had been unceremoniously sacked by Lloyd George, who had developed a strong animus against the Admiralty. (Churchill, then minister of munitions, had immediately employed him as his permanent secretary, where he remained until the ministry was disbanded in 1920 and he retired.) No one appears to have considered the deficiencies in the Admiralty's case against Turner which Aspinall had exposed during these sessions, or the implications of the phantom signal. If these issues had been understood, it is likely that the transcript of the closed sessions would not have seen the light of day until it would automatically have been released under the fifty-year limit in 1965. Oddly, Churchill and Oliver, the last remaining protagonists in the Admiralty's decision to pursue Turner, both died that year.

CHAPTER 12

The Mayer Liability Trial

T he lawyers who represented American survivors and the families of those who had died in the disaster firmly believed that they had a case in law against Cunard for compensatory damages on grounds of negligence. In all, nearly seventy actions were taken out in New York, Illinois and a number of other states. These were eventually consolidated into one lawsuit with the petitioners claiming damages of nearly $5.9 million, mostly for loss of life. Their case was heard in the United States district court, southern district of New York before Judge Julius Mayer, who had presided over a similar action brought against the White Star Line by *Titanic* survivors and dependents of those who had lost their lives in that tragedy. Mayer heard the case without a jury. Like Mersey, he was an establishment judge. He had been active in Republican politics and had served as Attorney-General of the State of New York before he had been appointed to the federal bench by President Taft.

By the time the case came to court in April 1918, America had been at war with Germany for a year and it was decided that thirty-three British witnesses, including Alfred Booth, Captain Turner and *Lusitania*'s designer Leonard Peskett, should be deposed in London rather than force them to cross the Atlantic in wartime. This process, including cross-examination, took place before commissioner R V Wynne in June 1917. A further complication arose from the Admiralty's adamant refusal to allow the evidence taken in the in camera sessions of the Mersey inquiry to be adduced in the American courts. They quite understandably invoked the national interest, pointing out that any release of such secret documents would provide valuable information to the enemy. Equally, Cunard would have committed a serious breach of the Defence of the Realm Acts had it handed over the evidence it had in its possession. The Admiralty declared that its instructions to Turner were not relevant to the case and Alfred Booth went so far as to swear an affidavit to this effect. The unavailability of this evidence was a severe blow to the claimants, several of whom unsuccessfully argued that the hearing be postponed until after the war when it could presumably have been disclosed. The plaintiff lawyers also prepared some seventy-nine interrogatories for Cunard to answer in writing which were then sworn in testimony. The line responded to the interrogatories in a remarkably open manner.

Before the case came to court, lawyers for both sides agreed to remove any allegations that *Lusitania*'s passengers had included Canadian troops or that she had been carrying guns or any ammunition including explosives and other munitions of war including aircraft and submarine components. This latter assertion was never credible since the liner's limited cargo space was too small to carry large prefabricated steel components. Nearly three years after the sinking, no evidence had emerged to justify these accusations, which had emerged from the fertile imagination of the German propaganda machine. Whatever Turner's shortcomings may have been, he was an honest man and he had testified under oath before Mersey that *Lusitania* was unarmed and that no Canadian soldiers had been on board. The plaintiff lawyers had discarded the weakest element in their case, which would have faced determined opposition from Cunard's lawyers. When he learnt of this agreement, Judge Mayer remarked somewhat prematurely: 'That story is forever disposed of, as far as we are concerned'.

Fate had not been kind to Turner. In December 1916 he had taken over command of the Cunarder *Ivernia*, then serving as a troopship in the Mediterranean. On New Year's Day 1917 *Ivernia* was torpedoed thirty miles west of Crete. Thirty-six men went down with her but once again Turner was rescued. He had been zigzagging at the time and the experience had left him unconvinced of the manoeuvre's effectiveness. Two years after the tragedy of *Lusitania*, Turner was still distressed by the loss of his ship. He told the Wynne hearings: 'I have been trying to forget the thing and I cannot'. He was not at ease in the witness box and he was occasionally irascible under cross-examination. He once retorted that he could paper the walls with the volume of Admiralty instructions which he had received. On this point, a large number of naval officers would have agreed with him. Once again he testified that *Lusitania* was unarmed and carried no high explosives.

In these hearings Turner was cross-examined on his navigation by his old adversary, Thomas Scanlan, once again acting for the passengers. He continued to insist on the necessity of steering a straight course for thirty minutes so as to take a four-point bearing although other captains had testified that an accurate position could be obtained by taking cross bearings in only three minutes. Turner's attitude to zigzagging had subtly changed since his appearance before Mersey when he had declared that he had not understood the procedure. He stated his belief that zigzagging was not suitable for a fast ship like *Lusitania*. Scanlan read the wording of the Admiralty document that 'fast steamers can considerably reduce the chance of a successful surprise submarine attack by zigzagging'. The resultant exchange went as follows:

Turner: Exactly so. It was a simply a suggestion; it was not an order.
Scanlan: You knew that that was what the Admiralty meant to convey?
Turner: Exactly.
Scanlan: And you took it upon yourself not to do it?
Turner: I did not think it [zigzagging] was requisite, with a ship like that.
Scanlan: You took it upon yourself not to do it?
Turner: Just so: it was not an order: it was only a suggestion.
Scanlan: You knew that it is a course invariably adopted by warships?
Turner: Yes, and I was torpedoed while I was doing it in one ship [*Ivernia*].

Despite this rebuff, Scanlan went on to question Turner about his reaction to the Admiralty's instructions. He freely admitted that the Admiralty's information was based on their experience of how submarine commanders operated and where they often cruised, *ie* in the vicinity of ports and headlands. He insisted that he had implemented the instructions in as far as he thought them consistent with the welfare of the ship.

Scanlan: You do concede that in some respects you carried out your own judgement?
Turner: Yes.
Scanlan: In spite of what the Admiralty had said?
Turner: Yes. I did not know that I did. I consider I pretty well did as they wanted me to do according to my own idea of it.

Scanlan then asked Turner a pointed question which, in essence, allowed him to divert blame towards the Admiralty: 'Do you consider that some of the instructions given by the Admiralty were not consistent with the safety of the ship.'

Turner: Yes, that is right with regard to the last telegram I got from them about that submarine off Coningbeg.

Scanlan: Can you indicate now ... which instructions of the Admiralty you thought it was prudent to deviate from and to take your own course?

Turner: By keeping to a mid-channel course I would have run foul of a submarine off Coningbeg.

Scanlan: You think you were right in disregarding the warning which the Admiralty gave you about Coningbeg?

Turner: No. I am sure that I was right: I do not think I was right. I am sure that I was right ... We never got that far ... if we had gone on the mid-channel course we should have run right into him ... we should have been looking for him and probably found him: and no doubt there were half-a-dozen more ...[1]

Scanlan was being tendentious as Turner had certainly not disregarded the warning. In this vigorous exchange the Captain had acquitted himself remarkably well.

In many respects the Mayer trial was a replay of the Mersey inquiry, although the navigation of the liner was now discussed in open court. Thirty-four witnesses had testified at the Mersey open hearings. Thirty-three British witnesses had been deposed before Wynne and a further thirty-seven, technical experts and survivors, among them Charles Lauriat, appeared in person before Mayer. The most impressive of the expert witnesses was Professor William Hovgaard of the Massachusetts Institute of Technology, who was examined by counsel on the causes of the liner's sinking, which he ascribed to instability resulting from flooding.[2]

Betts [counsel for the plaintiffs]: Would the action of the ship in sinking, as has been described, at the angle of 30 degrees by the head, be consistent with the flooding of No 1 boiler room?

Hovgaard: Not caused by that alone; *only if water gradually finds its way to the forward part of the ship and fills that up completely.* Then practically any angle is passed ultimately and the fore body is filled with water and the after body is air filled then ... ships will go down ...

Betts: Do you know whether this ship was constructed so that she would float with one boiler room flooded and the adjacent coal bunkers on one side?

Hovgaard: I have not made a calculation as to that but I would say from my general knowledge that she would undoubtedly stand the flooding of one boiler room and two adjacent bunkers without danger to her buoyancy.

Betts: What would you say about flooding the two boiler rooms and the adjacent bunkers on one side.

Hovgaard: . . . apart from the heeling effect, I should say that the ship would come very near to her bulkhead deck by sinkage.

Betts: If we assume that there were no air ports or air openings in the side of the ship open, what should you say as to whether the ship would float under these conditions?

Hovgaard: I should think she would float in safety, provided the water has no means of spreading beyond the two main bulkheads; *and provided that no opening in the side admits the water to the interior of the ship* [author's italics].

In reply to a question by Mayer, Hovgaard confirmed that *Lusitania*'s list would have been approximately the same whether one or two boiler rooms had been flooded. He did stress that the ship's stiffness may have been so much reduced with two boiler rooms flooded that the heel produced would be greater. During cross-examination, Mayer asked Hovgaard whether the evidence (of firemen Madden and Macdermott) to the Mersey Inquiry that both No 1 and No 2 boiler rooms had flooded would indicate that the point of impact was nearer No 2. He replied: 'Yes, it would indicate that it took place in the after part of boiler room No 1.'

Hovgaard placed considerable emphasis on the serious consequences of the large number of portholes, which had been left open. In a dramatic phrase one survivor testified that he saw water pouring into the saloon-class dining-room and the adjacent passage way on D deck like a kind of young Niagara. At a reasonable estimate some seventy starboard-side portholes were open at the time the torpedo struck. Hovgaard testified that a porthole of the type installed on *Lusitania* would admit water at a rate of 3.75 tons per minute, if submerged to a depth of eighteen inches. By extension, seventy portholes would have admitted about 260 tons of water per minute or nearly 5,000 tons in the eighteen minutes *Lusitania* remained afloat after she was torpedoed. Asked by Betts what would be the effect of the admission of water into the ship through the portholes on E deck on her stability or list, Hovgaard replied that: 'It would seriously reduce the stability, because in a very short time a great amount of water would pour in on the starboard side and would reduce the metacentric height – that is, the stiffness of the ship – and gradually the water accumulated would greatly increase the heel, the inclination of the ship.' Later in his testimony, Judge Mayer asked him the same question. His response was that the admission of water would greatly increase the heel of the ship and ultimately cause her to capsize.

Cunard counsel advanced one powerful argument. Under international law Turner could rely on the convention that unless he offered resistance or refused to stop when challenged, his ship would not be attacked. They pointed out that in May 1915 no large passenger liner had been attacked by a U-boat and that plaintiff criticism of his navigation owed much to hindsight. Several witnesses, including a French submarine commander, reiterated the belief that speed was the best defence against a submarine attack. Cunard counsel rebutted this evidence, arguing that mere speed did not render a ship invulnerable to such an attack. Commodore John Jamison of the IMM subsidiary, American Lines, appeared for the plaintiffs and was examined on the subject of navigation.[3] He did not believe in the necessity of taking a four-point bearing, telling the court that shortly before *Lusitania* had been torpedoed, he had commanded the liner *St. Louis* on a New York-Liverpool-New York round voyage. He testified that due to bad weather he had not seen the Irish coast on either leg of his voyage, keeping thirty miles offshore and had no difficulty in maintaining his correct position. In his view, taking a four-point bearing on Fastnet or the Old Head was not necessary, unless he were making for Queenstown. This last admission somewhat discounts the value of Commodore Jamison's testimony as he had conceded the necessity of taking an accurate fix before making port. He does not seem to have been asked whether he was taking a mid-channel course to avoid any likelihood of running his ship ashore owing to his inability to take a fix or what bearings he had taken in his final approach to Liverpool.

John Lewis, one of *Lusitania*'s two surviving third officers, gave evidence that cross-bearings and sun-line observations gave a position as accurate as a fix with an error factor of only a quarter of a mile, adding that Cunard regulations required sun-line observations to be taken daily whenever the sun was visible and that Turner had no valid excuse for not plotting a noon sun observation. Lewis testified that on 7 May the fog had burnt off by 11am and that in full sunlight cross bearings had been taken routinely off Galley Head and the Old Head of Kinsale.[4]

From Cunard's viewpoint, Lewis seems to have been a hostile witness and his evidence, implying that it was unnecessary for Turner to have taken a fix in the clear weather conditions on 7 May, was hardly objective. An error factor of a mile might have been acceptable in perfect weather but it would not suffice in darkness or fog, particularly if a ship was impelled to take a close inshore course. It also ignored the possibility of creeping error, that the original inaccuracy would multiply as the voyage proceeded. His testimony that cross bearings were taken off Galley Head was irrelevant. The liner was then steaming nearly twenty miles offshore, a distance too great to calculate accurate bearings.

Mayer delivered his judgment on 23 August 1918, clearing Cunard of any negligence for the loss of *Lusitania*. He followed Mersey's precedent and held the cause of the sinking, which he called one of the most indefensible acts of modern times, to be an illegal action by Imperial Germany. As a result of Mayer's decision, the plaintiffs could claim damages only from the German government. Mayer has been criticised for a number of errors in his judgment. He stated that the torpedo had been sighted promptly and that all watertight doors had been closed from the bridge although it would appear that a number of them had been knocked out by the force of the explosion. Despite survivor evidence to the contrary, he concluded that the lifesaving equipment was in good working order and that the crew had handled the launching of the lifeboats competently. In strict terms of law, Mayer was correct. These shortcomings could not have prevented the sinking although better attention to the equipment and crew training might have mitigated the loss of life. He chose to disregard Professor Hovgaard's evidence and decided that the open portholes 'were a very trifling influence . . . in accelerating the time within which the ship sank'.

We should not, however, be unduly derogatory of Mayer's judgment in the light of the Mersey precedent or of the contemporary animosity towards Imperial Germany. The decision was well received by the press, with the *New York Times* commenting in a thoughtful editorial that the ruling 'will take its place beside other American opinions that have so notably contributed to the determination of law . . .'[5] By the time Mayer reached his decision, Pershing's army had already made its mark at Belleau Wood and Chateau Thierry and was engaged in heavy fighting with the Germans on the Argonne. The revelations of German chicanery in the affair of the Zimmermann telegram, which will be discussed in a later chapter, had created a strongly held antagonism against all acts committed by the enemy. This hostility had been stimulated by an effective and unprecedented propaganda campaign run by the Committee on Public Information, appointed by the President, and headed by an energetic career newspaperman, George Creel. His efforts were boosted by Hollywood, who turned out a succession of strongly anti-German films, one of which was extravagantly titled *The Kaiser, The Beast of Berlin*. The Westminster Kennel Club even banned dachshunds from their 1918 dog show in Madison Square Gardens.[6] Significantly, and whatever their criticisms of Mayer, the plaintiff lawyers never appealed his decision. In 1921 President Harding appointed Mayer to the United States court of appeal for the second circuit.

The process of obtaining compensation from Germany proved protracted. Diplomatic relations between the two countries were not restored until August 1921. The two governments took a further year to agree the terms of reference for the mixed claims commission which was set up to handle negotiations. The commission had received claims from *Lusitania* survivors and relatives amounting in total to $15.5 million, chiefly for loss of life. Final agreement on compensation was not reached until December 1925, when Germany paid $2.531 million, including $2,214 million on account of loss of life and personal injury. In allocating the compensation to individual claimants, the commission had applied a formula which was based on the earning power of each victim, rather than on pure loss of life.

This formula had the odd effect of weighting the compensation towards the more wealthy victims at the expense of the less well-off. A widow of a businessman and her three children received the largest single payment, $140,000. The widow of another saloon-class passenger, Thomas Bloomfield, a successful reinsurance underwriter, received $45,000. Warren Pearl and his wife Amy, who were moving their family to Britain, received $19,714 for the loss of their personal effects, but only $11,000 for the loss of their two daughters. Another doctor, Carl Foss, had never fully recovered from the ill-effects of floating for more than three hours in the sea and had died in February 1924, aged only thirty-six. His estate received $23,500. Under the commission's formula, the estates of the two richest American passengers,

Alfred Vanderbilt and Charles Frohman, received no compensation. Vanderbilt had had left $15.6 million and the Commission argued that their beneficiaries had actually gained by virtue of their inheritance.[7]

CHAPTER 13

The War of the Notes

Two days before Schwieger docked at Wilhelmshaven, the American Government delivered the first of its notes concerning the sinking to Berlin. The widespread criticism of Wilson's 'too proud to fight' speech and the rapid crystallisation of public opinion ensured that it would be strongly worded and would reject the German note sent to Washington on 10 May. This had stated that:

> The German Government desires to express its deepest sympathy with the loss of American lives aboard *Lusitania*. The responsibility rests with the British Government, which through its plan of starving the civilian population of Germany, has forced Germany to resort to retaliatory measures.
>
> Despite the German offer to stop the submarine warfare if the starvation plan was given up the British Government has taken even more stringent blockade measures. British merchant vessels being generally armed with guns and having repeatedly attempted to ram submarines, so that previous search was impossible. They cannot, therefore be treated as ordinary merchant vessels ... Besides it is openly admitted in the British press that *Lusitania* on previous voyages repeatedly carried large quantities of war material.
>
> On the present voyage *Lusitania* carried 5,400 cases of ammunition, while the rest of the cargo consisted chiefly of contraband of war. If England, after repeated official and unofficial German warnings, considered herself able to declare that the boat ran no risk, she thus light-heartedly assumed responsibility for the human lives aboard. *Lusitania* with its cargo of armament was liable to destruction.
>
> The German Government cannot but regret that Americans felt more inclined to trust English promises rather than pay attention to the warnings from the German side.

Apart from its somewhat hectoring tone, the note contained a number of errors. The Allies had rejected the German offer to stop submarine warfare as Berlin had in return demanded an end to armament purchases in America. This was totally unacceptable as it would have placed the Allies at a disadvantage to Germany and its huge armament industry. The inference that *Lusitania* was armed was an invention, for like most British merchant ships she had no means of defending herself. The attempt to defend the loss of life by comparison to the starvation allegedly caused in Germany by the Allied blockade was far-fetched indeed.

The anglophile ambassador Page told Wilson after the tragedy that British public opinion believed that the United States should declare war or run the risk of losing European respect. Theodore Roosevelt was one of those who had understood the real implications of the tragedy of *Lusitania*. His reaction to the embassy's advertisement was characteristic. Had he been President he would have summoned Bernstorff, given him his passports and put him aboard the liner under guard.[1] He told a friend that he had not previously wished to take part in a European war. After the sinking, he unceasingly demanded greater military and naval preparations to be made as he now feared that America would inevitably become involved. Only a small minority, chiefly on the eastern seaboard, supported Roosevelt or Page in advocating war. An equally small faction, isolationists and pacifists, were opposed to any action, diplomatic or otherwise. They were supported by the large German-American community and by many Irish-Americans, who had nursed a venomous dislike of Britain arising out of their forebears' sufferings during the potato famine seventy years earlier. Public opinion, appalled by this example of German frightfulness, fiercely condemned the sinking but did not consider the deaths of American citizens on a British ship as a sufficient justification for going to war. Most Americans wanted to see Washington impose vigorous diplomatic pressure on Germany and demand an assurance that there would be no further attacks on passenger liners. On the day after the sinking, the British ambassador in Washington, Sir Cecil Spring-Rice, told the foreign office that the feeling that America should not go to war over the sinking of Lusitania was strongly held in many parts of the country, particularly in the Mid-West.[2] The *New York Sun*'s banner headlines were succinct:

PEOPLE WANT FIRM STAND WITH GERMANY

President is Urged to Act Quickly

but Few Persons Talk of War[3]

Wilson drafted the American note of 13 May on the portable typewriter which he had used since his days as a university professor. He protested against what he called an inhumane application of submarine warfare and demanded that the rights of American citizens on the high seas be respected. He was adamant that Americans, travelling on legitimate business, had the indubitable right to sail on any ship of their choice, including those of belligerent countries, in the expectation that they would arrive safely at their destination. He expected Berlin to disavow the sinking, offer compensation for the loss of life and take immediate steps to ensure that there would be no repetition of the tragedy. The note was well-received by the American press and public opinion. *The Times*, appreciating Wilson's approach, called it a literary masterpiece. The German media, not surprisingly, was sour. Although the Berlin *Vossiche Zeitung*, unlike its contemporary in Cologne, did manage to express regret for the loss of life, it announced that 'the responsibility for the deaths of so many American citizens ... falls upon the American Government'.

The sinking of *Lusitania* put Bryan in a quandary. As a pacifist he sympathised with the arguments of those who saw no reason to harry Berlin over the loss of life on a British ship and he found himself increasingly at odds both with the President and with public opinion. On 17 May, Bryan told the Austrian ambassador, Constantin Dumba, quite correctly, that America did not seek war and wished to reach a peaceful solution to her differences with Germany. He ineptly managed to give the envoy the impression that the note was really intended for public consumption and to assuage the widespread anger caused by the loss of American life. Dumba lost no time in telegraphing this revelation not only to the foreign ministry in Vienna but to its counterpart in Berlin.

On the following day, Ambassador Gerard gave a lunch party at which the under-secretary at the foreign office, Arthur Zimmermann, was one of the guests. Gerard noticed that Zimmermann was deep in conversation with an American lady who was married to a German. After lunch she told Gerard that Zimmermann, whose tongue was clearly loosened by a large quantity of the Ambassador's Moselle, had assured her that there would be no break with the United States as Wilson did not mean the note to be taken seriously. Gerard immediately asked Zimmermann to reveal the source of his information. He was shown Dumba's cable.[4] The ambassador's intervention had disastrous consequences. The German government was now convinced that they could carry on their submarine campaign without any American repercussions and that they had no need to consider any of Wilson's demands. Their contemptuous view of the American political system and public opinion was confirmed and the incident ensured that their reply to the American note would not be conciliatory.

The second German note of 28 May reiterated, indeed, enlarged on the complaints contained in its predecessor of 10 May. While regret was once again expressed over the loss of American life, the blame was firmly attributed to the British and their blockade. Berlin went on to list a succession of inaccurate and irrelevant accusations which in their eyes justified the torpedoing. They raised the old charge that *Lusitania* had been built with government funding as an armed auxiliary cruiser and was listed as such in the authoritative *Brassey's Naval Annual.* In reality, the 1914 edition of *Brassey* had listed her as a potential armed cruiser which might or might not be requisitioned in wartime, and since the 1890s her German counterparts had also been designed to be converted into auxiliary cruiser role in wartime. The note wrongly asserted that *Lusitania* was carrying concealed guns and had trained gun crews on board. As we know, the liner's conversion into an armed merchant cruiser had been halted before her guns could be fitted. On 31 May, Spring-Rice had categorically assured Bryan that *Lusitania* had not carried guns on any of her wartime voyages.[5]

Berlin added the fresh allegation that the passengers included a draft of Canadian troops bound for the Western Front, a charge which Washington rightly regarded as absurd, and implied that the sinking could be justified by Churchill's order that British merchant ships should ram submarines, which had been followed by a rash of attacks on U-boats. This assertion was immaterial as the torpedo had not been sighted until it was too late for anyone on *Lusitania*'s bridge to take any kind of evasive or retaliatory action against *U-20*. Without any supporting evidence, Berlin contended that the liner had sunk so rapidly because of the detonation of high explosive ammunition in the cargo.

The notes of 10 and 28 May reflect an unfortunate trait in Imperial German diplomacy. Berlin was all too prone to present itself as the aggrieved party in any dispute and to complain bitterly, almost extravagantly, about the actions of other countries. Unfortunately the detailed negotiations with America were handled by Zimmermann, an archetypal Prussian bully. He considered himself an expert on all matters American although he had only ever spent ten days in the United States. At one of his meetings with Gerard after the sinking, he worked himself into a fury and told the startled ambassador that: 'the United States does not dare to do anything against Germany because we have 500,000 German reservists in America, who will rise in arms against your Government if [it] should dare to take any action against Germany'. Gerard calmly called Zimmermann's bluff, replying: '. . . we had 500,001 lamp posts in America and that was where the German reservists would find themselves if they tried any uprising.'[6] In February 1916, towards the end of the protracted war of the paper bullets between Berlin and Washington which followed the sinking, Zimmermann hectored the State Department in almost hysterical terms: 'You Americans must not push your demands too far. You must not attempt to humiliate Germany.'[7]

In the light of the worldwide anger at the torpedoing and the loss of life, an apology on the lines advocated by Ballin, and more consistently by Bernstorff, placing the blame on the exigencies of war, might have improved relations between the two countries. Through a combination of German haughtiness and American diplomatic errors, the opportunity was missed and the tone of the notes made it impossible for either Wilson or mainstream opinion to accept them. The President was now honour bound to respond in strong terms. The prevailing sentiment was tersely expressed in a famous cartoon by William Alan Rogers. The urbane Bernstorff was depicted delivering the second German note to Wilson, who was sitting in the Oval Office, surrounded by the ghosts of the little lost children of *Lusitania*. The ambassador was saying that he had expected to find the President alone.

Bernstorff argued that Germany's interests would be best served by admitting liability for sinking *Lusitania*, thereby providing the Imperial Government with some moral credibility. He would then pressure the President to impel Britain to ease the blockade. Acting on his own initiative, Bernstorff met the President on 2 June. In his report to Berlin, he described his conversation as being friendly and that, despite his public stance, Wilson was looking beyond the question of liability for the loss of *Lusitania* and compensation for the loss of life. If Germany gave up submarine warfare, Wilson would press the British Government to suspend the blockade, adding that he believed that the Asquith cabinet would be prepared to agree terms. (He presumably based this judgement on the good relations House had established with Grey.) Wilson even hinted that he might be prepared to implement an arms embargo. These proposals, taken at face value, were so advantageous to Germany that Bernstorff sent an emissary, Anton Meyer-Gerhard, the German Red Cross representative in Washington, to Berlin to explain them more fully. They foundered on the objections of Tirpitz who was not prepared either to disavow the sinking of *Lusitania* or to offer Wilson a concession which he saw as tantamount to abandoning submarine warfare. Bernstorff ruefully conceded that Meyer-Gerhard's mission had achieved nothing.[8]

The breach between Wilson and Bryan was now final, the two men holding diametrically opposed perceptions of the rights of Americans travelling on the high sea. Bryan was prepared to limit the freedom of Americans in wartime by forbidding them to sail on the ships of belligerent nations. There was some justification in Bryan's position, which would be embodied in the Neutrality Acts passed by Congress in the 1930s. He could also claim precedent. During the Russo-Japanese War ten years earlier, British consuls-general in the Far East had advised their nationals not to sail in ships of either belligerent. Wilson remained insistent that the doctrine of the freedom of the seas allowed Americans the privilege to travel on any ship, refusing to consider pleas by congressional leaders in his own party to stop American citizens sailing into the war zone in Allied ships. He argued that Berlin's intransigence made it impossible to implement any limitations on travel, which would be widely perceived as kow-towing to Germany.

After the sinking of *Lusitania*, Wilson had effectively abandoned, at least in public, the concept of impartial neutrality. Bryan believed that America should remain impartial as between the warring European powers and he wanted to protest against the British blockade and the disruption it was causing to American trade. On 2 June Wilson overrode him, stating bluntly that 'England's violation of neutral rights is different from Germany's violation of the rights of humanity'.[9] At odds with the President, most of his advisers and public opinion, Bryan resigned on 8 June, another casualty of the sinking of *Lusitania*.

Wilson promoted Robert Lansing to succeed him. Like his predecessor, Lansing was a lawyer but one of a very different stripe. He had specialised in international law and was an acknowledged expert in the field of international mediation treaties. He came from the conservative wing of the Democratic party and he had strong Wall Street connections. His family could boast a remarkable record of public service. His father-in-law, John W Foster, had been Secretary of State under President Benjamin Harrison in the 1890s and his nephew and protégé, John Foster Dulles, was to hold the same office in the Eisenhower administration. Another nephew, Allen Dulles, had a distinguished career in the Office of Strategic Services (OSS) the forerunner of the CIA in the Second World War and later became director of the CIA. The sinking of *Lusitania* had destroyed any illusions Lansing may have harboured about Imperial Germany. He noted in his diary that 'the German Government is utterly hostile to all nations with democratic institutions because those who comprise it see in democracy a menace to absolutism . . . and the German ambition for world domination'.[10] Lansing was quite prepared to take a tough line with anyone in the German or Austrian embassies who had any truck with industrial espionage. Before the end of 1915, he had expelled the two trouble-making service attachés, von Papen and Boy-Ed, as well as the vexatious Austrian ambassador, Dumba.

On 5 June, four days before the second American note was sent to Berlin, Germany again backed away from unrestricted submarine warfare. The almost universal perception that the sinking of *Lusitania* had been a brutal and unnecessary act, which had done great harm to Germany, had strengthened the hand of the less hawkish elements in Berlin. In particular the army general staff did not want to be embroiled with any neutral country. The Kaiser, uneasy about the sinking, issued an order that passenger liners, Allied or neutral, were not to be attacked. His instruction was bitterly opposed by the German admiralty and Tirpitz and Admiral Gustav Bachmann, the chief of the Admiralstab; both promptly resigned in protest. The Kaiser refused to accept either resignation and Tirpitz stayed in office until March 1916. On 6 September, Bachmann, who had fallen out with Admiral Muller, the Kaiser's personal naval adviser, was replaced by Admiral Henning von Holtzendorff. The Kaiser gave Holtzendorff, who had the reputation of being opposed to unrestricted submarine warfare, the specific brief of curbing the U-boat hawks.

In the second American note, Wilson and Lansing effectively called Germany's bluff. They sharply denied the allegations made about *Lusitania* in the two earlier notes, demanding that Berlin provide proof to substantiate their claims. In an eloquent passage, which Wilson himself drafted, the note declared that 'The Government of the United States is contending for something much greater than mere rights of property or privileges of commerce. It is contending for nothing less high and sacred than the rights of humanity.' They demanded safeguards for the protection of American life and property, reminding Berlin that these principles had been reasserted at the outset of the war. The German government cooled their heels for a month before replying. In their third note, dated 9 July, they proposed a safe-conduct scheme for American ships, which was based on a suggestion originally made by Gerard. No contraband could be carried and each ship should prominently display the Stars and Stripes on their hulls. Ship movements would be agreed in advance between American and German authorities. The note made no further reference to the accusations that the liner had been armed or had been carrying Canadian troops or to the ramming of U-boats, thus implicitly accepting that their earlier charges had been specious or irrelevant.

Wilson decided that the note had not addressed any of the differences between Washington and Berlin, rejecting the safe-conduct proposal as a fundamental breach of his concept of freedom of the seas. He instructed Lansing to reiterate his earlier demands for a disavowal of the sinking and for reparation for the loss of life. Lansing, unaware of the Kaiser's instruction of 5 June which had not been made public, added a further demand, that Germany must undertake not to attack passenger liners in future. He embodied these points in the third American note of 21 July. The note was couched in formal diplomatic language, asserting that:

> the very value which this Government sets upon the long and unbroken friendship [with Germany] impels it to press very solemnly upon the Imperial German Government the necessity for a scrupulous observation of neutral rights [in the freedom of the seas] ... Repetition by the commanders of German naval vessels in contravention of the rights must be regarded ... when they affect American citizens as deliberately unfriendly.

Lansing was implying that a repetition of the sinking of *Lusitania* would lead at least to a breach in diplomatic relations.

The Kaiser was given to writing disparaging comments on the margins of official documents. Despite the restrained terms in which Lansing had drafted the note, his reaction was volcanic, scribbling: 'Utterly impertinent' and 'outrageous' and finally 'This is the most insolent thing in tone and bearing that I have had to read since the Japanese note last August. It ends with a direct threat.' His response was typical of the contemptuous German attitude towards America and its disregard for Bernstorff's well-reasoned advice.[11]

On 19 August, in contravention of the Kaiser's order, *U-24*, commanded by KapitanLeutnant Rudolf Schneider, torpedoed and sank the White Star liner *Arabic*, outward bound for New York, off the south of Ireland. Forty-four people were lost including two Americans. *Arabic*, which had evaded Schwieger the day before he sank *Lusitania*, was over 600 feet long and should have been identifiable as a passenger ship. Schneider's rather weak excuse was that *Arabic* had changed course towards him and he believed she was attempting to ram him. She was quite possibly zigzagging. On the same day HMS *Baralong*, a British Q-ship (a small merchant ship, sometimes a converted trawler, equipped with concealed guns, which was used as a decoy to entrap submarines) created a diplomatic incident which led to serious repercussions in Washington and imperilled the pro-British attitude which had been strengthened by the sinking of *Lusitania.*

Baralong had been on patrol about 100 miles from *Arabic* when the liner was torpedoed and had picked up her calls for assistance. Her captain, Lieutenant-Commander Godfrey Herbert, and her crew, including a detachment of Royal Marines, were not feeling particularly well-disposed towards German submariners when, later that day, they encountered *U-27*, commanded by KapitanLeutnant Bernhard Wegener, shelling the Leyland Line steamer *Nicosian*, carrying a cargo of mules, and whose crew had already taken to the boats. *Baralong*, with the Stars and Stripes painted prominently on her sides, signalled that she intended to rescue the crew. The U-boat disappeared from Herbert's view behind *Nicosian*'s stern, enabling him to run up the White Ensign and bring out his guns. Once he had the U-boat in his sights, he opened fire, sinking her within a few minutes. About a dozen of her crew jumped overboard and swam towards *Nicosian* intending to climb her ropes which had been left dangling after her boats had been launched. Fearing that they might scuttle the freighter, Herbert ordered his Marines to open fire on the swimmers, killing half of them. The boarding party, which he had sent to regain control of *Nicosian*, ignored the remaining Germans' offer to surrender and shot them in cold blood.

By any standards, this inexcusable action was a total breach of the conventions of war. It can only be explained as a reaction to the hostility against German submarine crews engendered by the sinking of *Lusitania* and further inflamed, in the minds of Herbert and his men, by the torpedoing of *Arabic* earlier that day. The muleteers on *Nicosian* were American citizens and were understandably shocked by what they had seen. When they returned to New Orleans a month later they provided affidavits to the German consul in the city. The affidavits were forwarded to Lansing who quickly grasped their significance. He told Wilson that he was shocked by the British conduct and that he hoped that the incident would not become public. Inevitably, the news did break early in October 1915 and was universally condemned in the American press. Wilson took a particularly dim view of the incident. He clearly expected a higher standard of ethics from the British than he did from the Germans and his tacit support for the Allies started to erode. The British naval historian, Captain Stephen Roskill, noted that: 'It is no exaggeration to say that the *Baralong* incident contributed to . . . Wilson and . . . Lansing executing almost a 16-point turn in their attitude toward us in 1916.' The German government protested strongly against what was, for once, a real British atrocity but their propaganda machine had cried wolf so often that their objections had little effect. The Admiralty successfully managed to cover the matter up until several years after the war had ended.[12]

On 4 September, Schwieger, in *U-20*, sank another British liner, *Hesperian*, some eighty-five miles southwest of Fastnet. Thirty-two of her passengers and crew, none of them American, went down with her. His reception on his return was frigid. He was ordered to Berlin where he was carpeted by Holtzendorff and asked to explain why he had sunk the liner in defiance of a specific order. His excuse that he had assumed that *Hesperian* was an armed merchant cruiser was not readily accepted and he received a severe dressing-down, about which he complained bitterly to his superior, Bauer. In November a third passenger liner, the Italian owned *Ancona*, was torpedoed in the Mediterranean by the *U-38*, which was operating out of the Austrian naval base at Cattaro in what is now Croatia and was flying the Austrian flag at the time of the attack. Two hundred lives, including twenty Americans, were lost. Lansing took a hard line with the Austrian Government and eventually forced them to admit that the U-boat commander had exceeded his instructions. Austria undertook to pay an indemnity for the loss of life and agreed that German sub-marines, flying Austrian colours, should not, in future, attack Allied passenger ships.

Wilson was understandably annoyed by the incidence of three attacks on passenger liners in just four months and Lansing was told to keep a firm pressure on Berlin, who had still not offered any reparation for the deaths on *Lusitania*. The activities of the German espionage team had not gone unnoticed by the federal authorities. A week after *Lusitania* was sunk, Wilson instructed the secret service to put both German and Austrian diplomats under surveillance. Captain Gaunt was more discreet than his German opposite numbers. One of his most valuable agents was a Czech named Voska, who controlled a network of moles inside the German and Austrian embassies and in the HAPAG offices. Voska's agents discovered that couriers, carrying classified information to Berlin and Vienna, were sailing on every eastbound neutral liner. When the Holland-Amerika liner *Rotterdam* called in at Falmouth in the first week in September, naval intelligence took a courier named John Archibald off the ship. Captain Hall had a rich haul and sent ambassador Page a number of documents which impli-cated the Austrian ambassador, Dumba, in fomenting strikes by Hungarian workers in munitions factories and Von Papen and Boy-Ed in various acts of sabotage. Although Wilson declined to eject the two service attachés, Lansing, irked by German intransigence over *Lusitania*, secured Dumba's expulsion.

After the sinking of *Ancona*, House and Lansing produced evi-dence that the two attachés had been involved in a plan to restore Wilson's Mexican nemesis, Huerta, to power and they were declared *persona non grata*. Wilson and Lansing only permitted Bernstorff to remain because he was considered indispensable to retaining any semblance of reasonable relations with Berlin. By the end of 1915, the German espionage and propaganda effort in New York had effectively been reduced to impotence.

Sadly, this was not to be Franz von Papen's last encounter with history. In June 1932, he became Chancellor of the already decay-ing Weimar Republic, the unloved successor to Imperial Germany. In his five months in office, he distinguished himself by sacking the elected state government of Prussia, a flagrant breach of the constitution. He was conceited enough to believe that he could control Hitler, helping to pave the way for his rise to power. During the Third Reich, Papen served as vice-chancellor and as ambassador to Austria although Hitler had two of his principal aides murdered in the so-called 'Night of the Long Knives' in June 1934. Papen used his talent for intrigue and espionage to undermine Austrian independence and prepare for the forcible Nazi takeover in March 1938. During the Second World War he was ambassador to Turkey. In 1945 he was arraigned at Nuremberg as a war criminal but was acquitted, later serving two years in prison on a denazification charge.

*   *   *

In the autumn of 1915 the widower-President took on a new lease of life. In October Edith Galt accepted Wilson's proposal and they were married a week before Christmas, sixteen months after Ellen's death. Spring-Rice officiously sacked a second secretary in the British embassy for retailing a story circulated by irrepressible Washington gossips which had the new First Lady telling her friends that 'When Woodrow proposed to me, I do declare that I was so surprised that I fell right out of bed!'

Early in 1916, Wilson took Edith on a speaking tour in the midwest, thus beginning his campaign for the presidential elections, now less than a year away. During his tour, he discovered that public opinion in the midwest was far less belligerent about U-boat warfare than he had believed and that there was no desire for a breach with Germany over the loss of *Lusitania*. He adroitly made a U-turn, ordering Lansing to seek an accommodation with the Germans. After an undignified squabble over wording had been resolved, Washington and Berlin reached a tentative agreement on 16 February. Without accepting that the attack on *Lusitania* was illegal, Germany conceded that retaliation against neutral citizens was unjustified and offered profound regret for the loss of American life. She assumed liability and undertook to pay an indemnity. Germany pledged that passenger liners would not be attacked provided that they did not attempt to escape or resist inspection and even suggested that the two countries should cooperate to uphold the freedom of the seas, presumably against Britain.[13] Wilson did not find the new agreement entirely satisfactory as from his point of view Germany could be deemed to have taken two steps forward followed by one back. Six days earlier the Admiralstab had moved once more towards unrestricted submarine warfare, announcing that it would treat Allied armed merchant ships as auxiliary cruisers and sink them without warning – a reversal of policy he found alarming.

For some months Holtzendorff had been concentrating U-boat operations in the Mediterranean and against naval targets. With more submarines in commission, he was now ready to step up his attacks on merchant shipping. Falkenhayn, the Chief of the General Staff, was increasingly concerned at the strain the army was experiencing fighting a war on three fronts, in the west against Britain and France, in the east against Russia and in the Balkans following Bulgaria's entry into the war on Germany's side. To make matters worse, the military weakness of Austria-Hungary, Germany's principal ally, was a constant worry to the General Staff. Falkenhayn feared that the Dutch, whose merchant marine had taken the brunt of the unrestricted submarine conflict, might go to war, opening up another front to which he would have to divert troops. He was thus strongly opposed to any action which might antagonise the neutral powers and insisted that the submarines should only attack Allied merchant shipping. The army and navy were for the time being prepared to support Bethmann-Hollweg and the Foreign Office in conciliating the United States and other neutral countries.

On 24 March, the French cross-channel ferry *Sussex* was torpedoed off Dieppe by *UB-29*. The sea was calm and many of the passengers were on deck enjoying the fine weather. Her captain had seen the track of the approaching torpedo and had put the helm hard over to starboard. There was insufficient time to avoid the missile, which only hit the ferry a glancing blow. Although she managed to make port, eighty of her 325 passengers were killed or wounded and four Americans were among the injured. Although *Sussex* had been steaming well to the west of the direct cross-channel route taken by troopships, the U-boat commander, Postkuchen, initially claimed that the passengers thronging the decks were troops. Berlin attempted to evade responsibility, telling Lansing that the ferry had hit a mine. Bernstorff concluded that this note was the most unfortunate ever sent from Berlin to Washington. Confronted by the Captain's testimony and evidence of torpedo attack including fragments of a warhead found aboard *Sussex*, the Foreign Office was forced to admit that a mistake had been made.

The attack was a flagrant breach of the agreement reached with Washington only five weeks earlier. On 20 April, Wilson and Lansing, understandably furious, sent Berlin an ultimatum. Unless Imperial Germany immediately abandoned attacking passenger liners and freighters without warning and adhered to cruiser rules, the United States would sever diplomatic relations. Bernstorff bluntly told the Foreign Office that Wilson was in earnest in demanding that Germany back down, noting that: 'Wilson wants rather to risk a break than be ridiculed as an unsuccessful note writer.' He added that with the presidential election due in six months time a break in relations would become inevitable unless Wilson gained the concession he was seeking. Four days later, under pressure from the Kaiser and Bethmann-Hollweg, Holtzendorff backed down and ordered the U-boat command to observe cruiser rules. On 4 May Berlin accepted the ultimatum. With Bernstorff's assistance, American diplomacy had won a considerable success. A wary truce persisted between the two countries for the rest of 1916.[14]

CHAPTER 14

The Myths of Lusitania

From the day she was torpedoed, the saga of *Lusitania* has become encrusted with legends and myths. One of these legends is entirely fictional. Among the memorable characters Evelyn Waugh created in *Scoop*, a novel loosely based on the Italian-Abyssinian war of 1935, was the unscrupulous Wenlock Jakes, whom he portrayed as '. . . the highest paid journalist of the United States, [who] scooped the world with an eye-witness story of the sinking of the *Lusitania* four hours before she was hit.'[1]

The proposition that Walther Schwieger had been sent to the south coast of Ireland with the specific mission of sinking the mighty ship arises out of a misinterpretation of the famous newspaper advertisement which was published on the morning the liner sailed from New York. In reality, the advertisement had not been specially aimed at *Lusitania* and, as has been noted, the Washington embassy had originally intended it to appear a week earlier. As there was little effective co-operation between the German foreign ministry and either of the armed services, it is doubtful whether the Admiralstab was even aware of the advertisement.

U-20 and her sisters had been ordered to sea with detailed objectives, to patrol designated areas, in *U-20*'s case the Irish Sea between England and Ireland. The boundaries of the Irish Sea could be defined as lying between St George's Channel to the south and the North Channel between Ulster and Scotland to the north. Schwieger had been forced to disregard his instructions owing to lack of fuel and on 7 May he was almost 200 miles from his intended patrol zone. If *Lusitania* had been designated as Schwieger's main target, the most suitable place for an attack would have been in Liverpool Bay, through which she would have had to pass before she crossed the Mersey Bar. The War Risks Association had indeed identified the bay as an area of particular danger. Nor would Schwieger have been allowed to advertise his presence by sinking three ships, one of only 132 tons, directly in *Lusitania*'s path. The dates of his voyage do not fit with the supposition. If *U-20* had sailed on 25 April, as originally intended, she would have been well to the north of Ireland on her way home to Emden by 7 May.

The sinking of *Lusitania* was to be freely exploited by the propaganda machines in both Britain and Germany. As early as 8 May, Spring-Rice had reported that German agencies in America were working to lay the blame on Britain.[2] Many of the myths which have grown up about the liner can directly be traced back to the German propaganda machine and its willing accomplices in the United States. They had a vested interest in portraying the sunk liner as a warship and therefore as a legitimate target which had been carrying a lethal and explosive cargo. They never hesitated in seeking to justify death by drowning by comparison to death by deprivation and starvation which they alleged had been caused by the Allied blockade of Germany. The propagandists in Berlin were desperate to find any issue which could usefully divert American and other neutral public opinion from the report severely indicting German behaviour in occupied Belgium, which was due to be published in the week following the sinking. Although it was later found to have included many exaggerations, this damning document had been prepared by a commission headed by Lord Bryce, a distinguished historian and former Liberal cabinet minister and ambassador in Washington, whose veracity could not easily be questioned.

The assertion that *Lusitania* was carrying guns originated from German misinformation circulated in New York and other American cities during the weekend after she was sunk. The *New York Tribune* cabled Alfred Booth and asked him to comment on an official German allegation in New York that the liner had been armed. His response was emphatic: '*Lusitania* was not armed in any way. She was built under the company's agreement with the British Government, under which she could be requisitioned for service as an armed cruiser. As a matter of fact, she was never so used at any period of her career, and no guns of any description were ever put on board the ship.' The embattled Booth then went on the offensive: 'any statement to the contrary is, therefore, false and is a typical German method of covering up the wilful murdering of non-combatants and women and children.'[3] On behalf of the Admiralty, Graham Greene was equally blunt: 'the statement appearing in some newspapers that the *Lusitania* was armed is totally false.'[4] In their sworn depositions for the Mayer liability trial, Turner and Leonard Peskett, Cunard's marine architect, who had designed *Lusitania*, both testified that the liner had never been converted into an armed merchant cruiser. Albert Worley, an inspector of munitions at the Woolwich Arsenal, who had been sent to America to work with Bethlehem Steel on the purchasing programme, travelled on the liner's last westbound voyage. With a keen professional interest in gunnery, Worley surveyed every part of the liner where guns could have been mounted and concluded that none had ever been installed, noting that he could find no closed-off areas and no sign of any gun crew.[5]

Charles Lauriat, a man with an analytical turn of mind, studied the reaction of the German press in the days immediately after the disaster for inclusion in his book. He selected an article from the *Frankfurter Zeitung* of 9 May, which he considered 'much saner' than those he had read in other papers. This allegedly sane journal repeated many of the myths with which Imperial Germany sought not only to justify the destruction of *Lusitania* but to portray itself as an injured party with no responsibility for whatever happened in the course of the war. In one passage in which it boasts of the superiority of German weapons it decries the British and Americans:

> ... have they a right to accuse us, those who allowed their friends and relatives to entrust themselves to a ship, whose destruction was announced with perfect clarity in advance, to a ship equipped like a *cruiser*, more powerful than any German protected cruiser, with twelve 15 centimetre guns? They mocked at us when we gave warning. Let them turn to those who committed the *crime* of allowing passengers to travel on a war vessel.

The *Frankfurter Zeitung* was apparently untroubled by the dubious morality of seeking to excuse a crime by announcing it in advance. It sought to deflect neutral criticism of the sinking:

> The impression created by the sinking of the *Lusitania* will extend far beyond the borders of Germany and England and we may at once assume that neutral voices will arise to deeply deplore the loss of a large number of passengers. Every human life is, of course, valuable and its loss deplorable, but, measured by the methods introduced by our enemies, forcing us to retaliatory measures in self-defence, the death of non-combatants is a matter of no consequence.

Lauriat noted that the anonymous author 'continues with the usual incantation attacking England's war of starvation against Germany and the shipment of thousands of millions [*sic*] of arms and munitions from America. He did not of course remind his readers that Germany had by far the largest armaments industry in Europe which it could supplement by purchases from manufacturers in European neutral countries.' Strangely enough, Lauriat did not comment on the accusation that *Lusitania* was an armed cruiser, since in his own words: 'I was keenly interested in all that was done aboard ship . . . and throughout the voyage I kept my eyes unusually wide open' and thus knew with reasonable certainty that she carried no guns.[6]

Albert Ballin, who had originally criticised the sinking, wrote to Arndt von Holtzendorff, HAPAG's representative in Berlin, and brother of the Admiral:

> Whether it was right to torpedo *Lusitania* with 1,600 [*sic*] passengers, most of them neutral, is a question I will leave aside for the moment. But every intelligent man will admit that our entire U-boat action has contributed to reducing the arrogance of the English and to complicating enormously the situation in England. It was certainly the only thing we could undertake against England . . . and I am now more than ever convinced of the correctness of our U-boat action. If the British are not completely godforsaken, this action must show them how necessary it is for them in the future to engage in a form of World policing with Germany. If they do not perceive this now then in the next war – which we will certainly not be spared – we will obtain with 200 submarines that which strange visionaries already foresee: we will bring England to its knees and destroy its power.[7]

This is a remarkable letter not only for its insight into the future but also for the reaction of its author, who knew far more about the world outside Germany than many of his contemporaries. Several years before the war Ballin had become opposed to Tirpitz's continued and frenetic expansion of the navy, correctly believing that it would endanger Anglo-German relations. In the heated climate of war he was now advocating the destruction of England in terms as extreme as any hawk in Berlin.

Most of the articles, which alleged the presence of guns aboard *Lusitania*, appeared in two New York publications, George Viereck's *The Fatherland*, and the *Gaelic American*, which had strong links with the radical wing of the Irish Nationalist movement and was ever ready to start a donnybrook with the British. Viereck was well pleased with himself for having written an article in the 8 May issue of *Fatherland* which had gone to press before the sinking, in which he forecast not only the torpedoing of *Lusitania* but of *Transylvania*, the Cunarder due to sail that day.

These publications had no scruples whatsoever in sacrificing accuracy to their editorial objectives. With glee they seized on a report in the *New York Tribune* in June 1913:

> The reason why the crack liner *Lusitania* is so long delayed at Liverpool has been announced to be that her turbine engines are being completely replaced but Cunard officials acknowledged . . . today that the greyhound is being equipped with high power naval rifles in conformity with England's new policy of arming passenger boats. So when the great ship next appears in New York Harbor about the end of August she will be the first British merchantman for more than a century sailing up the Lower Bay with her guns bristling over the sides.[8]

This report was itself inaccurate. *Lusitania*'s wartime role as a potential armed merchant cruiser had never been a secret. The liner had entered drydock in Liverpool on 12 May 1913 and was not returned to service until 21 July, ten weeks later. *Lusitania* and *Mauretania* normally went into drydock at intervals of a year to eighteen months for routine refits and inspection and maintenance of worn-out equipment. In particular, turbine blades, which ran continuously at high speed, required regular replacement. The timing of this particular refit indicates that it was not scheduled. Cunard refitted their express liners during the winter, not in the middle of the summer peak traffic season and *Lusitania* had been in drydock for a periodic refit from October to December 1912.

In May 1913 an error by one of *Lusitania*'s junior engineers had resulted in severe damage to one of her turbines and she had to be taken out of service to implement its complete replacement. The engineer officer was sacked and the chief transferred out of the vessel. The overall cost of the refit, before management overheads, came to £53,363 of which the turbine repairs accounted for £35,221. The extent of the damage to the turbines can be measured by the sale of £5,533 of damaged blades for scrap. Only £3,358 was spent on repairs to the ship and there is no indication of any expenditure on altering bunkers or cargo holds to instal magazines.[9] No one in New York was to see the bristling guns of *Lusitania* for the simple reason that they were never installed either during this refit or later. At some time in her career, gun-mountings had been installed on her shelter deck and were concealed by coiled ropes. Her complement of guns was not delivered to Liverpool until November 1913 and was then stored to be fitted if war was to be declared. When the Admiralty decided not to use the liner in AMC mode the guns, always in short supply in wartime, were no doubt reclaimed to be used elsewhere.

Viereck commissioned an article for *The Fatherland* by an alleged marine engineer named Koester, who went to absurd lengths to prove that *Lusitania* was a warship and thus a legitimate target. He described the liner, when armed with twelve 6in guns, as being as formidable a warship as any dreadnought. In May 1915 the Royal Navy had in service twenty-four dreadnoughts and ten battlecruisers, all with primary armament of 12in guns or more. Koester alleged that the guns had been concealed below deck or in the coal bunkers and could be brought out once the liner was at sea. A 6in gun with its mounting and shield weighs several tons and is too large to be easily concealed even on a spacious liner like *Lusitania*. Nor could these guns possibly be manhandled into position on their designated mountings on the forecastle and shelter deck let alone brought up several decks from the holds. In practice, 6in guns could only have been installed when the liner was in dockyard hands with the use of cranes and would in any case have required calibration before they could be used.[10]

It has often been argued that, even if the guns were never installed, they had been concealed in *Lusitania*'s holds and that her transversal coal bunker, immediately ahead of No 1 boiler room, had been converted into a magazine. Chronology does not support this supposition. It will be remembered that *Lusitania* returned to Liverpool on the completion of voyage 92 on 11 August 1914. On the same day the Admiralty decided that they did not require the two large Cunarders as armed merchant cruisers. Although the Admiralty files in the PRO do not record what further use was found for the guns, which had been earmarked for the vessels if they had been converted, it would have made no sense, particularly in wartime, to have stored these badly needed weapons in the liner's holds. Apart from any other consideration they would have taken up considerable cargo space which was urgently required for the transport of war supplies.

Reports have periodically surfaced, including one in a *Times* leader in August 1990, of Admiralty dives on *Lusitania* after the Second World War with the alleged objective of recovering these fictional guns or, alternatively, explosives from the holds. John

Light, the American who made nearly forty dives on her wreck in the 1960s, which he bought from the War Risks Association for £1,000 in 1967, discovered steel cables lying near the wreck which he assumed had been left by an earlier salvage effort. On one dive he found an object which he took to be a gun. Light was an accomplished diver but in examining the liner's port side which lies some 230 feet below sea level, he was working almost at the limits of endurance in conditions of extremely poor visibility. The object might as easily have been a hollow spar.

As recently as October 1997, a former chief salvage officer of the US Navy told a seminar that a British ship, allegedly owned by the specialist marine recovery firm of Risdon Beazley, had been stationed over the wreck for two weeks in the 1950s and that the guns had been removed during that dive. It is difficult to conceive that after forty years the Admiralty would have spent scarce budgetary resources on the expensive process of recovering guns or explosives from the wreck.

Risdon Beazley was a recognised leader in the recovery of non-ferrous metals from wrecks and after two world wars the waters off the south of Ireland were clearly a happy hunting ground. In 1955, their recovery ship, *Droxford*, was based at Cobh and habitually calibrated its underwater search equipment, such as sonar and echo sounders, on the wreck of *Lusitania*. Its position was known with complete accuracy and was close to *Droxford's* usual westward course out of Cobh. As the ship would have been stationary over the site of the wreck for some period of time, it is not surprising that local fishermen or observers ashore would have concluded that it was engaged in a diving operation. In his book *Wealth from the Sea*, Alan Crothall, a retired managing director of Risdon Beazley, is emphatic:

> It is true that the ill-fated ship carried small quantities of copper and brass amongst her cargo but they were not considered worthy of recovery by Risdon Beazley. In view of some later highly imaginative accounts of Beazley's having put a grab into the cargo and 'entirely cleaning it out, leaving grab tooth marks on the bulkheads', I am glad to . . . state that Beazley's never put any moorings down around the wreck, or interfered with it in any way.[11]

A former Risdon Beazley executive has confirmed that any attempt to remove cargo from the liner's holds, using then available technology, would have left a large access hole in her hull.[12] This would have been clearly visible when Dr Robert Ballard inspected the wreck with both manned and unmanned submarines in 1993. He found no evidence of any such hole.

The German propaganda machine went to considerable lengths to suppress any evidence which might contradict their claim that the liner was armed. Morris Spiers, the owner of the newsreel company, whose film of *Lusitania*'s departure from New York was being widely shown after the sinking, was visited by a German national, presumably an undercover agent, who offered to buy the negative of the film from him. Suspecting that the purchaser intended to destroy the negative as it conclusively proved that the liner was unarmed, Spiers declined the offer and invited the British consul-general in Philadelphia to view the film. The consul reported to the embassy in Washington that he and Captain Gaunt had seen the film, which showed a clear picture of *Lusitania*'s decks and that there was no sign of any guns.[13]

At the instigation of German agents, a number of affidavits were filed in New York declaring that the liner had been carrying guns on her last voyage. One complainant was a gullible clergyman named Brueckner, who alleged that he had seen *Lusitania*'s guns from a ferryboat.[14] Other affidavits protested that the manifests had been faked. These allegations questioned the consignment of furs and asserted that a quantity of acid for the production of explosives had been concealed under false documentation. One complainant, Gustav Stahl, testified that he had helped a steward named Leach, who was lost in the disaster, bring his luggage on board *Lusitania* on the evening before she sailed and had noticed four guns, two mounted forward and two more aft. Stahl, who had probably been bribed into making this statement, was a stooge of the HAPAG security manager and undercover agent, Paul Koenig, who conveniently disappeared when Stahl was indicted for perjury. Interestingly, two months earlier, another HAPAG manager, Buenz, had been one of five men indicted for producing false manifests for four neutral ships which were being provisioned the previous August to supply the cruiser *Karlsruhe* and the armed liner *Kaiser Wilhelm Der Grosse*. Dudley Field Malone produced a statement sworn by fifty witnesses testifying that there had been no guns aboard. Faced with this evidence, Stahl pleaded guilty and was sentenced to eighteen months imprisonment.

One of the most persistent of the legends of *Lusitania* was that she was sunk by an explosion of the ammunition in her cargo. This legend, like that of the guns, and for similar reasons, had been created by German propagandists and has been equally long-lived. With the benefit of modern technology, it can now be disregarded. In February 1924, Sir William Graham Greene wrote to his successor at the Admiralty, Sir Oswyn Murray. His letter was prompted by an article in an undergraduate magazine, the *Oxford Outlook*, which was then edited by his nephew Graham, the future novelist. The article, written by one Bernard Causton, with a strongly pro-German bias, had quoted Dudley Field Malone as telling *The Times* in December 1922 that *Lusitania* had been carrying 5,400 cases of ammunition. Greene told Murray that the author was clearly arguing that the presence of such cargo justified the sinking. In a strange piece of reasoning, since Germany had already introduced unrestricted submarine warfare, Greene added that as the cargo had not been explosive, it could have been carried without justifying the risk of hostile attack. He asked Murray to confirm the facts about the war supplies in the liner's cargo to assist him in writing a letter of rebuttal to the *Outlook*.

Murray's reply indicated a subtle difference of opinion with his predecessor. He quoted from the official naval historian, Sir Julian Corbett:

> The Germans maintain that only one torpedo was fired and that the second explosion was due to a consignment of explosives. If this was so she [*Lusitania*] would of course have been blown to pieces . . . in fact she carried no ammunition except 5,500 cases of rifle cartridges and shrapnel of a total weight of only 173 tons. *They were stowed right forward where a torpedo hitting amidships could not have affected them* . . . the Germans . . . did attempt . . . to argue that the ship would not have sunk so fast had this ammunition not, as they alleged, exploded.

Murray expressed the current Admiralty view that '. . . it is better to let sleeping dogs lie'.[15] This opaque answer implies that the Admiralty had, quite reasonably, no desire to renew the controversy over the loss of the mighty ship or to draw any further attention to their part in the tragedy or their rather questionable conduct after the event.

Greene contented himself with writing to his nephew, pointing out that the only ammunition being carried was rifle cartridges which he again argued did not justify the sinking. The younger Greene revealed this correspondence in a letter to *The Times* nearly fifty years later, after the publication of Colin Simpson's book, *Lusitania,* and a BBC programme had rekindled public interest in the loss of the liner.[16] The Admiralty's preference for secrecy, all too typical of British government departments, had an unfortunate effect. It perpetuated the legend that *Lusitania* had been destroyed by the explosion of her cargo for almost seventy years until Dr Robert Ballard made the first detailed examination of the wreck in 1993. He himself had been influenced by the legend and fully expected to find evidence of an explosion in the area of the cargo holds. To his surprise he could detect none and concluded that her loss was due to other causes.

The apologists in the New York press made other allegations of British misuse of merchant shipping, which on closer examination proved to be false. They charged that *U-29*, commanded by Kapitanleutnant Otto Weddigen, had been sunk by a decoy ship. Weddigen, who had torpedoed HMS *Aboukir* and her sister-ships in September 1914, had been the first U-boat commander to demonstrate the submarine's offensive potential and had become a hero to many Germans. *U-29* had, in fact, been rammed and sunk by HMS *Dreadnought*, Jacky Fisher's pioneer all-big-gun battleship. Both sides used decoys during the war as Germany had from the outset and the Kriegsmarine had shown no hesitation in painting merchant ships in Allied colours. In June 1914, Stanley Goodall, the future Director of Naval Construction, was a member of a group from the Admiralty, who were invited on board the HAPAG cruise liner *Konigin Luise* at Southampton to inspect a new hydraulic propulsion system. Goodall's keen eye noticed the heavy duty sponsons fitted to the liner's boat deck. He decided that the only possible use for these sponsons was to lay mines and that by implication Germany was actively planning for war.[17] His presentiment was correct. *Konigin Luise*, painted in the house colours of the Great Eastern Railway, was detected laying mines off Harwich and was sunk by the destroyer HMS *Lance* on the second night of the war. The armed merchant cruiser *Cap Trafalgar* had similarly been painted in Cunard colours at the time of her duel with *Carmania*.

On one occasion the Kriegsmarine descended to what could reasonably be called piracy. On 28 March 1915 Captain Charles Fryatt of the Great Eastern Railway ferry *Brussels* made a sharp turn towards *U-33* off the Dutch coast forcing the submarine to dive. Fryatt was following an Admiralty directive but the Germans never forgave him. In June 1916 two German destroyers ambushed *Brussels* and escorted her into Zeebrugge. Fryatt was court-martialled as a *franc-tireur*, a civilian who had committed a hostile action against the German armed forces. Despite a torrent of neutral criticism, led by Gerard, who demanded that he be accorded legal representation, Fryatt was shot. Notwithstanding the rebuff to his ambassador and the evidence that the execution had been ordered at top level in the Admiralstab, Wilson seems to have been much less annoyed by this incident than he had been over HMS *Baralong*.[18]

The first German note to Washington and the editorial in the *Kolnische Volkszeitung* reiterated another constant theme: the starvation of German children due to lack of food caused by the allied blockade justified the drowning of American children aboard *Lusitania*. As a well-argued editorial in the *New York Times* pointed out, blockade was a recognised method of warfare. An instruction signed by Lincoln during the Civil War expressly stated: 'War is not carried on by arms alone. It is lawful to starve a hostile belligerent, armed or unarmed, so that it leads to the speedier subjection of the enemy.' Bismarck had expressed a similar view. This allegation is dishonest as in the spring of 1915 there was little shortage of food in Germany, let alone any deaths by starvation. Nevertheless, German propagandists have repeated the fallacy that during the war 750,000 Germans died from starvation so relentlessly that this figure has become widely accepted, even by some British and American historians. A recent and more objective view concludes that: 'British naval strategy failed to starve German citizens into submission.'[19] The accusation is in any case sanctimonious as Imperial Germany abandoned any responsibility for feeding the civilian populations of occupied Belgium and Northern France to the international relief committees set up by Herbert Hoover and other humanitarians.

In his well-argued book *The First World War, An Agrarian Assessment*, Dr Avner Offer, a leading authority on the effects of the blockade, quoted a study in Munich in February 1915 which found that calorie intake was still at prewar levels. He discovered that the incidence for infant mortality in Germany, expressed as deaths per 1,000 children aged under a year, was marginally less in 1915 than in 1913, the last full year of peace.[20] Gerard mentioned the efforts of the *Frauendienst*, the service for women, a volunteer body, set up in Berlin on the first day of the war, which taught women how to cook without milk, eggs or fat and ensured that the children got a daily milk ration. He credited the *Frauendienst* with actually reducing the infant mortality rate in the city between 1914 and 1916. In the summer of 1916 the indefatigable Gerard and his wife took a weekend break at the Baltic resort of Heringsdorf. He noticed that the local hotels were still offering their guests four meals every day and were providing them with large sandwiches to eat on the beach if pangs of hunger overtook them between meals. When Gerard left Germany in February 1917 he concluded that the Allies were in far greater danger of starvation than the Germans.[21]

Shortages of food did not become noticeable until the winter of 1915/16 when the first food riots occurred and did not become really acute until the so-called 'turnip-winter' of 1916/17 which followed that year's harvest which had been poor throughout the world. Offer traced the letters of Ethel Cooper, a self-reliant and outspoken Australian music-teacher, who lived in Leipzig throughout the war, and which convey a vivid impression of urban life in wartime Germany. In September 1918 she wrote:

> Most people complain of being under-nourished – probably the average German, accustomed to very fatty food and much beer, feels the change more than I do . . . it is deadly monotonous but I can't say that I feel under-fed – I am certainly always hungry but I never felt better or fitter in my life, and I can't understand why so few people seem able to adapt themselves to the same regime.[22]

Dr Offer concludes that the German people were often cold and hungry. But, whatever their complaints, they did not starve either in May 1915 or later.

The second German note of 28 May asserted that *Lusitania* was carrying a large detachment of Canadian troops. This charge was presumably based on the anomaly that her passenger list included 345 Canadians, or more precisely, 345 people who had addresses in Canada. Until 1947 there was no separate Canadian citizenship and Canadians travelled abroad on British passports. In Mersey's report the total of British and Canadian passengers were thus listed together.

When Mersey recalled Captain Turner to the witness stand on 1 July 1915 and asked him whether any Canadian troops had been aboard *Lusitania*, he replied forthrightly in the negative. Despite the categorical denials made at the time, this allegation will not die. As late as October 1972, the author Colin Simpson wrote in a letter to *The Times* that the liner was carrying a draft from the 6th Winnipeg Rifles.[23] Although he did not mention the charge in his book *Lusitania*, published in the same year, he had noted Judge Mayer's somewhat premature reaction 'Good, now that story is forever disposed of' when the lawyers in the liability case decided to drop this allegation.

Many of the Canadian passengers were married couples and others, like Mrs Stephens, were accompanied by servants. The Department of National Defence in Ottawa investigated Simpson's accusation in detail, focussing on the 104 unaccompanied males on the passenger list with Canadian points of origin. Twenty-nine of these came from Toronto, eighteen from Montreal and only twelve from Winnipeg – not large enough to make up a draft. One passenger with a Winnipeg point of origin was travelling in saloon and the other eleven in second cabin. As officers were entitled to saloon, warrant officers and sergeants to second cabin and corporals and privates were placed in third class, a draft of this composition might be described as 'all chiefs and no Indians' and makes little military sense.

Fifty-three of these 104 passengers were lost in the disaster. None of their names appear in the official list of the Canadian war dead.[24] The evidence is persuasive that no draft of Canadian troops was aboard *Lusitania* on her last voyage. The suggestion that a body of troops in uniform could have been sent to New York by train and then transferred from the rail terminal to the Cunard pier without the federal agents, the police or the press, who were present in considerable numbers at the pier, noticing is totally implausible. As Berlin well knew, Canadian units sailed directly to Europe from Halifax or Montreal on British troopships. Washington, careful to maintain the appearance of neutrality, did not permit Canadian military forces to enter, let alone pass through, American territory. In November 1915, citing humanitarian reasons, Spring-Rice asked that wounded Canadian troops, who had been landed at Halifax, might be transported by the more direct rail link to Montreal and Toronto which passed through Maine. Lansing turned him down sharply.[25]

*   *   *

After the sinking, a Munich goldsmith, Karl Goetz, produced a medal celebrating Schwieger's achievement. Under an inscription 'No Contraband' the obverse side of the medal shows the liner sinking, guns clearly visible on her deck, over a further inscription: 'The liner *Lusitania* sunk by a German submarine

May 5 1915.' The message on the reverse was even more shame-less. Under the legend 'Business above all' passengers were shown lining up to buy tickets at a Cunard booking office manned by a skeleton. They were depicted as ignoring a man reading a newspaper with a banner headline 'U Boat danger' and a top-hatted Bernstorff, shaking a warning finger. The implica-tion was clear – the passengers who had died had only themselves to blame.

Goetz was a well-known creator of medals and a Dutch dealer featured his *Lusitania* medal in his catalogue. By mid-1916 British Naval Intelligence had discovered its existence and the astute Captain Hall quickly grasped its potential as a propaganda weapon. Goetz's treatment had been both heavy-handed and satirical and his mistake in bringing forward the date of the sink-ing by two days enabled Hall to claim that it had been planned in advance. At Hall's request, Gordon Selfridge, the owner of the London department store, reproduced 300,000 copies of Goetze's medal, which were widely distributed in neutral coun-tries, particularly in Norway and Sweden, to demonstrate German indifference to the loss of life. The British copies were sold in a presentation box costing a shilling for the benefit of war charities, which showed the mighty ship steaming at speed with an inscription that she had been sunk on her return journey from the United States by a German submarine. A powerful message inside the box read:

> An exact replica of the medal which was designed in Germany and distributed to commemorate the sinking . . . This indicates the true feeling the War Lords endeavour to stimulate and is proof positive that such crimes are not only regarded favourably but are given every encouragement in the land of Kultur.

An accompanying leaflet, headed a 'German Naval Victory', quoting the damning phrase from the *Kolnische Volkzeitung* edi-torial 'With joyful pride we contemplate this latest deed of our Navy' pointedly concluded that 'This picture seeks apparently to propound the theory that if a murderer warns a victim of his intention, the guilt of the crime will rest with the victim and not with the murderer'.

Although Goetz's medal had been purely a private venture, Allied propaganda successfully portrayed it as an official German project. Speaking in November 1916, Arthur Balfour strongly attacked the Kriegsmarine's war on commerce. He contrasted the high-minded proposals for conducting war at sea which Germany had presented at the 1909 Hague Conference with repeated examples of their wartime frightfulness including the recent sinking of a Norwegian merchant ship. Balfour ended with a ringing peroration: 'What are we to make of a nation which makes such a speech . . . at an assembly . . . considering international law and a few years afterwards strikes a medal for sinking the *Lusitania*.'[26]

Vivid posters of the sinking liner were rushed out with captions in bold print such as 'Lest We Forget'. The best known of these 'Take up the Sword of Justice' was produced by the illustrator and *Punch* cartoonist Bernard Partridge. Justice was depicted as an Amazonian figure rising from the sea brandishing her sword as the mighty ship sinks in the background while survivors can be seen fighting for their lives alongside corpses floating on the waves. In another effort, the Kaiser was satirised as a ferocious pirate complete with top hat and cloaked in skull and crossbones. In a widely publicised but inaccurate allegation British propaganda asserted that the Kaiser had ordered a school holiday to commemorate the sinking, thus subtly suggesting that he had encouraged German schoolchildren to celebrate the deaths of ninety-four of their British, American and Canadian contemporaries from drowning or hypothermia.

Partridge's poster had some success in boosting army recruitment and in inflaming the animosity that British troops on the Western Front felt towards the Germans. While the legend that whole battalions went into battle shouting 'Avenge the *Lusitania*' is probably unfounded, retribution for acts of German frightfulness was sometimes extracted. One British soldier recalled: '. . . we killed in cold blood because it was our duty to kill as much as we could. I thought many a time of the *Lusitania*. I had actually prayed for that day [of revenge] and when I got it, I killed just as much as I hoped fate would allow me to kill.'[27]

*   *   *

The British had one great advantage in the propaganda war. As a recent historian of the First World War noted:

> . . . when based on truth as in the case of the Belgian atrocities and the sinking of *Lusitania* Allied propaganda was effective in bolstering the will to fight. They were able to make a powerful appeal to the strong humanitarian instincts at home and in Allied and neutral

countries, publishing graphic details of the tragedy and the experiences of survivors in print and in picture.[28]

Cunard was fast off the mark. One of their employees, H S Taylor wrote of:

> ... the sinking of the *Lusitania* ... at which time I was with the Cunard ... Freight Department in Rumford Street, Liverpool, round the corner from the main office in Water Street. On the day following the disaster the basement of a building in Rumford Street had been converted for the purpose of displaying press type photos of the bodies of passengers (and crew) lying on the shore where they had come to rest as the tides receded. One I particularly remember was of a young mother still holding a baby in each arm but many of the photographs were too horrible for words. Each incoming tide floated in a further pathetic quota ...[29]

In contrast, the German propaganda effort throughout the war was crude and ill-directed. In the aftermath of the torpedoing of the liner its allegations could all too easily disproved. They strangely failed to concentrate sufficiently on the weakest point in the British case: that *Lusitania* was carrying both passengers and war supplies. German inability to perceive that morally they were in the wrong and that they had thoroughly alienated public opinion in the United States and other neutral countries prevented them from taking the alternative course of damage control. An admission that Germany had erred in sinking the liner and an assurance that passenger ships would not be attacked in future could have regained much of the moral ground lost. Such an approach would even have provided Berlin with some leverage in negotiating with Wilson and Lansing. German arrogance after the sinking of *Lusitania* and the ill-advised executions of Edith Cavell and Captain Fryatt handed the Allies an easy victory in the public relations war. The German propagandists never seem to have understood that the British held the trump cards – the powerful and highly emotive image of women and children fighting for their lives in the unfriendly waters of the Irish Sea and the scenes of horror in the Queenstown mortuaries so vividly recorded in *The Times*. As Churchill wrote in 1937: 'The poor babies who perished in the ocean struck a blow at the German power more deadly than could have been achieved by the sacrifice of a hundred thousand fighting men.'[30]

Two myths require special scrutiny. Was the liner's loss due to a conspiracy? The sinking of *Lusitania* is widely believed to have led directly to the American declaration of war in April 1917. These myths are examined in detail in the chapters *Conspiracy?* and *America Goes to War.*

CHAPTER 15

Conspiracy?

A thoughtful article recently appeared in the editorial pages of the *Wall Street Journal,* discussing the apparently inexorable rise of the conspiracty theory, concluded that: 'Conspiracy is now routinely invoked to explain events across the political and cultural spectrum . . . Conspiracy has even acquired a certain cachet.' Its author, Eric Gibson, specifically mentioned death and destruction.[1] It is hardly surprising that the destruction of a famous liner in dramatic and unprecedented circumstances with heavy loss of life attracted the attention of conspiracy theorists. The first of these theories emerged within the Admiralty itself and briefly attracted the support of Churchill and Fisher. Both men endorsed the Webb report's submission that German-American employees inside Cunard's New York office might have leaked details of *Lusitania*'s course to German agents in the city. As we have noted, this supposition was so unlikely that it was speedily discarded.

A more serious allegation, which has often been repeated over the years, has its origin in the Admiralty's perceived lack of action, notably the failure to provide a destroyer escort, in the forty-eight hours before Lusitania's sinking. The conspiracy advocates have inaccurately asserted that Churchill, aware that *U-20* was operating directly in the liner's course, had deliberately exposed her to submarine attack. They have maintained that his objective was to inflame American public opinion, furious at the loss of American life, into demanding war with Germany. Several commentators have asserted that the cruiser HMS *Juno* had been earmarked to act as an anti-submarine escort to the liner as she steamed along the south coast of Ireland, and had been withdrawn on Admiralty instructions, thus exposing the latter to submarine attack. There is no evidence to support this assertion. Rear-Admiral Hood, commanding the 11th Cruiser Squadron at Queenstown, is on record as having reported to the War Staff that *Juno* and the other ships in his Squadron were totally unsuited for use in an anti-submarine role. *Juno* was twenty-two years old in 1915 and her top speed of 19 knots was achievable, if at all, only for a very short period, due to the age and deterioration of her machinery. She would have had great difficulty in keeping up with *Lusitania* even at the latter's reduced speed of 18 knots and none at all at the liner's normal wartime cruising speed of 21 knots.[2]

Politicians who, like Churchill, habitually adopt a high profile are extremely susceptible to attack by conspiracy theorists. Unfounded allegations of conspiracy have been made against, amongst others, Franklin D Roosevelt over Pearl Harbor, and Harold Macmillan over the forced repatriation of the Cossacks and anti-communist Yugoslavs to Stalin and Tito in 1945. Fortunately, such theories almost invariably unravel when subjected to logical analysis and convincing arguments to the contrary can generally be mustered.

The opportunist element in Churchill's character and his fascination with, and deep involvement in, the sometimes murky world of secret intelligence attracted repeated accusations of conspiracy throughout his long career. During the Second World War he was accused of having suppressed his prior knowledge of the Luftwaffe's large-scale bombing attack on Coventry in November 1940 to preserve the secrets of Ultra, the British ability to read the German codes, and of having failed to pass on intelligence of the Japanese attack on Pearl Harbor. These allegations can both be convincingly rebutted.

Churchill was a determined man who was quite capable of taking ruthless action to protect the national interest in time of war. In July 1940 he ordered the destruction of the French Fleet at Mers-el-Kebir in Algeria to prevent it falling into German hands. This action, which resulted in considerable loss of life, was reported to Parliament and the press at the time and Churchill recorded the incident in his *The Second World War*.[3] Moreover, there is a considerable difference between Churchill's position as Prime Minister with absolute authority over defence strategy in the Second World War and his standing in the early months of the First World War when he was merely a member of a group of senior cabinet ministers co-ordinating the war effort and was directly responsible only for the Admiralty. Some theorists have argued that as one of his overriding intentions as Prime Minister in 1940/41 was 'to drag the Americans into the war' he was pursuing a similar objective in 1915.

The allegations of conspiracy have been pursued by several authors including Patrick Beesly, the historian of British Naval

Intelligence in the First World War. (Beesly was a cousin of the unfortunate Paul Crompton, who was lost on *Lusitania* with all his family.) They were strongly implied in an American television documentary shown as recently as the spring of 1997. The accusation of conspiracy against Churchill in the case of *Lusitania* is based on a letter he wrote to his cabinet colleague, Walter Runciman, President of the Board of Trade, on 12 February 1915. The letter reads in full:

> My Dear Walter,
> It is most important to attract neutral shipping to our shores in the hope especially of embroiling the United States with Germany. The German formal announcement of indiscriminate submarining has been made to the United States to produce a deterrent effect upon traffic. For our part, we want the traffic – the more the better and if some of it gets into trouble, better still. Therefore please furbish up at once your insurance offer to neutrals trading with us after February 18th. (The more that come the greater our safety and the German embarrassment). Please act promptly so that the announcement may synchronise with our impending policy.[4]

Conspiracy theorists usually construe the first sentence of this letter as indicating Churchill's intention of forcing America into the war at an early date. A more careful reading would suggest that he merely sought to 'embroil' America in a diplomatic or commercial impasse with Germany. Such a dispute would have intensified pro-Allied sentiment in America and thus have safeguarded the important munitions purchasing programme.

It is improbable, to say the least, that Churchill, or anyone else in a position of authority in the Admiralty, would purposely hazard a valuable ship like *Lusitania* on which they held a lien. At December 1914, some £1.7 million of the original construction loan of £2.6 million remained unpaid and the Admiralty was, in effect, the liner's owner of last resort. She was carrying a cargo of ammunition and other components and machinery urgently required for the war effort. The conspiracy theorists conveniently overlook the fact that Churchill had left the Admiralty to travel to Paris on official business several hours before Schwieger had announced his presence off the south coast of Ireland by sinking *Earl of Lathom.* His actions on and immediately after 7 May do not suggest that he was the mastermind behind a conspiracy to engineer *Lusitania*'s destruction. Had he been so involved, he would surely have returned post haste to London on hearing the news of her sinking to actively direct the next stage of the alleged plan

– luring America into the war. Instead, he lingered in France for three days.

Although Fisher's mental condition was fast declining, it is difficult to envisage him taking part in a plan to abandon *Lusitania* to her fate. In any case Churchill and Fisher were barely on speaking terms and it is absurd to suggest that the two men could have conspired together on any subject. By mid-May 1915 Fisher's antipathy to Churchill had become paranoid and he would have had no hesitation whatsoever in leaking the details of a conspiracy to abandon *Lusitania* had one existed. He had at least two opportunities to reveal a conspiracy. First, he wrote to Asquith on 13 May in terms bitterly critical of Churchill. Secondly, two days later, he leaked the news of his dispute with Churchill and his subsequent resignation to Bonar Law, thus precipitating the crisis which led to the change of government. On neither occasion did he mention any conspiracy. It is even more difficult to imagine admirals of the stature of Arthur Wilson or Henry Oliver or the operations staff in the Admiralty taking part in such a scheme. Too many officers would have known of it and it is worth noting that a secret shared is too often a secret lost. The Sea Lords would surely have threatened to resign en masse if it had been suggested to them. Churchill was in no position to direct a conspiracy without the connivance of Asquith and Grey and it is impossible to conceive that either man would have had any part in it. Evidence suggests that Churchill and his cabinet colleagues were perfectly content that the United States should stay neutral and continue to finance and supply the war effort on a major scale. As the perceptive Washington correspondent of the *Morning Post* wrote: 'The United States is physically unable to make war. She cannot send an army to Europe. It is true she might send her fleet to join those of the allies, but public opinion would in all probability oppose the Navy leaving the American coast defenceless.'[5] It was only later in 1915, well after the sinking of *Lusitania,* that Wilson sent proposals for increasing military and naval readiness to Congress.

A further argument can be adduced in Churchill's favour. His mother was American and, unlike most British politicians, he had visited America and had many highly-placed American friends. With his considerable intellectual curiosity, he would undoubtedly have known that the Constitution had granted the prerogative of declaring war to Congress. He would have appreciated that in May 1915 there were not enough votes, particularly in the Senate, elected on a geographical basis, to have sustained a declaration of war on Germany. Interviewed by Sir Ludovic Kennedy in 1982, the naval historian Stephen Roskill, who was by no means uncritical of Churchill, totally rejected the conjecture that he could have acted so ruthlessly as to purposely allow *Lusitania* to steam into danger.[6] David Stafford, author of the work *Churchill And Secret Service*, an acclaimed history of his long involvement in the world of intelligence and clandestine operations, dismisses the theory tersely: 'Churchill was not the mainspring of a conspiracy to sink the *Lusitania* since none existed.'[7] John Charmley, Churchill's most hostile biographer, who is highly critical of his performance at the Admiralty in 1914/15, does not even mention *Lusitania*.

A more realistic explanation is that the over-centralised and ineffective staff system inside the Admiralty had simply become overwhelmed by the exigencies of the first large-scale war at sea in a century, whose implications the War Staff, like most naval officers in both Britain and Germany, did not then fully understand. In his 1982 interview, Roskill was pressed to explain the Admiralty's omissions. He cited: '. . . bad control of merchant shipping, because we hadn't learnt how to do it . . . bad use of intelligence as regards merchant ships . . . inefficiencies and excessive secrecies in all parts of the Admiralty.'[8] We will examine his conclusion in the chapters *The Reasons Why*. Yet the accusations of conspiracy will not die down and can be fanned to life at any time. It is difficult to disagree with the thoughtful *Times* leader in August 1990, which concluded that: 'The British Government should lay to rest the many ghosts which haunt this tragedy by making a comprehensive statement of the facts.'[9]

CHAPTER 16

Post Mortem

*T*itanic and *Lusitania*, wrecked within three years of each other, are firmly linked in popular perception. In reality, the losses are not comparable, the effect of hitting an iceberg being rather different from that of being struck by a torpedo. *Titanic* was a passenger liner of conventional design, subdivided into a number of watertight sections by transverse bulkheads, which extended high enough to enable the vessel to stay afloat if three compartments were to be flooded. After she had collided with the iceberg, her naval architect, Thomas Andrews, discovered that she had been holed in five compartments and told her captain, E J Smith, that the unfortunate liner was doomed. She sank bow first as the water level slowly rose over the tops of successive bulkheads to flood the next compartment astern. She remained on an even keel, allowing both port and starboard side lifeboats to be launched.

The 1994 exploration of the wreck by the French institution IFREMER tends to confirm a thesis originally put forward at the Mersey inquiry into the loss of *Titanic* by Edward Wilding, Thomas Andrews's deputy. Wilding concluded that the damage inflicted by the iceberg as it bumped down the liner's side consisted of a number of small gashes. The IFREMER research confirmed that the gashes amounted in all to twelve square feet. The incursion of sea water was relatively slow and its depth in the bilges increased slowly enough to enable the engineers to reduce pressure and thus avert the threat of a boiler explosion. Power was maintained until the last boiler room flooded. During his submarine exploration, Dr Ballard sighted several boilers lying intact on the sea-bed, near the wreck, confirming that they did not explode.

The circumstances in which *Lusitania* was lost bear some resemblance to the torpedoing, in the early months of the war, of the old cruisers, HMS *Aboukir, Hogue* and *Cressy* and the pre-dreadnought battleships HMS *Formidable* and *Goliath*. These warships had all been designed in the late 1890s before there was any predictable risk of a submarine-delivered torpedo attack. Unlike

Lusitania, their engine rooms and, in some cases, their boiler rooms had centreline bulkheads. They also had longitudinal bulkheads, similar to those on the liner, outboard of the machinery spaces and adjacent to the ships' sides, which formed coal bunkers. A combination of these design features, which was usual in British warships of that period, proved highly vulnerable to torpedo attack and consequent asymmetrical flooding. In each case the stricken ship immediately developed a pronounced list and became unstable, foundering in a relatively short time with heavy loss of life. In percentage terms the loss of life on *Formidable,* only 233 of whose crew of 780 survived, and on *Goliath* was actually higher than on *Lusitania.* Admittedly, *Formidable* was sunk in rough weather but *Goliath* was torpedoed at anchor in lee of the Turkish coast.

Unlike *Titanic, Lusitania* had been primarily designed for speed and could be rapidly converted into an armed merchant cruiser. As ship design inevitably results in compromise, her naval architect, Leonard Peskett, was faced with a particularly difficult task in accommodating the Admiralty's requirements. As the submarine did not constitute a major factor in naval warfare at the time *Lusitania* was being designed between 1903 and 1905, neither the Admiralty nor Peskett can be blamed for their failure to anticipate its implications. The Admiralty had specified the use of high-tensile steel amidships above the lower deck in what it held to be the area of highest vulnerability to gunfire. Mild steel, as normally specified for passenger liners, was used below the waterline where the probability of damage was not then thought to be high.

Although earlier authors have generally ascribed *Lusitania*'s loss to the second explosion, current opinion suggests convincingly that the effect on the liner's stability resulting from the impact of Schwieger's torpedo was by itself sufficiently lethal to ensure her destruction. The second explosion is thus probably much less significant than has often been assumed. Although state-of-the-art underwater camera and computer technology, enabling detailed forensic examination of shipwrecks, is now available, the mounting of such an expedition is extremely expensive, well beyond the resources even of wealthy individuals. The IFREMER dive on *Titanic* was directly funded by the French Government whose objective was to further the development of the commercial and defence applications of the technology. Mr Gregg Bemis, the present owner of the wreck of *Lusitania,* has so far failed to secure the funding for a similar expedition. Even if a forensic examination of the interior of *Lusitania* is eventually undertaken, it is doubtful whether a survey of the starboard side of No 1 boiler room would be practicable as it is underneath the rest of the hull, due to the attitude of the ship as it lies on the seabed. In 1993 Dr Robert Ballard explored the wreck with his mini-submarine *Delta* and three remote-controlled vehicles which enabled his team to undertake a detailed underwater survey of her exterior, significantly advancing our knowledge of what occurred on that fateful May afternoon. However, he did not have access to the technology used by IFREMER and thus could not inspect her interior. In the absence of forensic inspection of the liner's boiler rooms, along the lines used by IFREMER on the wreck of *Titanic*, the enigma of what caused the second explosion may never be solved. The conclusions reached below are therefore unconfirmed and subject to the caveat that future exploration and research may render them erroneous.

Many commentators have been intrigued that *Lusitania* succumbed to a single torpedo when, on the previous day, Schwieger had been forced to use gunfire to sink *Candidate* and a second torpedo to finish off *Centurion*, which had both remained obstinately afloat after he had attacked them. He had been playing cat-and-mouse with the cargo liners in the fog and thus he had to take the best shot he could. It is possible that they flooded across the hull and that their holds might have been small enough for the resultant damage from a single torpedo to have been insufficient for them to have sunk quickly. Schwieger could not afford to hang around in the hope they would eventually go down and thus sank *Candidate* by gunfire to make sure that he had destroyed his prey. On the following day the weather was fine and he was able to lie in wait for *Lusitania* and take the favoured flank shot at a 90 degree angle, giving him the optimum chance for a successful hit. Schwieger was a cautious man, who was sceptical about the effectiveness of his torpedoes. Even in the Second World War, the magnetic and contact pistols on German torpedoes were unreliable and it was only when the Kriegsmarine captured a British torpedo and copied its pistol design that the German torpedo became a dependable weapon. With his experience of sinking much smaller ships on the day before clear in his mind, he intended to take no chances in attacking such a prime target, knowing the prestige that a successful strike on a large ship would earn for him and his crew. To this end, he set his torpedo to run shallow to ensure that it did not miss by passing under the liner's hull.

Schwieger, watching through his periscope, saw the torpedo strike the liner on her starboard side abaft the bridge. He noted two almost instantaneous explosions, the second of which produced the dramatic plume of smoke, coal dust and water which towered high above the bridge. By deduction from Schwieger's account, the torpedo clearly struck in No 1 Boiler Room but as the liner rests leaning over to starboard, the exact point of impact cannot be accurately identified. The authors of *Titanic and Lusitania, a Final Forensic Analysis*, a paper published by the Society of Naval Architects and Marine Engineers (SNAME), made a comprehensive study of the sinking of both liners.[1] They suggested that the explosion of the torpedo opened up a substantial hole in *Lusitania*'s side, possibly as large as twenty foot long by ten foot high or an area of about 200 square feet through which water could flow and if the warhead had detonated on impact with the hull plating that its force would have penetrated at least ten feet into the hull. Any delay in the warhead exploding would have greatly increased the extent of damage within the ship. The SNAME paper concluded that the explosion of the torpedo seriously damaged the longitudinal bulkhead between the coal bunkers and No 1 and No 2 boiler rooms. Even if these bulkheads had withstood the force of detonation of the warhead, the influx of water would have rapidly spread to the boiler room through the large coal handling doors which were cut in them. As the surviving fireman from No 1 boiler room, Thomas Madden, pointed out to the Mersey inquiry these doors had to be kept open to maintain the supply of coal to the boilers. Several of them would have been open at the time the torpedo struck.

Schwieger ascribed the cause of the second detonation to an explosion either in the boiler room or of the coal dust in the bunkers or of the cargo. When Dr Ballard explored the wreck, he found no evidence of any blast hole in the area of the cargo hold. He deduced that the distance between the hold and the torpedo's point of impact was too great to have touched off a detonation. *Lusitania*'s one transverse bunker, forty feet deep, lay between No 1 boiler room and the cargo hold. The SNAME paper reaches a similar conclusion. Although suspicion has fallen on certain items listed in the manifest, notably the furs and the oysters, we have no definite knowledge that explosive guncotton or tetrachloride were being carried as was alleged at the time. In any case, with the possible exception of the aluminium powder, there do not appear to have been any readily explosive items in the cargo.

An explosion of the aluminium powder is theoretically possible, given the metal's propensity to oxidise and catch fire. The theory that an explosion of the aluminium powder in the cargo hold could have caused the loss of the liner has recently been advanced. A scientist, who has been involved in the application of aluminium powder as a propellant for aircraft-delivered guided missiles, points out that it tends to burn rather than explode. In his view the explosive energy even from a direct torpedo hit on the stored powder would have been inadequate to have ignited it. He added that any detonation of the powder would be minor in comparison to the explosion which almost certainly did occur in the boiler room and that it could not of itself account for the loss of a ship of the size of *Lusitania*.[2]

Scientific experience with aluminium powder strongly suggests that its burn rate increases exponentially with the decrease in particle size and the optimum rate for burn would occur with one of 0.2 microns. The technology which was available in 1915 could not have milled such a very fine powder. Even with modern technology, the process of manufacturing this consistency is extremely complex. It would therefore be logical to conclude that it would have been difficult, if not impossible, for the powder in the liner's cargo hold to have been ignited accidentally. The hold was located on the far side of two major bulkheads almost 150 feet forward of the torpedo's point of impact, whose explosive effect the SNAME paper considered was limited to twenty feet. Any large explosion within the hold would also have vented upwards, using the point of least resistance, through the hatch covers. There is no eyewitness evidence of any such explosion occurring ahead of the bridge and, as already noted, Ballard could find no sign of any damage to that area of the hull. The theory, originally circulated by German propagandists, that the second explosion was caused by a detonation of the cargo can thus reasonably be discounted.

Ballard noted a trail of coal stretching along the seabed aft of the wreck and deduced that the coal had been blown into the water by an explosion of coal dust in the bunkers, which had become depleted towards the end of the voyage and would thus contain a great quantity of coal dust. Whilst Ballard's theory cannot entirely be ruled out, it seems unlikely. There is no evidence of a coal dust explosion occurring in any of the other coal-burning ships which were torpedoed in either World War. Before the First World War, coal was considered to be a defence against gunfire and torpedo attack and attempts to simulate a coal dust explosion proved unsuccessful. Some of these tests took place on ships whose bunkers were partially empty as *Lusitania*'s were on the day she was torpedoed.

Schwieger's torpedo had struck the liner at a point where she was exceptionally vulnerable. When Captain Dow prepared his contingency plan during the liner's February voyage, he believed that he could keep his ship afloat for at least an hour after she was hit by a torpedo, *providing that she was not hit in the boiler room.* (author's emphasis). Dow had every reason to be wary of the consequences of an explosion in any of the boiler rooms. *Lusitania* had twenty-five Scotch boilers, of the type generically known as fire-tube, because the furnace gases went through the tubes which operated at a pressure of 215 pounds per square inch and produced steam at a temperature of 390 degrees Fahrenheit. Their greatest area of weakness was the fire-box, where the hot gas from the burning coal passed from the furnace to the fire-tubes. Scotch boilers held a large amount of water at the saturation temperature of the steam pressure. Theoretical analysis in the SNAME paper suggests that the massive in-rush of cold sea-water at a temperature of 55 degrees Fahrenheit would cause high stress in the furnace side of the boiler, as also would differential expansion of the boiler shell, due to the quenching of the outer surface, and that the latter would be sufficient to cause failure of the riveted boiler shell joints, allowing the escape of water and steam into the boiler room. The flow of cold water into the furnaces would have extinguished the fires but in doing so some of it would have been converted into steam, much of which would have escaped up the funnel, carrying with it soot and debris. To this could well be added steam escaping from the boiler into the furnace space, due to the rupture of its fire-box, which was in turn caused by its sudden quenching with cold sea-water. This phenomenon would also explain the expulsion of the two passengers, Margaret Gwyer and William Pierpoint, who had been sucked into No 3 funnel as No 3 boiler room flooded in the ship's last moments. The boiler room crew would have had no time to open the safety valves and reduce boiler pressure as had been done on *Titanic*. With seven boilers, and almost ninety feet long, No 1 was the largest of *Lusitania*'s four boiler rooms. An array of pipes carrying steam to the turbines and generators was located above the boilers with 'take down' joints every ten feet and expansion joints every thirty-five.

It is important to differentiate between an actual boiler explosion and an explosion which took place within a boiler room. In the early days of steam, boiler rooms were dangerous places as explosions, which very few survived, were not uncommon. Those who were not scalded to death were suffocated as the steam displaced the air in the boiler room. By the time *Lusitania* was built, the design of boilers had been greatly improved with the use of better materials and the much safer cylindrical boilers had replaced the earlier and more vulnerable rectangular models. Her engineers, with years of experience behind them, knew well how to operate their boilers correctly. Interestingly, the effect of a large volume of cold water flooding into a boiler room and coming into contact with boilers operating at a high temperature has never been experimentally investigated. An examination of the events, which followed immediately after the torpedo struck, would indicate that the boilers did not explode. If a true boiler explosion had taken place, it is most unlikely that Fireman Madden, the sole survivor from No 1 boiler room, would have lived to tell his tale to Lord Mersey. He would have been engulfed by the force of the explosion as he escaped through the air intakes. An explosion of the boilers would have caused serious damage to the section of *Lusitania*'s decks which was directly above No 1 boiler room and anyone on deck would have had no doubts as to what had occurred. There is no evidence of any such damage.

All we know is that a second explosion occurred in the vicinity of No 1 boiler room almost immediately after the torpedo hit. Its possible causes were explored in considerable depth in the SNAME paper, which concluded that either a boiler had ruptured or more probably that a main steam pipe had fractured, both of which were theoretically possible. If the torpedo had exploded close to a boiler, its shell might have ruptured. The steam pipes were located above the boilers and high in the compartment, rendering them more vulnerable to the impact of a shallow-running warhead.

Since the publication of the SNAME paper, the author has unearthed further information in the shape of Third Engineer George Little's evidence before the Mersey inquiry.[3] He testified that he had been on watch in the engine room at the time the

211

torpedo hit. He noticed that, immediately after the explosion, the steam pressure at the engine room manifold had rapidly dropped to 50 pounds per square inch. He also stated that the turbo generators ran down and stopped, presumably due to the lack of steam, approximately three minutes after the explosion. The testimony of the passenger, James Brooks, who was on deck immediately above the site where the torpedo hit, and who was enveloped in a cloud of steam so dense that he found difficulty in breathing, indicated that whatever caused the second explosion, a massive amount of steam had escaped from No 1 boiler room.

There really appears to be no single ascertainable cause of the second explosion and the rapid loss of steam. It is possible that the explosion of the torpedo might have caused the shell of the nearest boiler to rupture or that it may have failed from thermal shock. Equally, a steam pipe might have fractured as a result of the explosion or from water hammer, caused by a boiler priming rapidly. A powerful release of energy comparable to an explosion would have resulted in either situation. If one or more boilers were perforated and the steam pipes had survived intact, it is unlikely that steam from the rest of the system could have escaped along that path. Where two or more boilers are connected together, it is normal marine engineering practice for the stop valves on the boiler steam outlets to be of a type known as non-return. These valves shut off automatically should the flow of steam be reversed, protecting the machinery and limiting damage in the event of a boiler failure. It is certain that *Lusitania* would have been so fitted.

The balance of probabilities suggests a fracture of a main steam pipe, which would drain the engines of steam and cause the steam cloud which enveloped James Brooks, whose experience was more characteristic of such a fracture than of a boiler explosion. This thesis is backed up by contemporary opinion. Two days after the sinking *The Times* special correspondent in Queenstown reported that Captain Turner was convinced that the torpedo had entered the forward boiler room and had broken the main steam pipe, completely paralyzing the engines. Turner reiterated his assertion in his interview with the *New York Times* in November 1915 and again two years later in his deposition for the Mayer trial: '. . . the torpedo burst the steam pipe and put the engines out of commission. . . .'

Third Engineer Little testified that, immediately after the torpedo hit and following a pre-arranged procedure, the telegraph was put to Full Astern, and then almost immediately to Full Ahead. He stated that the intention of the signal was to maintain the best speed possible in the circumstances and he did not alter the setting of the main engine throttles. Turner maintained, both during the inquiry and later, that he had intended to try to run the ship aground to prevent her sinking. Once No 1 and No 2 had flooded, it would have been impossible for No 3 as the only remaining undamaged boiler room in operation to have maintained steam pressure at the normal 215 pounds per square inch, even if the steam pipes had been left intact, unless the main throttle valves had been reset for a much lower speed. In effect, *Lusitania* had suffered a colossal engineering disaster, which left her dead in the water only three minutes after the torpedo had hit.

The effect of a hit on a main steam pipe was described by a survivor of the destroyer HMS *Tipperary*, sunk by gunfire at Jutland: '. . . the enemy's second salvo hit and burst one of our main steam pipes and the afterpart of the ship was enveloped in a cloud of steam, through which I could see nothing. Losing all their steam the turbines were brought to a standstill and we dropped astern out of the action . . .'[4] His account seems eerily similar to the misfortunes which overtook *Lusitania* after she was struck by the torpedo. It may be of some interest to note that in the 1960s everyone in the boiler room of the British aircraft carrier HMS *Centaur* was killed when a steam pipe, some six inches in diameter, fractured.[5]

The longitudinal bunkers in the forward part of No 1 boiler room were approximately ten feet wide, whilst further amidships in the same boiler room the bunkers were sixteen feet wide. These bunkers were thus extremely narrow in ratio to *Lusitania*'s beam of eighty-eight feet and were also stepped inwards at about the mid-point of that boiler room, creating a major element of weakness. Fireman Madden told the Mersey inquiry that the force of the incoming water, which he stated came from the side of the ship, was strong enough to knock him down and that there had been an explosion in the starboard boiler. It is possible that he was describing the explosive effect of the steam piping fracturing.[6]

Madden's testimony suggests that the inner bulkheads between the bunkers and No 1 boiler room were breached by the force of the impact. Merchant ships like *Lusitania* were equipped with interconnecting doors at floorplate level in the transverse bulkheads to allow the engineers access from one compartment to another. These doors were fitted with remote hydraulically-powered closing mechanisms with an accumulator to sustain the pressure, thus ensuring that they were not dependent on an external source of power. They were controlled from the bridge. It is unknown whether or not the system functioned correctly on this occasion although Third Engineer Little testified that the doors in the engine room did close. These watertight doors had been designed to withstand the inflow of water following a collision and it is probable that the system installed on board *Lusitania* could not operate fast enough to cope with the consequences of a torpedo hit and the resultant degree of internal damage. The available drawings do not indicate whether the access doors from the longitudinal bunkers to the boiler rooms were included in this system.

The only survivor from No 2 boiler room, Fireman Eugene McDermott, testified before Mersey that '. . . a rush of water met me and knocked me off my feet and I was struggling in the water for two or three minutes'. Asked whether the water appeared to come from the direction of the watertight door, he replied, like Madden, that it had come from the side of the ship.[7] His evidence would confirm the SNAME paper's conclusion that the rapid flooding of No 2 boiler room through the coal doors in the longitudinal bulkhead was exacerbated by the failure of the transverse bulkhead dividing the bunkers supplying the two forward boiler rooms. Seawater, now surging through the gaping breach in *Lusitania*'s hull at a rate initially as high as a hundred tons per second, was able to cascade into the two cavernous boiler rooms and the adjacent longitudinal bunkers adding to the free surface and contributing massively to the liner's instability. As a result she immediately developed a fifteen degree list to starboard and her bow trim rapidly increased (in layman's terms she began to sink by the bow). Even if there had not been an explosion within the boiler room, the mighty ship was now doomed and would inevitably founder within a matter of minutes.

As *Lusitania* settled deeper the flooding was aggravated by water pouring in through the portholes which had been left open on the upper decks. First Officer Jones and Charles Lauriat had both noted the large number of portholes left open in the saloon-class dining room and other areas of the ship. Lauriat, who had gone down to his cabin to recover some of his personal effects, saw water entering through portholes on B deck. Other closed portholes were probably fractured by the impact. As

Professor Hovgaard testified at the Mayer trial, a standard eigh-teen-inch porthole submerged by as little as three feet can admit three and three quarter tons of water per minute. At least seventy starboard portholes had been left open. The loss of *Titanic*'s sister ship *Britannic*, which sank in less than an hour after hitting a mine in the Mediterranean in November 1916 while serving as a hospital ship, has been ascribed to asymmetrical flooding, due in part to the large number of open portholes.

As *Lusitania*'s bow sank further into the water, it eventually came to rest on the seabed, some 300 feet below the surface and the ship pivoted to starboard, creating colossal stress to her hull as she settled rapidly. The liner's back broke between her third and fourth funnels in the area of the saloon-class dining-room and lounge, caused by massive stress of the structure of her hull as the flooded fore part was resting on the sea bed and the after-part continued to sink. This stress was exacerbated by the large holes cut on the strength deck to pass the boiler uptakes and to provide for the engine room trunking, necessary for the removal and replacement of machinery, and to create the vast saloon-class dining- and smoking-rooms, the former of which reached through two decks. These features substantially reduced the amount of steel which could otherwise have absorbed the longi-tudinal bending stresses on the hull at a location where these had high magnitude. *Titanic*'s back had also broken in much the same area but as the sea was relatively shallow at the point where she sank, *Lusitania*, unlike *Titanic*, did not break in two in her final plunge. Ballard's cameras show the effect of considerable damage to her hull in the area of her bows as she came into contact with the granite seabed.

The second explosion seems to have led to the loss of power but it was not the deciding factor in the loss of *Lusitania*. The liner would have sunk quickly even if there had never been a sec-ond explosion. The breach, approximately 200 square feet, torn in her hull by the impact of the torpedo, was nearly seventeen times as extensive as the gashes which sufficed to sink *Titanic*. The heavy list which *Lusitania* developed immediately after she was hit is evidence of the massive instability due to asymmetrical flooding in her forward boiler rooms and the adjacent bunkers, exacerbated by the inrush of water through the open portholes as high as B deck. Professor Hovgaard had testified to this effect before Judge Mayer. The loss of the battleships and cruisers in the early months of the war, can be ascribed to severe instability caused by the volume of water which poured into their hulls after they were torpedoed. Instability was a factor in the loss of HMS *Royal Oak*, a battleship designed before the First World War, which capsized after she was torpedoed at anchor at Scapa Flow in October 1939, also with heavy loss of life. A similar fate befell several of the battleships of the American Pacific Fleet, also of First World War design, when they were torpedoed by Japanese naval aircraft at Pearl Harbor.

Ships, which were designed with large undivided spaces such as massive boiler rooms or car decks, are particularly vulnerable to instability caused by flooding. In recent years the car ferry *Estonia* was lost in the Baltic when the bow doors to the car deck failed during a storm. The cross-channel car ferry *Herald Of Free Enterprise* foundered within minutes of leaving her berth in the Belgian port of Zeebrugge because one of her bow doors had accidentally been left open. The ship suffered no damage and her sinking was entirely due to the loss of stability resulting from the volume of water which flowed in through the opening into the car deck, running both the length and the beam of the vessel. The actual amount of water required to create instability on the car deck, relatively high up in the ferry, is not as great as might be thought. Thus the destabilising effect of water entering through the open portholes on *Lusitania*'s higher decks was probably even more serious than Professor Hovgaard had suggested.

A consultant to a recent TV documentary entitled *Secrets of The Deep, The Mystery of The Lusitania*, surmised that if the flooding had been confined to only one compartment, namely the starboard longitudinal bunker servicing No 1 boiler room where the torpedo actually struck, *Lusitania* would probably not have sunk.[8] Whilst this thesis may well be correct, there would have been no reason for her naval architects, working between 1903 and 1905, or indeed any contemporary designers of large merchant ships, to have built in the necessary high degree of watertight integrity to have confined the flooding to one particular area. The need to store and provide access to large quantities of coal adjacent to the boiler rooms necessitated designing openings in what would have otherwise been watertight bulkheads. It should be remembered that the system of watertight bulkheads and doors, particularly below the waterline, with which *Lusitania* was equipped, had been designed to cope with the effects of a collision and not with those of a torpedo impact. If only No 1 boiler room had flooded, the liner might have survived for long enough to allow for a more orderly evacuation as Captain Dow had envisaged. In the event, the flooding of both forward boiler rooms, together with the total loss of power and the open port holes, proved fatal and led to her foundering only eighteen minutes after Schwieger's torpedo had struck.

The rapidity with which *Lusitania* sank resulted from an unfortunate combination of circumstances. She had been designed long before passenger liners had ever been thought to be a likely target in time of war or the implications of the submarine as an offensive warship had ever been considered either by the Admiralty or by naval architects. Her design rendered her extremely susceptible to asymmetrical flooding and as a result she was highly exposed to the consequences of being struck by a torpedo. As fate would have it the mighty ship had been hit in an area where she was particularly vulnerable and her doom was sealed.

CHAPTER 17

The Reasons Why – I

Someone had blunder'd
Theirs not to make reply
Theirs not to reason why
Theirs but to do and die

T hus Tennyson on an earlier British military disaster, the charge of the Light Brigade during the battle of Balaclava in the Crimean War, which was the direct result of sloppy staffwork, exacerbated by animosities among senior commanders which bordered on the venomous. In her masterly book on the charge, *The Reason Why*, Cecil Woodham-Smith observed that the succession of orders sent by the Commander-in-Chief to the cavalry commanders were '. . . vague, obscure, the work of an amateur, an invitation to disaster'.[1] The poet's lines might equally apply to those who died on *Lusitania*.

Mersey had laid the blame for the disaster firmly at the door of Imperial Germany. Since the publication of his war diary, Walther Schwieger has stood condemned for the loss of life caused by his torpedo. He was a cautious man who was not readily going to exceed his orders which specifically instructed him to attack Allied merchant ships, warships and troop transports. As we now know, he was unaware of his victim's identity although her silhouette clearly identified her as British. The real onus must rest with his superiors in the naval hierarchy. If the Royal Navy suffered from bureaucracy and excessive centralisation, the Kriegsmarine bore some resemblance to the hydra, that mythical creature with many heads. Tirpitz, as state secretary for the imperial naval office, was responsible for finance, warship design and construction. Operations were controlled by the Admiralstab, then headed by Admiral Bachmann.

This situation was further complicated by a third centre of authority, the Kaiser's naval cabinet, whose chief, Admiral Georg von Muller, was a suave behind-the-scenes operator. No love was lost between Tirpitz and Muller. As could be expected this system led to constant infighting and certainly did not provide a background for effective decision-making. Germany lacked any institution similar to the British Committee of Imperial Defence, which had been set up to examine and coordinate strategy at high level. The Kaiser was the only authority who could coordinate military and naval operations. He was notorious for his short attention span and as the war went on he was increasingly excluded from the decision-making process. In the mind-set of the German military establishment the end generally justified the means.

The introduction of unrestricted submarine warfare in February 1915 was characteristic of contemporary German decision-making. Before 1914 the Kriegsmarine, like its British counterpart, had not understood the strategic potential of the submarine. Technology had advanced faster than the conventions of war and there were no international agreements governing the use of submarines. The existing Hague Convention rules were cumbersome and inappropriate. Within two months the instruction had to be sharply modified, forbidding attacks on neutral shipping. Despite his failings, the Kaiser was far from being the bloodthirsty monster portrayed by Allied propaganda. He had always loved great ships and his distress at the sinking of *Lusitania* and the devastating loss of life was undoubtedly genuine. In June 1915, against the advice of his admirals he had ordered that passenger liners were not to be attacked. In October of that year he told Gerard that he would not have permitted the liner to be torpedoed, if he had known about it, and that no gentleman would kill so many women and children.[2] In 1917 Schwieger was awarded the highest German decoration Pour Le Merité. Significantly, the citation did not mention that he had torpedoed *Lusitania*, merely noting that he had sunk 190,000 tons of Allied shipping. Nevertheless, it is legitimate to criticise Imperial Germany for enacting such a radical change in the conventions of war without any apparent attempt to think out the consequences.

While Mersey's judgment served its purpose in wartime it is inherently inadequate. British errors contributed towards the loss of the mighty ship. In Tennyson's phrase, someone had blundered, but whom? The controversy over who was responsible for her loss has raged for more than eighty years. Captain Webb's report, placing the onus squarely on Turner, largely set the tone for the continuing debate. Webb's objective, or more precisely that of his superiors in the war staff, was to let the Admiralty off the hook and set the hapless Captain up as a scapegoat for the loss of his ship.

To cast the entire blame onto Captain Turner as the War Staff attempted in the aftermath of the sinking of the liner, which was under direct Admiralty control when at sea and as other commentators, notably Thomas Bailey and Paul Ryan, in their 1975 book *The Lusitania Disaster,* have done since, is to ignore the complex and largely unprecedented circumstances which had an influence on the tragedy. In a newspaper article he wrote in 1937, Churchill was being equally subjective when he absolved the Admiralty and, by extension himself, from any responsibility. The Admiralty's case against Turner would have been more credible if their instructions had been more detailed, explicit and regular, particularly after the three sinkings on 5 and 6 May, all of them directly in *Lusitania*'s course, and if he had received any briefing when the liner was in Liverpool before she sailed on her last westbound voyage and during the week she was berthed in New York.

Although Webb's report does not stand up to detailed examination, Churchill essentially repeated its conclusions when he wrote about the loss of the liner in *World Crisis*, published in 1923. As recently as 1994 Sir Martin Gilbert, Churchill's authorised biographer, followed the same line in his generally authoritative *The First World War*, once again placing the blame on Turner. In his statement in the House of Commons three days after the sinking, Churchill had categorically told Bonar Law that two warning signals had been sent to *Lusitania*. In Gilbert's account the number of signals had risen to six.[3]

The number is, however, not really relevant. A much more significant issue must be considered: were the warnings adequate? Gilbert, like other commentators, does not address this point. In April 1975, Edward Beach, a retired captain USN, Second World War submariner and author of the acclaimed book *Run Silent, Run Deep*, wrote to Paul Ryan, whom he was assisting in his research for *The Lusitania Disaster*. He put forward a totally different perspective. Although he was not uncritical of Turner, Beach concluded that the amount of warnings and cautionary instructions he (Turner) received were not really adequate in the circumstances. Beach told Ryan that the real controversy of *Lusitania* lay in this area and compared the situation faced by Turner with Pearl Harbor. He pointed out that Admiral Husband Kimmel, the C-in-C Pacific Fleet, who was made a scapegoat for the Japanese attack, stoutly insisted that the routine warnings sent to him were by no means adequate given the far more exten-

sive knowledge that Washington possessed of Japanese intentions. Kimmel later appeared before a review board which found
that he had acted properly in the light of the information which
he had been given.[4]

As master of *Lusitania*, Turner was responsible for his ship and,
to his credit, he never sought to shirk his responsibility for her
loss. There is inevitably a difference between responsibility and
blame for what happened. What degree of blame did Cunard or
Turner bear for the disaster? Ample survivor evidence testified to
the lack of crew training in handling the lifeboats and the failure
to hold any passenger musters. The collapsible boats proved to
be almost useless. Passengers should ideally have been required
to wear or at least carry lifebelts with them once the liner had
entered the war zone. There is an aura of hindsight about some
of these charges. The criticism of Turner for ordering passengers
out of lifeboats and for any delay in launching them while the vessel was still under way is misplaced as they could not safely be lowered until she had virtually stopped. Collapsible boats had not
been used in any comparable shipwreck since their introduction
after the loss of *Titanic* and were thus untried. Although one
Lusitania survivor, George Kessler, told Purser McCubbin: 'It's all
right drilling crew but why don't you drill passengers?' another,
John McConnel, was remarkably candid on the subject of
lifebelts: 'We should have been drilled but we would not have
stood for it at the time.' Professor Ian Holborn had been outspoken about the inadequacy of the lifeboat drills. Another
saloon-class passenger took him aside and stated that he was
speaking for a group of his fellows. He asked the professor to
desist as he was alarming the ladies. The witty Holborn promptly
christened the group the Ostrich Club.

In May 1915 the reality of modern war was by no means properly
understood either by the officers of the Merchant Navy or by their
passengers. Cunard took justifiable pride in an exemplary safety
record of never having lost a passenger in peacetime. A degree of
complacency, that silent foe of and ever present danger to a successful business, seems to have crept in. The comfortable illusion
that *Lusitania* could outrun any U-boat was still widespread and her
officers would doubtless have maintained that: 'We are good.
Nothing is going to happen to us'. Their contemporaries on other
ships would certainly have echoed such sentiments.

A more intuitive man than Turner, a Fairweather Dow or an
Arthur Rostron, might well have prepared a comprehensive con-

tingency plan in the event that the liner might be torpedoed. On the night he steered *Carpathia* northwards through the ice to rescue the *Titanic* survivors, Rostron implemented a twenty-four point plan involving every department on his ship in the rescue operation, and Dow had done likewise in the flap at the beginning of February. Turner can reasonably be criticised for neglecting to make a more detailed plan and for failing to ensure that the portholes were closed. It must be said that more attention to lifeboat drill or compelling unwilling passengers to wear lifebelts could at best only have mitigated the loss of life. Such precautions would not have prevented the tragedy. Almost two thousand people were on board. The liner immediately developed a pronounced list to starboard preventing the port side boats from being launched and sank so rapidly that in the circumstances a heavy death toll was unavoidable.

As expounded by Captain Webb, the Admiralty charged that Turner had ignored their three directives, thereby hazarding his ship. He had reduced speed, he had failed to zigzag and he had come inshore, close to an important port and to prominent headlands. His reason for cutting his speed to 18 knots was valid as he had no intention of arriving at the Mersey Bar too early and thus having to wait until the flood tide could carry him across. He was complying with the War Risks Association's instruction to masters, which Aspinall had quoted during the closed sessions of the inquiry 'to avoid anchoring or reducing speed whilst making the entrances to the Mersey'. As George Little had testified during his deposition, the engine room had been instructed to keep a good head of steam at all times should a sudden increase of speed become necessary.

The Admiralty's prevailing belief that speed per se could enable a merchant ship to escape from a submarine was illustrated in an exchange of letters in the week following the sinking between Graham Greene and Harold Sanderson, Chairman of the White Star Line, understandably concerned as their liner *Adriatic* was due to sail from Liverpool to New York on 12 May. Sanderson wrote:

> ... it has all along been authoratively [*sic*] stated to us that vessels of good speed were regarded as almost immune from the consequences of torpedo fire from submarines, but in view of the disaster ... I should be glad to be informed whether the expert view continues unaltered or whether the sinking of the *Lusitania* was attended by circumstances which are not likely to repeat themselves ... [He then

pointedly asked] whether it is the intention of the Admiralty to afford any special protection to vessels engaged in the Atlantic passenger traffic in . . . the danger zone.

In a memo to Greene, Captain Webb had noted that the White Star passenger liners currently in service had speeds of between 15 and 17.5 knots, *ie* slower than *Lusitania* was steaming when she was torpedoed and that they could not be classed as slow ships. Greene replied:

> . . . I am commanded by Their Lordships to advise you that vessels of high speed are, as compared with slow ships, relatively immune from submarine attack. They cannot be successfully attacked by a gun, as their speed enables them to outpace a submarine. It is absolutely essential that the course which will be followed and the time of arrival should be kept secret; if this precaution is omitted, it is possible for enemy submarines to lie in wait for a particular ship . . . In respect of torpedo attack their immunity is not absolute, but the risk is not great if the advice given by the Admiralty is closely followed, and if a sharp and properly organised lookout is continuously maintained . . . No special protection which it is in the power of the Admiralty to afford would be of service to protecting fast liners as they could not come into action until the submarine was sighted by which time, the danger as far as a fast ship is concerned is at an end.[5]

This answer begs a number of questions. Sanderson was not warned that a submarine had considerable scope of vision and on a clear day could see a ship, particularly a large one, from a considerable distance thus giving it a good opportunity to manoeuvre into a position to attack. Coal burning steam ships could not avoid emitting smoke from their funnels and the bigger the ship the more the smoke. On a windy day, smoke would be dispersed rapidly, but in calm conditions it tended to rise in a plume and to advertise the presence of a ship, even when the hull was invisible below the horizon. May 7 off southern Ireland was such a day, with no wind and high atmospheric pressure, and the quantity of smoke rising from *Lusitania*'s three large active funnels, would have been visible at up to twenty miles away, providing early evidence of her approach and giving Schwieger ample time to set up *U-20* to attack. Writing after *Lusitania* had been torpedoed, Greene did not advise Sanderson that his captains should observe any of the three points which Webb had accused Turner of neglecting: maintaining top speed, zigzagging and keeping a distance from land. *Adriatic*'s cruising speed was 16.5 knots, slower than *Lusitania* had been steaming when she was torpedoed.

One highly respected contemporary authority did not share the Admiralty's conventional wisdom. Three days after the tragedy, J R Thursfield, the veteran naval correspondent of *The Times*, wrote:

> But even if the vessel had been proceeding at full speed, providing that she was placed favourably for the discharge of a torpedo from a lurking submarine, this alone would not have been sufficient to save her. As I have pointed out, over and over again, the rate at which a ship is travelling is no certain protection against torpedo attack if all the other circumstances are favourable and if the speed is a known factor.

Thursfield was correct to state that if a ship wanders into the arc of submarine attack, as *Lusitania* did, speed alone would not suffice to save her. However, the faster a target was steaming, the less time a U-boat commander had to prepare his attack, and greater likelihood there was of his torpedo missing.[6]

In his war diary, Walther Schwieger noted that he had sighted *Lusitania* at 1420 CET, fifty minutes before he fired at her. He was able to manoeuvre *U-20* into an excellent position where he could lay in wait for a flank shot with ten minutes to spare. Even if the liner had been steaming at her top achievable speed of 21 knots and not, as she was, at 18 knots, she would still have been in range of Schwieger's torpedo. The charge that Turner hazarded *Lusitania* by reducing her speed by three knots cannot be sustained.

The second Admiralty charge was that Turner had failed to zigzag in accordance with their directive issued on 16 April. This is a complex issue. Some writers have suggested that the directive was not distributed until well after Turner had sailed from Liverpool on the following day and it does not seem to have been signed by Churchill until 25 April. If this supposition had been correct, Aspinall would have strenuously objected to the directive being adduced by Carson during the Mersey inquiry. We have already noted Captain Frederick's failure to brief Turner on any matter, including the new directive, before *Lusitania* sailed on her last westbound voyage. The responsibility for Turner's misunderstanding the document must at least be shared by SNO Liverpool.

The Admiralty directive prescribed a random series of nine changes of course, ranging from 17 degrees to as much as 90 degrees at intervals of between five and twenty minutes over a two-hour period at the end of which the vessel would have returned to its original course and the manoeuvre would have been repeated. Masters received the directive with scepticism. Zigzagging was doubtless acceptable for destroyers, even for battlecruisers, but in their view it was wholly unsuitable for passenger liners. Merchant navy captains had their own governing priorities, which totally differed from those of their opposite numbers in the Royal Navy. The voyage should be completed on schedule, fuel consumption should be minimised and passengers should be kept happy and comfortable. No captain wanted to be confronted by head office with a sheaf of angry letters of complaint. Zigzagging on a liner nearly 800 feet in length and with a beam of 88 feet would inevitably have been an uncomfortable experience. In consequence the directive was widely ignored, at least in the months immediately after it was introduced.

Zigzagging was not really feasible close inshore, nor was it a panacea. In drafting the directive the Admiralty had subconsciously admitted a significant flaw: 'The underwater speed of a submarine is very low. It is exceedingly difficult for her to get into position to deliver an attack *unless she can observe and predict the course of the ship to be attacked*' [author's emphasis]. This commentary was to prove only too accurate. After the war, the surviving U-boat captain, Kiesewalter, told Frank Mason, the Hearst correspondent in Berlin and a former army intelligence officer, of the tactics he and his contemporaries used to counter the manoeuvre. They would take up a bow position ahead of their intended prey, knowing that its captain would duly change course either to port or starboard, in both cases presenting them with a favourable flank shot.[7] In essence such tactics were a variant of those used by Schwieger against *Lusitania* and it is at least arguable that, in the circumstances, he could have torpedoed the liner even if she had been zigzagging. In the Second World War, submariners were adamant that zigzagging was not an effective defence and, like Schwieger before them, they were much more wary of destroyer screens. As we know, the unfortunate Turner was torpedoed for a second time when commanding *Ivernia*, which was zigzagging at the time she was hit.

In practice the manoeuvre only proved effective for fast merchant ships sailing on random courses away from normal trade routes. In 1918 *Aquitania*, *Mauretania* and two other express liners were serving as troopships ferrying Pershing's army to

France. They sailed alone and their captains were instructed to maintain their top achievable speed at all times, to steer a random course and to zigzag. It was still found necessary to provide them with an escort of four destroyers once they reached longitude 15 West, some 200 miles west of Ireland.[8] As the effectiveness of the manoeuvre had not been established in May 1915, the Admiralty's charge against Turner is at best unproven.

The most serious accusation raised against Turner was that he had failed to steer a mid-channel course, disregarding directives to avoid headlands. During the inquiry Aspinall had rigorously cited the ambiguous nature of a number of Admiralty instructions to merchant shipping, notably the failure to define what was meant by a mid-channel course and to which sea lanes they were referring. The Admiralty could have identified the relevant areas more precisely by stating latitude and longitude. The Admiralty also disregarded the effect of the fateful signal received on board *Lusitania* at 11.52am on 7 May: 'Submarines active in southern part of Irish Channel, last heard of twenty miles south of Coningbeg Light vessel.' The Admiralty's instruction to Queenstown to make sure *Lusitania* received this signal might indicate that it had been sent in response to Alfred Booth's intervention with Admiral Stileman earlier that morning. If this supposition is correct, it is ironic that his concern for the ship's safety was to contribute to such a tragic outcome. The signal told Turner that submarines had been seen directly in his course. It did not inform him that two merchant ships had been sunk off Coningbeg or that that they had been torpedoed nearly twenty-four hours before. More importantly, it failed to tell him that the two ships had been attacked without warning or to give him any instructions as to the course he should take. In effect, he was left on his own. In his deposition for the Mayer trial, Turner had confirmed that he thought it correct to disregard the Admiralty's instruction to maintain a mid-channel course. F E Smith had effectively supported Turner by admitting that it would have been pedantic of him to continue his previous course.

Until he had received this signal, and despite the Admiralty's criticism after the event, Turner had steered what could reasonably have been described as a mid-channel course. He had intended to clear both the Old Head and Coningbeg by between eighteen and twenty miles. The table set out below shows the distances by which *Lusitania* had cleared prominent land features on her wartime eastbound voyages.[9] It also illustrates that Turner had kept further out to sea than Dow had on both the voyages in which he had been in command.

Departure	Voyage	Captain	Fastnet	Old Head	Coninbeg
Nov 4	95	Dow	1	2.25	1.5
Dec 5	96	Dow	2	2.5	1
Dec 30	97	Dow	14	2	1.5
Jan. 30	98	Dow	8	3	7
Feb 27	99	Dow	3	3.5	6
Apr 4	100	Turner	10	12	13
May 1	101	Turner	18.5	12	

Faced with the information that submarines were operating on his course, Turner had no other option but to use his own judgment. It was his responsibility to bring his large and valuable ship, with nearly two thousand people on board, into Liverpool safely and expeditiously. He had several concerns to take into account. He had to navigate St George's Channel at night with the likelihood of being delayed by fog and he had to cross the Mersey Bar before 9.30am on the following morning. In such a situation his first priority, as an experienced and cautious master, would have been to establish his actual position. He must have had some doubts as to what action he should take. According to his evidence to the Mersey inquiry, he summoned his two immediate subordinates, Anderson and Chief Officer Piper to the bridge, sometime after noon. Anderson had commanded Cunarders and he and Piper both held master's certificates. No one can envy these three officers left alone on *Lusitania*'s bridge to take such a difficult decision on totally insufficient information. Between them they had nearly a hundred years of seagoing experience but all their accumulated knowledge could not equip them for the task of navigating under the threat of submarine attack. In reality they were operating in a dimension which was as unfamiliar to them as it was to their counterparts of the Royal Navy.

Effectively, they had two choices: to come inshore or to stand further out to sea. Had either Anderson or Piper survived, Aspinall would certainly have called them as witnesses in the closed session of the Mersey inquiry and it would have been more difficult for the Admiralty to have maintained their line that Turner was an obstinate and recalcitrant man, on whom they could cast the entire onus for the tragedy.

The plaintiff lawyers and witnesses during the Mayer liability trial and subsequent commentators, notably Bailey and Ryan, have maintained that Turner could have safely navigated

Lusitania into Liverpool Bay without taking a four-point bearing fix. Such censure is both inherently subjective and the outcome of hindsight. It is more relevant to attempt to understand why Turner and his subordinates, reliant on magnetic compasses and sextants, acted as they did. Aspinall's defence of Turner was doughty but he could perhaps have spelled out the problems which he confronted more directly. A modern-day master would not be affected by the navigational difficulties which properly concerned Turner and his officers. With radio, X-band radar and satellite navigation aids at his disposal, he would call for and receive an instant and totally accurate fix but a 1915 problem cannot be solved by 2000 technology. Turner's critics totally over-look the errors which could and often did creep into navigation by dead reckoning. To illustrate the potential for error, the wreck of *Titanic* was discovered nearly twelve nautical miles from her last reported position.[10]

Few navigators would blame Turner for deciding to obtain a four-point bearing fix off the Old Head after he had changed course to steam parallel to the coast at 1.40pm. He would certainly have had intended to take a fix before reaching Coningbeg and turning up St George's Channel as night fell. The information he had received from the Admiralty indicated that the submarines were operating close to the lightship, 75 nautical miles or four hours steaming time ahead of him at his current speed of 18 knots. On this basis he would have been justified in believing that he could steer the steady course for the thirty minutes or so required to take the bearing without hazarding his vessel. Once the bearing had been completed, he could set course to pass close to Coningbeg and devote his entire attention to coping with the submarine menace.

The second option, to stand out to sea, had one major disadvantage. It would have added several hours to the time the vessel had to stay at sea in an area in which the Admiralty had just advised them that submarines were operating, thus increasing her exposure to attack. While we know that there was only one submarine off the south coast of Ireland, the three officers on the liner's bridge did not. At noon on 7 May *Lusitania* was about to clear Fastnet with 210 miles of her voyage remaining. Steaming at 18 knots on a mid-channel course keeping twenty miles off the Irish coast she would have reached the Mersey bar around 1.20am on 8 May. Turner would, therefore, have been compelled to have sailed a further forty-eight miles in the Irish Sea before he could return to the bar at 4.00am, the earliest time he could safely cross the obstacle.

If Turner and his colleagues had decided to stand out to sea, they would have needed to clear Coningbeg by at least forty miles to allow a sufficient margin of safety to avoid the reported submarines. This would have entailed a 30-degree turn to starboard to take up a new course which would have kept the liner between forty and fifty miles off the Irish coast. They would then have turned north close to the Smalls, the rocks approximately forty miles from Coningbeg, which marked the eastern or Welsh side of the sea lane through St George's Channel. If *Lusitania* had maintained her current speed of 18 knots, such a change of course would have lengthened the voyage by approximately fifty miles or almost three hours additional steaming time. She would have arrived at the Mersey bar in time for the flood tide which would have carried her across at 4.00am. The irony is that Turner had the time to spare to stand out to sea and to reach the Mersey bar during the window of five and a half hours, between 4.00am and 9.30am on the following morning, when there would have been sufficient depth of water for *Lusitania* to cross. He also had to consider one adverse factor: the ever-present danger of heavy fog in a relatively narrow sea lane. If he had been forced to reduce speed severely in heavy fog in St George's Channel, he could conceivably have run the risk of missing the tide at the bar in an area of maximum danger to the ship: a risk which no captain could accept in wartime.

In contrast, to bring *Lusitania* inshore shortened the time she had to remain at sea, retaining the current advantage of having time in hand to meet the tide at the Mersey bar. Turner would also be able to take the accurate four-point bearing fix he needed to steer a safe course up St George's Channel at night and ready his vessel for her final approach to Liverpool. Turner had no margin for error in taking an inshore course at night and as he had pointedly told Mersey: 'My Lord, I do not navigate my ship by guesswork'.[11] He would no doubt have reasoned that by steering an inshore course, almost identical to his peacetime route, he would have put sufficient distance between *Lusitania* and the reported position of the U-boats to enable him to avoid them.

Their instinct and experience would have led Turner and his officers to opt for an inshore course. This decision was to cost Anderson and Piper their lives and was to haunt Turner for the rest of his days. Yet in light of the inadequate information and the absence of any instructions provided by the Admiralty, the deci-sion reached by these three experienced professionals appears rational and defensible. Thus the die was cast and at 12.40pm, Turner ordered a change of course of 30 degrees to port. *Lusitania* and *U-20*, William Thomas Turner and Walther Schwieger, were now on a collision course. An examination of the allegations laid against Turner by the Admiralty would indicate that on the charge of failure to zigzag, the Scottish Law verdict of not proven might be applicable. Their other charges – the reduc-tion of speed and the decision to steer an inshore course – do not stand up to careful scrutiny. In his report, Captain Webb was crit-ical of Turner for not steering a course well out of sight of the Irish coast. This was written with the benefit of hindsight and begs the question of why Turner never received any explicit instruction as to the course he should steer.

Although Turner was criticised heavily by the Admiralty for the course he took after sighting the Irish coast at Fastnet, study of the track chart prepared specially for this book shows that his choice of S87E magnetic (074 true) was entirely rational, in relation to the information in his possession and that it did confirm to the (admittedly vague) Admiralty instruction. It kept him well clear of the Irish coast and would have brought him into a good position to alter course to the northwards at the appropriate time, enter-ing St George's Channel midway between Coningbeg and the Smalls. At the point at which this decision was made, the distance between the Irish and Cornish coasts is about 120 nautical miles and it is difficult to construe this as being a channel.

Previous commentators have tacitly assumed that *U-20* could not have attacked *Lusitania* if the liner had maintained her orig-inal course but this is not really the case. When Turner altered course 30 degrees to port, the liner moved inshore at right angles to her original course, by half the distance she travelled. When he turned to starboard one hour later and resumed his original course of S 87 E magnetic, *Lusitania*, steaming at 18 knots, was approximately nine nautical miles closer inshore, ignoring tidal effects. It will be remembered that Schwieger had sighted the liner as early as 1.20pm and had concluded that he could not intercept her if she maintained her then course of N 63 E. In his war diary he recorded that he submerged to periscope depth at 1.25pm: '. . . and proceeded at high speed on intercepting course toward steamer in the hope that the steamer will alter course to starboard along the Irish Coast. At 1440 CET (1.40pm GMT) the steamer turns to starboard . . . permitting an approach for a shot. Proceed at high speed until 1500 (2pm GMT) in order to gain bearing . . .' He had therefore sailed for thirty-five minutes at his top submerged speed of 8–9 knots to get into a position where he could torpedo the liner. In that time he would have travelled between four and a half and five nautical miles.

Although Schwieger did not record his position at the time he decided to intercept the liner, it is clear that *U-20* must then have been well to the south of the track that Turner was steering between 12.40pm and 1.40pm as his course was taking his ship away from *U-20*. Even when Turner resumed his original track of S 87 E, *U-20* had to travel at her maximum submerged speed to get within striking range of *Lusitania*. It is at least arguable that had Turner held the course which he was steering before 12.40pm, *Lusitania* would have passed relatively close to the position where *U-20* originally sighted her. As visibility was excellent, Schwieger might easily have sighted the liner before 1.20pm, steering a parallel course but south of his position, and as he would not have so far to travel to get into range, she would have been a relatively easy target to attack. Turner's decision to alter course and come inshore made Schwieger's task more difficult, but, alas, not difficult enough to save the liner.

An examination of the track chart indicates that the alteration of course inshore at 12.40pm, which had so greatly exercised Captain Webb and the Mersey inquiry, had only a minimal bearing of *Lusitania*'s sinking. No evidence exists that the inquiry ever studied a chart of the liner's course. The position of *U-20* in relation to the liner was such that Schwieger had a ready opportunity to get into range for a torpedo attack, provided that Turner maintained a course of S 87 E whether he was steaming at ten or eighteen miles off the coast. If Turner had taken his peacetime course, passing the Irish headlands at a distance of about one mile, Schwieger would probably have been unable to have intercepted the liner. The Admiralty charge that, by moving inshore, Turner increased the risk to his ship does not stand up to explicit scrutiny.

Another exercise in examining Turner's culpability for the disaster is to establish Cunard's reaction to the loss of one of their finest ships. The Cunard historian, Professor Francis Hyde, wrote: ' . . . there is evidence to show that . . . Turner was apprehensive about the voyage, there is reason to believe that, within the limits of the resources available to him, he took adequate precautions.'[12] Cunard did not abandon Turner – an indication that they did not hold him to blame – and he was retained as a relief captain. Towards the end of 1915 he went back to sea in command of the 4,750-ton freighter *Ultonia*. He was grateful for the opportunity although command of the veteran freighter, one of the smallest vessels in Cunard's fleet, was a considerable comedown from the sleek and prestigious *Lusitania*. He told Alfred Booth, who had apologised for giving him such a small command, that he would go to sea in a barge if necessary to get afloat again as he was tired of being idle and on shore when everyone else was away at sea. In December 1916 he had relieved Arthur Rostron, who had rescued the Titanic survivors when he was master of *Carpathia*, in command of the liner *Ivernia* (14,506 tons), then serving as a troopship in the Mediterranean. As we have seen, Turner's luck was out for once again he was torpedoed, although once again he survived. He never went to sea again and spent the rest of 1917 in command of *Mauretania*, then laid up in the Clyde. He was, however, appointed Commodore of the Line. When the liner went to sea as a troopship in the spring of 1918, she was commanded by Rostron. That year Turner was awarded the newly-instituted Order of the British Empire for his wartime services. He stayed in Cunard's service until he retired under the line's age rule in 1919.

CHAPTER 18

The Reasons Why – II

By October 1914 passenger traffic on the North Atlantic had dropped sharply and could have been comfortably accommodated on the smaller intermediate liners. If Alfred Booth had not been subject to the constraints of the Inverclyde/Selborne agreement and had been free to exercise his commercial judgement, *Lusitania* would have been laid up like her sisters and the White Star's *Olympic.* Since the liner had returned to the North Atlantic run in September 1914, she had been under Admiralty instructions when she was at sea, with Cunard even forbidden to contact her master. By assuming operational control over *Lusitania*, the Admiralty had also taken responsibility for her safe routing. Was the Admiralty thus to blame for her loss?

The Royal Navy had won its reputation in the Napoleonic wars with a series of successful fleet actions, due in large measure to superior leadership, which culminated in Nelson's epic victory at Trafalgar. In the Victorian navy, fleets and squadrons were manoeuvred by commanding admirals according to the fighting instructions and the signal book which became holy writ rather than the reference points which they had been in Nelson's time. In a command system where decision-making was increasingly centralised, the quality of initiative, which Nelson had prized so highly in his captains, the famous band of brothers, inevitably became inconsequential. As Correlli Barnett, an historian of the Royal Navy in the Second World War, noted: '. . . in the tranquil decades of the Victorian peace, the Royal Navy's whole system of command and control, its doctrines and its style of leadership had become the reverse of Nelsonian . . .'[1]

Throughout the 1900s the Admiralty had stoutly resisted the introduction of a general staff or of a staff college, where officers could be educated to bear the responsibilities of higher command. Only one senior Admiral, Beresford, had ever seriously advocated setting up a naval staff. Even Fisher, dynamic reformer though he was, had never attempted to modernise the Navy's command and control system. In truth, he was as bitterly opposed to the introduction of a naval staff as the admirals whom he loved to deride. In 1911 the shortcomings of the system were to be mercilessly exposed.

The Agadir incident in July 1911, when two German warships were dispatched to Morocco, which lay within the French sphere of influence, resulted in a high-level examination of the war plans of both the Royal Navy and the army. The navy's exposition of its strategy was unimpressive. Asquith was prodded into action by his close political ally, the Secretary of State for War, R B Haldane, whose criticisms of the Admiralty had been trenchant. He wrote to Asquith: '. . . the Admirals live in a world of their own. The Fisher method . . . that war plans should be locked in the brain of the First Sea Lord is out of date and impractical. Our problems of defence are far too numerous and complex to be treated in that way.'[2] The solution was obvious. A naval war staff had to be instituted as a matter of urgency. In a cabinet reshuffle in October 1911, Winston Churchill became First Lord of the Admiralty.

With his customary drive, Churchill set about the task of establishing a naval war staff along the lines of the Imperial General Staff which Haldane had successfully instituted at the War Office. To introduce a staff system over the objections of virtually every serving admiral required not only persistence, which Churchill possessed in full measure, but tact and patience, which were not Churchillian characteristics. He was ever in a hurry. By the summer of 1912, Churchill had apparently achieved his objective: the War Staff was formed and a war college to train staff officers instituted. His achievement was not as considerable as it might appear. In his haste, he had failed to institute effective terms of reference for the new staff system and to define the degree of control which the Admiralty would exercise over operations. In essence, the Admiralty's centralised power increased and those of fleet and squadron commanders diminished. The division of responsibility between the First Sea Lord and the Chief of the Naval War Staff, a post created in the reforms, was to cause serious problems. The two positions were merged in 1917 when the First Sea Lord took over responsibility for the War Staff.

The Admiralty's reputation as a highly conservative institution, inherently suspicious of technological innovation, has largely been refuted by recent historical research. It had unhesitatingly accepted the arrival of wireless telegraphy which gave it the opportunity to maintain centralised control over fleets, stations and squadrons around the world. This detailed control was increased by the adoption of a staff system and later by signals intelligence (SIGINT). Peter Drucker, the well-known writer on the theory and practice of management, commented on the decentralised management structure introduced into General Motors by Alfred P Sloan, its CEO in the 1920s, which was to prove the key to the company's success. Drucker wrote that 'General Motors could not function if every decision had to be approved by a few overworked men in New York or Detroit.' Substitute Royal Navy for General Motors and the Admiralty for New York or Detroit and the analogy illustrates the difficulties under which the service was operating in 1914–15.

When the First World War dawned in August 1914, the Navy had not fought a fleet action for nearly ninety years, since Sir Edward Codrington, who had been one of Nelson's band of brothers, had defeated the Turkish Navy at Navarino. It was sixty years since it had fought against another European navy. It was thirty years since its big guns had fired in anger and then only against Egyptian forts. The British ships which fought in the Crimean war were recognisably the descendants of those who had defeated the Armada, nearly three hundred years before. During the second half of the century of *Pax Britannica*, technological progress on all fronts was rapid and warships changed beyond all recognition. Iron and then steel replaced wood in ship construction. Sail gave way to steam, culminating in Parsons' marine turbine, which permitted surface warships to achieve previously unimagined speeds. Muzzle-loading cannon, which were fired broadside and which had a range of no more than 3,000 yards, had been replaced by long-range guns in revolving turrets. In 1914 the Royal Navy's newest battleships, the *Queen Elizabeth* class of 26,000 tons with a speed of 24 knots, had a primary armament of eight 15in guns, in twin turrets, firing a high explosive shell weighing nearly a ton with a range of over 20,000 yards. The introduction of wireless telegraphy had revolutionised communications at sea and the rapid development of the marine diesel engine in the years immediately before 1914 had enabled the submarine to acquire its offensive capability. The problems caused by the vastly increased scale of operations and the consequent need for decentralising operational control had still to be recognised.

Another great unknown at the outset of the 1914–18 war was that of risk-assessment. As Lord Chatfield, Beatty's flag captain at Jutland and First Sea Lord in the 1930s, wrote: 'Nelson knew exactly the risks he ran and accurately allowed for them.' The admirals and captains of the First War, in both the Kriegsmarine and the Royal Navy, had no such advantage. As Chatfield noted: 'It is not easy to go to school again when you are middle-aged, to find a new world growing up ... which you do not know much about, a time without precedent in naval history ... It was difficult for them to act as a senior officer should.'[3] The data to make accurate risk assessments just did not exist. The resultant lack of experience led those of a rash disposition and even some careful men to take what in retrospect seem to be insane risks and others to act with what appears to be craven care, because they did not realise what they were doing. Looking back, it is unreasonable to censure a man for not reacting in what we might regard as the correct way to a situation that was outside his or anyone else's experience. It is no surprise that the Royal Navy and the Kriegsmarine both had to feel their way until they had secured sufficient operating experience in war conditions to understand the capabilities and limitations of their warships and their armament. Prior to the event, it probably never occurred to any senior naval officer on either side, or for that matter to Walther Schwieger, that a single torpedo could sink a liner of over 30,000 tons, like *Lusitania*, in only eighteen minutes.

In August 1914 the Naval War Staff had been in existence for barely two years and was ill-equipped to deal with the problems of modern marine warfare. The Royal Navy was still critically short of trained staff officers, most of whom were either at sea or if they were serving in the Admiralty were actively lobbying to get back to the fleet. Vice-Admiral Sir Peter Gretton, a distinguished escort group commander in World War Two and later Vice-Chief of the Naval Staff, noted 'the weakness [in 1914] of the Naval War Staff and indeed of almost every officer concerned with the Admiralty direction of the war.'[4] Admiral Sir Rosslyn Wemyss, First Sea Lord from 1917 to 1919, and highly respected throughout the service, in which he was inevitably known as Rosy, acknowledged that the Admiralty needed a large and efficient staff organisation and that at the outset of the war this had been inadequate. Criticism of the degree of over-centralisation would have been equally justified.

Illustrating the old adage that nothing fails like success, the service had become a victim of *Pax Britannica*, in large measure its own achievement. From a command and control standpoint, the service was by no means ready for war. Arthur Marder, doyen of naval historians, noted that although it was 'numerically a very imposing force . . . In reality, the British Navy . . . had run in a rut for nearly a century.'[5] The effects of over-centralisation and the lack of battle experience and risk assessment soon became apparent. During Hipper's raid on the English east coast in December 1914 and on two occasions during Jutland, Admirals declined to open fire on the grounds that they had not received the necessary orders from their superiors.[6] In August 1914 the author's father, a graduate of the second course of the war college, who was later to have a distinguished career in the Second World War, was serving in a triple capacity as Flag Lieutenant, Squadron Signals Officer and War Staff Officer to Vice-Admiral Sir Douglas Gamble, commanding the Fourth Battle Squadron in the Grand Fleet. Like many contemporary admirals, Gamble resented the institution of the War Staff and the author's father wrote of him: 'He won't admit that a knowledge of war is the least necessary for any officers until they come to flag rank but how they are to learn it then I don't know . . . the old school will not admit that any one junior to them can have any ideas at all.' He noted that the fleet's command and control system was too rigid and the tactics were too inflexible, adding presciently that: 'I do hope we get a day of good visibility, then I think we shall wipe them off the map. A low visibility is unpleasant and anything may happen.'[7] Jutland was fought in poor visibility and the deficiencies of an over-centralised command system were all too clearly demonstrated.

One of Fisher's first actions after his recall had been to ease the then Chief of the Naval War Staff, Vice-Admiral Sir Doveton Sturdee, a protégé of Beresford's whom he loathed, out of the Admiralty by giving him command of the battlecruisers sent to the South Atlantic to hunt down Von Spee. He replaced him by Vice-Admiral Henry Oliver, the former director of naval intelligence, a highly-regarded figure in the service and a more able man than his predecessor. He owed his nickname 'Dummy' to a reputation for being taciturn.

Unfortunately, and even by contemporary naval standards, Oliver was an arch-centraliser, who insisted in drafting almost every important signal himself. Captain (later Admiral Sir) Herbert Richmond, then assistant director of operations, noted that 'he held all the strings in his hands – indeed too much so. He was so busy allocating craft for convoys of troops across the Channel . . . that he has no time for strategical schemes . . . It is impossible for work to be done properly in such a way. The principle of decentralising and trusting subordinates has not yet gained ground; so seniors are worked to death and juniors find no use for their brains.'[8] Anyone who has read through the Admiralty files in the Public Record Office on the sinking of *Lusitania* cannot fail to notice the huge volume of routine signals which flowed across the desks of Churchill, Fisher, Wilson and Oliver. A flood of paper ended up on the desks of junior staff officers, most of whom had neither the training nor the experience to distinguish between the meaningful and the insignificant. In hindsight this was no way to run a large fleet in wartime, but in the early months of the conflict, the defects in the system were not obvious to anyone, even to men of outstanding ability as Churchill was or as Fisher had been in his prime. Fisher's generally sympathetic biographer, Ruddock Mackay, is critical of the old Admiral for his failure to take any steps to improve the effectiveness of the staff after his return to the Admiralty. By May 1915 his capability was declining almost by the day. To make matters worse, one of the Admiralty's most senior staff officers, the director of operations, Rear-Admiral Thomas Jackson, was palpably not up to the job.

In the autumn of 1914, through a number of fortuitous circumstances, British naval intelligence enjoyed a stroke, or to be more precise, three strokes of monumental good fortune, acquiring all three of the Kriegsmarine's most important naval codes. By the end of 1914, the cryptographic section in Room 40 of the Admiralty was able to intercept and read all the principal German naval codes and as a result were aware in almost minute detail of the High Seas Fleet's movements and plans. By November 1914 the Admiralty possessed the order of battle for the entire High Seas Fleet. Churchill delighted in this coup. As David Stafford, the historian of his involvement with secret intelligence, wrote: 'Churchill stood head and shoulders above his political contemporaries in grasping the importance of intelligence. Secret service with all its romance and melodrama, trickery, deception, plot and counter-plot, certainly appealed to the schoolboy within him.'[9] He took a close interest in Room 40 and rigorously examined its output.

If the Kriegsmarine had made too free a use of wireless telegraphy and paid little heed to any resultant security risk, Churchill was well aware of the paramount need to prevent the Germans from realising that their codes were being read. He insisted on maintaining a high degree of secrecy, tightly restricting access both to the decrypts and to the operational analyses regularly produced by the highly capable Commander Herbert Hope. It is not easy to hold a balance between using intelligence received from decrypts and running the risk of compromising its source and in practice the balance has generally erred on the side of discretion. In pursuit of this policy, Churchill ordered that only one copy should be made of each decrypt and that this should be sent to Oliver as Chief of the War Staff. He in turn circulated it to a small group of recipients including Fisher, Wilson, Hall, Jackson and his assistant, Richmond, and the duty captains in the War Staff. The fleet commanders, Jellicoe and Beatty, the C-in-Cs ashore, including Coke at Queenstown, and Captain Webb, as director of the trade division, were not in the loop and only received this intelligence at Oliver's discretion.

Unfortunately, this system impeded the development of an effective interface between intelligence and operations. It was to have dangerous consequences. During the fleet actions of the Dogger Bank and Jutland, there were serious delays in transmitting vital decrypts to Jellicoe and intelligence of the route on which the High Seas Fleet was returning home after Jutland was not properly communicated to him. It was only after Jutland that Room 40 was placed under the control of Hall's naval intelligence division which should have been its proper home from the outset.

When the Admiralstab initiated unrestricted submarine warfare in February 1915, its U-boats were already operating in the Irish Sea against merchant ships carrying cargoes of war supplies from America. Hope was by now producing a daily analysis of the strength, movement and location of the German U-boats. This report was restricted to Churchill, Fisher, Wilson and Oliver. Room 40's task was made easier by the frequency of the German radio traffic, some of which was extremely precise in its instructions. (Another example of the over-centralisation which wireless almost encouraged.) This traffic continued for the first two or three days of each U-boat's voyage until they passed beyond radio range. This information was of great potential value to the Admiralty as it gave it the power to track each U-boat's path with a reasonable degree of accuracy at least in the early stages of its voyage, and to warn local commanders of the threat to warships and merchant shipping and where the submarine was likely to penetrate.

In their zeal to pile blame on the unfortunate Turner, Bailey and Ryan commented: 'Turner ... had no contact with submarine operations and little knowledge of how to counter attacks by U-boats . . . he regarded his judgment, based on peace-time experience with surface ships, as superior to that of the officers in the Admiralty, who had been studying these problems for years and more recently in costly combat.'[10] Although the first part of this statement is true, the second is almost completely inaccurate. Before August 1914, neither the Royal Navy nor the Kriegsmarine had regarded the submarine as being anything other than a defensive weapon. In 1913 Fisher, supported by the former Conservative Prime Minister, Arthur Balfour, produced a series of prescient papers on what he considered to be the potential menace of the submarine. He wrote: 'I don't think it is even faintly realised the immense impending revolution which submarines will effect as offensive weapons of war.'[11] In a paper entitled *Submarines and Commerce* he asserted:

> . . . Germany, by stationing submarines off our principal commercial ports, may occasion greater damage than we can effect by means of our whole sea power . . . again it will be impossible to deal with merchant ships in accordance with international law. Is it presumed that they will disregard this and sink any vessel heading for an English commercial port?.[12]

Fisher was retired and Balfour out of office and neither man was believed. The conventional view within the Admiralty was represented by Jellicoe, then Second Sea Lord, who wrote in May 1913: 'I cannot conceive that submarines will sink merchant ships without warning.' Churchill wrote to Fisher on New Years Day 1914: '. . . there are a few points on which I am not convinced. Of these the greatest is the question of the use of submarines to sink merchant ships. I do not believe this would ever be done by a civilised power. These are frankly unthinkable propositions and the excellence of your paper is to some extent marred by the prominence assigned to them . . .'[13] Fisher's warnings went unheeded, and during the remaining months of peace little if anything other than defensively arming some merchant ships was done to develop any coherent anti-submarine strategy. In May 1914, Fisher wrote to Asquith: 'the recent arming of our merchant ships is unfortunate, for it gives the hostile submarine an excellent excuse (if she needs one) for sinking them.'[14] No research had been initiated into devices which could locate or destroy submerged submarines, the principal danger to seaborne trade.

The torpedoing of HMS *Aboukir* and two other cruisers by a single U-boat on one morning had dramatically illustrated the submarine's considerable offensive potential. This disaster resulted in what Commodore Reginald Tyrwhitt, the commander of the Harwich Force and one of the most able naval leaders of the war, sardonically described as a severe attack of 'submarinitis' both at the Admiralty and in the Grand Fleet. During the fleet action of the Dogger Bank in January 1915, Beatty had ordered a sharp turn to port away from the German battlecruisers, a move that was sharply to his disadvantage, because a lookout on his flagship HMS *Lion* thought he had seen a periscope. (If Oliver had sent all the relevant decrypts to Beatty, he would have known that there were no U-boats within forty miles of his fleet. This episode is a typical example of the misuse of intelligence by the over-centralised system inside the Admiralty.)

In 1915 the War Staff's cardinal priority was keeping watch on the High Seas Fleet at Wilhelmshaven and ensuring that the Grand Fleet was at prime readiness to deal with any German sortie into the North Sea. They shared Jellicoe's concern that he had a negligible superiority in destroyers and were thus loath to detach any from the fleet for escort duty. Their second priority was the Dardanelles operation, Churchill's concept, which urgently required the dispatch of warships from home ports to enable the Navy to continue supporting and supplying the army, now uncomfortably sandwiched between the Turks and the sea. Anti-submarine warfare and the protection of merchant ships had a low priority. Although, by January 1915, U-boats had already sunk a number of Allied merchant ships, the submarine menace was by no means well understood.

In February 1915, the trade division issued a document headed 'Instructions for Owners and Masters of British Merchant Ships with reference to the Operations of German Submarines against British Shipping', which displayed a startling ignorance of a U-boat's capabilities. A section called 'Information Respecting Submarines' stated:

> A submarine cannot see under water. When submerged she is obliged at frequent intervals to put up a long tube, known as a periscope, in order to see where she is going. Some submarines are armed with a gun, but this is an inferior weapon, incapable of inflicting serious injury upon an iron steamer manned by a resolute crew.
>
> All submarines carry torpedoes, but their supply is limited, and they will be very averse from firing them at merchant vessels. It is very difficult for a submarine to hit a moving ship with a torpedo, especially if she is kept nearly end on, and experience has shown that a

great many torpedoes are fired without any result . . . Gun-fire from most submarines is not dangerous.[15]

It would be difficult to imagine a more misleading or inept piece of staff work. During the Mersey inquiry Inglefield had contradicted the argument that a submarine could not see underwater and confirmed that its range of vision, using its periscope, was five miles. Although the Kriegsmarine had yet to implement a concerted programme aimed at Allied merchant shipping their vulnerability to both gunfire and torpedo attack should have been firmly established. Indeed, one wonders whether there was any contact between the trade division and the rest of the War Staff, and complacency about what actions could be taken to protect merchant ships against the U-boats seems only too evident.

In essence, the Admiralty had, at the outset of the war, adopted the policy outlined by Churchill in the House of Commons after the sinking of *Lusitania*. Merchant ships should sail independently and fend for themselves, taking evasive action whenever they were confronted by a submarine. The shipping lines took a more or less similar view. This conventional wisdom was stoutly maintained until its total failure became evident after Holtzendorff had resumed unrestricted submarine warfare with a much larger U-boat fleet in February 1917 and his submarines had succeeded in sinking 860,000 tons of merchant shipping in the following April. It was only when Great Britain was facing disaster that the Admiralty belatedly instituted a convoy system, which resulted in losses being reduced, more or less immediately, to manageable proportions.

The already overworked Oliver and his staff had to react to circumstances which had never been anticipated before the war. The procedures which were adopted after the loss of HMS *Aboukir* and her sisters, *ie* sailing at high speed, zigzagging and the provision of destroyer screens, proved reasonably effective in protecting warships but were less suited to safeguarding merchant ships. In effect, the only available methods of defending merchant ships were intelligence and actual sightings of U-boats. The system in operation was fallible as the trade division, headed by Captain Webb, was chiefly involved in policy and had no real authority over merchant ship movements. Nor was it in the loop to receive Room 40 decrypts. Indeed, the Admiralty lacked the central intelligence and communication system which was to prove essential to controlling merchant shipping. It was not until the Second World War that a comprehensive system was set up in Liverpool under the aegis of the C-in-C Western Approaches.

*   *   *

Four charges can be laid against the war staff over the loss of *Lusitania*. First, there had been a clear failure to grasp the significance of the Western Approaches, the sea lanes south of Ireland through which passed virtually all British merchant traffic eastward bound from North America. In peacetime the post of Vice-Admiral Queenstown was held by a flag officer who was not going any further in the service – a pleasant prelude to retirement. Sir Charles Coke was no Beatty or Tyrwhitt, who on his own initiative might have lobbied unceasingly to be given more or better equipped ships or wider operational authority. Second, despite the knowledge that a U-boat was operating off the south Coast of Ireland, *Lusitania* had not been given a destroyer escort, the accusation which had been raised in the *Morning Post* editorial on 10 May and reiterated by Beresford and Houston in the House of Commons. Third, the instructions sent to Turner had been ambiguous and insufficient, notably the failure to divert the liner to the North Channel. Finally, the telegram inaccurately stating that *submarines* were operating south of Coningbeg is yet a further instance of the lack of interface between intelligence and operations which occurred during the early years of the war. By deduction from the decrypts, it should have been evident to the war staff that only one submarine was in the area. Under the prevalent centralisation, this information was only narrowly circulated within the staff and was never transmitted to Coke. These criticisms reflect the war staff's inexperience, particularly in the area of risk-assessment.

After the sinking, Coke rather belatedly concluded that the resources available to the Queenstown command were inadequate. On 12 May he wrote to Graham Greene, using the customary words used by supplicant admirals requesting action from the Sea Lords: 'I have the honour to request that you will bring the following to the notice of their Lordships . . . recent events have emphasized the urgent need of a force of destroyers to be based at Queenstown. In my opinion 12 are necessary.'[16] Rear-Admiral the Hon Horace Hood, Commanding the 11th Cruiser Squadron or Cruiser Force B as it was also styled and flying his flag in HMS *Juno*, was more outspoken. Hood, known on the lower deck as the

'On 'Orace 'Ood, was a direct descendant of the great Lord Hood, a distinguished admiral in the Napoleonic Wars, and was widely considered to be one of the ablest flag officers in the service. He was one of the legion of admirals who had fallen foul of the increasingly vindictive and erratic Fisher, who had removed him as Rear-Admiral, Dover, and exiled him to command the squadron of obsolete cruisers stationed at Queenstown.

Hood had raised his flag on 10 April, only a month before the sinking. In his signal to the Admiralty he pointed out that his cruisers had already been forced to patrol up to 100 miles out from the south coast and advocated their replacement by a force of destroyers. He was explicit: 'I do not think that Cruiser Force B, as presently constituted, is of any use for the protection of trade to and from the North Atlantic,' adding that: 'the facilities at Queenstown could support a greatly increased force of trawlers and yachts.'[17] When these signals were circulated in the war staff, Captain Webb concurred. Oliver did not agree with either admiral, noting that there were higher priorities for employing destroyers elsewhere. His reaction suggests that he still did not appreciate the critical importance of protecting merchant shipping off the south coast of Ireland.

One admiral, Alexander Duff, saw the situation with clarity. Duff was then Rear-Admiral, Fourth Battle Squadron in the Grand Fleet but later in the war became the first director of the Admiralty's anti- submarine division and then assistant chief of the naval staff responsible for the entire campaign against the U-boats. His opinions must carry some weight as he is credited with much of the success for their eventual defeat. Marder described him as one of the few admirals of that war holding the four aces necessary for successful command: a gift for leadership, a fertile imagination with a creative brain, ability to make full use of the ideas of his juniors and offensive spirit. Duff commented trenchantly in his diary: '. . . *Lusitania* is sunk off the Irish coast . . . the disaster lies at the hands of the Admiralty. They knew that the ship was marked as an object lesson of German "frightfulness" and yet they allowed her to run at scheduled time and normal course and provided no protection. Indirectly the Dardanelles operation contributed; the T.B.Ds [destroyers] that should be guarding merchant shipping are being used there.'[18]

He was not alone in holding this opinion. Three days after the sinking, the consul-general in Rotterdam, Maxse, reported to the foreign office that Dutch naval officers were surprised at the inadequate protection which the Admiralty had provided to the liner.[19] Duff had highlighted a major problem. As a result of the Dardanelles operation, destroyers were urgently needed in the Mediterranean for escort duty and destroyers were the one class of ship in which the Royal Navy had a negligible superiority over the Germans. In May 1915, the Grand Fleet and the Harwich Force could muster between them only 96 destroyers as against 90–110 in the High Seas Fleet. No fleet commander has ever believed that he had sufficient ships. Nelson had once famously remarked that the lack of frigates would be emblazoned on his heart, and Jellicoe was understandably loath to part with any of his precious destroyers. Consequently, only a small number of destroyers were available for trade protection in home waters, even for valuable ships like *Lusitania.*

Lusitania had been escorted by the navy on earlier voyages. In November 1914 she had been accompanied westbound across the Atlantic by the battlecruiser HMS *Princess Royal* which Fisher had ordered to the West Indies in case Admiral von Spee had traversed the newly-completed Panama Canal. The War Staff were also concerned about the cruiser SMS *Karlsruhe* which they erroneously believed was still operating in the Atlantic but which had, however, blown up earlier that month. On 3 March Oliver received a decrypt advising U-boats that *Lusitania* was due to reach Liverpool on 5 March – a clear indication that she was regarded as a prime target. He reacted by ordering two 'L' class destroyers to meet her in St George's Channel and escort her into Liverpool. The destroyers, however, failed to make contact until the liner was off North Wales on the last leg of her voyage. Compared to its response to earlier threats to the liner, the Admiralty's puzzling inaction on 6 and 7 May has led some commentators, notably Patrick Beesly, to infer the existence of a conspiracy to abandon the vessel.

On 25 April, Room 40 decoded Bauer's instructions to *U-30* setting out the patrol areas for her and her two sisters, including Schwieger's *U-20*, detailed for the Irish Sea. On 1 May, the day after *U-20* had left Emden, Hope recorded that she was at sea since 30 April, gone NW, under orders for Irish Sea. This intelligence was neither sent to Coke nor to Webb. Oliver issued detailed orders to warships. The battleship HMS *Orion* had been refitting in Devonport and was due to rejoin the Grand Fleet at Scapa Flow. Oliver delayed her departure by two days until he could be reasonably certain that *U-30* was no longer in the sea lanes southwest of England. He finally instructed her to sail on 4 May, escorted by four destroyers, and with specific orders to steer a course fifty miles west of the Scilly Islands and one hundred miles off the Irish coast. The cruiser HMS *Gloucester*, returning from the Mediterranean Fleet, was ordered to keep sixty miles west of Finisterre, the westernmost point of the French coast, and to steer a mid-channel course when south of Ireland, whilst zigzagging and maintaining a speed of twenty knots. At 12.51pm on 7 May, less than two hours before *Lusitania* was torpedoed, Oliver sent a signal to the Admiral at Devonport with instructions for the cruiser HMS *Duke of Edinburgh*, due to sail for Scapa. She was to keep one hundred miles off the coast of Ireland and pass fifty 50 miles west of the Scottish island of St Kilda.[20] The precision of these orders contrasts sharply with the signals sent to the masters of merchant ships, including Turner aboard *Lusitania*, which seem almost as vague and obscure as the messages which had doomed the Light Brigade at Balaclava.

Four of the destroyers, which Houston had suggested in his Parliamentary question on 17 May were available for escort duty, had already been sent north with HMS *Orion*. Four 'L' class destroyers had been detached to escort troopships which were ferrying an Irish division from Dublin to Liverpool, a task which was successfully completed on the morning of 6 May. Oliver then ordered them to return to their base at Milford Haven to refuel and escort another battleship, HMS *Colossus*, which was proceeding to Devonport to refit. On the completion of this task, two destroyers were ordered back to Milford Haven and the other two were detailed to wait in Devonport to escort the troopships *Ascania* and *Ivernia*, Cunarders which had been chartered by the Admiralty's transport division, and which were due to sail on the night of 10 May.[21] As warships and troopships had priority, for all practical purposes the Navy had no destroyers available to escort *Lusitania*.

Anyone attempting to answer the problem of 'who had blunder'd' should eschew hindsight. As Aspinall had prudently reminded Mersey during the inquiry: 'we have the very great advantage of knowing so much now which was not known to him [Turner] then; we are sitting on the matter in cool judgment'. Fortunately, we have access to the account of a contemporary observer who had no axe to grind: Walther Schwieger. After he had torpedoed *Lusitania*, he kept an eagle eye on the outside world through his periscope. At 1715 CET, he noted to his surprise:

Round about are visible from time to time six smoke clouds from large inbound and outbound steamers. It is especially remarkable that so much traffic could be found here today, although the day before two large vessels were sunk south of St. George's Channel. *It remains inexplicable why* Lusitania *wasn't sent through North Channel.* [author's emphasis] The waters south of Ireland between Fastnet and St. George's Channel and between 30 and 50 miles from the coast will remain one of the best regions for the war on commercial traffic. Vessels cannot pass here at night if they want to enter the Irish Sea at night. It is unlikely that they will be convoyed by destroyers when at sea; therefore the attack on shipping will be easier to mount here than in the vicinity of harbours or lightships . . .[22]

A KapitanLeutnant of the Kriegsmarine had correctly summed up a situation which the War Staff had failed to recognise. Schwieger's question requires answering. Despite the lack of escorts, the War Staff could have taken alternative steps to protect *Lusitania* against submarine attack. First, she could have been diverted into Queenstown as *Transylvania* and *Ausonia* had been three months before. Submarines habitually prowled around the entrances to ports, as the Admiralty's directives had indicated. A diversion into Queenstown thus involved a degree of risk. In hindsight, the failure to divert the liner round the north of Ireland is, in Schwieger's phrase, more inexplicable as this course of action could have been adopted without incurring any risk as late as the evening of 6 May. Captain Casey Morgan USN testified as an expert witness in the in camera sessions of the Mayer trial that if Turner had been instructed to detour round the north coast at 8pm on 6 May, the diversion would have added approximately 110 miles or five and a quarter hours sailing time to the voyage at the liner's top attainable speed of 21 knots. He would have arrived at the Mersey bar at approx. 6.45am on 8 May with time in hand to have crossed the bar on the flood tide.

By the evening of 6 May the war staff knew that *Candidate* had been sunk off Coningbeg without warning earlier that day and was probably aware of the loss of *Centurion* and that the decrypts revealed that there were no U-boats off the northern Irish coast. The north Channel had been barred to merchant shipping in March on the grounds that mines had been laid there and as at its narrowest point the distance between County Antrim on the Irish side and Wigtonshire on the Scottish was only twenty-two miles as opposed to the clear sea lane of thirty-five miles in St George's Channel between the Tuskars and the Smalls. The mines had, however, been cleared and on 2 May the trade division had advised shipping lines that the channel had been reopened to merchant ships.

A week after *Lusitania* had been torpedoed, Admiral Hood was on patrol in HMS *Juno*. Aware that *U-27* was somewhere south of Ireland, and that Viereck had threatened that she would share the fate of her fellow-Cunarder, he ordered *Transylvania*, which had left New York on 8 May, to divert round the north of Ireland. In an almost *opera bouffe* incident, his instructions were countermanded by the shore station at Crosshaven, which came under Coke's command. *Transylvania*'s understandably confused captain complained that he could not deal with conflicting orders. Hood was listening in to this interchange and intervened, overruling Crosshaven.[23] The liner reached Liverpool safely. Before Churchill left the Admiralty, he made amends to Hood and rescued him from the naval Siberia to which the vengeful Fisher had exiled him, giving him command of the Third Battlecruiser Squadron in the Grand Fleet. His battlecruisers fought extremely well at Jutland but his flagship HMS *Invincible*, momentarily silhouetted against the setting sun, was hit by a shell from the battlecruiser *Derfflinger*, which penetrated her magazine, blowing the ship up. Hood and all but six of her crew were killed. His death was a severe loss to the service.

Six days after *Lusitania* was sunk, Fisher went behind Churchill's back and wrote to Asquith:

> . . . I honestly feel that I cannot remain where I am much longer as there is a . . . never-ceasing drain . . . of our resources in the decisive theatre of the war. But that is not the worst – instead of the whole of the Admiralty being concentrated on the daily increasing submarine menace in Home Waters, we are all diverted to the Dardanelles and the unceasing activities of the First Lord, both by day and night, are engaged in the ceaseless prodding of everyone . . . afloat and ashore in the interests of the Dardanelles Fleet . . .[24]

Fisher's objective was clearly to discredit Churchill but his letter is equally a damaging admission of his declining powers. He had been the one Admiral who had accurately foreseen the submarine's sinister potential and his failure to counter the U-boat offensive must have been galling. In his heyday, to use his own vivid phrase, hell itself would have frozen over before he could have been dissuaded from pursuing such an important objective.

Within two months of the loss of *Lusitania*, the Admiralty tacitly admitted that the powers and resources provided to Coke were totally inadequate for such a vital sea lane. The pressure for the resultant changes at Queenstown did not, however, originate from the war staff. Jellicoe and Beatty, realising that the current organisation at the Admiralty could not cope with the challenges of anti-submarine warfare, lobbied the new First Sea Lord, Sir Henry Jackson, for the appointment of a senior admiral who would be solely responsibility for coordinating operations against the U-boats. As Jellicoe wrote 'the War Staff have no time to do it'.[25] Although Jackson did not fully agree with the fleet commanders and a specialist anti-submarine division of the war staff was not established until Jellicoe became First Sea Lord in December 1916, their lobbying bore some fruit.

Admiral Coke had held the appointment at Queenstown for four years. He was sixty-one and he was overdue for relief. The Admiralty could thus safely dispense with his services without any official admission that his departure reflected any responsibility on their part for the loss of *Lusitania*. He hauled down his flag on 25 July and retired. His successor, Vice-Admiral Sir Lewis Bayly, known in the service as Luigi, was one of its best-known characters. Fisher had sacked Bayly as C-in-C Channel Fleet following the torpedoing of HMS *Formidable* on New Year's Day 1915 and had relegated him to the command of the naval college at Greenwich. Bayly's ships had not been zigzagging at the time and it is instructive to compare Fisher's relatively lenient treatment of Bayly with his vindictive onslaught on Turner four months later. Jellicoe had argued that Bayly's talents were being wasted at Greenwich and vigorously advocated that he be appointed to the vital post at Queenstown. Bayly was styled Vice-Admiral (later C-in-C) Western Approaches and was given vastly increased authority and resources. Under his command he had a flotilla of sloops, small destroyers without torpedoes, designed for escort duty, which were used to protect the more valuable ships on final approach to British ports. Bayly forged a considerable reputation at Queenstown and won the respect and the admiration of the US Navy, several of whose destroyer divisions were stationed there after America came into the war.

Lusitania was doomed by what might be described as Admiralty overload, which resulted from over-centralisation, the lack of operational experience and risk-assessment and the inadequate interface between intelligence and operations which was to plague the Navy for the first two years of the war, most notably during the battle of Jutland. As Admiral Duff had noted, the War Staff had overlooked the ominous significance of the advertisement that had appeared in the New York papers under the byline of the German embassy on the day that *Lusitania* sailed and which Captain Gaunt had promptly reported to the Admiralty. The staff's actions to protect the liner taken after they had received intelligence of Schwieger's presence off the south coast of Ireland, including the torpedoing of *Candidate* and *Centurion* without any warning, could be termed inadequate. Diversion or more explicit warnings would have averted disaster.

A point should, however, be entered in mitigation of the war staff. Churchill's instinct for intelligence had persuaded him that the use of invaluable decrypts within the Admiralty had to be carefully regulated. He rightly considered it imperative to prevent the Kriegsmarine from realising that their codes were being compromised and that the Admiralty had detailed intelligence about submarine movements. Indeed, it was not until the Second World War that a balance was achieved between the risk of compromising SIGINT and its effective application. In the early months of 1915, there were no accepted guidelines for its use. As a result the war staff consistently erred on the side of caution. As Oliver strongly suspected that the merchant navy's codes, including the 1st Edition MV code carried on *Lusitania*, had fallen into the hands of the Kriegsmarine, he was especially wary about relaying SIGINT to merchant ships. This understandable reluctance might explain why Oliver took no action over a decrypt from a German radio station announcing that the liner was due to sail on her next westbound voyage on 15 May. He may have reasoned that as she had survived a U-boat threat on her March eastbound voyage when the destroyers from Milford Haven almost failed to make contact with her, she could well do so again. The exchange of correspondence between Graham Greene and Sanderson after *Lusitania* had been torpedoed indicates the Admiralty's prevailing belief – which we now know to be incorrect – that speed per se was sufficient to enable fast liners to evade U-boats. The War Staff might have concluded that in framing their signals to Turner there was no necessity to endanger valuable SIGINT. In retrospect this was a serious error.

It would be inequitable to place the blame on any one individual. Coke could be criticised for failing to send more of the ships under his command to sea on the morning of 7 May as *Lusitania* steamed along the south coast of Ireland. Even if they could not locate Schwieger, they might have forced him to keep below periscope depth. However, he had been given inadequate resources and terms of reference and, like many contemporary flag officers, he was not a man given to acting on his own initiative. Oliver, the Admiral most directly concerned, was grossly overworked and Fisher's mental powers were fading fast. Modern technology had made the first important war at sea in a century much more complex than any earlier conflict; a factor to which the Navy's command structure in 1915, operating in what might be called uncharted waters, could not properly respond. The historian, David Stafford, notes: 'The Admiralty's mindset [was] slow to wake up to the ruthless nature of modern war at sea and still convinced that merchant ships should be treated differently from warships.'[26] The service had not only fought relentlessly against the introduction of a staff system but had neglected to train its officers in higher command. As Churchill himself wrote: 'We had competent administrators, brilliant experts of every description, unequaled navigators, good disciplinarians, fine sea officers, brave and devoted hearts, but at the outset of the conflict we had more captains of ships than captains of war.'[27]

The penchant of both Churchill and Oliver for running a one-man show had unfortunate results. However, the Admiralty's failure to realise the need for decentralised control of operations was a more important factor in the tragedy. The report of the Dardanelles Commission, set up to review that ill-fated operation, described the way that many senior officers of both services conducted operations in the early years of the First World War: 'We are of the opinion that Lord Kitchener did not sufficiently avail himself of the services of his General Staff, with the result that more work was undertaken by him than was possible for one man to do, and confusion and want of efficiency resulted.' Although Kitchener was Secretary of State for War, he also acted throughout 1915 as if he were de facto chief of the imperial general staff. The Commission's observation about the dangerous consequences of excessive centralisation, could, with equal justification, have been made about the Admiralty in May 1915.

In theory, and under the British concept of Ministerial Responsibility, the 'buck stopped' with Churchill. He had been appointed First Lord with the specific remit of establishing the war staff and he could be faulted for not ensuring that it was operating effectively. Indeed, he seems to have lost interest in the staff once it had been set up. His habitual interference in operations did not make the staff's task any easier. His most recent biographer, Professor Norman Rose, noted of his second term at the Admiralty in 1939–40: 'Churchill generated vitality. The Admiralty buzzed with "electricity" when he was present. While he was away, it was dead, dead, dead.'[28] The comment is equally true of his first term. If Churchill had not been away from the Admiralty on 6 and 7 May, his ready intuition might conceivably have appreciated the dangers lurking off the Irish coast and he might have demanded that more specific instructions and warnings be sent to Turner, thereby reducing the odds against disaster. In effect the 1,198 men, women and children who died on *Lusitania*, were victims of failures in a system, which had beaten even the energies of Churchill.

CHAPTER 19

Aftermath: America Goes to War

O ne of the most enduring myths of *Lusitania* was that her sinking led inexorably to American entry into the war. The future Cunard commodore, James Bisset, who had lost friends and old shipmates aboard the liner, expressed this widely held, but erroneous, view in his memoirs:

> We learnt the terrible news which stunned the world and, in a sense, altered the course of the war and of human history. It was the sinking of the *Lusitania* by a torpedo fired without warning by a German U-Boat – a man-made disaster made more horrifying for that reason than the wreck of the *Titanic* three years previously – that aroused the intense indignation and hatred against Germany which eventually brought the U.S.A. into the war. That was the turning point in American public opinion which, until then, had been isolationist and neutral.[1]

As recently as August 1990 in an editorial named 'Laying *Lusitania*'s Ghosts', *The Times* declared: 'Although two years were to elapse before the United States joined Britain's side, the destruction of so large a merchant vessel played a large part in that decision.'[2]

In reality, the United States declared war for reasons which had little to do with the torpedoing of the great liner. In May 1915, American public opinion overwhelmingly wished to avert war. In June of that year, House wrote to Sir Edward Grey that 'the vast majority of our people desire the President to be very firm in his attitude towards Germany and yet avoid war'.[3] The Austro-Hungarian military attaché in Washington, on holiday that summer on the New Jersey shore, noticed an increasing animosity against Germany and her allies but, like most of his colleagues, doubted that it was strong enough to lead to war.[4] We have seen how Wilson had taken the mood of the American people at the end of 1915 and that he and Lansing had succeeded in achieving a diplomatic solution to the acrimonious dispute with Germany which had followed the sinking. Matters might well have rested there in the absence of three seemingly unrelated events which occurred later in 1916, the inconclusive battle of Jutland, a significant change in the power structure inside Germany and the poor harvest worldwide.

The German government declared Jutland to be a great victory on the basis that their losses in both ships and men were much less than the British. Indeed, they had sunk three British battlecruisers for the loss of only one of their own and the German dead and wounded were less than half those of the British. Five days after the battle, the Kaiser went to Wilhelmshaven to congratulate the Kriegsmarine. Addressing the crew of the flagship *Friedrich Der Grosse*, he declared rather extravagantly that the spell of Trafalgar had been broken. In fact, the German High Seas Fleet had had a lucky escape, due to an unhappy succession of communication failures and uninspired leadership which had once again plagued the Grand Fleet. The fleet commander, Admiral Reinhard Scheer, had to remind Wilhelm that he had only ten dreadnoughts and a single battlecruiser ready for sea and that the British had more than twice that number.[5] A month later, reporting to the Kaiser on the battle, he emphasised: 'there can be no doubt that even the most successful result of a high sea battle will not compel England to make peace. A victorious end to the war at not too distant a date can only be sought by the crushing of English economic life through U-boat action against English commerce.'[6] The star of the submarine hawks was once again waxing.

Wilhelm was meanwhile losing faith in Falkenhayn. In August 1916 he was made a scapegoat for the costly failure at Verdun and was demoted to a field command in the Balkans. He was replaced by the formidable combination of Hindenburg and Ludendorff, formerly C-in-C and Chief of Staff on the eastern front. Although Hindenburg enjoyed huge prestige for his victory over the Russians at Tannenberg, he was essentially a front man and the real power rested with the belligerent Ludendorff. Citing the exigencies of war, the duo demanded and received extensive powers over all aspects of national life and economic activity.

Germany gradually drifted into military dictatorship. Bernstorff had been on leave in Germany when war broke out in August 1914. When he returned to Washington, his American wife Jeanne had remained behind to support their recently widowed daughter. In August 1916, Ballin arranged a passage for her to New York on a Danish liner. Before she sailed she had a meeting with Bethmann-Hollweg. Her close friend, Erika von Watzdorf, who had accompanied her to this meeting, wrote:

To Jeanne's repeated requests that the total submarine war would mean America's entry into the war, Bethmann replied in pain that he knew that but that he was powerless against the will of the Supreme Command and the Pan-Germans. It was a sad spectacle to see the Chancellor of the German Empire in this helpless fatalistic condition in the hour of greatest . . . danger.[7]

In October 1916, Holtzendorff intensified the submarine warfare campaign against commercial targets. As a result of the priority given to submarine construction, he now had 87 U-boats available for operations out of a total fleet of 119 as against only 25 when the previous offensive began in February 1915. Many new U-boats had a long range and some could even cross the Atlantic. In October 1916 the *U-53* had appeared off Newport, Rhode Island, creating a considerable stir, and torpedoed five ships, two of them neutral, on one occasion asking the captain of an American destroyer to move out of the way so that she could get a better shot at her target. From a German point of view the results were impressive. Although the Kriegsmarine was still observing cruiser rules, over the four months to the end of January 1917, 757 ships with an average monthly tonnage of 326,000 were sunk, more than double the figure achieved in May 1915, including *Lusitania*. Early in November the P & O liner *Arabia* was sunk in the Mediterranean without any warning. An explosion in her boiler room killed eleven of her crew. Good seamanship and the prompt arrival of rescue ships allowed her 439 passengers including a large number of women and children to be saved. This action was a flagrant breach both of the Kaiser's instructions that unarmed passenger liners were not to be attacked and of the agreements which Wilson and Lansing had so painstakingly achieved with Berlin earlier in the year. Lansing protested strongly to Bernstorff but in return the Germans prevaricated and offered excuses. Their recalcitrant reaction indicated the growing influence of the hawks within the German command and control structure.

In November, Wilson won a second term, campaigning on the slogan 'He kept us out of war' which his diplomatic success had made possible. He was again returned on a minority of the electoral vote and as in 1912 he owed this somewhat underwhelming victory to Republican feuding. The powerful Governor of California, Hiram Johnson, had fallen out with and refused to support or endorse his party's presidential candidate, Charles Evans Hughes. By a margin of less than two thousand votes the golden state went Democrat, enabling Wilson to scrape back to the White House. By the end of 1916 he had become somewhat disenchanted with the Allies and especially with the British. He had been offended firstly by their breach of international convention in the *Baralong* incident and later by the severity of the sentences handed out to the ringleaders of the Easter rising in Dublin and by the heavy loss of life on the Somme. In this mood he had conceived the unrealistic concept of peace without victory, which he expounded in a speech on 22 January 1917, lecturing both sides to renounce their ambitions. As might be expected his theories went down badly in London and Paris, with the British, who had gone to war to defend the integrity of Belgium, being understandably exasperated. Theodore Roosevelt, always a incisive critic, reasonably pointed out that Wilson's belief that there was little difference in morality between the Allies and Germany was 'wickedly false'.[8]

By December 1916 the once-sceptical Holtzendorff had become an adherent of unrestricted submarine warfare. Despite the successes of the autumn campaign, he had accepted the arguments forcefully presented by Scheer and his chief of staff, the bellicose Adolf von Trotha. They reasoned that if the navy continued to operate under cruiser rules, the submarine would never become a decisive weapon and that Britain could not be defeated. Trotha maintained that the Admiralstab had deferred to American diplomatic pressure for too long and that it was time that the blunt end of the sword be presented to the enemy. Holtzendorff and his economic advisers concluded that Britain, with her extensive overseas resources, was effectively maintaining her allies and that if she was knocked out of the war, France and Italy would be forced to sue for peace.[9]

They argued that the failure of the 1916 harvest throughout Europe and in the chief cereal producing areas in North America and in Argentina provided an unrepeatable opportunity for decisive action. Holtzendorff's experts concluded that Britain would not be able to buy their full requirement of wheat and other grains from the United States and Canada after February 1917. They asserted that Britain would have to make good this deficiency by importing wheat from Australia, which would entail the diversion of 750,000 tons of much-needed shipping. With one hundred submarines available in January 1917 and a return to unrestricted submarine warfare, the Admiralstab concluded that they could sink in excess of 600,000 tons per month or double the current level of losses. With the Allied merchant navies suffering such heavy losses and believing that neutral shipowners would react to unrestricted warfare by keeping their fleets in port, they reckoned that they could force Britain into submission in six months. They urged that the unrestricted campaign should start no later than 1 February so as to achieve its objective before the 1917 harvest could provide the British with any relief.

On 9 January 1917, an imperial conference met at Pless in Silesia, ostensibly to consider Holtzendorff's plan. In reality the outcome was a foregone conclusion. As early as August 1916, Hindenburg and Ludendorff had advised the Kaiser to revert to unrestricted submarine warfare. Before Christmas they had decided to support the Kriegsmarine even at the cost of risking an American declaration of war. After Holtzendorff had expounded on the scheme, Bethmann-Hollweg rose to object, quoting the views of Bernstorff and other diplomats who knew the country well, that American entry into the war would strongly reinforce the Allies and would be greatly to Germany's disadvantage. He made the mistake of rambling on for nearly an hour, thoroughly irritating the Kaiser. Holtzendorff, carried away by hubris, retorted: 'I will give Your Majesty my word as a naval officer that not one American will set foot on the Continent.'[10] Hindenburg told Wilhelm: 'We can take care of America.' Ignorance of and contempt for America was the order of the day at Pless. Holtzendorff's attitude is particularly surprising as he was presumably aware of the strength of the American Navy, whose twelve dreadnoughts, fifty-six destroyers and fifty submarines made it a force to be reckoned with.

The Chancellor no longer carried much weight and within a few months was to be pushed out of office by Ludendorff. Alfred von Valentini, Chief of the Kaiser's Civil Cabinet, overheard the distraught Bethmann-Hollweg mutter 'Finis Germaniae'. So the die was cast, the agreement reached with Washington the previous February was unilaterally torn up and Holtzendorff was authorised to resume unrestricted submarine warfare on 1 February. America and the other neutral countries were not to be told of the decision until the previous evening. It was a massive gambler's throw and one which came uncomfortably close to succeeding.

In November 1916, the relatively moderate foreign minister, Von Jagow, had been replaced by his deputy, Arthur Zimmermann. Unlike his predecessor, who had shared Bernstorff's objections to a unrestricted submarine campaign, the new minister was a blustering hawk. Ballin, who had a low opinion of many German diplomats, was particularly contemptuous of Zimmermann, remarking that if he had been a HAPAG employee he would not have risen above the level of porter.[11] The new foreign minister now proposed a scheme to inveigle America into trouble in her own backyard, thus making her entry into war with Germany even less likely. Since the Mexican revolution of 1910, relations between the two countries had been at best uneasy. Wilson's ham-fisted intervention in the internecine world of Mexican politics had made matters worse. In April 1914 he had ordered the Marines to forcibly occupy the port of Veracruz to prevent the HAPAG cargo liner *Ypiranga* landing guns and ammunition for the then President, Huerta, whom he detested. Ballin had been personally involved in planning this consignment. Nineteen Americans and over a hundred Mexicans were killed in an operation which achieved nothing. Later that year Huerta was driven out by his rival, Carranza. The new President was not in complete control of the country. In March 1916, the warlord Pancho Villa crossed the border and torched the town of Columbus, New Mexico, killing some twenty people. It is possible that German agents, acting behind Bernstorff's back, who had been actively interfering in Mexican affairs since the 1910 revolution, had incited this action. In response, Wilson had sent an expeditionary force, commanded by General J J (Black Jack) Pershing, in what proved to a futile effort to hunt Villa down. Pershing's troops had only recently been recalled and an uneasy peace now prevailed.

Zimmermann convinced Ludendorff that Carranza could be encouraged to resume hostilities and proposed an alliance with Mexico against the United States. On January 16th he sent a telegram to Bernstorff for onwards transmission 'by a safe route' to Heinrich Von Eckhardt, the German Minister to Mexico. It read . . .

WE SHALL COMMENCE UNRESTRICTED SUBMARINE WARFARE ON FEGRUARY 1ST. WE SHALL ENDEAVOUR . . . TO KEEP THE UNITED STATES NEUTRAL. IN THE EVENT OF THIS NOT SUCCEEDING, WE MAKE MEXICO A PROPOSAL OF ALLIANCE . . . MAKE WAR TOGETHER, MAKE PEACE TOGETHER, GENEROUS FINANCIAL SUPPORT AND AN UNDERSTANDING ON OUR PART THAT MEXICO IS TO RECONQUER THE LOST TERRITORIES IN TEXAS, NEW MEXICO AND ARIZONA.

YOU WILL INFORM THE PRESIDENT OF MEXICO OF THE ABOVE MOST SECRETLY AS SOON AS THE OUTBREAK OF WAR WITH THE UNITED

STATES IS CERTAIN AND ADD THE SUGGESTION THAT HE SHOULD, ON HIS OWN INITIATIVE INVITE JAPAN TO IMMEDIATE ADHERENCE AND AT THE SAME TIME MEDIATE BETWEEN JAPAN AND OURSELVES. PLEASE CALL THE PRESIDENT'S ATTENTION TO THE FACT THAT THE UNRE- STRICTED EMPLOYMENT OF OUR SUBMARINES NOW OFFERS THE PROSPECT OF COMPELLING ENGLAND TO MAKE PEACE WITHIN A FEW MONTHS.

It is worth remembering that Japan was allied to Britain by treaty and had declared war on Germany in August 1914. Although the Japanese government had scrupulously upheld its treaty obliga- tions, Berlin had long dreamt of inducing Japan to break her alliance. Their efforts had achieved nothing. To ensure its arrival, Zimmermann sent his telegram in code by three different routes, including the State Department's own cable system. Room 40 plucked the signal out of the ether on each of the three routes. Hastily summoned by his cryptologists, 'Blinker' Hall, now a rear- admiral, quickly realised that the naval intelligence division had struck gold. As no spymaster wishes to take any action which might reveal to the enemy that he is reading their codes, Hall astutely locked the damning decrypts in his safe and waited for events to unfold.

On the morning of 18 January, Lansing, who disliked the state department's network being used for messages between Bernstorff and Berlin, handed Zimmermann's telegram to the ambassador, not without apprehension. Bernstorff decoded the message and sent it in the same code to Eckhardt in Mexico City, via Western Union. He knew the consequences for Germany of the resumption of the submarine campaign and fought valiantly to the bitter end to get the decision revoked. As early as February 1916, the influential Hamburg banker, Max Warburg, who had close contacts on Wall Street, had opposed any return to unre- stricted submarine warfare as it would alienate Washington. On January 26 he repeated his warning: 'if we end up at war with America we will face an enemy with such strength . . . that we will have nothing more to hope for.'[12] No one in Berlin took any more notice of Bernstorff or Warburg than they had of Bethmann-Hollweg. On the afternoon of 31 January, the ambas- sador called on Lansing to inform him of the new campaign. The normally reserved Lansing realised that all Bernstoff's efforts to preserve peace between America and Germany now lay in ruins. In a gesture of sympathy he escorted him to his car with his arm around the disconsolate ambassador's shoulder. When the news was released the next day, the Dow Jones Index fell by 7.2 per cent, the third largest decline since its inception in 1895.

A stunned Wilson was loath to break with neutrality and clung to the concept of peace without victory. He was still vacillating when the cabinet met on 2 February, telling the secretary for agriculture, David Houston, that he did not want either side to win. He was now expounding similar views to those held by Bryan at the time *Lusitania* had been sunk. By the next day he finally decided not to declare war on Germany but only to break off diplomatic relations, hand Bernstorff his passport and post armed guards on American merchant ships.

Admiral Hall had, like Wall Street, expected Wilson to go to war thus relieving him of the necessity of disclosing the dynamite telegram. Two days later he revealed its contents to the British foreign office. By 19 February Room 40 had successfully decoded the entire message and Hall's agents in Mexico City had got hold of Bernstorff's signal to Eckhardt. The time was ripe. Arthur Balfour, now Foreign Secretary in Lloyd George's Government, authorised Hall to show the telegram to ambassador Page, who was deeply frustrated by Wilson's continuing insistence on neutrality. On the morning of 24 February Page cabled the Zimmermann telegram to Washington. Wilson was furious with the German chicanery, not least by their misuse of the State Department cable facility, which he himself had so incautiously authorised. His bill to arm merchant ships was in trouble in the Senate where a group of antiwar senators was seeking to kill it by filibustering.

To force the issue he released the details of the telegram to the newspapers. The story broke on the morning of 1 March. The banner headlines of the *New York Times* thundered:

GERMANY SEEKS ALLIANCE AGAINST U.S.

ASKS JAPAN AND MEXICO TO JOIN HER

FULL TEXT OF PROPOSALS MADE PUBLIC[13]

There were many in America who could not believe what they read. The Mexican and Japanese governments quickly denied any knowledge of the affair. True to form, George Sylvester Viereck, whose paper *The Fatherland* had disseminated so many lies about *Lusitania*, rushed into print to declare the telegram 'a brazen forgery planted by British agents – a preposterous document, obviously faked.'[14] They were all to be trumped. On 3

March Zimmermann, compounding his earlier arrogance in sending such a message over the wires, inexplicably revealed that he had indeed sent the telegram.

The Prussian invasion plot, as the media rapidly christened the telegram, crystallized opinion across America. To most of the population the war had been remote and the issues far from clear. The sinking of *Lusitania* had alerted Americans to German frightfulness and left them with a deeply rooted aversion to their war machine and its ruthless disregard for human life. However, the diplomatic war of the paper bullets which had followed her torpedoing and later losses like *Arabic, Sussex, Ancona* or the Cunarder *Laconia*, sunk in February 1917 with the loss of two American lives, had not greatly aroused their interest. The mass of Americans who lived far from the sea still felt remote from, and unaffected by, the war.

Zimmermann and his telegram radically changed this comfortable perception. In her book *The Zimmermann Telegram*, the historian Barbara Tuchman summed up the situation aptly: 'This was different. This was Germany proposing to attack the United States, conspiring with America's neighbour to snatch American territory: worse, conspiring to set an Oriental foe on America's back. This was a direct threat upon the body of America, which most Americans had never dreamt was a German intention.'[15] The Washington correspondent of *The Times* reported: '. . . the Mexican revelations had aroused the public more than anything else since the outbreak of war . . . it was worth a dozen *Laconia* outrages . . . that the West had never been touched by the submarine issue but that the Mexican plot and Bernstorff's complicity had touched everybody . . . to the quick.'[16]

Throughout America, public opinion reluctantly accepted that the machinations of Germany would involve them in war. The *Chicago Tribune*, owned and edited by the isolationist Colonel Robert McCormick, expressed a typical reaction, asking its readers to realise 'without delay that Germany recognises us as an enemy' and that the country could no longer avoid 'active participation in the present conflict.' These sentiments were mild in comparison to their contemporaries in Texas or on the west coast. The *El Paso Times* derided Prussian militarism as 'writhing in the slime of intrigue' and the *Sacramento Bee* denounced Germany for its 'treacherous enmity, underhanded, nasty intriguing.'[17]

Viereck readily recognised that at a stroke Zimmermann's admission had destroyed the political influence of the German-

American community. It is difficult to have much sympathy for him but it is ironic that he should have been betrayed by the very men in Berlin for whose cause he had so loyally propagated such flagrant lies. German-owned papers in the midwest, which had followed Viereck in denouncing the telegram as a forgery, either lapsed into a sheepish silence or rapidly announced that they and their readers were and always had been loyal Americans. After Hitler came to power, Viereck showed his true allegiance, becoming a leading light in the German-American Bund, the local off-shoot of the Nazi Party.

Bernstorff was meanwhile having a miserable journey back to Germany. On the day *Lusitania* had left New York for the last time, three other liners had also sailed for European ports. Over the ensuing two years North Atlantic passenger schedules had declined almost to the point of being non-existent. In 1916 the Dutch, enraged by the sinking of three liners and the torpedoing of a fourth, the Holland-Amerika *Ryndam*, which barely managed to make port, had cancelled all services for the duration. The ejected ambassador, his wife and his staff found passage on the Danish liner *Frederik VIII*, which sailed from New York on 15 February. They were seen off by Dudley Field Malone, several secret service agents and a crowd of newspapermen. The British granted Bernstorff safe passage on the condition that the liner should call at Halifax for a detailed search. In this diversion the hand of the crafty Hall can be detected. The Admiral had a high regard for Bernstorff's powers of persuasion and worried that even at this late hour he might be able to argue Berlin away from a confrontation with the United States. Taking no chances Hall held *Frederik VIII* in Halifax for twelve days, only authorising her departure after the telegram had safely been in the hands of the State Department for seventy-two hours. In reality Bernstorff had absolutely no influence with the military rulers of Germany and their ultra-nationalist allies. When he finally reached Berlin in the third week in March, the Kaiser ungratefully refused to see him.

Wilhelm eventually relented and later in 1917 he appointed Bernstorff as ambassador to Turkey where he served until the end of the war. He refused any further office and for seven years he was a member of the Reichstag. During the Weimar Republic, Bernstorff was scurrilously attacked by ultra-nationalists for having damaged the best interests of Imperial Germany by appeasing President Wilson during his term as ambassador. These criticisms were as illogical as they were inequitable for had

Bernstorff succeeded in his prime objective of keeping America out of the war, Germany might well have escaped the catastrophe which befell her in October and November of 1918. Harold Nicolson, reviewing Bernstorff's memoirs from an Allied point of view, offered a far more realistic assessment of his achievements: 'He was our most formidable diplomatic adversary during the war and had his Government followed his advice, we might never have achieved victory ...' Bernstorff left Germany for ever in 1933 when Hitler became Chancellor, dying in exile in Geneva in October 1939. His American widow, fearing a German invasion of Switzerland and the long arm of the Gestapo, returned home and died in Washington in 1943.[18]

With extraordinary complacency, it never seems to have occurred to Zimmermann or his subordinates that their codes might have been broken. Despite Eckhardt's efforts, President Carranza decided not take the German bait so that the entire exercise had been in vain. Zimmermann had succeeded in creating one of history's greatest unforced errors. In July 1917 he was sacked, never to hold office again.

When the anti-war senators filibustered out his bill to arm merchant ships, Wilson issued an executive order putting the guards aboard. German U-boats had meanwhile sunk five American ships without warning, three of them on 18 March, with the loss of thirty-six lives, further inflaming anti-German feelings. By the middle of March the neutralists were in total disarray and public opinion had run ahead of the President. When Americans of such different political views as Theodore Roosevelt, who had once been in a small minority in advocating war, and the pacifist and teetotaler Josephus Daniels, whom Wilson had unsuitably made Secretary of the Navy, agreed that conflict was now inevitable, he had to act. The March revolution in Russia, ousting the Czar, removed the last block in Wilson's mind. He could reasonably justify his complete change of position by claiming that America would be fighting a war to save democracy.

On 21 March, Wilson summoned a special session of Congress for the evening of 2 April to receive a message about 'grave matters of national policy'. Despite the late hour and a steady spring drizzle, a large crowd had gathered to watch Wilson drive down Pennsylvania Avenue with a cavalry escort on his way to Capitol Hill. He sat rigid inside the car staring fixedly in front of him. Who can guess at the thoughts which may have passed through the mind of the complex man which lay behind the icy

Calvinist mask. Was he back a half-century in time, once again the boy tending the Confederate wounded in his father's church, or did he, as in the Rogers cartoon, feel the spectral presence of the ghosts of *Lusitania*, seeking vengeance?

Inside the great chamber of the House of Representatives, not a seat was to be had. Washington society had, like the President, dined early and flocked to Capitol Hill to hear the historic announcement. Many congressmen were wearing miniature Stars and Stripes in their buttonholes. The justices of the Supreme Court in their black robes and the chiefs of staff of the army and navy were in the audience. House and Tumulty sat with Lansing and other Cabinet members. Nearby were the Allied ambassadors, relief almost perceptible on their faces.

On the stroke of 8.30pm the sergeant-at-arms appeared on the floor of the House and announced the President. Wilson strode to the rostrum and began his address, asking Congress to 'declare the recent course of the Imperial German Government to be in fact nothing less than war against the government and people of the United States'. He described the submarines as out-laws and referring to the Zimmermann telegram, he reminded the legislators that Germany 'means to stir enemies against us at our very doors.' When he declared that 'there is one choice we cannot make . . . we will not choose the path of submission' the venerable Chief Justice, Edward White, who had fought in the Confederate army during the Civil War, was so moved that tears ran down his cheeks. By House's calculation, Wilson reached his eloquent peroration after speaking for thirty-two minutes[19] asserting that:

> the German Government was a natural foe of liberty . . . that the world must be made safe for democracy . . . that America must fight for the principles that gave her birth. To such a task we can dedicate our lives and our fortunes, everything we are and everything we have, with the pride of those who know that the day has come when America is privileged to spend her blood and her might for the principles which gave her birth and happiness and the peace which she has treasured. God helping her, she can do no else.

It was perhaps Wilson's finest moment. The provocation which Germany had heaped on America had led him reluctantly to pro-pose war to Congress and Wilson had the support of a united nation to an extent which would certainly not have been possible after the loss of *Lusitania*. Even his most implacable adversary,

Theodore Roosevelt, conceded: 'The President's great message was literally unanswerable. Of course when a war is on, all minor considerations, including all partisan considerations, vanish at once. All good Americans will back the President with single minded loyalty.'[20] Congress and the gallery gave Wilson a standing ovation which one reporter called 'a roar like a storm'. When the President returned to the White House, his mask slipped for a minute and he remarked to Tumulty: 'Think of what they were applauding. My message today was a message of death for our young men. How strange it seems to applaud that.' The Senate voted for war by 82 to 6, the House by 373 to 50. At noon Washington time on 6 April 1917, Wilson signed the formal declaration. To borrow the words of Admiral Yamamoto after Pearl Harbor, Imperial Germany had recklessly raised the slumbering giant against her and had thereby sealed her fate. The ghosts of *Lusitania* had been assuaged.

CHAPTER 20

The Captains and the Kings Depart

The tumult and the shouting dies
The captains and the kings depart:
RUDYARD KIPLING *Recessional*

S everal writers have pronounced that the sinking of *Titanic* heralded the end of the age of innocence. The loss of a large luxury liner, declared by the media to be unsinkable, after striking an iceberg and with heavy loss of life, certainly challenged the comfortable wisdom that technology had mastered the elements. In the eyes of passengers on the North Atlantic, and despite the new regulations hurriedly introduced after the tragedy, life on the express liners went on in much the same fashion as before. Yet in the two years which separated the sinking of *Titanic* from the outbreak of war the first two of Ballin's trio of giant liners, *Vaterland* and *Imperator*, each of them 10,000 tons larger than *Titanic* and *Lusitania*'s larger sister *Aquitania*, all three if anything more ornate than the lost liner, went into service.

An American poet, Alan Seeger, then serving with the French Foreign Legion and who was later killed on the Somme, wrote to his mother three days after the sinking of *Lusitania*: 'I cannot understand the American state of mind, nor why Americans have the temerity to venture into a war zone, much less let their wives and children go there when anyone with a grain of sense might have foreseen what has happened. They might just as well come over and go maying in front of our barbed wire.'[1]

Seeger was expressing an opinion which many were to echo. In retrospect it is difficult to understand why so many of the passengers, including women and children and couples on honeymoon, were on board *Lusitania* nine months into a major war. Alfred Vanderbilt was going to Britain to attend a meeting of the International Horse Show Association and Charles Frohman to book acts for his autumn shows, a function which could presumably have been left to his associates in London. The Cunard advertisement which appeared immediately above Viereck's notice on 1 May still offered round-the-world tours and bookings

266

to all principal ports. The men and women who booked passage on *Lusitania* knew a world of stability, the godchild of *Pax Britannica*. International laws were universally upheld. Piracy had long since been stamped out and international terrorism was hidden half a century in the future. The ominous advertisement was thus greeted with disbelief and in the main ignored. Many passengers firmly believed that the Royal Navy, whose forebears had created the peace which had endured for a century, would ensure that they arrived safely in Liverpool.

Today's long-distance travellers, as inured to a world of violence as their predecessors in 1915 were accustomed to one of stability, are far more wary. The terrible images of terrorism, the hijacking of passengers for political ends, the rolling of bombs into airports crowded with Christmas holidaymakers, the throwing overboard of an elderly man in a wheelchair from a hijacked cruise liner, are indelible. During the Gulf War, *Lusitania*'s lineal descendants, the wide-bodied jets, flew almost empty across the Atlantic in response to Saddam Hussein's threats of terror, hollow though they proved to be. *Lusitania*'s passengers were, in essence, sailing into uncharted waters, where none had gone before. Theodore Roosevelt said of the sinking of the mighty ship: 'This . . . represents piracy on a vaster scale of murder than old-time pirates ever practiced. It is warfare against innocent men, women and children.'[2] Their victims had at least some understanding of the risks they were running in venturing into those waters which old-time pirates had frequented. If the war staff could not contemplate that one of the world's largest liners could sink in only eighteen minutes with the consequent loss of 1,200 lives, neither could her passengers be expected to visualise such a fate and their decision to set sail from New York becomes more explicable.

The deaths of so many women and children on *Lusitania* was a major influence in making the civilian population in both combatant and neutral countries aware of the uncomfortable realities of modern warfare. 1915 saw not only the loss of *Lusitania*. It was the year of Gallipoli, Ypres and Loos and the recognition of the full horrors of the trench war stalemate, the year that Imperial Germany launched poison gas as a weapon of war and shot Edith Cavell. Lyn Macdonald, an acclaimed British historian of World War One, named her book on 1915 *The End of Innocence* and her choice of year seems much more realistic than that of the commentators on *Titanic*.

The Admiralty instructed Cunard to make *Mauretania* ready for sea to replace her lost sister but before she could sail they once again changed their minds and requisitioned her as a troopship. Commanded by a reinvigorated Captain Dow, she sailed for the Greek island of Lemnos at the end of May 1915, the first of several voyages in which she carried reinforcements for the Gallipoli campaign. On one of these voyages, on 9 September 1915, *Mauretania*, ever a lucky ship, evaded a German torpedo. The lookouts reported the danger in sufficient time for Dow to put the helm hard over and the torpedo passed harmlessly down her side. The outcome was a tribute both to Dow's consummate seamanship, for which he was congratulated by the Cunard board, and to the agility built into the design of these great ships. One week later, the Admiralty took the opportunity of the loss of *Lusitania* to cut the annual operating subsidy from £150,000 to £90,000.[3]

On the day that Wilson signed the declaration of war against Germany, American boarding parties successfully commandeered the HAPAG and NDL liners, including the giant *Vaterland*, which had been laid up in American east coast ports since August 1914. Earlier attempts to sabotage their machinery did not prove effective. Once the damage had been made good, they were given American names (*Vaterland* being renamed *Leviathan*) and commissioned as troopships ferrying Pershing's army to France, serving alongside *Mauretania* and *Aquitania*.

By the summer of 1917, with increasing experience of modern sea warfare, the institution of a specialist anti-submarine division and the introduction of convoy, the Admiralty was pioneering the development of effective equipment and operational systems which enabled the American army to be safely transported to France and which led to the eventual defeat of the U-boats. In so doing, the Royal Navy redeemed the reversals which it had experienced in the earlier days of the war and made a major contribution to the allied victory. Two outstanding naval officers, Admiral Duff and Captain W W Fisher, known throughout the service as The Great Agrippa because he was immensely tall, deserve great credit for this achievement. Working closely with the Royal Navy in the appropriately named Operation Pull Together, directed by Admiral Bayly at Queenstown, the US Navy's destroyer divisions were to play a significant role in this success.

Walther Schwieger remained in command of *U-20* until she ran aground off Jutland in fog in November 1916. She had been attempting to help *U-30*, whose engines had broken down. As she could not be dislodged, her crew was taken off and she was blown up. He was then given command of the larger and newer *U-88*, which was sunk with the loss of all hands by the British Q-ship HMS *Stonecrop* in the Bay of Biscay in September 1917. Only six other U-boat commanders had sunk more Allied ships in terms of tonnage. Early in 1920, Frank Mason, the Hearst correspondent in Berlin, obtained a copy of Schwieger's war diary from a German naval officer. Quickly recognising its significance, he had the entire document photographed before his source, pressured by naval intelligence, could grab it back. In April of that year, the diary was published in Britain in the *Sunday Chronicle* and in France in the magazine *L' Illustration* and was widely syndicated in America. The revelations that only one torpedo had sunk *Lusitania*, not two as Lord Mersey had concluded, and of Schwieger's ice-cold reaction to the plight of the survivors created a media sensation.[4]

Before the war was over, the bell tolled cruelly for Albert Ballin, who had served Germany with great distinction. Only when it was too late did Ballin realise that its leaders were directing the country to disaster. In May 1917 his disillusion was showing and he was less confident about U-boat warfare than he had been two years earlier. He wrote of a meeting with the Kaiser:

> I found him full of optimism, far more so than I thought was justi-
> fied. Both he and Ludendorff seem to put too much faith in the suc-
> cess of submarines but they fail to see that this weapon is procuring
> for us the enmity of the world and the promise held out by its advo-
> cates that Great Britain will be bought to its knees in two months is,
> to put it mildly, extremely doubtful . . .[5]

By November 1918, with his gift of foresight, Ballin was predicting red revolution in Germany, the draconian terms of what he called a Clemenceau peace and the break-up of his beloved HAPAG which he had led to the stars. On 3 November the High Seas Fleet mutinied at Kiel and the revolt spread to the other ports where self-styled committees of workers and sailors – in reality Communist thugs – took control. Five days later a band of these thugs burst into the HAPAG offices and beat Ballin up. They were driven out by police but the shipowner, who had been in poor health for years, went home and, overcome by depression, took an overdose of sleeping tablets. Although doctors were summoned and his stomach pumped out, his heart collapsed under the strain and he died during the night. It was a tragic end for the man who had made such an enormous contribution to the world of shipping. As a Jew he was, however, to be spared the Holocaust which was to come.[6]

Ballin's fears for HAPAG proved all too prophetic. Under the terms of the Versailles Treaty, the Americans retained the commandeered *Leviathan*. His two other giant liners, *Imperator* and the uncompleted *Bismarck*, were handed over to the British as reparations for *Lusitania* and *Britannic*, becoming respectively the Cunarder *Berengaria*, named after the wife of Richard the Lionheart, and the White Star liner *Majestic*. Deprived of Ballin's dynamic leadership, HAPAG never recovered the pre-eminent position which the line had held in 1914.

When the German merchant marine recovered toward the end of the 1920s it was NDL, whom HAPAG had pushed into second place, who reintroduced an Atlantic express liner service with their highly successful new generation liners *Bremen* and *Europa*. On her maiden voyage in July 1929 *Bremen* recaptured the Blue Riband, knocking eighteen hours off the record which *Mauretania* had held so long. The veteran Cunarder did not surrender easily. In the following month she made her best time ever over the Atlantic. Her chief engineer, Andrew Cockburn, who had been senior second engineer on *Lusitania*'s last voyage, did wonders with her engines and her time from Southampton to New York was only four hours outside the new record.[7]

Two days after Ballin's death, the first of the captains and kings of our saga vanished from the pages of history. To no one's regret, the Kaiser abdicated and slipped across the Dutch frontier. When he arrived at Amerongen he asked his astonished host, Count Bentinck, if he could have a cup of good English tea. Wilhelm, who had spent more than four years of his reign afloat, cruising on his beloved *Hohenzollern*, never saw the sea again. He passed much of the twenty-two remaining years of his life chopping wood. He had plenty of time to reflect on the hubris which had cost him his throne and all his Imperial possessions.

In January 1918, Woodrow Wilson announced his famous Fourteen Points, the second of which incorporated his tenet of the freedom of the seas, to which he had adhered so vigorously at the time *Lusitania* was sunk. The Fourteen Points made him an international figure and his credo helped to bring the war to an end when the military defeats that autumn led to the final collapse of Germany. Throughout Wilson's career he had paid little heed to unwelcome advice and he imperiously overrode his advisers, who had almost unanimously implored him not to go to Versailles for the peace conference. Although the Republicans now controlled Congress and any treaty required the Senate's confirmation, he made the serious mistake of not including any senator of either party in his delegation. On 4 December he sailed from Hoboken on *George Washington*, despite her name one of the commandeered German liners. New York Harbour gave the departing President a tumultuous send-off, with tugs and ferries sounding their sirens, nineteen-gun salute from the escorting warships and an airship circling overhead, rivalling the greeting it had given to *Lusitania* eleven years earlier.

During the protracted and often acrimonious discussions at Versailles, Wilson became increasingly obsessed with his concept of the League of Nations. One historian noted: 'Once the League was up and running, he thought, it could correct whatever flaws existed in the treaties of peace. In effect Wilson put all his eggs in one basket.'[8] On 7 May 1919, four years to the day after Schwieger had torpedoed *Lusitania*, the Allies presented Germany with their peace terms, the draconian Clemenceau peace which Ballin had astutely foreseen. The German delegation was given no option but to accept. After Clemenceau had stage-managed the formal signature of the treaty in the hall of mirrors at Versailles on the fifth anniversary of the assassination of the Archduke in Sarajevo, Wilson returned to Washington to oversee the passing of the treaty through the Senate.

As three-quarters of the Senate and a majority of American public opinion would have accepted the principle of the League, the President should have achieved his objective. Wilson was in no mood to compromise with the fifty senators who had reservations that the League conflicted with the Constitution. Rather than negotiate, he decided to go over the heads of the Senate to the people. Against the advice of both Edith Wilson and Dr Grayson, the President embarked on a strenuous coast to coast speaking programme. In the rarefied atmosphere of Pueblo, Colorado, three weeks into the tour, he suffered a stroke. Grayson ordered the presidential train back to Washington. Four days after he returned, Wilson had a further stroke from which he never fully recovered.

For the remaining eighteen months of his term, the President of the United States of America was physically disabled. Edith Wilson jealously guarded the presidential sickbed and succeeded in ousting Robert Lansing. Enfeebled, Wilson refused to make any concession to Lodge and the Treaty never secured the two-thirds majority needed for confirmation. Without American participation, the League was deprived of any hope that it might ever have proved effective. For all his gifts, Wilson's career ended in bitter failure, due in no small measure to his own intransigence.

Within two years, the third of our captains and kings, Winston Churchill, was back in government as Minister of Munitions, Lloyd George overcoming heated Conservative opposition to his appointment. His drive served him well and he made a sterling contribution to the victory in 1918. Between 1917 and 1929 he held high office almost continuously. A bitter enemy of Soviet Russia, Churchill had moved to the right by the mid-twenties and had rejoined the Conservatives, becoming Chancellor of the Exchequer in Stanley Baldwin's Government. Controversy dogged him, both at the War Office where he promoted the ultimately unsuccessful Allied intervention in Russia and at the Treasury where, possibly against his better judgement, he returned Britain to the gold standard. Despite the pressure of office, he still found the time to research and write *World Crisis*, his memoirs of the war. Arthur Balfour made the famous quip that Churchill had written a brilliant autobiography disguised as a history of the universe[9] and there is certainly an element of self-justification in *World Crisis*, not least about his tenure of the Admiralty.

When Captain Turner retired in 1919, he moved to Yelverton in South Devon. Two years later he set off for Australia in what proved to be an unavailing effort to find his two sons who had moved there with his estranged wife and with whom he had lost touch. His failure to locate them added to the emotional turmoil caused by the sinking of *Lusitania* from which he never recovered and about which he would seldom, if ever, talk. He eventually moved back to a house in the Liverpool suburb of Crosby, looked after by the devoted Mabel Every. A year before Turner died Albert Bestic, one of the liner's surviving deck officers, visited him. Although he had by then been bedridden for two years, and age and poor health had combined to soften his once abrupt quarterdeck manner, Bestic found him still alert with the piercing blue eyes which he remembered. Turner confirmed that he had come inshore after learning the news of the submarines in mid-channel. He told Bestic that after the torpedo had struck, he had intended to keep way on the liner and run her aground but that he had been thwarted by the loss of power. In any case he could have never have kept the vessel afloat for long enough to have beached her given the lethal damage caused by the impact of the torpedo. Turner left Bestic in no doubt as to the bitterness he harboured towards the Admiralty for the lack of information he had been given before the sinking. His housekeeper, Mabel Every, was emphatic that Turner was equally bitter towards Churchill for the treatment he meted out to him in attempting to scapegoat him for the loss of the ship, an accusation he repeated in *World Crisis*.

On the eighteenth anniversary of the tragedy in May 1933, Turner was interviewed by the *Daily Mail*, breaking his long silence for the first and only time since he had talked to the *New York Times* in November 1915. He vividly described *Lusitania*'s last minutes:

> . . . Most of the passengers were still in the dining room at 2.10 p.m. on May 7. I was on the bridge, looking forward to getting a good night's sleep when I got to Liverpool.
>
> Then, from out of the empty sea, came that one messenger of death. There was no warning.
>
> I did not see anything, although some passengers said later that they saw a submarine's periscope just before we were hit. The torpedo caught us amidships.
>
> The 32,000 tons ship quivered and slowly heeled to starboard. Officers on the bridge turned to me. No one spoke. A hole had been torn in our side large enough for a tramway-car to pass through and the water just rolled in.
>
> Then someone moved. I turned to the telegraph and my officers went away to their jobs. The watertight doors were closed and messengers sped to calm the passengers. Like lightning the boats on the starboard side were manned.
>
> In the steerage there was a panic. Officers had to rush and fight to keep the ways clear.
>
> Then from every companion-way, there burst an endless stream of passengers. The boat-deck was crammed with a silent crowd – mothers and fathers clasping their little ones, sons searching for their parents, and sweethearts clinging to each other, all wide eyed with terror.
>
> The ship sank lower and lower. More boats got away. But still the deck was black with people.

By this time frayed nerves were giving way and terrible, hopeless confusion reigned.

Helplessly I turned away. The waves seemed to jump on our decks. Soon it was all over. The whole ship seemed to be plucked from my feet by a giant hand and I found myself being dragged down into the depths. It seemed an age before I broke the surface again and what a ghastly sight met my eyes!

Hundreds of bodies were being whirled about among the wreckage. Men, woman and children were drifting between planks, lifeboats and an indescribable litter.

The instinct to live kept me swimming until I was picked up by a lifeboat. Then I lay exhausted until destroyers came and rescued us. That is my simple story.[10]

Turner had told the *New York Times* that he believed that *Lusitania* had been struck by two torpedoes. His reference to 'one messenger of death' would indicate that he now accepted that the liner had only been hit by one. He may, of course, have read Schwieger's war diary. He confirmed the evidence of Schwieger and other eye-witnesses where the torpedo had struck. As other survivors had done, he noted that a degree of panic had set in among the steerage-class passengers. Turner revealed no sign of the bitterness he felt about his subsequent treatment by the Admiralty. Indeed, he referred to the Admiralty rather charitably, showing the reporter an old log which read: 'Arrived in New York April 23rd 1915. During the time in New York the Germans put in the papers a warning to passengers not to go in the ship as she would be torpedoed.' He told the reporter: 'all the time we were in New York, warnings kept coming to me that my ship would be caught by the submarines. Even the Admiralty sent word that we should have to take the greatest care because of the threats'.

After eighteen years Turner's memory was playing tricks on him. Although the press advertisement was assumed to have been specifically aimed at *Lusitania,* in reality, as has been noted, it was directed against all Allied passenger liners. There is no evidence that Turner received any warnings in the week he was in New York about the liner's safety from the Admiralty or any other source. Nor had he been rescued by a destroyer. As we know there were no destroyers in the Queenstown command in May 1915 and he had finally reached port on the trawler *Bluebell.*

On 24 June 1933, seven weeks after giving the interview, William Thomas Turner died, aged seventy-six. He was accorded the traditional Cunard funeral for a great sea captain. Neither of his sons attended and the only family mourners were his surviving sister and his actress-niece, Mercedes Desmore. Six Cunard quartermasters carried his coffin, draped in a Union Jack, into church and then to the graveside. Captain Luke Ward, Cunard's principal marine superintendent, and five serving captains led a large gathering of mourners, serving employees and pensioners, from the line and from the Liverpool shipping world – evidence, if such is needed, of the regard in which this rather remote, sometimes gruff and often maligned man was held. In 1993 Turner's decorations, the OBE, the Silver Medal for Saving Life, the Transport Medal and South African and First World War Stars, were sold at auction at Crewkerne in Somerset. The anonymous vendor was alleged to be a relative of Mabel Every, Turner's housekeeper. They realised £5,000, at the top end of the auctioneer's estimate, the purchaser being a well-known dealer and collector of decorations.

During the war Cunard and its subsidiaries had lost *Lusitania* and forty-four other ships. Despite these losses Cunard had survived the war in reasonably good shape and was able to order replacement ships. In 1919 the UK terminal for Cunard's express Atlantic service was moved from Liverpool to Southampton, a step which had been contemplated as early as 1907. Cunard management had long been concerned at the difficulty in operating a rapid turn-round service when *Lusitania* and *Mauretania* could only cross the Mersey Bar in twelve hours out of twenty-four, a factor which had played an important part in determining the speed Turner had steamed on that fateful 7 May. Essentially, Cunard was taking over a service, including a stop at Cherbourg, which had previously been the preserve of the two German lines. By 1922 their three express liners, *Mauretania, Aquitania* and *Berengaria*, had all been converted to burn oil.

Alfred Booth's health broke down that year and he was forced to retire as Chairman of Cunard although he remained a non-executive director until 1945. His successor, Sir Thomas Royden, and his deputy, Sir Percy Bates, both of whom came from Liverpool shipping families, were to be the dominating figures in Cunard throughout the interwar years. They had to face some serious problems. In 1921, the United States Congress passed new restrictive immigration legislation, which led to the virtual loss of the profitable emigrant trade. Despite the Admiralty's culpability for the loss of *Lusitania*, the British Government never forgave any portion of the construction loan, no doubt justifying their stance on the grounds that the War Risks Association, which they had reinsured, had paid out Cunard in full. The loan was repaid on schedule in 1927, twenty years after *Lusitania*'s maiden voyage. Whitehall even made the line pay for *Berengaria*. To make matters worse, the former HAPAG liner proved uneconomic in service. Surmounting many difficulties, Cunard's competent management team kept the line profitable throughout the 1920s, with major innovations like the first round-the-world cruise in the newly completed *Laconia* in 1923. In the 1920s, careful attention to service helped to build Cunard into one of the great brand names of the world.

As early as 1926, Royden and Bates had turned their attention to replacing the existing express liners, all of whom had entered service before 1914. They reasoned that advances in marine engineering would allow them to introduce a new generation of liners who could operate a weekly service with only two vessels rather than the existing three. The new ships would be much larger than their predecessors, at least 75,000 tons, but as Bates once said: 'they were the smallest and slowest which can fulfil properly all the essential economic conditions'.[11] In April 1930, Percy Bates became Chairman of Cunard and in the following December the keel of an 81,000-ton giant, code named No 534 to be funded from the line's own resources, was laid in the same berth at John Brown in Clydebank where *Lusitania* had been built. Within months the full fury of the depression fell upon Cunard and the line could no longer afford to finance the construction of the new vessel. Two weeks before Christmas 1931, work stopped on No 534, bringing destitution to the people of Clydebank.

History had repeated itself. As Inverclyde had before him, Percy Bates was forced to go to Whitehall to ask for government financial assistance for the construction of a new North Atlantic liner. By a strange coincidence, the Chancellor of the Exchequer was Neville Chamberlain, whose father Joseph had served on the Cabinet committee which had recommended that the Balfour Government provide the construction loan and operating subsidy for *Lusitania* and *Mauretania*. Chamberlain turned Cunard down flatly on the grounds that national security was not an issue as it had been in 1902. For two years Bates tenaciously argued for his big ships concept. He could muster two powerful arguments.

First, government construction subsidies advanced to French and Italian shipping lines had funded new liners including the giant *Normandie*, a vessel of about the same size as No 534, then fitting out in a French shipyard. Second, the experience with the new NDL liners *Bremen* and *Europa* showed that modern ships could cream off whatever traffic was available at the expense of the older vessels. In short, Cunard needed the new liner if a viable British presence was to remain on the North Atlantic.

Early in 1934 the Treasury agreed to advance a £5 million loan to complete No 534 and provide extra working capital. If the vessel proved a commercial success, a further £4.5 million would be advanced to fund the construction of a proposed sister ship. Under the terms of the agreement, Cunard and the now almost moribund White Star Line merged, effectively a Cunard takeover of its old rival.

In April 1934 work on No 534 resumed. Five months later Queen Mary launched her and gave the vessel her name. From the day *Queen Mary* went into service in May 1936, she was highly profitable and extremely popular with passengers, restoring Cunard's fortunes as *Lusitania* and *Mauretania* had done thirty years before. As fast troopships, *Queen Mary* and her sister *Queen Elizabeth* followed the tradition set by *Aquitania* and *Mauretania* in 1918. *Queen Mary*, and her sister ship *Queen Elizabeth*, made a colossal contribution to Allied victory in the Second World War. Between them they carried over a million American and Canadian servicemen across the Atlantic. In a single voyage they could transport 15,000 troops, equivalent to a fully-equipped infantry division with personal arms from New York to Scotland in less than a week. Military historians have estimated that their availability shortened the war in Europe by a full year.

Twice in thirty years, two chairmen of Cunard, both of them astute and tenacious, had gone to Whitehall seeking and eventually obtaining government assistance for their North Atlantic express passenger service. On both occasions the intervention proved successful, the line was reinvigorated, its profitability restored and Britain regained its premier position on the route. In the light of the priceless contribution to Allied victory in the Second World War by the two great Cunarders, the loan support advanced to Cunard in 1934, repaid in full and on time, could rank as the best investment a British government ever made.

In June 1937 Winston Churchill revisited the subject of *Lusitania* in an article in the London Sunday paper *The News Of*

The World. From the distance of twenty-two years, his commentary on the sinking had subtly altered since he had written *World Crisis*, in which he had placed the blame solely on Turner. He conceded that Turner, whom he had once threatened to pursue without check, had taken precautions and he merely chided him gently for his failure to zigzag, probably the weakest charge the Admiralty had made against him. Churchill cited four different messages sent to Turner on 6 and 7 May concluding, at least to his own satisfaction, that: 'No one can say the Admiralty was remiss'. He did not mention that he had been First Lord at the time or that the ship had been under Admiralty instructions when she was at sea. One wonders whether he would have taken such a complacent view if someone else had held that office in May 1915.

The article is marred by some strange errors. Although he must have learnt both from the decrypts which he had so assiduously studied as First Lord and from Schwieger's published war diary that the liner had been sunk by one torpedo, he repeated, as he had in *World Crisis*, Mersey's conclusion that she had been hit by two. His account of the lowering of the lifeboats was by no means accurate and he described the liner's final moments in purple Churchillian prose:

> At last the bow went under altogether. The stern rose out of the water . . . the *Lusitania* hung thus for a moment and then went down. The sea closed over her, forming an immense wave which thundered down upon the boats and the swimmers, battering them with debris and the bodies of the dead. Many had already been drowned and the great wave took heavy toll of those who still survived.

This account conflicts with the testimony of the survivors who were adamant that the mighty ship had gone down without causing anything more than a momentary seething of the waters. In another passage he recounted that: 'for a little while the German submarine had remained on the surface and its officers had surveyed their handiwork of horror from its work as if in a play'. There is no evidence that the cautious Schwieger, short of fuel and anxious to avoid any retribution, ever came above periscope depth.

When he wrote the article Churchill had been in the political wilderness for seven years and fighting his lone crusade for rearmament and against the aggressive ambitions of Nazi Germany for four. His purpose was clear: to remind his readers of one of the worst examples of German frightfulness in the previous war. He castigated Germany in much the same terms which Carson had used in his opening address to the Mersey inquiry, accusing her of caring little for the traditions of the sea and denouncing her for 'a grisly act which hitherto had never been practised deliberately except by pirates'. By extension Churchill was warning of the horrors which might be expected at sea in the event of another conflict and of the fate which Nazi Germany might expect if, as in 1917, the United States were to go to war against her.[12]

In one respect, the lesson of the loss of *Lusitania* was not learnt. It had taken 1,200 deaths to bring home to the Admiralty the importance of the Western Approaches and of the naval base at Queenstown. During the negotiations for Irish independence in 1921, Churchill proposed to Michael Collins, leading the Irish delegation, that the British should retain three naval bases in southern Ireland including Queenstown. At his request, Beatty, then First Sea Lord, made a presentation to Collins, who told Churchill: 'Of course you should have the ports: they are necessary for your life.' The Treaty provided for British retention of the three bases and no great objection to the provision was ever raised.

In 1938, Neville Chamberlain, now Prime Minister, was renegotiating the 1921 Treaty with his Irish opposite number, Eamon De Valera. The Irish included a request that the British give up their rights to the bases as a bargaining counter to be discarded once their primary objectives had been secured. To De Valera's astonishment, Chamberlain unconditionally gave away these rights. Even more astonishingly, the then First Sea Lord, Chatfield, offered no objections to the Prime Minister's decision. Chatfield was a gunnery officer and a battleship enthusiast, who had been Beatty's flag captain throughout the First War. It is difficult to envisage Admirals like Bayly and Duff, who had played leading parts in the anti-submarine campaign, agreeing with Chatfield on this issue. Churchill fought valiantly against Chamberlain's surrender of the ports but he was supported only by the Ulster MPs. No one will ever know how many lives were lost during the Second World War as a result of this gratuitous act of appeasement.[13]

When war broke out on 3 September 1939, Chamberlain brought Churchill back as First Lord of the Admiralty, the post he had left in despair twenty-four years before. That evening the signal 'Winston is back' went out to every ship in the navy. History was to repeat itself ere that day was out. Leutnant F J

Lemp, commanding a new *U-30*, torpedoed the Donaldson liner *Athenia* (13,581 tons) outward bound from Liverpool for Montreal. One hundred and twelve lives were lost, including eighteen Americans. While Schwieger had acted within his instructions, Lemp had exceeded his. At the outset of the war, Hitler had ordered his U-boat commanders to observe the Hague Convention and not to attack passenger liners. In reaching this decision, the Fuhrer was not motivated by any concern for humanity but by his intention to offer peace terms to Britain and France once he had conquered Poland. When it became clear that the Allies were not interested in his overtures, he removed any restrictions on submarine operations. By mid-November 1939, he had ordered that any clearly identifiable Allied ships, including passenger liners, could be attacked without warning.

When Lemp returned home, he was carpeted by Admiral Doenitz, then commanding the U-boat service, and explained his action by stating that in the twilight he had mistaken *Athenia* for a merchant cruiser. Doenitz concluded that Lemp had not taken sufficient precautions to establish the identity of the ship before attacking her and placed him temporarily under cabin arrest. Berlin refused to admit any responsibility for the loss of *Athenia*, as they had when *Lusitania* had been sunk, and, without proof of German complicity, Washington decided to take no diplomatic action. The British press had no doubts as to who was responsible and, evoking the memory of *Lusitania*, they roundly condemned the sinking as another example of German frightfulness on the high seas. On 22 October the Nazi propaganda minister, Josef Goebbels, delivered an inflammatory speech in which he blamed the sinking of *Athenia* on the 'Archmurderer Churchill', an eerie repetition of the groundless accusation that Churchill had deliberately abandoned *Lusitania* to her fate. The absurdity of Goebbels's charge was revealed when Doenitz eventually revealed the truth in his testimony at Nuremberg. Churchill had been in office for only four hours when Lemp sunk the liner, no time even to consider, let alone organise, a conspiracy.[14]

Neville Chamberlain was no more suited to be a war leader than Asquith had been before him and by the spring of 1940 his government was being widely criticised for its complacency. Churchill's star was rising. His pent-up vitality had reinvigorated the Admiralty. The sinking of the pocket battleship *Admiral Graf Spee* and Captain Philip Vian's audacious rescue of the merchant navy prisoners from the German supply ship *Altmark* had bolstered his image as a decisive leader. The ill-starred Norwegian campaign, for which, incidentally, Churchill must bear much responsibility, led to an ill-tempered debate of no confidence. Thirty Conservative MPs voted against the Government and sixty more abstained.

As in 1915 it was evident that an all-party government had to be formed. The Labour Party, who detested Chamberlain, refused to serve under him, rendering his position untenable, and the succession passed to Churchill. The criticisms, which can validly be raised against Churchill as a defence minister in either war, pale into insignificance in comparison to his inspiring and indomitable leadership of Britain during the Second World War, his dogged refusal to contemplate defeat and his success in keeping the fragile flame of hope alive in Nazi-occupied Europe.

In the Second World War the Royal Navy was to be tested far more thoroughly than it had been in the First. Led by a new generation of fleet commanders, several of whom had made their mark as destroyer captains in the earlier war, and backed up by an effective staff system, the service fully recovered its reputation for skill and professionalism. To use the words of the wise medieval Bishop, the officers and men of the Navy had once again kept the sea, which is the wall of England, as their forebears had in the days of Drake and Nelson. Nazi Germany finally surrendered on 7 May 1945, the thirtieth anniversary of the sinking of *Lusitania*.[15]

*   *   *

The captains and the kings are long gone. Henry Oliver, the longest-lived of them, reached the rank of Admiral of the Fleet and died in 1965 aged one-hundred, some months after Churchill passed on and was honoured by a state funeral befitting a national hero. Shortly before his death in 1918, D A Thomas was raised to the peerage as Viscount Rhondda. Margaret Mackworth had been his only child and by special dispensation she inherited the title. The battle for women's suffrage won, she became the publisher and editor of the right-wing weekly *Time and Tide*. She divorced her husband shortly after the war and never remarried. As she had no children the peerage became extinct when she died in 1958. Charles Lauriat ran his bookselling firm, which was in business until quite recently, until he died in 1937. Oliver Bernard is best remembered as the designer of the Lyons Corner Houses, enormously popular in the 1930s and 1940s, which he laid out in a vivid art deco style.

Warren Pearl worked alongside the bereaved Antoine Depage at his hospital at La Panne and then became the head of the American Red Cross in Europe. His family made their permanent home in England. They often visited America, always travelling on Cunard to take advantage of the 25 per cent discount which the line gave to all *Lusitania* survivors. Audrey Pearl, now the Hon. Mrs Hugh Lawson Johnston, remembers sailing with her mother on *Queen Mary*'s maiden eastbound voyage in June 1936. On another journey on *Queen Mary* in the summer of 1939, they met the steward who had looked after the family on *Lusitania's* last voyage. Audrey and the intrepid Alice Lines became lifelong friends and Alice nursed her children and her grandchildren. She married twice and on 18 December 1996 she celebrated her hundredth birthday. She died in November 1997 and Audrey Lawson Johnston, with three generations of her family, headed the mourners at the funeral for the gallant nanny who had saved her life eighty-two years before. As far as the author can determine, she is now the last remaining *Lusitania* survivor although no one meeting her would readily believe that she has passed four score years.[16]

* * *

There is now a golf course on the approaches to the lighthouse on the Old Head and outside its entrance stands a circular memorial in the local granite. It was dedicated on the eightieth anniversary of the tragedy and its inscription reads: 'In memory of the 1198 civilian lives lost on the Lusitania 7th May 1915 off the Old Head of Kinsale'. It is surmounted by a bronze depicting a girl with a baby in her arms, clinging to a lifeboat, with the great ship sinking in the background. On that same day, the Courtmacsherry lifeboat retraced the epic mission that her predecessor *Kezia Gwilt* had undertaken on that fateful 7 May and laid a wreath over the wreck of the ship. As the lifeboat moved slowly over her hull from bow to stern, her echo sounder made a record of her wreck which shows her lying in one piece on the seabed.[17]

Every year the sea encroaches a little further on the wreck of *Lusitania*, shrouded in the local fishermen's nets, on which Dr

Ballard's unmanned mini-submarine so nearly got snagged during his exploration. She has suffered so severely from the erosion caused by the fierce currents that Ballard described the wreck as 'marine junk'. Nor has she escaped the attentions of the marine salvage companies or of unauthorised divers, some of whom have resorted to looting artifacts. Three of her four high tensile brass propellers have been removed. One of these, salvaged in 1982, was later presented to the Merseyside Maritime Museum and is on display in the adjacent Albert Dock complex. Its inscription reminds us that it was one of the new propellers fitted in 1909, which increased *Lusitania*'s speed by one knot. Nor is the mighty ship forgotten by the people of her old home port, whose forebears, in her heyday, had affectionately called her Lucy. Every year on the anniversary of her sinking a service to the memory of those who died on her last voyage is held outside the Maritime Museum.

Until that day, perhaps a century or more from now, when time and tide finally do their work, the hull of the mighty ship should be allowed to remain undisturbed, a memorial to those who sailed on her last voyage, those who died, and particularly the nine hundred who, like Alfred Vanderbilt and John Stephens, Greta Lorenzen and the two little Pearl sisters and Second Officer Percy Hefford and Fireman Dan Daly, have no known grave but the sea.

Requiescat *Lusitania* in pace

APPENDIX 1

The Four-Point Bearing Fix

Before the development of radar, a four-point bearing fix was used by mariners to ascertain the position of their ships in relation to land when only one reference point on shore, normally a headland, was visible.

The technique used was for the ship to proceed on a steady course at a constant speed. The exact time was noted, when the headland bore 45 degrees from the ship's head, or 4 points (1 point is 11° 15') in the terminology used with magnetic compasses, such as those installed on *Lusitania.* The ship would steam on the same course until the headland was perpendicular to the ship, or abeam in nautical parlance. Once again the time was noted and the period of time which elapsed between taking the two bearings was ascertained. Together with the ship's speed, the distance travelled during the period could be calculated. Because the bearings and the distance travelled formed a right-handed equilateral triangle, the distance that the ship had steamed between taking the two bearings was also the distance from the headland. This fix enabled the mariner to plot a fairly accurate position of his ship on his chart. No bearing taken on a steel ship with a magnetic compass of the type installed on *Lusitania* can be quite as precise as one taken with a gyro compass. A master in 1915 would have to allow for unquantified errors in taking bearings off headlands, which resulted in corresponding errors in the ship's position. For example, an error of 1 degree in taking a bearing at a range of twenty miles, would cause an error of approximately 0.35 miles in a ship's position.

The principal error which could occur when using this technique was the effect of the tidal current in the locality. This could be ascertained to a reasonable degree of accuracy from charts and tide tables for many, if not all, headlands. Since the direction and speed of the tidal flow are not constant and may well be at an angle to the ship's course, some uncertainty might exist about the distance the ship ran *over the ground* as opposed to *through the water,* the latter being the measurement taken directly on board the ship. As it is extremely difficult to achieve an accurate direct measurement of *rate*, errors can effect the calculation of the assumed distance run, if the ship's speed varies slightly or the course steered wanders. The state of the wind and sea can also effect the actual speed and true course steered but these are not of great significance. The ship's log is not especially accurate as a method of measuring the ship's speed, although its errors would be sufficiently well known for a navigator to allow for them.

It is also important to know the exact point on the land being used to take the bearing. Fortunately, landmarks such as lighthouses stand on many headlands, particularly those in areas of heavy sea traffic such as the Old Head of Kinsale. As these are shown on charts, a navigator can rely on an accurate position.

Taking everything into account, a four-point bearing would probably have been accurate to within one mile, sufficient for most navigational purposes, although not as accurate as a simultaneous sight taken on two landmarks. It was, however, preferable to dead reckoning, which might have been all that was available to a navigator as he closed land at the end of an ocean voyage if weather conditions prevented him from taking sun or star sights to ascertain his ship's position more accurately.

The distance from the headland selected to take this kind of fix was important. With a ship close inshore, the rate of change of the bearing would be high, leading to difficulty and risk of error in taking exact bearings at the right moment. With the ship too far off the land, the run would take a considerable time, as much as an hour. It is not easy to take accurate bearings of objects so distant as to be only barely visible and the magnitude of such errors would only increase the further the ship was offshore.

Although a four-point bearing was a great deal better than navigating a ship by guesswork, to use Captain Turner's phrase, it could be inconvenient to implement and could contain errors which are difficult to quantify. It is not a substitute for a fix taken simultaneously off two separate landmarks ashore.

APPENDIX 2

The Parsons Marine Steam Turbine

A turbine is a device which converts kinetic energy into mechanical energy. A steam turbine converts the thermal energy stored in steam into work. It consists of a shaft, or rotor, supported by a bearing arrangement and encased in a cylindrical casing. Steam issuing from nozzles located on the periphery of the turbine cylinder is directed by fixed vanes on to the rotor blades, causing them to turn. To work efficiently, the turbine blades on the rotor must move at high speed, conventionally half the speed of the steam emerging from the nozzles which drive them. To achieve this, the turbine rotor must either rotate or should be of large diameter. This creates a fundamental problem because to maximise efficiency, propellers should rotate at slow speeds – for many merchant ships at less than one hundred revolutions per minute. This difficultly was initially resolved by coupling large diameter turbine rotors directly to the propellers as no alternative technology then existed. Thus the turbines aboard *Lusitania* were large diameter and revolved slowly. The problem of reconciling turbine and propeller speeds was solved some ten years after the initial introduction of turbine-powered ships through the development of large reduction gears and the gear cutting machine tools necessary for their production. This innovation enabled turbines to rotate at high speed, reducing their size and allowing low propeller speeds, improving propulsion energy. It was now practicable to design both High Power (HP) and Low Power (LP) turbines small enough to be connected to one set of gearing, thus reducing the number of shafts compared with direct drive. This configuration allowed the condenser to be slung underneath the LP turbine, providing for a more compact engine assembly, saving considerable space compared with direct drive, where the condensers had to be situated either above the turbines or in a separate compartment. The geared turbine constituted a major advance in ship propulsion, second only to the development of the turbine itself.

Parsons scrapped the original equipment fitted on *Turbinia* and replaced it with a three-stage axial flow steam turbine driving

286

three shafts, each fitted with three propellers, 18 inches in diameter and 24 inches in pitch, which enabled his invention to reach its full potential. He had selected this propeller design after exhaustive testing to overcome the problem of cavitation, cavities which formed behind rotating propeller blades, seriously reducing their thrust and severely limiting the efficiency of the propulsion system.

This description is adapted from *The Story of Charles Parsons and His Ocean Greyhound* by Ken Smith, published by Newcastle Libraries and Informatioin Services and Tyne and Wear Museums. *Turbinia*, restored to her original condition and evoking sleekness and power, is on display at the Discovery Museum in Newcastle-on-Tyne.

APPENDIX 3

Explanation of 'Priming' and 'Water Hammer'

Priming

A boiler is said to prime when a quantity of water is carried over with the steam into the pipework system attached to the boiler. In a ship, this condition is normally caused by contaminated water in the boiler, the most usual contaminant being salt, which causes the boiler to effervesce. A sudden shock, such as the impact of a torpedo or projectile, can induce priming in boilers adjacent to the point of strike. Other causes of priming include maloperation allowing the boiler to overfill with water with the same effect: water enters the steam pipe system, where it can result in water hammer.

Water hammer

Water hammer occurs in steam pipes when they are suddenly presented with water in addition to steam. This results in rapid local condensation of the steam, thus generating a shock wave, resulting in leaking joints or, in the worst case, a catastrophic failure of the entire system. In the case of *Lusitania*, the SNAME paper, 'The *Titanic* and *Lusitania*: a Final Forensic Analysis', estimated the magnitude of this shock wave as being up to twenty-three times the normal pressure.

Water hammer is so called because it produces a loud and repeated clanging noise as if the pipework was suddenly being struck by a large hammer. The steam pipe vibrates and often sheds much of its lagging. It is an experience which marine engineers do not enjoy and in normal steaming take care to avoid. A torpedo strike close to a boiler could cause very serious water hammer and pipe failure before any damage control could be implemented.

In normal circumstances, water hammer would be controlled by immediately draining the water out of the steam system through drain valves and automatic 'steam traps' whilst, at the same time, blowing down the boiler to remove any contaminants.

Bibliography

Lloyd E Ambrosius, *Wilsonian Statecraft, The Theory and Practice of Liberal Internationalism during World War I*, SR Books, Wilmington, Delaware 1991

Louis Auchincloss, *Woodrow Wilson*, Viking Penguin 2000

Thomas Bailey & Paul Ryan, *The Lusitania Disaster*, Free Press 1975

——, *Hitler Vs. Roosevelt*, Free Press 1979

Robert Ballard, *Exploring The Lusitania*, Warner Books 1995

Robert Ballard & Rick Archbold, *Lost Liners*, Hyperion 1997

Correlli Barnett, *Engage The Enemy More Closely*, W W Norton 1991

Philip Bates, *Bates Of Bellefield, Gyrn Castle and Manydown*, Privately Published 1994

Patrick Beesly, *Room 40*, Hamish Hamilton 1982

Oliver Bernard, *Cock Sparrow*, Jonathan Cape 1936

James Bisset & P R Stephenson, *Commodore: War, Peace and The Big Ships*, Angus & Robertson 1961

Robert Blake, *Bonar Law: The Unknown Prime Minister*, Eyre & Spottiswoode 1955

Robert Blake & Wm Roger Louis, *Churchill*, Oxford University Press 1993

David K Brown, *Warrior To Dreadnought: Warship Development 1860-1905*, Chatham Publishing 1997

Daniel Allen Butler, *The Lusitania:The Life, Loss and Legacy of an Ocean Legend*, Stackpole Books, Mechanicsburg, Pennsylvania 2000

David Butler, *Lusitania*, Macdonald & Co. 1981

Vincent P Carosso, *Morgans Private International Bankers 1854-1913*, Harvard 1987

Lamar Cecil, *Albert Ballin: Business & Politics In Imperial Germany 1888-1918*, Princeton 1967

W S Chalmers, *Full Cycle: The Biography of Admiral Sir Bertram Home Ramsay*, Hodder & Stoughton 1959

John Charmley, *Churchill: The End Of Glory*, Hodder & Stoughton 1993

Winston S Churchill, *World Crisis 1915*, Thornton Butterworth 1923

——, *The Second World War*, Cassell, Vol 1 1948, Vol 2 1949

Kendrick Clements, *Woodrow Wilson – World Statesman*, Twayne 1987

John Colville, *The Fringes Of Power*, Hodder & Stoughton 1985

Julian Corbett, *Naval Operations*, Longmans, Vol 1 1920

Allan Crothall, *Wealth From The Sea*, Starr Line, Orpington Kent 1993

Duncan Crow, *A Man Of Push And Go: A Life Of George Macaulay Booth*, Rupert Hart Davis 1965

Reinhard Dorries, *Imperial Challenge: Ambassador Count Bernstorff and German–American Relations 1908-1917*, University of North Carolina 1989

——, *Albrecht Count Von Bernstorff*, Bonn 1995

C L Droste & W H Tantum, *The Lusitania Case*, 7c's Press, Riverside Connecticut 1972

David Lloyd George, *The War Memoirs Of David Lloyd George*, Vol 1 1914-15, Little Brown, Boston 1933

Peter Drucker, *Concept Of The Corporation* 1946

Susan Els, *Titanic – Legacy Of The World?s Greatest Liner*, Time-Life Books 1997

Niall Ferguson, *The Pity Of War*, Allen Lane 1998

William H Garzke Jr and others, *The Titanic And Lusitania: A Final Forensic Analysis*, Society Of Naval Architects & Marine Engineers (SNAME), Jersey City NJ 1995

James W Gerard, *My Four Years In Germany*, Hodder & Stoughton 1917

Martin Gilbert, *Winston S Churchill*, Vol 3, Heinemann 1971

——, *The First World War*, Weidenfeld & Nicolson 1994

Andrew Gordon, *The Rules Of The Game*, John Murray 1996

Peter Gretton, *Former Naval Person: Winston Churchill And The Royal Navy*, Oxford University Press 1968

Paul Halpern, *A Naval History Of World War One*, US Naval Institute Press 1994

August Heckscher, *Woodrow Wilson*, Scribner 1991

Des Hickey & Gus Smith, *Seven Days To Disaster: The Sinking Of The Lusitania*, Collins 1981

J R Hill (ed), *The Oxford Illustrated History Of The Royal Navy*, Oxford University Press 1995

A A Hoehling and Mary Hoehling, *The Last Voyage Of The Lusitania*, Revised edition, Madison Books 1996

J J Horgan, *From Parnell To Pearse*, Browne & Nolan 1948

Archibald Hurd, *A Merchant Fleet At War*, Cassell 1920

Micheal Hurley, *Home From The Sea: The Story Of The Courtmacsherry Lifeboat 1825-1995*, Privately Published 1995

Francis Hyde, *Cunard and the North Atlantic 1840-1973*, Macmillan 1975

J H Isherwood, *Steamers Of The Past*, The Journal Of Commerce & Shipping Telegraph Liverpool 1966

William James, *The Eyes Of The Navy*, Methuen 1955

Roy Jenkins, *Asquith*, Collins 1964

Howard Johnson, *The Cunard Story*, Whittet Books 1987

Humfrey Jordan, *Mauretania*, Hodder & Stoughton 1936

John Keegan, *The Price Of Admiralty*, Century Hutchinson 1988

——, *The First World War*, Century Hutchinson 1999

Ludovic Kennedy, *Truth To Tell*, Bantam Books 1991

Thomas J Knock, *To End All Wars: Woodrow Wilson and the Quest for a New World Order*, Oxford University Press 1992

Charles Lauriat, *The Lusitania's Last Voyage*, Houghton Mifflin 1915

Robert Leckie, *The Wars Of America*, Vol II 1900 To 1992, Harper Collins 1992

Arthur Link, *Wilson: The Struggle For Neutrality*, Vols. III-V, Princeton 1960

——, *Wilson: Confusions And Crises*, Princeton 1964

Walter Lord, *The Night Lives On*, William Morrow 1986

John Lukacs, *A Thread Of Years*, Yale 1998

Walter McDougall, *Promised Land: Crusader State*, Houghton Mifflin 1997

Bibliography

Ruddock Mackay, *Fisher Of Kilverstone*, Oxford University Press 1974

Arthur Marder, *From Dreadnought To Scapa Flow*, Vols 1 & 2, Oxford University Press 1964

Robert Massie, *Dreadnought*, Hodder & Stoughton 1991

John Maxtone-Graham, *The Only Way To Cross*, Revised edition, Barnes & Noble 1997

Nathan Miller, *Theodore Roosevelt: A Life*, Quill William Morrow 1992

Avner Offer, *The First World War: An Agrarian Assessment*, Oxford University Press 1989

Patrick O'Sullivan, *The Lusitania: Unravelling The Mysteries*, Collins Press 1998

Norman Rose, *Churchill: The Unruly Giant*, Free Press 1995

Stephen Roskill, *Churchill And The Admirals*, Collins 1977

Eric Sauder & Ken Marschall, *RMS Lusitania: Triumph Of The Edwardian Age*, Transatlantic Designs 1991

Charles Seymour, *The Papers Of Col. House* Vols 1 and 2, Houghton Mifflin 1926

Colin Simpson, *Lusitania*, Longman 1972

Andrew Sinclair, *Corsair, The Life Of J. Pierpont Morgan*, Little Brown 1981

Ken Smith, *Turbinia:The Story Of Charles Parsons And His Ocean Greyhound*, Newcastle Libraries & Information Services & Tyne & Wear Museums 1996

——, *Mauretania: Pride Of The Tyne*, Newcastle Libraries 1997

David Stafford, *Churchill And Secret Service*, John Murray 1997

Jean Strouse, *Morgan: American Financier*, Random House 1999

Barbara Tuchman, *The Zimmermann Telegram*, Macmillan 1966

——, *The Guns Of August*, Anniversary edition, Macmillan 1988

Arthur T Vanderbilt II, *Fortune's Children: The Fall of the House of Vanderbilt*, William Morrow 1992

Ronald Warwick, *QE2*, second edition, W W Norton 1993

Evelyn Waugh, *Scoop*, Chapman & Hall 1937

Edwin A Weinstein, *Woodrow Wilson: A Medical and Psychological Biography*, Princeton 1981

Cecil Woodham Smith, *The Reason Why*, Constable 1953

Newspapers & Periodicals
Cork Examiner; Daily Mail, Interview with Captain Turner, May 8th 1933; *Engineering*, 'The Cunard Turbine-Driven Quadruple-Screw Atlantic Liner *Lusitania*' 1907; *Forbes*; *Illustrated London News*; *Imperial War Museum Review*; *Morning Post*; *New York Sun*; *New York Times*, Interview with Captain Turner, 21 November 1915; *New York Tribune*; *News Of The World*; *Rolls-Royce Magazine*, '*Turbinia* – The experiment which transformed the World's navies'. March 1991; *Spectator*; *The Sphere*; *The Nation*; *The Shipbuilder*; *The Times*; *Wall St. Journal.*

Official publications
Formal Investigation Into The Loss Of The S. S. *Lusitania*
(Open and Closed Sessions) June-July 1915

Report On The Loss Of S. S. *Lusitania* July 1915. (The Mersey Report)

Archival Sources
Churchill Archives Centre, Churchill College, Cambridge
Winston S. Churchill, Stephen Roskill and Viscount Weir papers

Cunard Archives, University Of Liverpool
Files: D42/C1/230, D42/C1/241, D42/PR3/24/6, D42/PR3/7/7, D42/PR/7, D42PR/10, D42/PR13/23, D641/6/1-9, D641/6/17, DA2/PR3/28/3A, Eaves Papers, Minutes of Annual General Meetings and Meetings of the Board of Directors and the Executive Committee.

Hoover Institution, Stanford University, Palo Alto, California
Thomas Bailey/Paul B Ryan, Karl F Falk and Frank E Mason Papers.

Imperial War Museum, London
A B Cross and H S Taylor Papers. Kennedy/Roskill Interview

Merseyside Maritime Museum, Liverpool

National Maritime Museum, Greenwich
Sir William Grahame Greene Papers. File GEE 13/F

Public Record Office, Kew
ADM Files: 1/8451, 1/9158, 53/45458, 116/1416, 137/113, 137/1052, 137/1058, 137/1062, 137/2958, 186/678.
Other Files: CAB 45/267, FO 371/2586, MT 9/1326, MT23/1400.

Notes

Prologue
1. Henderson quoted in the video *Last Voyage Of The Lusitania* (National Geographical Society 1994).

Chapter 1: Challenge and Response
1. Between 1891 and 1911 the population of Germany increased from 49 million to 65 million and over the same period her export trade grew by 200 per cent. Her merchant marine had increased from 1.2 million tons in 1890 to 3.3 million tons in 1913.
2. James W Gerard, *My Four Years in Germany* (Hodder & Stoughton 1917) p195.
3. David K Brown, *Warrior to Dreadnought: Warship Design 1860-1905* (Chatham Publishing 1997) p88.
4. Cunard Archives University of Liverpool D641/6/19.
5. Lamar Cecil, *Albert Ballin: Business & Politics in Imperial Germany 1888-1918* (Princeton 1967) p22.
6. Francis Hyde, *Cunard and the North Atlantic* (Macmillan 1975) p100.
7. Information from Arnold Kludas to the author 11 May 1998.
8. Robert Massie, *Dreadnought* (Hodder & Stoughton 1991) pp794-7. Sir Valentine Chirol, letter to *The Times*, 11 May 1915.
9. Ballin did not pioneer cruising as is often stated. In the late 1880s the London-based Orient Line dedicated several ships to cruising the Norwegian fjords and in the Mediterranean. In 1900 Ballin did commission the first purpose-built cruise liner *Prinzessen Viktoria Luise*. Information to the Author from Dr. Alan Jamieson, 3 November 2000.
10. Hyde p75.
11. Jean Strouse, *Morgan: American Financier* (Random House 1999) p199. According to one account, Morgan with a party of friends arrived in Liverpool on a Cunarder on a Christmas Eve in the early 1880s. The line's staff had gone home for the holidays and no porters were available. He was forced to make arrangements for getting the party's luggage off the ship, through customs and to the railway station. By the time he had completed this onerous task, the last London train had left and the party had to stay in Liverpool overnight. Morgan did not reach his London house until the afternoon of Christmas Day and he never forgave Cunard for this miserable incident. *Titanic Commutator* (Titanic Historical Society Vol 24 No 150 2000).
12. Hyde p81. Cunard archives, board minutes, 9 November 1897.
13. Cunard archives D42/PR3/24/6.
14. Cunard archives D241/2/25.
15. Quoted in Andrew Sinclair, *Corsair: The Life of Pierpont Morgan* (Little Brown 1981) p14.
16. Morgan's involvement with IMM is documented in Strouse pp457-81.
17. Cunard archives D42/PR3/25/3A, minutes of annual general meetings.
18. Thomas Bailey and Paul Ryan, *The Lusitania Disaster* (Free Press 1975) p49.
19. Selborne to Inverclyde 10 May 1902. Hyde p144.
20. Philip Bates, *Bates of Bellefield, Gyrn Castle and Manydown* (Privately published 1994). The details of this table read:

SPEED	CONSTRUCTION	HORSEPOWER	SUBSIDY
Knots			
20	£350,000	19,000	£900
21	£400,000	22,000	£19,500
22	£470,000	25,000	£40,500
23	£575,000	30,000	£67,500

24	£850,000	40,000	£110,500
25	£1M.	52,000	£149,000
26	£1.25M	68,000	£204,000

21. Quoted in Howard Johnson, *The Cunard Story* (Whittet Books 1987) p82.
22. Information to the author from David K Brown, 16 July 1997.

Chapter 2: The Birth of a Star
1. See Appendix 2. Detailed accounts of Charles Parsons' development of the marine turbine can be found in Ken Smith, *Turbinia: The Story of Charles Parsons and His Ocean Greyhound* (Tyne and Wear Museums 1995) and in 'Turbinia – the Experiment which Transformed the World's Navies', *Rolls-Royce Magazine*, March 1991.
2. Smith p28.
3. Cunard Archives, board minutes 24 March 1904.
4. Quoted in Johnson p73.
5. Robert Ballard and Rick Archbold, *Lost Liners* (Hyperion 1997) p48.
6. The writer, H V Morton, who accompanied Churchill to the Placentia Bay, Newfoundland, Conference on that ill-fated and unlucky ship, HMS *Prince of Wales* in August 1941, described conditions aboard a KG V class battleship: the noise was indescribable, the vibration persistent. Keith Aldritt *The Greatest of Friends* (St. Martins Press 1995) p55.
7. 'The Cunard Turbine-Driven Quadruple Screw Atlantic Liner *Lusitania*' *Engineering*, 1907 pp54-5. J H Isherwood, *Steamers of the Past.* 'Cunard Liner *Lusitania* of 1907', *The Journal of Commerce and Shipping Telegraph*, Liverpool 1966 p68.
8. Isherwood p68.
9. Cunard Archives, board minutes 21 September 1905.
10. Isherwood pp68-9.
11. Sinclair p188.
12. Hyde p114. Cunard archives D42/ PR3/28/3A.
13. These figures are taken from the inquiry into North Atlantic mail and passenger shipping by Lord Weir (December 1932). Weir Papers, Churchill Archives Centre, Churchill College, Cambridge.
14. Isherwood p69.
15. Private information to the author.
16. Hyde pp148-73. Between 1909 and 1914 Cunard's operating profits had increased from £273,000 to £718,000 and return on capital from 4.4 per cent to 11 per cent.
17. Cunard archives, board minutes 8 December 1910.

Chapter 3: The Brief Life of the Armed Merchant Cruiser
1. PRO MT/23/1400.
2. A more detailed account of the actions between armed merchant cruisers can be found in Paul Halpern, *A Naval History of World War One* (US Naval Institute Press 1994) pp78-82.
3. Julian Corbett, *Naval Operations*, Vol 1 (Longman 1920) pp29-31.
4. PRO MT/23/1400.
5. Duncan Crow, *A Man of Push and Go: The Life of George Macaulay Booth* (Rupert Hart-Davis 1975) p68.
6. Cunard archives D42/61/230, Alfred Booth memo, 18 May 1914.
7. Crow p79. Colin Simpson, *Lusitania* (Longman 1972) pp48-9.

Chapter 4: A Winter of Discontent
1. Edwin A Weinstein, *Woodrow Wilson: A Medical and Psychological Biography* (Princeton 1981) p44.
2. Weinstein pp15-18, 141, 164-5.
3. Weinstein p178.
4. August Heckscher, *Woodrow Wilson* (Scribners 1991) p374.
5. Simpson p76.
6. Charles Seymour, *The Private Papers of Colonel House* (Houghton Mifflin 1926) Vol 1 p157.

7. Dudley Field Malone to the editor, *The Nation,* 15 December 1922, published 3 January 1923. Karl F Falk Papers, Hoover Institution, Stanford University, Palo Alto, California.
8. Cunard archives, board minutes 21 January 1915.

Chapter 5: The Last Voyage
1. *New York Times,* 11 April 1915.
2. Louis Auchincloss, *Woodrow Wilson* (Viking Penguin 2000) p53.
3. These details are taken from a copy of the liner's manifest in the Thomas Bailey/Paul Ryan Papers, Hoover Institution. The original of this manifest is in the Franklin D Roosevelt Presidential Library, Hyde Park, New York. It was presented to Roosevelt, who collected maritime memorabilia, in 1940 by the then Collector of the Port of New York, Harry Durning.
4. Crow p74.
5. *The Times,* 3 May 1915.
6. *New York Tribune,* 2 May 1915.
7. A B Cross papers, Imperial War Museum.
8. *The Times,* 10 May 1915. *Forbes,* 11 October 1999.
9. Information to the author from the Hon Mrs Patricia Noel-Paton, great-granddaughter of Mrs Stephens, 7 October 1997.
10. Information to the author from M Wim Coumans, Director-General of the Belgian Red Cross, 6 August 1999. A A Hoehling and Mary Hoehling, *The Last Voyage of the Lusitania* (Revised edition, Madison Books 1996) p28.
11. Charles Lauriat, *The Lusitania's Last Voyage* (Houghton Mifflin 1915) p67.
12. *The Times,* 3 May 1915.
13. Hoehling p31-2.
14. Information to the author from Lord Rees-Mogg, 14 May 1998.
15. Quoted in Johnson pp86-7.
16. Quoted in Eric Sauder and Ken Marschall, *RMS Lusitania, Triumph of the Edwardian Era* (Transatlantic Designs 1991) p45.
17. Patrick Beesly, *Room 40* (Hamish Hamilton 1982) p102.
18. Information to the author from Captain Graeme Cubbin, archivist of the Harrison Line, 15 May 1999. The quotation is taken from German records as quoted by Mr R M Coppock of the UK Ministry of Defence in correspondence with Captain Cubbin.
19. PRO ADM 137/113/105.
20. PRO ADM 137/113/105.
21. The author has taken all extracts from KapitanLeutnant Schwieger's war diary from a translation from the original in the Bailey/Ryan Papers, Hoover Institution.
22. Simpson p114.
23. A B Cross Papers, Imperial War Museum.
24. Hennessy evidence to the Mayer trial 1918, quoted in Bailey & Ryan p136.

Chapter 6: The Titans of the Admiralty
1. Simpson pp113-4.
2. *New York Times,* 2 May 1915.
3. Interview with Lord Hailsham by Simon Sebag-Montefiore, *Spectator,* 9 November 1996.
4. Arthur Marder, *From Dreadnought to Scapa Flow,* Vol 2 (Oxford 1964) p87.
5. Martin Gilbert, *Winston S. Churchill,* Vol 3 (Heinemann 1971) p419.

Chapter 7: The Seventh Day of May
1. Seymour Vol 1 p432.
2. PRO ADM 1/8451.
3. Quoted in Sauder p46.
4. Lauriat's descriptions of the sinking can be found in *The Lusitania's Last Voyage* pp8-25 and 90-98.
5. Bailey & Ryan p196. Lehmann statement to the *New York Times,* 2 June 1915.
6. Arthur T Vanderbilt, *Fortune's Children: The Fall of the House of Vanderbilt* (William Morrow 1992), note 11 to Chapter 9, p311.

7. Warren Pearl interview with the *New York Sun*, 11 May 1915.
8. *New York Times*, 25 May 1915. C L Droste and W H Tantum, *The Lusitania Case* (7c's Press 1972) pp169-170.
9. PRO ADM 53/45458.
10. A B Cross Papers, Imperial War Museum.
11. Quoted in Dr Robert Ballard, *Exploring the Lusitania* (Warner Books 1995) pp105-6.
12. Hoehling p165.
13. Arthur Rowland Jones evidence to the Mersey inquiry. Transcript open sessions pp26-29.
14. *Morning Post*, 10 May 1915.
15. Leslie Morton evidence to the Mersey inquiry. Transcript open sessions pp16-19.
16. Chris Doncaster, 'The Wanderer's Finest Hour', *Best of British Magazine* March 1999. 'The Manx Lusitania Medals', *Sea Breezes*, April 2000. Additional information to the author from Mr Doncaster, including the letter from skipper Ball to Charles Morrison.
17. Micheal Hurley, *Home From The Sea: The Story Of The Courtmacsherry Lifeboat 1825-1995* (privately published) pp1-4.
18. Wesley Frost correspondence, Lusitania display, Cobh Heritage Centre.
19. Hall/Swinton correspondence, Lusitania display, Cobh Heritage Centre.
20. Lauriat p43-4.
21. *Cork Examiner*, 8 May 1915.
22. These figures are taken from the Cunard archives. The details are as follows:

Passengers	On board	Survivors	Lost
Saloon	291	113	178
Second Cabin	601	227	374
Third Class	373	134	239
Total Passengers	1,265	474	791
Crew	694	290	404
Suspected Agents	3	0	3
Total	1,962	764	1,198

23. *New York Sun*, 11 May 1915. Information to the author from the Hon Mrs. Hugh Lawson Johnston, daughter of Warren Pearl, 11 July 1997.
24. *Morning Post*, 10 May 1915.
25. Quoted in Hoehling pp217-8.
26. *The Times*, 10 May 1915.
27. Information to the author from Count Bertil Bernardotte, who heard the story from Dwight and Eileen Harris, 21 October 1999.
28. Quoted in Ballard pp116-7.

Chapter 8: Reaction
1. Kenrick Clements, *Woodrow Wilson World Statesman* (Twayne 1987) pp158-60.
2. Reinhard Dorries, *Imperial Challenge: Ambassador Count Bernstorff and German-American Relations 1908-1917* (University of North Carolina Press) p99.
3. *The Times*, 10 May 1915.
4. The accounts of the riots in Liverpool and other cities are taken from *The Times*, 10 and 11 May 1915 and the *New York Times*, 25 May 1915.
5. Correlli Barnett, 'Home Front: Front Line', *Spectator*, 4 July 1988.
6. Cunard archives, Booth to Sumner 8 May 1915.
7. *The Times*, 10 May 1915.
8. The *Kolnische Volkszeitung* editorial is as quoted in *The Times*, 10 May 1915.
9. The press comments on the sinking of *Lusitania* are taken from *The Times*, 10 May 1915 and from PRO ADM 116/1416.
10. PRO ADM 116/1416.
11. The account of the Kinsale inquest is taken from J J Horgan, *From Parnell To Pearse* (Browne and Nolan 1948) pp272-76.
12. *The Times* and the *New York Times*, 11 May 1915.

13. Hoehling p231.
14. Rosebery to the editor of *The Times*, 10 May 1915.
15. Ballin to Von Jagow, 17 May 1915, Frank E Mason Papers, Hoover Institution.
16. Dorries, note p277.
17. PRO ADM 137/113/623.
18. *New York Sun*, 11 May 1915.
19. Clements p158-60. Heckscher, *Woodrow Wilson*, p85.
20. Wilson to Edith Galt, 11 May 1915, quoted in Heckscher p385.
21. PRO ADM 137/113/1069.
22. *Sunday Express*, 5 May 1929.

Chapter 9: How are the Mighty Fallen
 1. *Morning Post*, 10 May 1915.
 2. The extracts from Question Time are taken from Hansard, 10 May 1915.
 3. PRO ADM 1/8931.
 4. PRO ADM 116/1416.
 5. PRO ADM 1/8937.
 6. The Webb report can be found in PRO ADM 137/1058.
 7. Fisher obituary, *Dictionary of National Biography 1911-1920*.
 8. May's grandson told the author that his grandparents never allowed Fisher's name to be mentioned in their house.
 9. Fisher's and Churchill's comments on the margin of the Webb report, ADM137/1058.
10. John Colville, *The Fringes of Power* (Hodder & Stoughton 1985) p126.
11. David Lloyd George, *War Memoirs*, Vol 1, 1914-15 (Little Brown 1933) pp198-202.
12. Ruddock Mackay, *Fisher of Kilverstone* (Oxford 1974) p502.
13. Mackay p 502.
14. John Charmley, *Churchill: The End of Glory* (Hodder & Stoughton 1993) p131.

Chapter 10: Lord Mersey Inquires
 1. Transcript open sessions Mersey inquiry (Mersey transcript) p35.
 2. Mersey transcript p38.
 3. Walter Lord, *The Night Lives On* (William Morrow 1986) p204.
 4. Information to the author from Mrs Imelda Lutyens, granddaughter of Admiral Inglefield, 12 April 1999.
 5. The accounts of the examination of witnesses are taken from the Mersey transcript.
 6. Cunard archives, PR13/23 10 June 1915.
 7. *Morning Post*, 10 May 1915.
 8. Hoehling p128.

Chapter 11: In Camera
 1. The account of the closed sessions of the Mersey inquiry are taken from the transcript of these proceedings.
 2. PRO ADM116/1416.
 3. PRO ADM137/1058.
 4. Cunard archives 13/7.
 5. Joseph Marichal evidence, Mersey transcript pp66-70.
 6. Information to author from Paul Banfield, associate archivist, Queen's University, Kingston, Ontario, Canada 3 April 1998.
 7. Inglefield papers.
 8. Lauriat criticism of Mersey report, Lauriat pp152-60.
 9. Turner interview *New York Times*, 21 November 1915.
10. PRO ADM 1/8937.

Chapter 12: The Mayer Liability Trial
 1. Bailey and Ryan pp272-3.
 2. Hovgaard evidence Mayer trial testimony, Vol II pp230-261, Bailey/Ryan Papers, Hoover Institution. Professor Hovgaard had a distinguished career. He had served in

the Danish navy for twenty-five years and had successfully passed out of a naval construction course at the Royal Naval College, Greenwich. He had considerable experience of shipbuilding, having worked for Denny Brothers on the Clyde and had later managed the Copenhagen shipbuilders, Burmeister & Wain. He had specialised in the study of subdivisions of both warships and merchant vessels.

3. Bailey and Ryan p223.
4. Bailey and Ryan p297.
5. *New York, Times,* 27 August 1918.
6. John Lukacs, *The Thread of Years* (Yale 1998) p134.
7. Decision of the Mixed Claims Commission, 21 February 1924. Dockets 244 (Pearl) and 245 (Bloomfield), provided to the author by the Hon Mrs Hugh Lawson Johnston. Bailey and Ryan p292 and 321-2.

Chapter 13: The War of the Notes
1. Nathan Miller, *Theodore Roosevelt: A Life* (Quill William Morrow 1992) p544.
2. PRO FO 2586/371.
3. *New York Sun,* 11 May 1915.
4. Gerard p161.
5. Spring-Rice to Bryan, 31 May 1915. PRO MT 9/1326/ M16243.
6. Gerard p165.
7. Quoted in Bailey and Ryan p271.
8. Dorries pp105-7.
9. Lloyd E Ambrosius, *Wilsonian Statecraft: Theory and Practice of Liberal Internationalism during World War I* (SR Books 1991) p40.
10. Ambrosius p41.
11. Dorries pp110-11.
12. The *Baralong* incident is described by Sir Ludovic Kennedy, *Truth To Tell* (Bantam Books 1991) pp120-3 and by Halpern p301. The Roskill quote appears in Kennedy p323.
13. PRO ADM 116/1416, Spring-Rice to Grey, 16 February 1916.
14. Dorries pp125-40.

Chapter 14: The Myths of Lusitania
1. Evelyn Waugh, *Scoop* (Little Brown 1937) paperback edition p92.
2. PRO FO 2586/371.
3. *New York Tribune,* 11 May 1915.
4. *The Times,* 10 May 1915.
5. Bailey and Ryan p65.
6. Lauriat pp100-13.
7. Ballin to Arndt Von Holtzendorff, 6 June 1915. Cecil pp285-6.
8. *New York Tribune,* 19 June 1913.
9. Cunard archives D42/C1/230, minutes of executive committee, May/June 1913.
10. Droste and Tantum pp46-53.
11. Allan Crothall, *Wealth From The Sea* (Starr Line 1993) p93.
12. Information to the author from Roy Martin, September-November 1998.
13. Colville Barclay, counsellor British Embassy, Washington, to Grey 22 June 1915, PRO MT/1326/M 18622.
14. PRO ADM 137/1058/257.
15. Greene to Murray, 27 February 1924. Murray to Greene, 10 March 1924, quoting Corbett, *Naval Operations* Vol 2, p323. Sir William Graham Greene papers (GEE 13/F) National Maritime Museum, Greenwich.
16. Graham Greene, letter to *The Times* 17 October 1972.
17. Information to the author from David K Brown 16 July 1997.
18. Gerard p133. Halpern p301.
19. Niall Ferguson, *The Pity Of War* (Allen Lane 1998) p291.
20. Avner Offer, *The First World War – An Agrarian Assessment* (Oxford University Press 1989) pp36 & 45.
21. Gerard pp213-4.
22. Offer p52.

23. Simpson, letter to *The Times*, 20 October 1972.
24. Correspondence between Ryan and the Canadian Department of National Defence, Bailey/Ryan Papers, Hoover Institution.
25. Bailey/Ryan p111.
26. Details of the Goetz Medal and the Bernard Partridge poster are taken from the *Imperial War Museum Review*, Vol 1, 1986.
27. Ferguson p383.
28. Ferguson p444.
29. H S Taylor papers, Imperial War Museum.
30. *News Of The World*, 6 June 1937.

Chapter 15: Conspiracy?
1. *Wall Street Journal*, 28 August 1998.
2. The same point is made in Des Hickey & Gus Smith, *Seven Days To Disaster:The Sinking Of The Lusitania* (Collins 1981) p133.
3. Winston S Churchill, *The Second World War*, Vol 2 (Cassell 1949) pp208-12.
4. Churchill to Runciman, 12 February 1915, Martin Gilbert *Winston S. Churchill Companion* Vol III, Part 1 (Heinemann 1973) p501.
5. *Morning Post*, 10 May 1915.
6. The typescript of this interview can be found in the Imperial War Museum.
7. David Stafford, *Churchill And Secret Service* (John Murray 1997) p73.
8. Kennedy/Roskill interview. See 6 above.
9. *The Times*, 8 August 1990.

Chapter 16: Post Mortem
1. The co-authors of this paper are Dr William Garzke, a partner in Gibbs & Cox, the well-known naval architects and designers of the ultimate transatlantic express liner *United States*, David K Brown, former Deputy Chief Naval Architect, Royal Corps of Naval Constructors, UK Ministry of Defence, Arthur D Sandiford, a retired naval architect, Professor John Woodward, University of Michigan, and Peter Hsu, Techmatics Inc, who produced computer-aided designs and illustrations.
2. Information to the author from Dr Joe A Martin, a PHD in Material Sciences, lately at the US Government Nuclear Design Centre at Los Alamos, New Mexico.
3. Mersey transcript p21. George Little Deposition PRO ADM 137/1058.
4. John Keegan, *The Price of Admiralty* (Century Hutchinson 1988) Penguin paperback edition p174.
5. Information to the author from Captain David Garstin RN, 13 April 2000.
6. Mersey transcript p47.
7. Mersey transcript p48.
8. *Secrets Of The Deep* was shown on Channel Four in December 1999.

Chapter 17: The Reasons Why (I)
1. Cecil Woodham-Smith, *The Reason Why* (Constable 1953) p255.
2. Gerard pp174-6.
3. Martin Gilbert, *The First World War* (Weidenfeld & Nicolson 1994) p157.
4. Beach to Ryan, 2 April 1975. Bailey/Ryan Papers, Hoover Institution. Beach to the author, 8 September 1998.
5. Sanderson to Greene, 10 May 1915. Greene to Sanderson, 15 May 1915. PRO ADM 137/1058.
6. *The Times*, 10 May 1915.
7. Frank E Mason papers, Hoover Institution.
8. Halpern p436.
9. Bailey and Ryan p280. The table, amended by the author to include *Lusitania* voyage numbers, is based on Answers to Cunard Interrogatories (pp11-12) taken for the Wynne Deposition (1917) of UK-based witnesses for the Mayer Liability Trial. On her last voyage (No.101) *Lusitania* had not completed taking a four-point bearing fix when she was torpedoed. The stated distances from Fastnet and the Old Head of Kinsale were presumably supplied by Captain Turner from memory, which were in

turn based on dead reckoning and should therefore be considered to be approximate.
10. Susan Els, *Titanic – Legacy of the World's Greatest Liner* (Time-Life Books 1997) p116.
11. Mersey closed sessions transcript p3.
12. Hyde p162.

Chapter 18: The Reasons Why (II)
1. Correlli Barnett, *Engage The Enemy More Closely* (W W Norton 1991) p7.
2. Massie p747.
3. Quoted in Andrew Gordon, *The Rules of The Game* (John Murray 1996) p352.
4. Sir Peter Gretton, *Former Naval Person: Winston Churchill and the Royal Navy* (Oxford 1968) p199.
5. Marder Vol 1 p6.
6. Gordon pp470-71.
7. W S Chalmers, *Full Cycle: The Biography of Admiral Sir Bertram Home Ramsay* (Hodder & Stoughton 1959) pp19-21. The author's father was Vice-Admiral, Dover at the time of the Dunkirk evacuation and C-in-C, Allied Naval Expeditionary Force for the Invasion of Normandy. In January 1915 Admiral Gamble was replaced as Vice-Admiral 4BS by Vice-Admiral Sturdee, the victor of the battle of the Falkland Islands.
8. Marder Vol 2 p92.
9. Stafford p363.
10. Bailey and Ryan p283.
11. Beesly p87.
12. Mackay pp447-53.
13. Mackay pp447-53.
14. Bailey and Ryan p10.
15. PRO ADM 116/1416, issued 10 February 1915.
16. Coke to Greene, 12 May, 1915 PRO ADM 137/1052/381.
17. PRO ADM 137/1062/459.
18. Churchill Archives Centre ROSK 3/20.
19. PRO FO 2586/371.
20. PRO ADM 137/113/611.
21. PRO ADM 137/113/105 & 107.
22. Schwieger war diary.
23. PRO ADM 137/1062/464.
24. Fisher to Asquith, 13 May 1915, Mackay p496.
25. Jellicoe to Jackson, 18 and 24 June 1915. Beatty to Admiralty, 25 June 1915. Quoted in Marder Vol 2 pp361-2.
26. Stafford p74.
27. Quoted in Keegan p174.
28. Norman Rose, *Churchill, The Unruly Giant* (Free Press 1995) p312.

Chapter 19: Aftermath: America Goes to War
1. Quoted in Johnson p87.
2. *The Times*, 8 August 1990.
3. Ambrosius p41.
4. Lukacs p132-3.
5. Halpern p326.
6. Scheer to the Kaiser, July 1916, Halpern pp328-9.
7. Dorries pp346-7.
8. Walter McDougall, *Promised Land: Crusader State* (Houghton Mifflin 1997) p136.
9. Halpern p336.
10. Holtzendorff's boast is quoted in Gilbert, *First World War* p306. A full account of the Pless conference can be found in Barbara Tuchman, *The Zimmerman Telegram* (Macmillan 1966) Ballantine Books paperback edition pp137-41.
11. Cecil p129.
12. Ferguson p284.
13. *New York Times*, 1 March 1917.

14. Tuchman p181.
15. Tuchman p194.
16. *The Times*, 3 March 1917.
17. Tuchman pp185-6.
18. Bernstorff's later career is described in Dorries pp9-15. Nicolson comment: Dorries, *Albrecht Graf Von Bernstorff* (Bonn 1995) p15.
19. Seymour Vol 2, p469.
20. Miller p544.

Chapter 20: The Captains and the Kings Depart
1. Joe H Kirchberger, *First World War Facts* (Oxford 1992) p160.
2. Miller p546.
3. Cunard archives board minutes, 9 and 16 September 1915.
4. Frank E Mason papers, Hoover Institution.
5. Cunard archives, private files.
6. Cecil p342.
7. John Maxtone Graham, *The Only Way To Cross* (revised edition Barnes & Noble 1996) p255.
8. McDougall p144.
9. Rose p159.
10. Hickey & Smyth pp319-320.
11. *Daily Mail*, 8 May 1933.
12. *News Of The World*, 6 June 1937.
13. Churchill, *The Second World War* Vol 1 (Cassell 1948) pp215-7.
14. Bailey and Ryan, *Hitler v Roosevelt* (Free Press 1979) pp55-7. Barnett p66.
15. Barnett p155.
16. Information to the author from the Hon Mrs Hugh Lawson Johnston.
17. Hurley p4.

Index